CORRUPTION

CORRUPTION

The New Corporate Challenge

Nick Kochan
and Robin Goodyear

To Ian

Good luck in your
whistleblowing

from

Nick Kochan

June 2012

palgrave
macmillan

First published 2011 by
PALGRAVE MACMILLAN

Palgrave Macmillan in the UK is an imprint of Macmillan Publishers Limited, registered in England, company number 785998, of Houndmills, Basingstoke, Hampshire RG21 6XS.

Palgrave Macmillan in the US is a division of St Martin's Press LLC, 175 Fifth Avenue, New York, NY 10010.

Palgrave Macmillan is the global academic imprint of the above companies and has companies and representatives throughout the world.

Palgrave® and Macmillan® are registered trademarks in the United States, the United Kingdom, Europe and other countries

ISBN-13: 978–0–230–29843–9

This book is printed on paper suitable for recycling and made from fully managed and sustained forest sources. Logging, pulping and manufacturing processes are expected to conform to the environmental regulations of the country of origin.

A catalogue record for this book is available from the British Library.

A catalog record for this book is available from the Library of Congress.

10 9 8 7 6 5 4 3 2 1
20 19 18 17 16 15 14 13 12 11

Printed and bound in Great Britain by
CPI Antony Rowe, Chippenham and Eastbourne

This book is dedicated to Miriam Kochan, mater familias

CONTENTS

CONTENTS

CONTENTS

CONTENTS

FIGURES AND TABLE

Figures

Table

PREFACE
A TIME TO ACT ON CORRUPTION

Bribery and corruption are topics that are resonating ever more loudly with business managers and their advisers. The noise surrounding the publication, passing, and finally implementation of the UK Bribery Act testifies to concern, interest, and fear in the ranks of business. The elephant in the room is trumpeting. Companies can no longer sit back from this most pressing of debates.

In the run-up to the delayed publication of the final guidance, a most fascinating debate took place between those who were anxious that the law would be draconian and would curtail the giving of every form of entertainment, and on the other, those advocating a strong law that ensured the United Kingdom dealt with concerns expressed by the OECD about the country's compliance with the OECD Convention and with international obligations.

Members of the second group also got wind of the government's plan to exempt companies whose only link with the United Kingdom was a stock exchange listing, arguing that it made a distinction for investors between foreign companies with business in the United Kingdom, which were covered by the Act, and those who did not have such business, and therefore were not. Did it produce a two-tier listed community, they enquired? This group were opposed to any watering-down or diminution of the Act's powers. They lost that particular argument.

Those fearing a draconian implementation of the Act were clearly in the majority. They raised many canards about the way the Act would impact on relationships and the perks they could offer clients. The world got to know about the extent business was done at Wimbledon between sets or at the Grand Prix after the chequered flag. Kenneth Clarke, the justice secretary. appeared to sympathize with their concern, and said, in his introduction to the "Guidance notes" for the Bribery Act, "Rest assured, no one wants to stop firms getting to know their clients by taking them to events like Wimbledon or the Grand Prix."[1] Others got exercised about the giving and receiving of champagne, or a first class flight.

But at the same time as the British, and to an extent global, business community were discussing excitedly the impact of the new law on their hospitality budgets, news was filtering through about the "Arab Spring," the refreshing upsurge in democratic activity in Tunisia, Egypt, Yemen, Bahrain, Syria, and then Libya. The remarkable expression of rebellion from the street was in part targeted at the privileges enjoyed by the unelected presidents and leaders. We started to learn about the extent of their fortunes, pillaged over the decades from their people at home, and now deposited in bank accounts in tax havens.

The overseas wealth of Ben Ali (of Tunisia), Mubarak (of Egypt), Ghaddafy (of Libya), the Assads (of Syria), and others has been scrutinized. These investigations take two forms. First, governments want to know who provided that wealth and how. Second, they want to know how the wealth left the countries and where it went. Countries want answers to the first question to understand better the business practices of the dictators, as well as those who supplied the wealth. They want answers to the second, better to track the wealth, and also to understand the extent of due diligence and anti-money laundering regimes of international banks. Once they have obtained both sets of information, the chances of retrieving and returning the wealth to the countries of its origin are enhanced.

On the first score, namely the way the wealth was obtained, countries' law enforcement departments need to look at the structure and politics of the regimes. Power and corruption are umbilically linked. The powerful person has the ability to influence the giving of contracts, and thus is most likely to be in a position to demand a bribe. The company that wants to receive a contract and lacks scruple will throw hospitality at the powerful person. The risk to the person who accepts the corrupt payment varies from regime to regime, from country to country. In this book, we look at countries' different systems of transparency and different systems of business mores. Companies active in countries where the risk of corruption is high face a greater task in exerting due diligence and carrying out auditing procedures.

Countries with dictatorships, whether the dictators are overweening families or overweening parties, are most prone to corruption. As Lord Acton, the great nineteenth-century historian, aptly commented, "Power tends to corrupt and absolute power corrupts absolutely."[2] Individuals or families that stay in power for a long time build up coteries that rely on the patronage of their leaders. Even if the country had a system requiring transparency and accountability when the individual came to power (and most did not), the loyal coterie (around the dictator) will override these systems to protect their sources of patronage and wealth. Family members are typically leading members of many of today's corrupt regimes. This is the context for the inclusion of "politically exposed persons" in anti-money-laundering legislation and directives.

It is no less pertinent to the context of bribery, and in particular to company systems for assessing corruption risk, and anti-bribery regimes. Companies that have signed a contract with a regime subsequently found to be corrupt may seek to review contractual arrangements if the regime is toppled.

The message we hope readers will take from this book is that the price for engaging with corrupt regimes, or corrupt individuals, is rising. It is clear that governments are pushing companies to scrutinize their anti-bribery systems. They are ratcheting up the offences (and consequent penalties) to which they are liable, should they be found to flout the law. They are spreading the responsibility more widely for monitoring processes (so directors who should have known what was going on are now vulnerable to prosecution). In short, the company itself is in the firing line if it is complicit in the bribe. The price of a failure to implement systems can be an unlimited fine.

However, criminal penalties resulting from a conviction may be only the least of the corporate's problems. For example, lawyers say that the cost of an internal investigation of a corruption allegation can easily cost as much as the fine. More than that, prosecutors are likely to require the corporate to appoint and pay for a monitor. This will be an external law firm that supervises the implementation of the anti-corruption processes. Substantial costs are likely to be incurred as this will need to be in place for a number of years.

The damage to the company will go much further than merely the financial burden. A conviction for corruption will poison its reputation. This in turn will cause a loss of morale amongst employees and other stakeholders, while shareholders will sell the stock.

There will also be implications for the board's ability to pursue its long-term strategy. The merest allegation of corruption can scupper the best-crafted deal and introduce uncertainty into all future plans. So claims that Rupert Murdoch's News International paid bribes to the Metropolitan Police (coupled with widespread allegations of phone hacking) forced the company on July 13, 2011, to withdraw its bid for the 61 percent of British Sky Broadcasting that it did not already own.

Debarment from international contracts and finance is a further risk to a company found to be engaged in corrupt behaviour. The World Bank, for example, debars firms and individuals from World Bank financed contracts if they have been sanctioned under its fraud and corruption policy. The institution has a publicly available list of companies that have been debarred.

Law enforcement will argue that the new law, even if not widely implemented, will add additional risk to those that participate in a corrupt relationship. The more anti-bribery legislation that is enacted, the more the risk of law enforcement's involvement, the more complex schemes will need to become, and this will push up the monetary price of a bribe. In short, the marketplace will chip away at the incidence of bribery.

But there is a wider message for readers of this book. This is that corruption undermines the global marketplace, and in due course weakens the way business is done for all its players. Those who give or receive corrupt payments make a short-term gain, but undermine their long-term prospects. By the same token, those who refuse to pay a bribe (and the numbers are growing) will take a short-term loss. The company that does not give or receive bribes should send out a message that it is being a good corporate citizen, that it is committed to principles of transparency and accountability.

The less the bribery, the greater the promise of a fairer marketplace for companies, of more distribution of wealth to the poor in countries where dictators have become corrupt, and of greater faith in the legitimacy of the business community, in an era of cynicism and greed. If this book strengthens that message, and those who adhere and practice it, it will have attained its goal.

Nick Kochan and Robin Goodyear
London, July 13, 2011

ACKNOWLEDGMENTS

We would like to express our considerable gratitude to a large number of researchers and writers who made this book possible. In many ways this is a communal effort, where many people pulled together to maximize the range of research, of knowledge, and of information.

We would like to express our gratitude to Richard Alderman, the director of the UK Serious Fraud Office, for agreeing to write a Foreword to the book, and to Vivian Robinson, the SFO's expert adviser on the UK Bribery Act, who gave of his time and knowledge unstintingly.

The City of London Police and their Overseas Anti-Corruption Unit have been immensely helpful over the last year. We are also grateful for the assistance provided by the Metropolitan Police's Proceeds of Corruption Unit.

The following people gave their time and assistance with particular chapters and topics. In no particular order of contribution or merit, we would like to thank: Lawrence Joffe, for his work on the BAE and al Yamamah affair; Gregory Husisian, of Foley and Lardner, LLP; Sam Hilton, for work on the US Foreign Corrupt Practices Act and corporate responses; Portia Roelofs for her work on Nigerian corruption; Barry Vitou, for his work on director liability under the UK Bribery Act, and his firm Pinsent Masons, for their charts; Helen Parry, for her work on bribery and corruption cases under UK and US law; Alan Doig for assisting with footnotes and textual accuracy; Stephanie Orme, for her work on the origins of anti-bribery and corruption legislation in the UK. We would further like to thank Lewis Lyons, for his sterling work in editing and organizing the book under severe time pressures, James Harrington for his work on the voluminous notes, and Thomas Brooks for his comments.

We would further like to thank Stephen Rutt of Palgrave Macmillan for his support of the project. Miriam Kochan compiled the index, and we are immensely grateful.

A number of people have spoken to us on condition of anonymity. We are grateful to them.

Nick Kochan and Robin Goodyear

FOREWORD

The fight against corruption is an absorbing topic for the many of us who care about this subject both personally and professionally. It is a story that has heroes, villains, and victims.

The victims are the many people in countries who suffer as a result of corruption. We see many examples of this in our work in the Serious Fraud Office. We see people (often the poorest members of society) dying or suffering serious illness because of corrupt deals struck by business with powerful members of those countries. We see damage to the infrastructure of countries, and we see damage to the environment. We see countries, which are rich in the quality of their natural resources and the talents of their citizens, that are held back by a culture of corruption that favors the few and causes great damage to the many.

We see villains as well. These are individuals and companies that do business with corrupt politicians and officials in jurisdictions knowing or not caring what the results will be for the people of those countries. They try to defend what they are doing by talking about the need to do business and the impossibility of doing business in these countries without using bribery. Unfortunately for them, the public reaction, whether in the countries where the bribery takes place or in their own home countries, is very different. The public are rightly intolerant of corporates and individuals who cause damage to victims and their societies through the use of corruption.

And, of course, there are heroes. There are many that I admire very greatly. One of the privileges of my role in the Serious Fraud Office is that I meet them from time to time. These heroes include the individuals (whether journalists, members of non-governmental organisations, private citizens, or others) in the countries that suffer from corruption who work at bringing to light corrupt activities and exposing what has happened. They do this at very great risk to themselves and to their families. I have come across cases where individuals have been killed because of their work.

Another group I would class as heroes consists of those individuals who work in enforcement authorities in these countries and who try to ensure that the rule of law is respected and that those who receive bribes are convicted and punished. Again, I know of cases where the regime in power has attempted to deal with a courageous law enforcement official through assassination.

All of the people I have mentioned are true heroes in my eyes and are worthy of very great respect from all of us.

What we also need to reflect on and welcome are the very important changes in our own societies that make the public much less tolerant of behaviour of this nature. This has been one of the most significant developments in this area. It is clear to me that there is great public hostility to corrupt activities. What I have also found interesting in my own work in the Serious Fraud Office is that this view is frequently shared by many in corporate organisations. They are working hard (often in very difficult and challenging circumstances) to create long-term value for their organisations and for society. Corruption can destroy their organisations just as much as it can eventually destroy societies. The individuals in companies I talk to see anti corruption as being an ethical issue that is important to them personally as well as to the organisation's ethical culture. Our best corporates do not always share with the public all that they are doing in combating corruption, but I believe they have a good story to tell.

I see corruption and the attack on corruption as being linked to many other fundamental issues. Corruption destroys the rule of law and democratic institutions. It is no coincidence that those countries with systemic corruption have no respect for the rule of law, do not respect the independence of the judges and the enforcement authorities, and do not observe democratic accountability. It is also no coincidence that this results in the impoverishment of the citizens of those countries.

Corruption also destroys the ability of ethical corporates and individuals to compete for business on level terms. Corporates have a choice between engaging ethically or not engaging at all. My view is that citizens of these societies will benefit from investment by good ethical companies. A system that favors those who use corruption will discourage those who want to do ethical business in that country, with the result that citizens of that country will be the poorer.

I am looking forward very much to the further opportunities to combat corruption that have been given to us by the UK's Bribery Act 2010. This Act came into force on July 1, 2011. Important guidance by the UK's Ministry of Justice has been published together with guidance from our Director of Public Prosecutions and by me.

The Bribery Act modernizes the UK's outdated law on corruption. It creates a new and very important offense at the corporate level of failing to prevent bribery with a defense of adequate procedures. And the Act also widens our jurisdiction in respect of foreign companies.

I want to see the SFO use the Bribery Act to the full in order to support our good ethical companies and to ensure a competitive market place for them. The Bribery Act gives us the tools for this and I look forward to using them.

Richard Alderman
Director, UK Serious Fraud Office

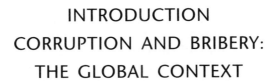

INTRODUCTION
CORRUPTION AND BRIBERY:
THE GLOBAL CONTEXT

Corruption is widely considered to be the cause of deep and enduring problems in government, business, and civil society. This has long been known and countenanced. But tolerance is diminishing. Governments in many countries are less prepared to overlook contracts going to undeserving parties to buy their favors. The tide is turning on corruption.

The context to this change in ethical climate is the fall of communism in Russia, growth of capitalism in China, and rise in global terrorism (with associated measures aimed at countering its financing). These have exposed multinational companies in all sectors to increased scrutiny into how they do business. While the increase in global trade has meant more opportunities for corruption, the post-cold war global economic order is characterized by an ever-increasing focus on the importance of ethical corporate behavior. This is partly because those Western states that have hitherto been the major drivers of globalization already have strong domestic laws and values against corruption, and partly because a major part of globalization is increased state membership in multilateral organizations and international networks which often commit parties to agree and enforce minimum standards of behavior.

The new pressure on bribery also arises from the rising incidence of corrupt practices over the last two decades: estimates of bribery's cost to business (in terms of contract prices) have risen from 5 percent to 30 percent, reaching 45 percent in highly competitive markets.[1] As a proportion of world trade, the value of bribes is phenomenal: US Attorney General Eric Holder concurs with recent World Bank estimates that more than US$ 1 trillion in bribes are paid each year out of a world economy of US$ 30 trillion: "That's a staggering three percent of the world's economy ... and the impact is particularly severe on foreign investment .... The World Bank estimates that corruption serves, essentially, as a 20 per cent tax."[2]

High-profile cases involving major companies have turned the spotlight on the extent to which bribery distorts global markets and destroys communities. National and international campaigning groups have also voiced their demands for greater transparency, with the result that

1

the corporate world is under growing pressure to adopt anti-corruption practices.

CIVIL SOCIETY'S CAMPAIGN AGAINST CORRUPTION

Recognition, investigation, and documentation of the ways in which corruption prevents change, constrains development, and damages the economic and social fabric of the countries where it occurs has fueled a burgeoning global protest movement and growing public intolerance of corrupt practices in both the developed and developing world.

Transnational anti-corruption networks are playing an increasingly significant role in setting the agenda, shaping the debate and direction of campaigns against bribery. In an interview with the authors, Paul Whatmore, Detective Inspector at the Metropolitan Police's Proceeds of Corruption Unit, emphasized that:

> There are major overall international drivers for [the anti-corruption agenda] ... Transparency International, Global Witness, Human Rights Watch all agitate in the international community. They say that companies have got to stop doing this, and if it doesn't start somewhere, no one else will follow.

Transparency International (TI) is the leading activist group in the field. This non-governmental organization has chapters in over 90 countries. Founded in Berlin in 1993 by Peter Eigen, a former regional director of the World Bank, TI draws attention to the problems created by corruption. TI campaigns to promote transparency in elections, public administration, procurement, and business, and lobbies governments to bring about change. The organization also develops and distributes practical guidance to help businesses operate ethically.

Its biggest achievement, however, has been to raise awareness in governments, businesses, and the general population – in its own words, to "challenge the inevitability of corruption." TI is best known for its annual Corruption Perceptions Index, a worldwide survey that ranks countries according to the perceived level of corruption in public life. In addition to other research, TI also publishes a Bribe Payers Index and, since September 2010, a Global Corruption Barometer, the only worldwide public opinion survey on corruption. TI has been directly involved in international anti-corruption agreements; it played a major part in establishing the Organization for Economic Co-operation and Development (OECD)'s Anti-Bribery Convention and in drafting the United Nations Convention against Corruption and the African Union Convention on Preventing and Combating Corruption.

Also established in 1993, Global Witness (GW) is a non-governmental organization (NGO) based in London and Washington, DC. It is an environmental group concerned with detecting and exposing the corruption and social problems associated with the exploitation of natural resources. In its mission statement the group says it is "motivated by a desire to tackle the underlying causes of conflict and poverty and to end the impunity of individuals, companies and governments that exploit natural resources for their own benefit at the expense of their people and the environment."[3] The group campaigns for financial transparency as a way to expose corrupt relationships.

According to GW, in 2008, exports of oil and minerals from Africa were worth roughly £242 billion ($393 billion) – over ten times the value of exported farm products (£23 billion/$38 billion) and nearly nine times the value of international aid (£27 billion/$44 billion). If used properly, this wealth could lift millions of people out of poverty. However the main benefits of resource extraction typically are diverted by political, military, and business elites in producer countries, and oil, mining, timber, and other companies overseas.

GW describes the concept of the resource curse – also known as the paradox of plenty:

> the phenomenon whereby countries rich in natural resources such as oil, gas or minerals end up poorer and more unequal than countries without them. This can be because of corruption, a decline in the competitiveness of other economic sectors, and volatility in commodity markets. ... Countries relying on oil and mining revenues are often poor, badly run, corrupt and prone to violent instability. This is in large part because the political elite place their own vested interests above their responsibilities to their population, undermining democracy and basic human rights.[4]

According to GW, countries that have successfully escaped the resource curse include Botswana and Norway.

The growing importance of transparency in government and business is illustrated by "Publish What You Pay," a global network of over 600 civil organizations that lobby for disclosure in the extractive industries. Transparency is also a principal concern for the Center for Public Integrity, an independent investigative organization whose mission is concerned with the interaction between private interests and government officials and its effect on public policy. The emergence of such single-issue groups has been crucial in focusing attention on the ways in which corruption affects particular business sectors, countries, and regions.

The internet has provided a new way for people to tell their stories of corrupt practices. Websites such as www.ipaidabribe.com expose corruption at the grassroots level while at the same time they provide a forum for people to discuss how best to avoid or reject demands for bribes. Public

FIGURE I.1 How natural resource corruption is facilitated and the need for a joined-up anti-corruption strategy to tackle it

Stages of process

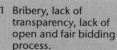

Allocation of natural resource licences
Crucial stage in establishing sound management of natural resources, and strong legal framework and institutions

Revenues from natural resource begin to flow
Often substantial licit financial flows pour into country. Huge potential for economic growth and development. Substantial risk of corruption

Corruption as money moves through government budgets
Corruption spreads beyond misappropriation of natural resource revenue as the country secures foreign loans and begins to spend new government revenue

Negative outcomes

1 Bribery, lack of transparency, lack of open and fair bidding process.
2 Companies with inadequate expertise gain contracts.
3 Lack of proper environmental or social impact assessments and safeguards.
4 Corrupt elite using natural resource allocation proceeds to develop patronage networks.
5 Corruption and poor management of natural resources and related revenue becomes the norm.

1 Lack of transparency in revenue payments to government coupled with weak institutions and accountability lead to widespread misappropriation.
2 Corrupt elite and patronage networks become deeply entrenched, and dependent on natural resource revenue.
3 Civil society and democratic institutions become sidelined as power concentrates in the hands of a corrupt few.

1 Loans provide advance on future revenue allowing corrupt elites to enrich themselves.
2 Corruption in state procurement becomes the norm, companies which pay bribes receive government contracts rather than legitimate development partners.
3 Companies linked to corruption in developing countries receive backing from wealthy states, further entrenching corruption.

Joined up UK anti-corruption strategy

1 Strong anti-bribery legislation.
2 Promote EITI (Extractive Industries Transparency Initiative) and require companies to publish all payments to foreign governments.
3 ODA should ensure open and transparent bidding rounds and work with governments to build strong and accountable government institutions and sound public financial management.
4 Work with other donors to hold leaders to account, making ongoing development assistance dependent on agreed governance reforms in the management of natural resources.
5 Work with other donors to create space for civil society and strong independent democratic institutions to monitor natural resource revenue and public finances, and hold the government to account.

1 Banks required to publish information on loans to sovereign governments and state-owned companies.
2 Ensure that states do not provide financial backing to companies with links to corrupt deals abroad.
3 Strong anti-bribery legislation.
4 Work with other donors to ensure strong public financial management as prerequisite to ongoing disbursement of ODA.

global witness

Illicit financial flows flow out of country
Foreign banks facilitate state-looting by accepting proceeds of corruption. Substantial tax revenue lost through lack of transparency and abusive tax avoidance through transfer mispricing.

Donor failure helps to entrench and subsidise corruption
Donors further entrench corrupt regimes by underwriting basic state services without securing governance reform, allowing state resources to be looted with impunity.

1. Revenue from natural resources never reaches government coffers as it is laundered offshore by corrupt elites.
2. Developing countries fail to benefit from tax revenue from natural resources.
3. Corrupt elites spend their money abroad with impunity.

1. Country fails to develop strong democratic institutions.
2. Natural resource revenue is wasted.
3. Corrupt regimes learn the language of democracy and human rights whilst side-stepping substantive issues and refusing to reform – their entrenched position makes engagement more difficult.
4. Risk of conflict and instability.

1. Ensure that banks enforce robust *know your customer due diligence* procedures.
2. Set international standard and publish register of beneficial ownership of companies.
3. Work with FATF to make 1 & 2 (above) international standards.
4. Ensure international accounting standards to require country by country reporting and ensure automatic international exchange of tax information.
5. Visa bans and asset freezes for corrupt foreign officials.

1. Make natural resource governance a cornerstone of initiatives in resource-rich, developing countries.
2. Require basic transparency and governance benchmarks to be met prior to the disbursement of aid.
3. Percentage of UK aid to go to non-state actors, to promote governance and accountability.
4. Push multilateral institutions to take the same approach.

Source: George Boden, Global Witness.

resentment of corruption has been expressed through social initiatives such as "Bribebusters" in India, currently being piloted by lawyer and entrepreneur Shaffi Mather, which shows that low-level bribery can be tackled at the grassroots level and doing business without bribery is possible. Individuals and companies confronted by a bribe request can hire Bribebusters, for a fee, to act on their behalf, using legal means. Mather says "I'm working to battle corruption, especially individual demands for bribes," such as street vendors paying officials or drivers stopped for traffic offenses paying police officers:

> It might be a small amount that each individual has to pay, but ... there are multiple studies done by the World Bank and Transparency International that estimate the bribes paid in 18 common services such as electricity, water and civic services ... are around $4.5bn. And we're not talking about the big scams or scandals, these are just bribes paid by the common man in their daily life.[5]

Local schemes such as this are complemented by organizations representing global businesses. So the International Chamber of Commerce has also adopted a program to combat bribery.

RECOGNITION BY GOVERNMENT: DOMESTIC RESPONSES WITH INTERNATIONAL IMPLICATIONS

Two pieces of legislation with significant international implications emanate from the United States and the United Kingdom. These are the 1977 US Foreign Corrupt Practices Act (FCPA) and the 2010 UK Bribery Act.

These two laws are feared by businesses because of their extraterritorial jurisdiction and potential for aggressive interpretation. The US FCPA, for example, is restricted to US citizens and nationals or those whose principal place of business is within the United States, but the US Department of Justice is increasingly expanding the remit of the law, to bring in more corporates. The UK Bribery Act has a potentially even wider reach; an SFO official explained that "In practice, a company registered anywhere in the world and having part of its business in the UK could be prosecuted for failing to prevent bribery on its behalf wherever in the world that bribe was paid." Recent guidance has excluded foreign companies whose only business in the United Kingdom is a stock exchange listing from the reach of the Bribery Act.

Businesses are also taking the Act seriously because it marks a new a trend in corruption legislation – it introduces a new corporate responsibility to put procedures in place to *prevent* corrupt practices. Previously, "knowledge" (however narrowly or widely interpreted) had been a key component in determining corporate liability for bribery. Robert Amaee, former head of the Serious Fraud Office (SFO)'s anti-corruption team, explains how the UK Bribery Act changes the rules of the game:

> The new Act sweeps away this requirement and introduces a new corporate offence of failing to prevent bribery. This is a novel concept under English law and one which we are likely to see more of the years to come. This makes a commercial organization criminally liable if one of its employees, agents or subsidiaries bribes another person, intending to obtain or retain business or an advantage in the conduct of business for the company.[6]

Legal firm McDermott Will & Emery suggests that national legislation such as the UK Bribery Act is likely to drive up standards in company policy. They observe that "due to the desirability of firm-wide consistency in corporate compliance programmes, the enaction of the Bribery Act may accelerate the process of raising the bar in this respect."[7] The Bribery Act's broad scope, harsh penalties, and narrow defences may be seen as a harbinger of other preventative minimum standards for businesses.

TRANSNATIONAL INITIATIVES

> The topic of fighting corruption has become more popular at global summits, for example at the G8 and G20. Previously the topics simply didn't exist, yet now it is being promoted by the heads of the largest states. This means that everybody understands that corruption is a global evil, and that countries need to coordinate their efforts.[8]

Corruption has long been acknowledged as a threat to business by developed states, but it is only relatively recently that coordinated international moves towards reducing corruption have been attempted with any vigor. As well as new domestic legislation criminalizing bribery, as in the UK Bribery Act, there is a move towards international agreements and collaborative action to combat corruption. Links between terrorist financing and money laundering have accelerated transnational attempts to address a whole range of financial misconduct.

The European Union

A conviction for corruption in the European Union can result in exclusion from tendering for contracts. In the EU Procurement Directive of 31 March 2004, on procedures for the award of public works contracts, public supply contracts, and public service contracts, Article 45 regulates the supply of goods and services to government bodies by companies and individuals. The Directive requires EU member states, for the first time, to exclude companies and individuals convicted of corruption from being awarded public procurement contracts, effectively introducing a debarment regime into the European Union.

The commentary on Article 45 states:

> The award of public contracts to economic operators who have participated in a criminal organization or who have been found guilty of corruption or of fraud to the detriment of the financial interests of the European Communities or of money laundering should be avoided. Where appropriate, the contracting authorities should ask candidates or tenderers to supply relevant documents and, where they have doubts concerning the personal situation of a candidate or tenderer, they may seek the cooperation of the competent authorities of the Member State concerned. The exclusion of such economic operators should take place as soon as the contracting authority has knowledge of a judgment concerning such offences rendered in accordance with national law.[9]

Although a conviction for corruption can result in a company being excluded from tendering for contracts, in other cases (for example in the case of a company that is convicted under the UK Bribery Act) such exclusion is not mandatory but a possible outcome. It is important to note that the EU Convention against Corruption does not have the force of law, and the World Trade Organization (WTO) has no binding rules concerning corruption in international trade and government contracting.

Other regions

Governments in other regions around the world have made public pronouncements about cracking down on bribery. Twenty-five countries have now adopted the 1996 Inter-American Convention against corruption, which criminalizes the paying or accepting of bribes by public officials. This marked a significant step in government response, as it was the first international judicial instrument dedicated to fighting corruption.

Governments belonging to the Association of Southeast Asian Nations (ASEAN) are also taking increased interest in tackling corruption, particularly in relation to "gifts" to public officials. This move has been given urgency by the links between corruption and terrorism in the region.

In Africa, the New Partnership for Africa's Development (NEPAD) has started to focus more closely on corruption and how it adversely affects one of its goals of poverty relief. The 29 countries that signed its memorandum of understanding are committed to "just, honest, transparent, accountable and participatory government and probity in public life." Recognition in African governments of the impact of corrupt politicians is illustrated by the transnational African Parliamentarians' Network Against Corruption (APNAC) which works to "strengthen parliamentary capacity to fight corruption and promote good governance." In December 2001, the 15 members of the Economic Community of West African States (ECOWAS) signed the Protocol on the Fight against Corruption, which requires all signatories to criminalize the paying and receiving of bribes, and provides an international cooperation framework to improve mutual law enforcement and facilitate asset confiscation.

As in other areas of development, there have also been increasing efforts at cooperation between developed and developing states. The deputy head of South Korea's anti-corruption watchdog stated at the 2010 G20 summit that "Our country, which has been trying to effectively address corruption issues that have inevitably arisen during the process of rapid economic growth, has been playing an active mediating role between advanced and developing countries at the Anti-Corruption Working Group."[10]

The OECD

Bribery is the cancer of globalization.
Angel Gurría, secretary general, OECD[11]

The OECD promotes democratic and free market principles in business transactions and development. It has been increasingly active on corruption and bribery, particularly since the 1997 OECD Convention on Combating Bribery of Foreign Public Officials in International Business Transactions, which established "legally binding standards to criminalize bribery of foreign public officials in international business transactions," along with monitoring and enforcement measures to make it effective. It is the first and only international anti-corruption agreement to focus on the "supply side" of the bribery transaction:

> This Convention deals with what, in the law of some countries, is called "active corruption" or "active bribery," meaning the offence committed by the person who promises or gives the bribe, as contrasted with "passive bribery," the offence committed by the official who receives the bribe.[12]

While it has no direct powers of enforcement, the 38 signatories to the Convention commit themselves to enforcing this expression of intent through domestic legislation. The OECD Convention on Bribery creates obligations for participating countries to translate the concepts and principles into domestic law, which consequently alters the legal obligations of companies. The OECD Working Group on Bribery in International Business Transactions is responsible for monitoring the implementation and enforcement of the 1997 Convention, in addition to the more recent "Recommendation on Further Combating Bribery of Foreign Bribery in International Business Transactions" (2009) and other related instruments. The OECD has been taking an increasingly active role in this area; the 2009 recommendation is geared towards helping signatories prevent, detect, and investigate allegations of foreign bribery, and includes "Good Practice Guidance on Internal Controls, Ethics and Compliance." All of the OECD's country reports detailing the current state of anti-bribery measures, and data collected from participating countries, are available on its website (www.oecd.org).

The OECD has also played a role in attempting to improve the anti-corruption regimes of specific geographic regions. To date, 28 countries have endorsed a joint plan by the Asian Development Bank/OECD Anti-Corruption Initiative for Asia and the Pacific, which aims to set minimum standards and safeguards to prevent corruption and bribery.

In addition to the work of the OECD, the growing governmental consensus that corruption is a threat to development is being entrenched by other strategic policy initiatives at the highest level. After Resolution 55/61 in 2000, the United Nations Convention Against Corruption entered into force in December 2005, with 140 signatories, and stressed the importance of the principles of prevention, criminalization, international cooperation, and asset recovery in countering the threat of corruption.

The UN Global Compact

Corporate social responsibility (CSR) initiatives have also illustrated top-level commitment from major companies to combating corruption. However, not all of the abstract principles lauded by the United Nations have received equal attention, from either governments or businesses. Coca-Cola's Chief Ethics and Compliance Officer pointed out that historically, multinational corporations have acted with relatively less urgency where corruption is concerned.[13] Recent events and high-profile cases (discussed later in the book) indicate that this is changing rapidly. This change is illustrated by the UN Global Compact, a strategic policy initiative created in 2000 comprising 5,300 businesses and six UN agencies, which describes itself as the "world's largest corporate citizenship and sustainability initiative." The network aims to place ten universal principles into business philosophy and everyday operation. These are:[14]

Human Rights
Principle 1: Businesses should support and respect the protection of internationally proclaimed human rights; and
Principle 2: make sure that they are not complicit in human rights abuses.

Labour
Principle 3: Businesses should uphold the freedom of association and the effective recognition of the right to collective bargaining;

Principle 4: the elimination of all forms of forced and compulsory labour;

Principle 5: the effective abolition of child labour; and

Principle 6: the elimination of discrimination in respect of employment and occupation.

Environment

Principle 7: Businesses should support a precautionary approach to environmental challenges;

Principle 8: undertake initiatives to promote greater environmental responsibility; and

Principle 9: encourage the development and diffusion of environmentally friendly technologies.

Anti-Corruption

Principle 10: Businesses should work against corruption in all its forms, including extortion and bribery.

The World Bank and other global organizations have recently paid considerable attention to combating corruption and bribery.

BUSINESS ATTITUDES TO BRIBERY

Some Western companies are prone to dismiss corrupt practices as norms that are intrinsic to the culture of certain countries, especially in the developing world. Executives may feel that certain locations, as well as particular people, are acceptable targets for corruption. Bribery may be dismissed as a necessary evil or be seen as an informal tax on operating in certain regions.

The corporation, like the state, might eschew morally ambiguous practices at home but embrace questionable ethical standards in foreign dealings. Faced with deliberate stalling by corrupt officials or simply with inefficient public administrations, corporations might turn a blind eye to the activities of their agents or subsidiaries in an effort to speed up their business transactions.

However, parent companies (or their subsidiaries and agents) that continue to operate with this mentality might find themselves in trouble when the UK Bribery Act comes into force. Tom Beezer, an expert in multi-jurisdictional law at law firm Bond Pearce, points out that:

Different areas of the world may have a completely different view of how a relationship should be properly constructed and what is acceptable. Your overseas representatives, who may not be aware of the UK legislation, might be doing something perfectly normal where they are based, but the UK mother ship could fall foul of the Act.[15]

11

Despite an increase in the number of UK companies that strive to eliminate corruption from their activities (and the activities of their associates), the necessary cultural shift has not yet occurred. A recent report by the UK Financial Services Authority (FSA) identifies a number of serious current concerns with British business and their relation to, and attitude towards, bribery:

- Weak governance of anti-bribery and corruption and a poor understanding of bribery and corruption risk among senior managers.
- Poor responses by many firms to significant bribery and corruption events, which should have led them to reassess the adequacy of their preventative systems and controls.
- Weak monitoring of third party relationships and payments, with a worrying lack of documentary evidence of due diligence taking place.
- Little or no specific training provided on anti-bribery and corruption, even for staff in higher-risk positions; and inadequate compliance and internal audit monitoring of anti-bribery and corruption work.[16]

This research suggests that the consequences of the UK Bribery Act might be a shock to many boards. When the FSA investigated 17 wholesale insurance intermediaries operating in the London market it found that:

insurance intermediaries have historically approached this area of their business far too informally (especially higher-risk business) and that, at present, many firms would not be able to demonstrate that they have in place adequate procedures to prevent bribery, as required by the Bribery Act 2010. As such, there is a significant risk of illicit payments being made to win business.[17]

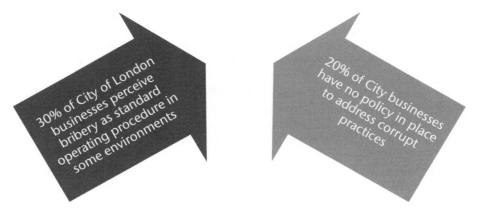

FIGURE I.2 **Complacency in the City of London**

Source: Pinsent Masons/Barry Vitou.

These FSA concerns are echoed by other research. Over a third of respondents to a Transparency International survey in 2010 thought that City of London businesses perceive bribery as standard operating procedure in some environments, and a survey by a City law firm showed that 20 percent of City businesses had no policy in place to address corrupt practices.[18] These worrying findings are not unique to British companies. All businesses that operate in a competitive environment may have an interest in tacitly condoning bribery in pursuit of profit.

THE PRISONER'S DILEMMA: IF WE DON'T PAY BRIBES OUR COMPETITORS WILL

The Prisoner's Dilemma is a tool borrowed from game theory, where it has been used to explain why two self-interested actors may not co-operate, even though it is ultimately in both their interests to do so. More specifically, it has been applied to the problem that businesses face when deciding whether or not to pay bribes. In an ideal world, all companies bidding for a contract or commodity would reject all requests for bribes. This would result in an optimal outcome: the initial price of the contract or commodity would be lower, the savings would be passed on to the end users, and the best bid would be the one that succeeds. However, this is not an ideal world. Companies are by no means certain that their competitors are behaving honestly, and are uncertain about their motives, and so bribes are paid, the price of goods soars, and corrupt officials flourish.

David Frost, director-general of the British Chambers of Commerce, epitomized this mentality when he raised concerns that "In a cut and thrust world of exporting what we don't want is the British playing with a straight bat and we find some of our competitors are not."[19] Businesses that would, ideally, reject all forms of bribery are held captive by their belief that bribery is universal and unavoidable, and may tacitly condone bribery out of suspicion or uncertainty about the methods of their competitors.

A crucial factor in this situation is the historical weakness of anti-corruption regimes and of what Professor Robert Sullivan of London University calls "nails in the club," tools for detection, enforcement, and deterrence. Although research indicates that effective deterrence may not always require the prospect of high penalties along with a significant prospect of detection,[20] companies may evaluate the likelihood of being caught (and the size of the fine should this occur) and conclude that in many cases it is cheaper to pay a bribe than to play fair.

The UK Bribery Act raises the possibility that private investigators may increasingly be used by companies in the future to demonstrate that their competitors are paying (or offering to pay) bribes. Once a board has consciously decided to stop any kind of bribe paying or facilitation payment, it becomes in its interest to ensure that other companies with which it is in direct competition are exposed and prosecuted. In this way, informal self-regulation may create the necessary momentum for the corporate "prisoners" to break out of the dilemma and create positive change in business culture.

This structural dilemma has only partial explanatory power; it ignores the individuals and organizations in the equation. Not all corporates pay bribes and not all officials request or demand them. When competing for a contract with another company that has a reputation for bribery (or in a country that is synonymous with corruption), a business may be more tempted to offer bribes. Because the decision to take or offer bribes is a highly individual one (and dependent on such factors as a person's psychology and economic situation), determining whether an executive or public official is susceptible to bribery can be a delicate art. Court papers in a recent US bribery scandal detailed one initial approach: "Mr. Rahal recounted how he would drop a $100 bill on the floor, then bend to pick it up, saying: 'You must have dropped this. Is it yours?' If the person said yes, Mr. Rahal considered him receptive."[21]

CULTURAL ATTITUDES TO BRIBERY: IT'S JUST HOW THINGS ARE DONE

While British legal authorities may not have a lot of sympathy with the kind of cultural relativism that accepts bribery as part of business in a country or sector, there is some evidence than not all bribes are equal in the eyes of the general public in particular countries. Analysis of a number of hypothetical scenarios appears to indicate that some forms of bribery are culturally condoned in Mauritius.[22] Some forms of the Chinese concept of "guanxi," defined as ongoing "relationships between or among individuals creating obligations for the continued exchange of favours," are closely associated with bribery and corrupt public officials; in other countries, this may be known as "blat," "bakshish," or "relationship marketing".[23] In light of the extraterritorial jurisdiction of the UK Bribery Act, much effort has gone into determining the extent to which "one culture's favor is another's bribe."[24]

There is a persistent argument in many countries that stopping bribery of foreign officials will mean they are not able to compete with other companies who will continue to bribe. Despite Lord Woolf dismissing the assertion that competitors will benefit from robust anti-corruption procedures as a thin excuse "made for not doing things that you know you should,"[25] there is evidence to suggest that (in the short term at least) it is not unfounded. It is estimated that, from 1977 to 2004, American companies lost 400 major contracts because of bribes given by competitors to foreign government officials.[26] When viewed from a short-term and superficial perspective, bribery can be perceived as a good thing by maintaining market dominance and increasing efficiency for a particular company, by reducing queuing time and thereby expediting essential processes.[27]

A BAD REPUTATION

Where an individual is seen as a potential future liability, government officials may be unlikely to want to be seen to have anything to do with them for fear of harming their own reputation. An individual's possible involvement with corruption and bribery can cause shunning by diplomatic officials in countries with strong anti-corruption values.

This fear of stigmatization, of being tarnished with the same brush if allegations are made in the future, could also cause indirect harm to associates of corrupt businesspeople. In this way, corruption erodes the trusting relationship that is crucial between government and business. Dan Roberts, the former deputy editor of the *Sunday Telegraph*, points out that "There are other convincing arguments against turning a blind eye to corruption. The most powerful ... is that being seen to flout international law is even more damaging to Britain's commercial reputation than it is politically."[28]

Research tends to focus on the economic consequences of bribery in the countries in which it occurs (that is to say, countries in which it is received), rather than on the consequences of being caught paying bribes. This is a serious omission, as it is clear that this impact can be grievous. The news that a firm (or subsidiary of a multinational corporation) is being prosecuted, or has been convicted of bribery, can immediately impact on the share price. In late 2010, shares in Panalpina dropped 4.1 percent on the news of its admission of guilt in a deferred prosecution agreement concerning the bribery of officials in at least seven countries.[29]

According to Sam Eastwood, a partner with lawyers Norton Rose:

As international anti-corruption policies impact increasingly on global companies and their dealings with other companies, a dynamic of "corporates policing corporates" is beginning to emerge. In order to protect themselves from liability attaching to them from other potentially corrupt business entities, commercial organisations are increasingly requesting details of the anti-corruption policies and procedures of the companies with which they enter into business relationships. Crucially this means that commercial organisations are becoming increasingly concerned with compliance with the Bribery Act and other jurisdictions' anti-corruption legislation, even if those laws do not directly apply to them.[30]

The 2010 UK Foreign Bribery Strategy recognizes the seriousness of the potential economic disadvantage of retreating from bribery, and states that the government will actively support "transparent companies with robust anti-corruption procedures" in order to "ensure that ethical business will not be undercut by unscrupulous competitors or disadvantaged in access to [government] support."[31] Demonstrating a robust bribery risk management strategy will surely become an essential component of all corporate bids tendering for government contracts as well as a cornerstone of CSR. As well as damage to its reputation, being caught bribing can result in severe economic consequences beyond the immediate fine or plea-bargain.

Disbarment for a period of years from tendering for future lucrative contracts can have severe consequences for a business. So the German construction company Lahmeyer International suffered severe losses after it was banned from tendering for seven years for World Bank-funded projects after a conviction for bribery in South Africa. The World Bank's Sanctions Committee found that Lahmeyer engaged in corrupt activities by bribing the Lesotho Highlands Development Authority's Chief Executive, Mr Masupha Sole, the government official responsible for contract. The World Bank told Lahmeyer on December 6, 2006, that the period of ineligibility may be reduced by four years if the Bank decides that Lahmeyer has met specific compliance conditions and fully cooperated with the Bank "in disclosing past sanctionable misconduct."[32]

While in some cases debarring is discretionary and might be avoided if promises to rectify the situation are made at the appropriate level (for example, with World Bank contracts), in others (for example under the European Union Procurement Directives), a purchasing body must exclude from tendering any company that has been convicted of corruption. The risk of mandatory disqualification from tenders is something boards need to take seriously.

Countries, as well as companies, that acquire a reputation for receiving bribes are also damaged. The developing country that is so stigmatized will jeopardize its eligibility to receive future aid payments; the Millennium Challenge Corporation only gives aid to those states that are judged to be implementing principles of good governance, which includes an evaluation of their control over corruption.[33] The closure of the UK investigation into BAE's activities in Saudi Arabia and elsewhere damaged the country's reputation for transparency. This weakened the efforts of British companies in bidding for contracts abroad.

The reputation for corruption serves as a bar on any form of business activity. To the extent that this form of abuse has hitherto been neglected, such tolerance is unlikely to be sustained. Individuals with a reputation for corruption will be excluded from the job market. They will also burn their bridges with influential public officials.

Companies perceived as corrupt face serious consequences in terms of their share price. They may also be precluded from tendering for lucrative contracts. Those stigmatized once are likely to attract the attention of regulators and law enforcement agencies. Developing nations' governments have particular reason to fear being deemed corrupt; a reputation as a country where bribery of public officials is encouraged or tolerated does nothing to help attract foreign direct investment and international aid.

PART I
THREATS

1

THE THREATS:
ECONOMIC, SOCIAL, AND POLITICAL
EFFECTS OF CORRUPTION AND BRIBERY

Bribery and corruption introduces an opaqueness into the relationship between buyers and sellers, between those who issue contracts and those who tender for them, between those who hold political power and citizens who must obey authority. This in turn leads to a weakening of trust in ostensibly fair practice at one level, and in disillusionment with political and market procedures at another level.

Markets and populations have long experienced deception and distortion, but it is argued that globalization has added to the problem. This is because it has enhanced the scale and speed of business activity beyond the capacity of regulators to ensure accountability.

Corrupt practices hit all levels of business and society, even in subtle ways that are not immediately apparent. In public works contracts, bribes paid to site inspectors can have devastating consequences in the long term if substandard labor or materials are used in the construction of infrastructure. In correspondence with the authors, Barry Vitou of law firm Pinsent Masons, who specializes in corporate risk and assurance, explained that "Poorly delivered goods and services are also a feature of corruption. For example, it is said that the tendency of buildings to collapse and roads to wash away in some poorer jurisdictions is due to corruption."[1] In other contexts, corruption can mean a few cents on the price of desperately needed medicine in the developing world. It can mean a 20 percent premium on the cost of a contract for public service provision. It can buy the silence of witnesses to corporate negligence or criminality, and it can fund terrorism and narco-trafficking.

The former director of the UK Serious Fraud Office (SFO), Robert Wardle, draws attention to how corruption acts as a barrier to positive change in the developing world: "Bribery in order to obtain business has long been recognized as a serious impediment to overseas development. It is a drain on the resources of the poorest countries and is uncompetitive and corrosive to standards of corporate behaviour."[2]

Because corrupt practices have such far-reaching negative consequences, eliminating them from the public and private sectors can bring

19

widespread beneficial effects. In the words of Angel Gurría, secretary-general of the Organization for Economic Co-operation and Development (OECD):

> All of us stand to benefit from a global economy where bribery and corruption have been ruled out. Corporations want to seek business opportunities based on the price, quality and pertinence of their goods and services, instead of having to look over their shoulders to check if their competitors are offering bribes to get the contract. Taxpayers want assurance that their taxes are reaching the people they were designed to help, and not being siphoned off into secret bank accounts.[3]

THE ECONOMIC EFFECTS OF CORRUPTION: BRIBERY AND BUSINESS

Bribery has a detrimental impact on the market by driving up prices through price fixing and backroom deals. In both developed and developing countries, a culture of bribery can prevent change and stifle competition. However this effect can also be brought about deliberately. Companies have sometimes resorted to bribery to maintain their dominant position in the market or to slow the pace of technological change that appears to be inevitable, or to resist efforts to improve environmental regulations and ban harmful fuel additives such as TEL (tetra-ethyl-lead) in developing countries. The SFO summary of the case of Innospec Limited stated that:

> In order to conduct its business in Indonesia, the company appointed agents to act on its behalf in seeking to win or continue contracts to supply TEL. Between 14 February 2002 and 31 December 2006 (the indictment period), the company paid $11.7 million to its agents. From these commissions, bribes were paid by the agents to staff at the state-owned petroleum refinery, Pertamina, and other public officials who were in a position to favour the company by purchasing orders of TEL .... One particular fund was structured to protect the interests of the lead based additives industry, whereas in truth and reality, it was no more than a slush fund to corrupt senior officials in various Ministries with the intention of blocking legislative moves to ban or enforce the ban on TEL on environmental grounds and/or seeking a higher level buy-in to continued yearly supplies of TEL to Pertamina.[4]

Corruption also undermines investor confidence across all sectors of business. A 2003 survey by the Foreign Policy Centre shows that the perceived level of corruption is the single biggest disincentive for companies wanting to invest in foreign markets.[5] However, the pernicious effects of corruption are not merely economic; they pervade all levels of society.

THE POLITICAL EFFECTS OF BRIBERY AND CORRUPTION

Corporations are among the principal stakeholders in a country's governance. They take part in virtually every element of a state's structure, going way beyond the commercial and business world. So they will engage, often at the highest level, with its justice system, its aid and trade bodies, its domestic security agencies, its employment and human resources administrations, and many more. They will likewise seek to lobby politicians, often as senior as the head of state. Corporations have immense resources at their disposal to achieve their particular ends.

While the corporation has so much economic power, local government officials' decisions have the power to affect outcomes. Those decisions are reached by balancing many complexities, ranging from economic and employment consequences, through issues of resource utilization and pressures from local interest groups. "Gray areas" abound in negotiations with the external enterprise. The successful outcome to a negotiation can be explained to all the participants and stakeholders. It respects transparency above all. When states and their officials cannot explain the route they traveled to reach an outcome to a negotiation, they make themselves and their stakeholders vulnerable to the charge of corruption. Corruption, like fraud, may be the result of a secret deal that occurs in the shadows.

The deal that cannot be tested at any point in its life or by any authority (judicial or political) risks unraveling through the force of rumor, allegation, and finally suspicion. The parties to the deal (and many who may have had no part) are likely to be touched and compromised in this process. Officials who acquire a reputation for negotiating privately rather than publicly, and in their own self-interest rather than that of the country, weaken their negotiating positions with other stakeholders.

Weak officials and corrupt states are prey to corporations. Worse still, they are likely to be seized upon and exploited by organized crime, terrorists and other traffickers of arms, people, and drugs. International efforts to combat narco-trafficking in Africa and South America have been crippled by corruption and bribery, in which cartels have been known to offer a choice to public officials between taking silver or lead.

Those who obtain profits corruptly, either by distorting the market or by selling state assets through secret negotiation, are required to engage in underhand practices to cover the trail of those profits. They then expose themselves to charges of money laundering and fraud. A Transparency International (TI) study of Vietnam found that bribery and corruption were associated with "the loss of state assets, reduction in business opportunities and competitiveness due to increased production costs, reduced foreign investor confidence, under-utilization and loss of competent civil servants and officials, increased social inequality and environmental degradation."[6]

Bribes can also impede the consolidation of democratic structures and processes. Academics and NGOs such as TI have argued that "money lost to corruption is the largest potential source of funding available to many new democratic governments aside from foreign direct investment."[7]

The wider effects of bribery are not restricted to hampering economic and social development, or weakening democratic governments. Bribes used by criminal executives to cover up their wrongdoing or dubious activities can have a corrosive effect on justice in the country in which they occur. There have been reports that American businesspeople have offered bribes to foreign public officials in order to thwart investigations being conducted by the US Securities and Exchange Commission into other financial misconduct.[8]

When bribery seeks to circumvent regulations, the environment and ecosystem of a country can be threatened, as well as the integrity of a government department implicated in such a scandal. In 2005, agrochemical giant Monsanto was fined US$1.5 million (£799,000) after it admitted that one executive paid $50,000 (£31,000) in bribes – which were hidden in the accounts as "consulting fees" – to officials in Indonesia's environment ministry, in an attempt to prevent environmental impact assessments being conducted on its genetically modified cotton.[9]

The global reach, economic power, and intelligence capabilities of the largest corporations now exceed those of many small and developing nations. The disparity between private and public power is no more evident than in the relationship between transnational corporations and developing states with weak governance. In these cases, bribery can misappropriate the infrastructure of developing countries for commercial gain. Swiss freight company Panalpina admitted, in a US$236.5 million settlement, to bribing Angolan military officials so the company could use military cargo aircraft to transport commercial goods. It also admitted paying bribes in hundreds of ways in seven nations between 2000 and 2007.[10] US prosecutors and courts would use this case to narrow down the scope of the facilitation payment defence, under the Foreign Corrupt Practices Act.

Where a particular government is synonymous with corruption, it can erode social capital and foster support for various forms of extremism. One UK weapons manufacturer famously said of Saudi Arabia, "Commissions make the world go round.... I don't know of a royal who'll get out of bed for less than five percent."[11] When interviewed by the author, Professor Robert Sullivan of University College, London argued that in Saudi Arabia this attitude has dangerous consequences that go far beyond popular disillusionment:

> There is no doubt at all that certain habits of these kleptocrats are a major bulwark against development .... There is real anger in the countries which are dominated by ruling elites, and the best example I know is Saudi Arabia. Just under the surface is enormous anger from the out-

group, and it is one of the major drivers of the jihadis and with every reason. They see a tremendous ongoing collusion between western interests and these rip-off elites. Both are playing the same game and they find the hypocrisy gut-wrenching.[12]

While the Saudi corruption that helps extremists to flourish is allegedly on a massive scale, involving huge sums of money and high-level officials, corruption on a far smaller scale can still have corrosive effects. Paying off border guards to ensure swift passage of entirely legal goods may seem fairly innocuous, but widespread low-level bribery subverts state sovereignty and contributes to a culture of lawlessness, which can facilitate activities such as organized crime and terrorism. The architect of the 2004 Beslan school massacre, Shamil Basayev, reportedly bribed Russian border guards to cross from Chechnya deep into Russia to conduct terrorist attacks.[13] Similarly, when ordinary Somalis suspect officials in Mogadishu of taking bribes from foreign trawler companies it reduces already weak trust in government and may increase support for both Al-Shabaab and for pirates.[14]

In all the countries in which it occurs, explains the former head of the UK Serious Fraud Office (SFO) anti-corruption team, "Not only does bribery distort markets, it leads to a wider loss of trust in the fabric of government and the administration of law."[15] This erosion of trust between the government and the people can ultimately fuel the forces of anarchy and revolution; the corruption surrounding over-powerful rulers has been repeatedly cited as a central reason for the uprisings currently taking place across North Africa and the Middle East.

Although it has not reached the same level, popular resentment at corruption in sub-Saharan Africa is a serious problem. There have been concerns that corruption in Kenya threatens to precipitate the country into organized violence as witnessed in the wake of the 2008 election.

THE IMPACT OF BRIBERY ON SOCIETY

As noted above, one of the major effects of widespread corruption is its hugely destabilizing impact on a country's social order. A culture of bribery can effectively hold society captive, slow or stop social progress, and empower despots. In systemically corrupt countries, bribery can be seen to increase the divide between the ruling elite and the dispossessed, with potentially devastating long-term consequences.

The anti-corruption pressure group TI publishes an annual Corruption Perceptions Index, which ranks 178 countries according to their perceived levels of public sector corruption, from Denmark, New Zealand, and Singapore to Myanmar, Afghanistan, and Somalia. Countries with low average income and high levels of inequality are very likely to be at the upper end of the index. TI's findings show that high levels of inequality in the

23

distribution of income predict high levels of corruption.[16] The Corruption Perceptions Index, supported by numerous other studies, shows that per capita income is inversely related to corruption, and that countries with greater economic inequalities are perceived as substantially more corrupt.

Exacerbating inequality and deprivation can contribute to social instability and create the conditions for popular uprising. This in turn damages investor confidence and depresses trade. When bribes are a matter of course in the distribution of goods in developing countries, payment is a burdensome extra expense, and non-payment can cause delays, increasing waiting times, and affecting all the businesses that depend on those goods. In the summary of the 2010 report, Huguette Labelle, chair of TI, stated:

> corruption remains an obstacle to achieving much needed progress ... Allowing corruption to continue is unacceptable; too many poor and vulnerable people continue to suffer its consequences around the world. We need to see more enforcement of existing rules and laws. There should be nowhere to hide for the corrupt or their money.[17]

The corrosive effect of corruption on social cohesion in China is increasingly evident. A report published in the *Pacific Economic Review* shows that increased inequality between the ruling elite and the rest of society is a major cause of popular resentment. The authors note that "high-level profiteering is a major cause of disaffection among the working class in China and was one of the main causes of the Tiananmen Square demonstrations."[18]

Official corruption becomes prevalent where economic change outpaces social and political development. In his 2007 study of global terrorism, *Brave New War*, author John Robb says of China, a country where this process has been particularly apparent:

> The rise of the role of the market, at the expense of the state, has in many cases stretched the state to breaking point.... The rapid pace of economic growth in the country has radically outpaced the capacity of the government to police it or mitigate its negative effects. The result has been a rapid rise in the number of economic protests from people demanding protection and/or support.[19]

In the former Soviet Union, the huge economic changes and rapid privatization of previously public assets after the fall of communism have created a corrupt shadow economy. In contemporary Russia, there are concerns that rampant bribery functions like a parallel tax system for the personal enrichment of elites – at the cost of the rest of society.

These examples serve as brief illustrations of the damage that corruption and bribery have on the economic, political, and social orders in the countries in which they occur. However they provide only a glimpse of the devastating consequences that corruption can have on citizens, businesses, and governments. Throughout the private and public sectors there is an increased acknowledgement of the gravity of the situation. This is due to a large extent to the work of civil society groups which have sought to raise the profile of corruption as a global evil to be confronted.

PART II
LAW

2

THE GLOBAL LEGAL CONTEXT

THE FOREIGN CORRUPT PRACTICES ACT:
THE UNITED STATES LEADS THE WAY

In 1977 the Foreign Corrupt Practices Act (FCPA) was enacted in the United States. The FCPA prohibits paying anything of value to foreign officials that could make them act contrary to their duties or to gain an unfair business advantage. The Act also requires corporations to keep accurate books, records, and accounts. This Act made the United States the first country to criminalize the payment of bribes by its citizens and companies to foreign officials overseas. The FCPA also applies to certain foreign issuers of securities and to anyone carrying out bribery within the United States. It can be called into effect even when there is no crime committed in the United States, and companies can be held responsible for acts of independent foreign subsidiaries. The FCPA allows facilitation payments for routine government action. This chapter looks at the history of the FCPA, what it says, how it works in practice, why it was introduced, and the effect it has had.

The history of the FCPA

Corrupt practices in American businesses used to be commonplace, and this came to the attention of the US government in the 1970s. The first hint was when, in 1970, the International Telephone and Telegraph Corporation (ITT) offered the CIA US\$1 million to block the election of a Marxist candidate in Chile. The CIA refused. To investigate this, the Subcommittee on Multinational Corporations was formed under Frank Church.[1] At the time bribery was not illegal under US law, but the Church Subcommittee decided that the acts of ITT had been unethical if not illegal.

The true extent of international bribery was only revealed following the Watergate scandal. In June 1972 five men were arrested for breaking into the Democratic National Committee headquarters at the Watergate hotel. This led to a series of political scandals as a huge number of illegal activities by those in power to maintain their power came to light over the next two years, which culminated in the resignation of President Nixon in August

1974.[2] These illegal activities included illegal campaign contributions from businesses. This led the US Securities and Exchange Commission (SEC) to investigate. They discovered that the companies that had been making the illegal campaign donations had used off-the-book "slush funds." These funds had also been used by US companies for bribing foreign public officials. Investigations under Frank Church showed that increasingly large bribes had been paid out by US companies throughout the 1960s and 1970s.

To cope with huge amount of cases the SEC launched a voluntary disclosure program in 1975, in which companies that came forward, admitted to bribery, and cooperated with investigations were unlikely to be prosecuted.[3] Over 400 American companies came forward and admitted making questionable payments abroad; between them they had paid bribes of over $300 million. In a congressional hearing in 1976 the Lockheed Corporation admitted to spending $24 million on bribes around the world. People that Lockheed had bribed included the Japanese prime minister and a member of the Dutch royal family. Lockheed claimed that bribery was just a part of business and was not illegal, and it did not promise to stop bribing.[4]

The issue of bribery by American corporations was discussed over a number of Senate meetings throughout the early 1970s. It was argued that US companies needed to pay bribes so that they could compete with multinational corporations based in other countries who paid bribes.[5] There were however also a lot of arguments for making bribery illegal. The effect of bribery on American foreign policy was certainly a significant factor, especially after the Lockheed scandal. The United States did not want its companies paying bribes to foreign politicians and possibly causing more scandals.

It is also important that the SEC was devoted to transparency and maximizing the disclosure of relevant financial information to stockholders. Furthermore bribery was seen by many as immoral. A strong US antibribery law could help companies resist corrupt demands abroad.[6] There was also the reputation of both the United States and of capitalist systems in general, which needed to be upheld. In 1976 the US secretary of commerce, Elliot Richardson, wrote that allowing bribery reduces the international acceptability of multinational corporations and makes them appear unaccountable to the law. He said that bribery erodes people's confidence in capitalism, in corporate responsibility, and in democracy. Furthermore he claimed that stopping bribes made by US companies trying to meet foreign competition would not lead to a significant loss of business.[7]

The Senate meetings moved on to look at how best to deal with these problems. The Ford administration suggested a Foreign Payments Disclosure Act whereby companies would have to report payments to foreign public officials and the foreign governments could choose whether to prosecute. Senator William Proxmire said that such an Act would allow companies to continue to pay bribes. He proposed that companies should be forced to disclose all payments over $1,000 to foreign officials, and that bribery payments should be criminalized. The SEC claimed that this would be impossible to monitor, and pushed for a system whereby corporations would have to monitor themselves. Proxmire revised his plan and drafted what became the FCPA.[8]

On December 19, 1977 the FCPA was signed into law by President Carter.[9] The Act stated that companies are responsible for establishing accounting controls, and criminalized bribery to foreign public officials, to retain or obtain business. It was fought for by anti-corruption champions such as Church and Proxmire. This was the first Act of its kind in the world. No other country had anything similar; in fact at the time in some Western countries companies could deduct money spent on bribes from tax returns as legitimate business expenses.[10] To ensure that American companies did not lose out in competition with other countries, the United States immediately tried to internationalize anti-bribery measures. It wanted to have a code of conduct drafted by the United Nations. However international divisions and opposition from multinationals impeded any decisive step. In 1979 the United States dropped this project.[11]

The FCPA received a lot of criticism throughout the rest of the 1970s and the 1980s from those who thought it was damaging American business. The main argument against the Act is that it reduced the ability of US companies to compete in an international market, especially without other countries having similar laws. The Act was also widely criticized for being unclear and ambiguous in both its anti-bribery provisions and its accounting provisions.

Opponents of the Act claimed that it was unclear what was prohibited and permitted, and in particular what payments could be regarded not as bribes but as facilitation payments. They claimed that this led companies to cease foreign trade rather than have to deal with these uncertainties, and this cost up to $1 billion annually in US export trade.[12] Similarly the accounting controls were criticized as being too costly and burdensome and for making companies overly cautious when trying to avoid possible penalties. It was argued that companies should only have to report details relating to the profits of the firm. Also that it was unfair to ask US firms to "play detective" and constantly monitor the actions of independent agents in foreign countries. Furthermore the Act was seen as a case of US ethno-centrism: it was the United States forcing its own moral views on the rest of the world when paying bribes is actually morally acceptable according to many cultures.[13]

It is not clear exactly how bad for business the FCPA was. Proxmire disputed the claim that the law reduced US exports by $1 billion annually. He said that this was a self-described "hit or miss" estimate that directly contradicted past testimony by administration officials.[14] In fact there has never been any conclusive evidence that the FCPA has put US companies at a competitive disadvantage.[15] Yet it seems quite probable that businesses were disadvantaged somewhat.

In 1981 the US General Accounting Office reported on the effects of the FCPA on business. It concluded that the FCPA appeared successful in reducing bribery and had led to a number of changes in business activities. Companies had introduced more accounting controls. There was a change and an increase in codes of conduct being given to employees, and an increase in written acknowledgements from employees that they would comply with the codes. However there was widespread confusion and controversy about exactly what the FCPA said, and the FCPA itself was vague and ambiguous. Furthermore 30 percent of companies claimed they had lost business overseas, and 60 percent believed they could not compete on equal terms with foreign companies.[16]

Throughout the 1980s there was a significant lull in FCPA prosecutions. During Reagan's eight years as president (1981–89) the SEC settled only two cases.[17] This led to a debate throughout the 1980s about whether to change the FCPA, water it down, or maybe scrap it altogether.[18] In 1988 the FCPA was amended as part of the Omnibus Trade and Competitiveness Act.

The amendment meant that there was now no accountability for failing to meet accounting provisions unless it had been done knowingly, and the provisions need be no more than those that would be put in place by a prudent man. A company needed to use its influence only in good faith to push firms that it did not control to maintain acceptable accounting controls. Furthermore simple negligence or foolishness was not a basis for liability for having bribed foreign intermediaries; instead deliberate ignorance was the criterion for a violation. The amendment provided definitions about what counted as bribing foreign officials. It explained the exception for facilitation payments, and stated that the Attorney General must offer advice about what is permissible within 30 days of a request. The fines for violations were increased and the amendment provided two affirmative defences (that the payments were legal under the written laws of the country or that they were genuine expenses).[19] The amendment to the FCPA in 1988 made prosecutions more difficult, by mandating that evidence of deliberate ignorance was required for prosecution and by providing the affirmative offenses. Despite more restrictions the amount of FCPA cases investigated increased into the 1990s.[20]

At the same time the US Congress set in motion procedures and negotiations with the OECD to put pressure on other countries, particularly those countries who were the United States' main competitors, to put in place legislation similar to the FCPA.

Talks with the OECD came to fruition when the OECD Convention on Combating Bribery of Foreign Public Officials in International Business Transactions was signed by 33 countries including the United States and the United Kingdom in December 1997.[21] The convention went into effect in 1999. The signatory countries all agreed to make it illegal to bribe a foreign public official to obtain an advantage in business.

The FCPA was amended to make it apply to foreign individuals or foreign companies who acted in any way that would lead to a corrupt payment while they were in the United States.[22] The amendment also prohibited bribery to obtain any improper business advantage from foreign officials, extended the jurisdiction for certain FCPA cases,[23] and redefined "foreign official" to include a member of a public international organization.[24]

In the 21st century, FCPA enforcement has increased massively. A number of other laws and changes to enforcement strategies were passed that led to changes in FCPA enforcement. Before 2002 fines were rarely above six figures, an amount that would never cripple a large multinational company, and FCPA compliance was not a huge issue. In 2002, following the Enron scandal in 2001 where false bookkeeping lost investors billions, the US Government passed the Sarbanes-Oxley Act (SOX), which required chief executives (CEOs) to sign off financial reports and thereby be responsible for their accuracy. SOX also supported whistleblowers. This led to a boost in the number of FCPA investigations. Over the next few years the SEC added hundreds of extra staff to help with FCPA enforcement. In 2007 the FBI created a new division that would work on FCPA cases, and again the number of cases rose. This allowed the SEC and the Department of Justice (DOJ) to use more methods to catch FCPA violators. For example in January 2010 the FBI arrested 22 executives after a sting operation where FBI agents posed as emissaries to an African defense minister who offered a large contract and let it be known that they wanted a bribe.[25]

In the last few years there have been a number of cases with record fines. In December 2008 Siemens, which had being paying bribes all around the world, had to pay $1.6 billion in fines for FCPA violations, the largest settlement so far. In 2009 KBR had to pay $579 million for its part in a bribery scheme in Nigeria, the largest fine paid by a US company,[26] and in 2010 the longest prison sentence, of 87 months, for an FCPA violation was given to Charles Jumet for bribing officials in Panama for Ports Engineering Consultants Corporation.[27] FCPA compliance is a huge issue for companies. We will later look in detail at exactly how FCPA enforcement takes place, how dangerous it really is for a company to be caught, and what is likely to happen to them. First we will look in more depth at exactly what the FCPA says.

What the FCPA says

The people and companies to which the FCPA applies are split into "issuers" and "domestic concerns." Many types of company in the United States are required to register with the SEC. This generally includes any US group involved in business. These domestic and foreign companies that are traded on any US stock exchange are known as issuers. A domestic concern is any individual or resident of the United States or any company which falls under US law or has its main business in US territory. This distinction is worth noting as some of the rules and enforcement differ for issuers and for domestic concerns. The FCPA also applies to foreign companies or nationals who do anything that leads to someone in the United States violating the FCPA themselves. They cannot pay bribes or violate the FCPA while they are in the United States, nor can they promote or encourage others to do so.

The FCPA has both anti-bribery provisions and accounting provisions. We will first look at the anti-bribery provisions. These prohibit the bribing of foreign officials for the purpose of obtaining or retaining business.[28]

The act of bribing is considered to be the payment or the promise of payment of "anything of value." The term "anything of value" is defined loosely. As well as cash it can include discounts, gifts, entertainment, travel, use of facilities, and promises of future employment. There is no minimum value for what has been given. The perception of the recipient and the subjective valuation in the eyes of the receiver, of the thing given, are used to consider whether a bribe has been paid. There is considerable focus on the purpose of the payment.

The term "foreign public official" is also interpreted quite broadly. A foreign public official can be considered to be anyone acting in an official position for any foreign government or international public organization. This includes employees of state-owned enterprises and employees of any companies over which the foreign state exercises considerable control, regardless of role or rank. It also includes candidates running for foreign political office.

The payment must be made with corrupt intent for it to violate the FCPA. It must be made with the intent of either encouraging an official to misuse his official position, or obtaining or retaining business or directing business to one particular party. To "obtain or retain business" can mean anything that gives the company an unfair competitive advantage, such as receiving special treatment or tax breaks. Furthermore the success of a bribe is not required for an FCPA violation.

The FCPA also states that US companies are also responsible for the acts of any foreign intermediaries that they use and for their foreign subsidiaries, even when no crime is committed on US territory. So it is illegal for a company to pay an intermediary when its staff know that, or consciously disregard the possibility that, the money will then be given to a foreign public official. To avoid the possibility of intermediaries paying bribes, companies are expected to practice some degree of due diligence. For example they should assess the risks of bribery in the place they are working and of the other companies they are working with, they should ask for written assurance of FCPA compliance, and keep an eye out for red flags.

The FCPA has an exception for facilitation payments. These are payments to ensure routine government action such as processing or providing permits, visas, and documentation, or providing police protection, power, water, mail, and anything similar to these. There is also an exception in the case of a company defending its property or its people.

There are also jurisdictional limitations that apply to the FCPA. For acts committed within the United States, to show a violation of anti-bribery provisions of FCPA by an issuer or a domestic concern, the use of an instrumentality of interstate commerce must be shown. This is satisfied by anything such as travel into the United States, travel between states, use of US mail or telephone, money passing through a US bank account, or even an email passing through US servers. This restriction does not apply for acts outside US territory. This restriction also does not apply to foreign nationals who fall under the FCPA.

The two possible affirmative defences are first, that the payment was legal under the written law of the country of the foreign official involved, and second, that the money was used for demonstrating a product or was part of a contractual obligation. However the onus is on the defence to show either of these was the case.

The DOJ has agreed to a number of measures to help companies comply with the FCPA. For example, the attorney-general will issue a decision in response to a specific request about what is permissible within 30 days of receiving the relevant information.

Enforcement of the FCPA is split between the DOJ and the SEC. The DOJ is responsible for all criminal cases and for civil cases involving domestic concerns or individuals who have violated the anti-bribery provisions. The SEC is responsible for civil enforcement of the anti-bribery provisions involving issuers.[29] A company or individuals can undergo both criminal and civil enforcement as a result of the same bribery case.

Under civil law, for violating the anti-bribery provisions, individuals or companies may be fined up to $10,000. The court can then impose another fine of a fixed amount that depends on the seriousness of the case, and can be at most $500,000 or up to the profit the violator expected to receive. However under criminal law, violating the anti-bribery provisions can mean that corporations are subject to a fine of up to $2,000,000 and individuals may be fined up to $100,000 and jailed for up to five years. Each of these fines can be levied for each violation of the FCPA. Also the Alternative Fines Act may increase any of these criminal fines to up to twice the gain or loss that was caused by the violation. Furthermore the SEC can disgorge companies' profits if they were made on contracts secured with improper payments. The fines on individuals cannot be paid by the company involved on the individual's behalf.

The SEC can also investigate and pass an injunction or other civil action against a person or a firm that it believes has violated, or is about to violate, the anti-bribery provisions.[30]

There also may be other repercussions for business or individuals. They may be barred from doing business with the federal government, be ruled ineligible to receive export licenses, be barred from the securities business, or barred from various programs with government agencies.

Violating the anti-bribery provisions of the FCPA may also give rise to a private cause of action, under the Racketeer Influenced and Corrupt Organizations Act (RICO), from a competitor who has lost out by the bribe for treble the damages they suffered, or to actions under other federal or state laws.[31]

The accounting provisions of the FCPA state that, first, issuers need to make and keep books and records that accurately and fairly reflect the transactions of the corporation and record all use of company assets. This prevents companies from hiding corrupt payments. Second, issuers must set up and maintain an adequate system of accounting controls. There are a number of reasons for these accounting controls. They enable the company to produce accurate financial statements, in which it can look for discrepancies between existing assets and recorded assets, and tell who is responsible for spending. These accounting controls limit individuals' access to a company's assets and thus help ensure that transactions carried out are in accordance with management decisions. The internal controls need to be such that they would satisfy a prudent official.[32]

Individuals involved with a company, such as directors, stockholders, and employees, can be subject to the accounting provisions. The accounting provisions extend to majority-owned foreign subsidiaries of an issuer. When an issuer holds less than or equal to 50 percent of a subsidiary's stock, then it is required to use its influence to a reasonable extent to encourage the subsidiary to devise and maintain accounting controls.

To prove civil violations of the accounting provisions no proof of intent is required. If a subsidiary breaks these rules, an issuer can be responsible for a civil violation even if the violation is unknown to the issuer.[33] Criminal violations are committed when a company or person deliberately violated the accounting provisions.

The accounting provisions do not apply if the rules are broken when a company is cooperating with the federal government on a matter concerning national security.[34]

Violation of the accounting provisions of the FCPA is always dealt with by the SEC. The fines for violating the accounting provisions are much larger than those for the bribery provisions. Under civil law, individuals can be fined up to $100,000 and corporations can be fined up to $500,000. Under criminal law individuals can be fined up to $5 million and jailed for up to 20 years, and companies can be fined up to $25 million. Once again these fines are levied for each violation of the FCPA, the Alternative Fines Act may increase any of the criminal fines to up to twice the gain or loss that was caused by the violation, and the fines on individuals cannot be paid by the company on the individual's behalf.

How it is enforced: the FCPA in practice

Normally when a company is charged under the anti-bribery rules, it will also face charges for false record keeping, as the bribery will almost certainly have been falsely recorded in the company's books.

Very seldom is there a case where a company is brought to court only because of its violating the record-keeping and internal control provisions of the FCPA. Normally such accusations are accompanied by more serious accusations of corruption.[35] Yet often it is false record keeping that a company will be charged with, and these accounting rules are hugely important in deterring bribers. Not only are the fines much higher, but it is often much easier for prosecutors to prove some wrongdoing. To prove a violation of the accounting rules in the civil courts there is no need to prove corrupt intent. In the criminal courts the accounting violations are much simpler to explain to a jury. There is no need to prove that a foreign official was involved or to show that a promise or offer of payment had been made. Most of the evidence is in documents, such as looking to see if records are false or insufficient. In many cases where evidence of bribery cannot be shown, companies still face huge repercussions for failing the record-keeping provisions.[36]

As well as the fines and the sanctions that can be placed on a company, the legal costs, and the loss of reputation, the SEC may also request that a company employ an independent compliance monitor. Since 2004 the SEC has regularly required this as a condition of a settlement with companies.[37] A monitor will do a number of different things. They will make sure the company keeps on the straight and narrow. They will ensure the company makes the changes it committed to make, and adheres to the terms of the settlement. They will review and evaluate the company's internal controls and the record-keeping procedure. The monitor may have to issue written reports,[38] and the company may be obliged to follow any recommendations made in those reports. Often the major cost for a company required to hire a monitor is not the monitor's fees but rather the cost of implementing the monitor's policy recommendations.[39] The monitor is authorized to disclose information should they find any evidence of corrupt payments.[40]

Although the introduction of a compliance monitor had been an increasing trend for FCPA cases in the last decade, it now seems to be on the decline. In 2008 the DOJ provided a policy for the selection and supervision of monitors. There has been a recent effort to rationalize the use of monitors. Instead of routinely requiring a monitor, the government is now using a more subtle approach, whereby it considers a number of factors such as how likely the company is to remain corrupt, the degree of the original transgression, and what procedures the company has voluntarily taken on to improve FCPA compliance.[41] The FCPA may consider other solutions, such as letting a company self-monitor.

There are other recent trends in FCPA prosecution. There has been a focus by the DOJ on investigating and prosecuting individuals rather than companies, in an attempt to deter people from corruption by the prospect of a prison sentence. The SEC and DOJ have also looked to target their investigations on sectors or industries that they feel are likely to have corrupt practices. For example the sting operation mentioned above that caught 22 executives was specifically aimed at the military and law enforcement products industry.

The enforcement agencies have also become noticeably more aggressive in their prosecution attempts over the last couple of years. They have begun using enforcement tactics such as the sting; they also try to use broad interpretations of the law, and they assume parent companies know about the crimes of their subsidiaries. They have also stepped up attempts to prosecute foreign nationals, and are even attempting to prosecute the foreign officials involved in bribery cases.

Both the SEC and DOJ encourage self-reporting, and have publicly announced that they will reward companies that self-report, cooperate with investigations, and voluntarily disclose information. This is made explicit in the US Principles of Federal Prosecution.[42] This reward will often take the form of deferred prosecution or even no prosecution for such companies. An increase in self-reporting has also been a factor in the recent increase in FCPA cases.

The SEC and DOJ have tried, and succeeded, to ensure that if an executive or any other member of a company discovers a bribe being paid, or records being falsified by an employee, intermediary or subsidiary of the company, it is almost always in the best interest of the company to self-report to the agencies (except in the smallest of cases where the matter can be handled internally). Self-reporting and cooperation can make it easier for a company to negotiate a favorable settlement with the SEC and DOJ. For example in a 2007 case Baker Hughes, a company in the oil services sector, pleaded guilty to paying bribes in Kazakhstan.[43] It had paid over $9 million in bribes, and had been previously accused of bribing in 2001, but it was only fined $21 million and made to disgorge profits of $23 million. The company could have been charged another $27 million, but the DOJ pushed for leniency due to Baker Hughes' "timely disclosure and exceptional cooperation."[44] In other cases self-reporting and cooperation have led to companies not being prosecuted at all.

It is not enough just to self report a case of FCPA violation and expect leniency. The enforcement agencies are also looking for companies that cooperate willingly with investigations, carry out their own investigations, take action against those involved, and increase compliance procedures.[45]

For example in 2004 the DOJ signed a non-prosecution agreement with InVision in return for cooperation, adopting an FCPA compliance program, paying a $8,000,000 fine, and accepting full responsibility.[46] InVision had a few years previously been using foreign sales agents and intermediaries in China, the Philippines, and Thailand, who were very likely to pay bribes to acquire contracts.[47]

Criminal corruption prosecutions may have significant consequences. A convicted company is almost always debarred from federal contracts in the United States. If it is convicted of corruption offenses it will also be excluded from government contracts in Europe. Many companies will therefore try to negotiate a settlement with the SEC or the DOJ that does not result in a criminal conviction, only a civil one. The DOJ may insist on a criminal plea from a subsidiary of the company but this does not lead to debarment of the company to the same extent.

The US government has been particularly sympathetic to companies with which it does a lot of work, where there would be collateral consequences for the government. For example in the Siemens case, which is examined in more detail elsewhere, the DOJ allowed the company to only plead guilty to violations of the accounting provisions of the FCPA and did not prosecute it for bribery.

The effect of the FCPA

The FCPA has had a significant global impact. Many companies from around the world are listed on the US stock exchange and thus have to comply with the FCPA. As has already been shown, the passing of the FCPA has accompanied American attempts to encourage the rest of the world to introduce anti-bribery laws. Thirty-eight of the world's richest countries have now signed the OECD Anti-bribery Convention.[48] In the UK, the City of London Police's Overseas Corruption Assessment Project collects data on the occurrence of corruption overseas, and, in the private sector, anti-corruption policies are being introduced into companies globally.[49]

American companies have reduced the amount of bribes paid and introduced various FCPA compliance measures. However American companies still pay bribes, and there are still corrupt companies in the United States.

Many companies are taking note of the increasing levels of FCPA enforcement that have been seen over the last decade. Adopting an FCPA compliance program is often seen as a necessity for large US businesses operating abroad,[50] as companies fear falling on the wrong side of the law. A 2010 Deloitte survey shows how FCPA compliance measures are increasing. The researchers questioned 216 senior professionals who were involved in business relationships outside the United States while working for US companies with a range of sizes and from a range of sectors, and 75 percent of participants said that companies in their industry had become more concerned about the FCPA in the previous three years. A total of 73 percent of correspondents said their company had increased compliance to reduce the risk of staff being caught paying bribes. Furthermore 65 percent said in the previous three years their companies had seen an increase in internal FCPA risk assessment. These figures were all higher for correspondents from larger companies. For example, of companies with annual revenues of $1 billion or more, 82 percent said there had been an increase in concern about FCPA compliance. Almost all the companies had some FCPA compliance, with larger companies doing more. Most of the larger companies (with revenues above or equal to $1 billion) provided training (87 percent) and had a formal system for reporting FCPA violations (73 percent).[51]

Of course, although this can be viewed as a great success in combating corruption, these results show that many companies still do not have the necessary due diligence controls in place that could prevent them from falling foul of the FCPA. The survey showed that only about 20 percent of companies always carry out detailed investigations before beginning business with another company. There is still a lack of compliance in US companies, and significant corruption remains.

This can be seen by looking at Transparency International's 2008 Bribery Perceptions Index (BPI), in which the United States only came ninth out of 22 countries.[52] The Bribery Perceptions Survey questioned thousands of executives from around the world about how corrupt they perceived business from various countries to be, then ranked the results. It showed first that no country is immune from corrupt corporations: all around the world businesses pay bribes. For the United States, 12 percent of correspondents thought American companies would be likely to bribe high-ranking politicians. 8 percent thought they would pay facilitation bribes to low-level government officials, and 11 percent thought they would use personal and familiar relationships to obtain contracts. The survey also showed that, globally, executives did not feel governments were adequately addressing the problems of bribery and corruption. For example only 28 percent of US business executives felt that their government was effective in stopping corruption. Corruption is decreasing, but it is far from gone from US companies.

Many people have criticized the FCPA by claiming that it impedes the ability of US companies to compete in a global market. This point may have been overstated, especially by opponents of the Act. They struggle to show that American companies have lost out at any stage in competing for contracts. Since 1977, although many other countries have stepped up their anti-bribery legislation, it is still argued by some that US companies are impeded by the FCPA. Certainly the FCPA has a negative effect on what business deals US companies are willing to enter into. For example in the Deloitte survey, 42 percent of participants said that their company had cancelled or renegotiated a deal abroad because of concerns about the FCPA.[53] The evidence also suggests that FCPA enforcement has led to a decrease in investment in countries where bribery is thought to be more common.[54] However this does not mean that there has been a significant inability to compete. In most cases where US companies have paid bribes, these were designed to win contracts from other US companies. Clearly stopping such bribes would have no effect on how the United States competes with other countries. Furthermore as we saw from Transparency International's BPI, the countries that are the US's main competitors in business are often even better at preventing bribes than is the United States. So it seems very far-fetched to say that US companies cannot compete in a global market.

It is interesting to consider companies' views of the FCPA. Some companies, in particular those that have been caught paying bribes, have claimed that paying the bribes was the only way they could compete. For example in a case in 2002 ARI, which paid over $500,000 in bribes, alleged that such bribery was necessary in order to compete with other companies.[55] In 2009 KBR, a subsidiary of Halliburton, which recently had to pay $600 million in fines as a result of distributing about $180 million in bribes, said that forcing the company to comply with the FCPA would put it at a competitive disadvantage.[56] More specifically, as part of the settlement KBR had to agree to retain an independent compliance monitor. It claimed that having to monitor the use of agents in international operations, and the compliance procedures the company had to put in place, could limit its use of agents in large-scale international business projects.

Not all businesses disagree with the FCPA. Some see that it has both advantages and disadvantages for US business.[57] Some of the steps that companies have to go through to ensure FCPA compliance can be seen as a nuisance,[58] yet at the same time, some businesspeople see that regulation is beneficial in increasing transparency and reducing the demand for bribes.[59]

Conclusion

The 1977 FCPA has had a significant impact on the scale of bribery and corruption. Almost all US companies now have comprehensive anti-corruption controls and accurate bookkeeping. Bribery is thought of in a very different way across the globe.

EXAMPLES OF FCPA ENFORCEMENT[60]

United States v. Faheem Mousa Salam

This case was heard in 2006. Salam was a translator working for a US company in Iraq. The bribery was connected to actions unrelated to his work as a translator. He paid $60,000 to a senior Iraqi policeman to push through the sale of a map printer and 1,000 armored vests to the Iraqi police, in a deal worth over $1,000,000. In 2006, Salam was convicted on one count of FCPA violation. He was sentenced to three years in prison, two years of supervised release, and 250 hours of community service.

United States v. SSI International Far East, Ltd and United States v. Schnitzer Steel Industries, Inc.

This case was heard in 2006. SSI International Far East, Ltd is a subsidiary wholly owned by Schnitzer Steel Industries (SSI), a US steel company. From 1995 to 2004 SSI-Korea paid $204,537 to foreign officials and $1,683,672 to employees of private customers in China and South Korea, in the form of refunds, gratuities, and commissions, to encourage them to buy scrap metal from the company. Most of this money was paid between 1999 and 2004 to government-owned steel mill managers in China. This would have produced profits of $61,606,935 ($6,279,095 from government entities and $55,327,840 from private entities).[61]

As well as these bribes the company spent about $138,000 on gifts. This included pens, perfume, jewelry, and providing entertainment to managers of other companies. Most these gifts were fairly small, some costing a few hundred dollars. Some were more pricy, such as a watch costing $2,400 and $10,000 in gift certificates.[62]

SSI discovered the payments in 2004, and voluntarily disclosed the information to the DOJ and SEC. At the time SSI had no FCPA compliance at all, yet it began a rigorous internal investigation, disclosing everything relevant to the authorities.[63]

In 2006 SSI-Korea pleaded guilty to violating the anti-bribery and accounting provisions of the FCPA and paid a $7,500,000 fine.[64] It entered into a three-year deferred prosecution agreement with the DOJ during which it was required to have an independent compliance monitor. Whether it was prosecuted after the three years would depend partly on the reports by the compliance monitor. Unusually the monitor was to review compliance with foreign anti-bribery laws, as well as with the FCPA. The monitor would make reports to the DOJ and SEC.[65] SSI had to agree to take on any recommendations in the monitor's reports. The company has now agreed a SEC cease-and-desist order, to disgorge the profits gained and interest on them, which came to $7,700,000, and to retain a compliance monitor for the present.[66] SSI itself was never convicted of a crime (only its subsidiary SSI-Korea was convicted).[67]

SSI-Korea fell within US jurisdiction because it had employees in the United States who participated in the bribery. Employees of SSI-Korea made wire transfers from the United States to off-the-books bank accounts in South Korea, of money which was used to bribe officials in Korea and China.[68] The bribes were paid to officials of state-owned enterprises, as opposed to government officials, yet this is enough for the FCPA to apply. Enforcers of the FCPA are increasingly trying to deter payments to officials of state-owned or partly state-owned enterprises.[69]

SEC v. Si Chan Wooh and United States v. Si Chan Wooh

Si Chan Wooh was a senior officer at SSI International who oversaw the bribery. He lost his job in the investigation in 2006, and in 2007 he pleaded guilty to violating the FCPA.[70] In 2007 he agreed to pay about $40,000 in civil penalties and disgorgement and interest. This shows how the enforcement agencies will often bring cases against individuals as well as companies at the same time.

SEC v. York International Corp

York International is a US company that supplies air conditioning and refrigeration and has subsidiaries around the world. This case related to contracts to supply air conditioners and other similar products to governmental entities in Iraq, the UAE, and a number of other countries.[71] Sometimes using intermediaries, various subsidiaries paid over $8,500,000, generally as kickbacks to secure contracts. They made hundreds of payments to secure government and private contracts in various countries. They were involved in the Oil-For-Food scandal: they used the United Nations Oil-For-Food scheme to pay bribes to Iraqi officials, through a Jordanian intermediary, in exchange for contracts. Overall the bribes made the company a profit of over $12,600,000 (almost $1 million of which was from the Oil-For-Food scheme).

In 2005 the United Nations told York that it had discovered possible corrupt transactions. York at the time was about to be taken over by Johnson Controls Inc. (JCI). York and JCI started an internal investigation and self-reported to the SEC and DOJ. In 2007 the SEC accused York of violating the FCPA's anti-bribery, bookkeeping, and internal controls provisions. York cooperated with the investigations, and the SEC took York's self-reporting and subsequent cooperation into account. York was forced to pay a $2,000,000 civil penalty and disgorge about $10,000,000 profit. It was also ordered to retain an independent compliance monitor. York also entered into a deferred prosecution agreement with the DOJ which will result in the company having to pay a $10,000,000 fine.[72]

United States v. Richard T Bistrong

This case was heard in 2010. Bistrong was vice-president of international sales for Armor Holdings Inc., a protective equipment company based in Florida. In total he paid about $4.4 million in bribes from 2001 to 2006. He, and others at Armor Holdings, paid bribes to obtain business deals in Nigeria and the Netherlands and with the United Nations. The payments were then hidden by falsifying invoices. Bistrong paid a UN official to obtain information about bids being submitted for a contract. He used an intermediary to pay a Dutch official to influence the National Police Services Agency of the Netherlands to form a contract with Armor Holdings, and paid a kickback to an official of the Independent National Election Commission of Nigeria in return for another contract. These bribes would have made about $8.4 million in business. Bistrong also authorized export of vests and helmets from the United States to the UAE without a license to do so.[73]

In 2007 Armor Holdings disclosed that one of its subsidiaries had received a written request for information from the UN Office for Internal Oversight Services relating to a former UN vendor, IHC Services, which had had dealings with Armor Holdings and had then been suspended as a result of allegations of corruption in 2005. Armor Holdings launched an internal investigation which resulted in the termination of several employees including Bistrong.[74] Armor Holdings cooperated closely with the DOJ and SEC, and implemented corrective measures. Later in 2007 BAE took over the company.

Bistrong agreed to cooperate with the DOJ and SEC. He became a key component of the sting operation designed to catch other corrupt members of the military and law enforcement products industry. This was the largest single operation in the history of FCPA enforcement.[75] It took two years and involved about 150 FBI agents.[76] An undercover FBI agent posed as a sales agent for a fictitious African minister of defence. He let it be known that he wanted a bribe of 20 percent for awarding sections of a $15 million contract to outfit the country's presidential guard. Twenty-two executives fell for the sting and agreed to pay the bribe. Bistrong helped the government build its case. He facilitated introductions between the undercover FBI agents and the executives, and was instrumental in introducing the FBI to some of the defendants.[77] The 22 executives were arrested on January 18, 2010, 21 of them in a single sweep at the annual firearms industry trade show being held in Las Vegas,[78] and indicted for conspiracy to violate the FCPA and conspiracy to engage in money laundering.

In September 2010 Bistrong himself pleaded guilty to charges of violating the FCPA's anti-bribery provision, its books and records provisions, and the Department of Commerce's export license requirements.[79]

On July 13, 2011, Armor Holdings entered into a non-prosecution agreement with the Department of Justice in connection with $222,750 in improper payments made to an agent, a portion of which was passed onto a UN procurement official, and the $4.4 million improperly recorded third-party commissions used to obtain business from government customers.

The company agreed to pay a $10.2 million criminal fine. Armor is required to report to the Department of Justice on the implementation of its remedies and its enhanced compliance efforts every six months until the end of the agreed period. The company has also reached a settlement with the SEC to disgorge over $1.5 million plus $458,438 in prejudgment interest and a criminal penalty of $3.68 million.[80]

SEC v. Willbros Group, Inc., Jason Steph, Gerald Jansen, Lloyd Biggers, Carlos Galvez
and
United States v. Jim Bob Brown
and
SEC v. Jim Bob Brown
and
United States v. Jason Edward Steph
and
United States v. Willbros Group, Inc
and
United States v. James K. Tillery and Paul G. Novak

This is an interesting case. It shows how different settlements can be negotiated with the government by the accused. It also shows how the SEC and the DOJ can both prosecute for the same crime, and that both the company and the main perpetrators can be prosecuted. Furthermore we see that other crimes such as money laundering often accompany bribery cases,

In the last decade Willbros International, part of Willbros Group, a Panamanian organization listed on the US stock exchange, paid over $11 million in bribes to secure contracts for oil and gas construction projects in Nigeria and Ecuador, to win business worth nearly $500 million. Action was taken against Willbros in both the criminal and civil courts by the SEC and the DOJ. A number of people who were involved in the bribe making were also taken to court and charged.

The bribes in Nigeria were being paid as far back as 1996 in order to obtain favorable treatment. A the time Jim Brown was the managing director of Willbros International's Nigerian and South American subsidiary operations, and James Tillery was an executive for Willbros International. Bribes were mainly made to obtain contracts for Willbros. By 2003 bribes which would over the next few years total over $6 million had begun to be paid to Nigerian governmental figures and to officials of the Nigerian National Petroleum Corporation (NNPC) to obtain contracts for a natural gas pipeline to be built and contracts to repair oil platforms off the Nigerian coast. Bribes were also paid to the state-owned company PetroEcuador to win oil contracts worth nearly $3.5 million in Ecuador. Willbros employees Jason Steph, Gerald Jansen, Lloyd Biggers, and others used false invoices to obtain money from the Willbros headquarters which they used for paying bribes. Tillery and others authorized Paul Novak, who represented two consulting companies, to pay the bribes to the Nigerian and Ecuadorian officials. These consulting companies were used as intermediaries to channel the corrupt payments.[81]

Willbros International also had a scheme to buy false invoices so that it could fraudulently claim VAT tax credits. This was put into practice by an employee called Carlos Galvez, working in Bolivia, who falsified records.

In 2006 Brown was accused of violating the FCPA. Brown agreed to cooperate with the government. In 2010 he was sentenced by the DOJ to 12 months and 1 day imprisonment and two years' supervised release, and payments of $17,600. So far he has not had to pay a civil penalty.

In 2007 Steph was charged with and pleaded guilty to one count of conspiracy to violate the FCPA and three counts of money laundering. He agreed to cooperate with the DOJ investigation of Willbros. The DOJ dismissed the money-laundering charges and reduced the sentence for violating the FCPA. Steph received 15 months imprisonment, two years of supervised release, and paid charges of $2,100.

In 2008 Steph, Jansen, Biggers, and Galvez were accused by the SEC of various offenses. Steph, Jansen, and Biggers were all accused of aiding and abetting the violation of the FCPA bookkeeping and internal control provisions. Steph was also accused of violating the bribery provisions of the FCPA, and Galvez was accused of falsifying records. Jansen and Galvez were fined $30,000 and $35,000 respectively.

In the same trial the SEC accused Willbros of violating the FCPA. Without admitting or denying the allegations Willbros agreed to pay $10.3 million in disgorgement of profits and interest. Willbros also had to undergo criminal prosecution by the DOJ in the same year. The company entered into a three-year deferred prosecution agreement and agreed to pay a fine of $22 million. These fines were each to be paid in four instalments over a number of years. By this point Willbros International and Willbros Group had implemented a compliance program and a review of their existing controls. They agreed to continue with this and also to hire an independent monitor for three years.

Also in 2008, Tillery and Novak were indicted in the criminal courts for one count of conspiracy to violate the FCPA, two counts of violating the FCPA, and one count of conspiracy to commit money laundering. Novak had his US passport revoked, and returned to the United States in 2008, where he was arrested. In 2009 his passport was returned. He later pleaded guilty to conspiracy to violate the FCPA and violating the FCPA. He was sentenced in 2010. At the beginning of 2010 Tillery remained a fugitive.[82] He was arrested in Nigeria in early 2010. In August he was awaiting possible extradition pending further hearing of the case in Lagos.[83]

Case study: Bribery and the CIA defense – James Giffen

Much of this material is drawn from United States v. James H. Giffen, et al. District Court Docket No: 03-CR-404-WHP Court of Appeals Docket No: 05-5782-CR.[84]

In November 2010, the case finally ended of James Giffen, accused at his indictment in 2003 of "making more than $78 million in unlawful payments to two senior officials of the Republic of Kazakhstan in connection with six separate oil transactions, in which the American oil companies Mobil Oil, Amoco, Texaco and Phillips Petroleum acquired valuable oil and gas rights in Kazakhstan."[85] Despite what one commentator called "slam-dunk documents" detailing Giffen's micro-payments through a Swiss bank account in classic money-laundering style, after seven years the prosecution suddenly dropped the charges and instead charged him with a misdemeanor tax violation, to which he pleaded guilty.[86] Giffen walked out the US District Court a free man, with no prison time and no fine to pay.

Giffen had claimed the "public authority" defense, which allows government operatives to perform illegal acts in the course of work affecting national security. There is some doubt whether Giffen was an official agent of the US government at all, or merely someone who had passed on information out of patriotic duty or in an attempt to gain favor. At any rate, the CIA refused to release documents that were essential to the prosecution's case and it had to be dropped. Was the whole thing simply a bold move by Giffen's lawyers that paid off? Did they bank on the fact that the CIA would not want to reveal the extent of cooperation between the US and Kazakh governments in sharing secrets and brokering oil deals? We will never know, as the only person in the court who had seen any of the documents in question was Judge William Pauley, who praised Giffen as a Cold War hero as he wound up the case.[87]

The public authority defense originally only applied to cases where an agency gave the actor permission to engage in otherwise illegal conduct, but has been extended to cover apparent or ostensible authority. It became known as the "CIA defense" after it was used by operatives in the Watergate affair. They had been instructed to break into the offices of Dr Lewis J. Fielding to search for confidential information concerning his patient, Daniel Ellsberg, who had leaked the confidential Vietnam War documents known as the Pentagon Papers to the *New York Times* in 1971. The accused operatives claimed to have been instructed to carry out this burglary by E. Howard Hunt, who had been a career CIA agent before being recruited to work for President's Nixon's Special Investigations Unit, known as "the plumbers."

James Giffen first went to Moscow in 1969 as a representative of a US metals trader, and over the next couple of decades became a frequent traveler between the United States and the Soviet Union, brokering business deals and building up high-level government contacts in both countries. After the collapse of the Soviet Union, Giffen shifted his attention to Kazakhstan in 1992, and ingratiated himself with President Nursultan Nazarbayev, known as The Boss, becoming his advisor, brokering oil deals and, the prosecution alleged, acting as Nazarbayev's personal banker and money launderer.

Indictment

In April 2003 a Grand Jury in New York indicted Giffen with making more than $78 million in payments to two senior officials in Kazakhstan in connection with six separate oil and gas rights deals between the Kazakhstan government and US oil companies Mobil, Amoco, Texaco, and Phillips Petroleum.[88]

In one of the transactions in question, concerning rights to the Tengiz oil field, one of the world's largest, Mobil agreed to pay success fees owed by the Kazakhstan government to Giffen and his company Mercator. Giffen then paid £22 million of these fees into Swiss bank accounts owned by two high-level Kazakh officials. Between 1995 and 2000, Giffen also diverted about $70 million that was paid by various oil companies into escrow accounts at Banque Indosuez in Switzerland to his own secret Swiss bank accounts. He claimed these transfers were for the purpose of paying Banque Indosuez's fees for the transactions.

The indictment alleged, however, that Banque Indosuez entered into a series of sham agreements under which 90 per cent of their fees were transferred to secret accounts controlled by Giffen. Giffen then used this money to make additional unlawful payments of $55 million to the two senior Kazakh officials by transferring money into Swiss accounts they beneficially owned. The officials used these payments, among other things, to buy jewelry worth more than $180,000 and pay for a daughter's education at a Swiss private school. Giffen allegedly kept a portion of the diverted funds for himself, and spent millions of dollars on luxury items and jewelry, some of which he gave to Kazakh officials.[89]

The indictment stated that in making these unlawful payments Giffen also defrauded the people of Kazakhstan out of the honest services of its officials, defrauded the Republic of Kazakhstan out of millions of dollars from oil transactions, and laundered money to promote and conceal his crimes. Giffen was charged with conspiring to violate the FCPA, conspiring to commit money laundering, committing mail and wire fraud, and filing false personal income tax returns. If convicted,

Giffen faced a jail term of up to 20 years imprisonment and a fine of up to $250,000.

Our man in Astana

On January 10, 2005, Giffen submitted a list of the classified information he wanted to reveal at trial in support of a proposed public authority defense. Giffen's lawyer, William Schwartz of Cooley LLP in New York, claimed that he had acted "with the intention of furthering the national interest of the United States and in reliance on his ongoing communications with" government agencies, and "not with the fraudulent and corrupt intent with which he is charged." He also asserted "his belief that his conduct was neither fraudulent nor corrupt, and that it was approved by the American government was confirmed by a government agency's repeated exhortations to remain close to the President of Kazakhstan and by our government's continued reliance on him in sensitive situations."[90]

Giffen described the decades of assistance that he had given to the United States, often as an unofficial conduit between leaders of the United States and the Soviet Union. He said that during this time he gave the US government information on political and economic developments in the Soviet Union, and then in Kazakhstan, and was regularly debriefed by US government officials. Giffen claimed that by the time of the transactions at the heart of the indictment, he understood himself to be working not only for the government of Kazakhstan, but also for US government agencies, and that he was acting with the approval of the CIA, National Security Council, State Department, and White House.

According to his account, in one of these debriefings he disclosed the existence of the Swiss bank accounts to an agent of the US government and told him they were approved by President Nazarbayev. He said he wanted this money to be under his control and available in order to pay fees and other expenses. He also told the US official that Banque Indosuez had offered to create off-balance sheet corporate accounts, maintained by Kazakh officials, so that the Kazakh government could have funds available to spend quickly and confidentially, and that bogus transactions were created to secretly move the proceeds of several oil deals.

Giffen also disclosed to the US official that the Kazakh government had requested that the Mobil payments in the Tengiz oil field deal should go to a Swiss bank account, and that a portion of the money was to be retained for the personal use of Kazakh government officials. He said he had carried out numerous transactions on behalf of the Kazakh government, including cash withdrawals for government delegations and jewelry purchases for Nazarayev. He also revealed that he had created a "pass-through" account in New York to facilitate payments in the United States.

Giffen stated that no US officials had ever told him that the off-balance sheet accounts were improper or that he should not be involved with such transactions. To the contrary, he said they repeatedly told him to stay close to the president and continue to report. He thus understood that the agency wanted him to remain in a position to serve the interests of the United States when called upon to do so. He believed that he was authorized to participate in these transactions, and he did not act with intent to defraud or with corrupt intent.

Charges dropped

In statements and hearings, Schwartz painted Giffen as a patriot who had furthered the interests of the United States by ensuring that US oil companies had access to Kazakhstan's oil wealth and that it did not fall into the hands of Russian or Chinese companies. Schwartz requested access to classified CIA documents that would document the agency's relationship with Giffen. The CIA refused, over a period of years, to provide this, which effectively stalled the case. The presiding judge, William Pauley, made it clear that Giffen had a constitutional right to the documents, and since these were not forthcoming, Giffen would be denied the right to a fair trial, which meant the prosecutors were not able to pursue the case.

After years of legal wrangling back and forth over the right to the CIA documents, the DOJ suddenly and unexpectedly dropped the charges in August 2010. Giffen was charged instead with failing to supply information about foreign bank accounts on his 1996 tax return, and he subsequently entered a plea agreement. Giffen pleaded guilty to failing to disclose that he was a signatory of a Swiss bank account for Condor Capital Management, for which Nazarbayev was the beneficiary. On behalf of his company, Mercator, Giffen also pleaded guilty to giving Nazarbayev a pair of $16,000 speedboats.

It was an embarrassing climbdown for the DOJ; one commentator called it "the Giffen Gaffe, the biggest blunder in the history of the FCPA."[91] Schwartz pursued a successful policy of trying to slow down the case with procedural matters, and guessed, rightly, that the CIA would not cooperate in releasing classified documents. It was a risk – had they done so, the court would have been treated to character-damaging reports of his client's notoriously hard-drinking, debauched, and luxurious lifestyle. According to energy journalist and author Steve LeVine, the CIA defense was a carefully considered bluff, as Giffen was not a US agent:

CIA officers of the era deny that Giffen was anything of the sort –

he walked into CIA headquarters on his own volition and talked to agency officers about Kazakhstan, they said, but that was very different from being a trusted asset on an informal assignment. In short, they asserted, Giffen was simply another dude talking.[92]

But that was not how Judge Pauley saw it. At the sentencing, he paid tribute to Giffen as a patriot who had been dreadfully wronged by the accusations, which had deprived the nation of his valuable services: "Mr. Giffen was a significant source of information for the US government and a conduit for secret communications to the Soviet Union and its leadership during the Cold War." In helping Kazakhstan develop its natural resources, "he advanced the strategic interests of the United States and its interest in Central Asia. These relationships, built up over a lifetime, were lost the day of his arrest .... This ordeal must end. How does Mr. Giffen reclaim his reputation? This court begins by acknowledging his service." Pauley ordered Mercator to pay a $32,000 fine, the value of the two speedboats, and sentenced Giffen to time served – the one night he spent behind bars after his arrest.[93]

Perhaps the DOJ prosecutors should have seen the writing on the wall in 2006, when Nazarayev, an accused co-conspirator in a high-profile bribery case, paid a state visit to the United States and was the guest of President Bush, both at the White House and at his family estate in Kennebunkport. In an era of both post-9/11 secrecy and fears over energy security, the CIA was never going to release documents that would incriminate a strategic partner. The fact that Kazakhstan ranked 111th in Transparency International's 2006 Corruption Perceptions Index did not prevent the Bush administration from maintaining close ties, at the same time that Bush was making speeches vowing to end international corruption.

As LeVine says:

> When [Schwartz] advanced the strategy, it was exquisitely timed – in among the strongest periods of the George W Bush administration, with its hyper-sensitivity about the release of even unclassified documents – under the premise that the CIA was unlikely to disgorge cables and what-not that would validate Giffen's claims. And if the CIA did refuse to so cooperate, Giffen could claim compellingly that he couldn't receive a fair trial.[94]

In the same year that the DOJ successfully pushed for the longest ever FCPA-related sentence in the case of Charles Jumet (see below), Giffen was let off. "Schwartz understood correctly that he could set up a collision between the Justice Department and the CIA in which the latter would probably prevail."[95]

51

Case study: The longest prison sentence for bribery: it's better to come clean – the Jumet case

In 2010 Charles Jumet was given a prison sentence of 87 months, the longest sentence ever imposed on an individual in an FCPA case.[96] The case involved the use of shell or front companies, share issues, and dividend payments to disguise bribes paid to government officials between 1997 and 2003, in connection with the navigation of the Panama Canal.[97] It clearly illustrates the dangers of lying to the authorities in an attempt to cover up bribery payments.

The following material is drawn from United States of America v. Charles Paul Edward Jumet, case 3:09-CR-00397-HEH November 10th 2009.[98]

In July 2004, the United States Department of Homeland Security, Immigration and Customs Enforcement began a criminal investigation into whether US citizens were involved in making payments to Panamanian officials in order to receive a contract from the Panamanian government. The FBI subsequently joined the investigation. The case revolved around accusations of a conspiracy between Charles Jumet and John Warwick to secretly pay money to government officials in return for a 20-year contract to collect lighthouse and buoy tariffs, conduct engineering studies, and maintain aids to navigation.

The corporate nexus

In order to do this, Jumet and Warwick set up a complex arrangement of companies. They set up the Panamanian company Ports Engineering Consultants Corporation (PECC); Overman Associates, an engineering firm with its principal place of business in Virginia Beach, Virginia; and Overman de Panama, a Panamanian company that was a holding company for investments that Overman Associates made in Panama. Overman de Panama also had a management interest in PECC. Jumet was vice president, then later president, of PECC, and vice president of Overman de Panama and Overman Associates. Warwick was president of Overman Associates and Overman de Panama.

The conspirators arranged for shell companies Warmspell and Soderville to be set up by Hugo Torrijos and Rubén Reyna, the administrator and deputy administrator of the Panamanian National Maritime Ports Authority, who were made shareholders in PECC so they could be used as a conduit for the corrupt payments in the form of "dividends." Jumet and Warwick also arranged for PECC to issue "to bearer" shares as a corrupt payment to the then president of Panama, Ernesto Perez Balladares.

After establishing these companies with the assistance of Torrijos and Reyna, Warwick and Jumet then submitted to the ports authority a proposal for the privatization of its engineering department, in which Overman Associates and Overman de Panama would provide engineering services. In 1997, the Panamanian government awarded PECC a no-bid 20-year concession.

The dividend payments

The plan was to authorize PECC to issue "dividend" payments totaling $300,000 to its shareholders, including Jumet, Warwick, and the shell companies Warmspell and Soderville. In addition Warwick signed an £18,000 "dividend" check from PECC, payable to the "portador" (bearer). The check was subsequently deposited into an account belonging to President Balladares.

In 2000, Panama's Comptroller General's Office suspended the contract while it investigated the government's decision to award PECC a contract without soliciting any bids from other firms, and suspended payments to PECC for services billed under the lighthouse and buoy contracts, in which Jumet and Warwick had agreed that PECC would pay $109,536.50 to Overman de Panama for work carried out. Warwick then brought a civil lawsuit in the Circuit Court for the City of Virginia Beach, Virginia, in which Overman de Panama sought a monetary

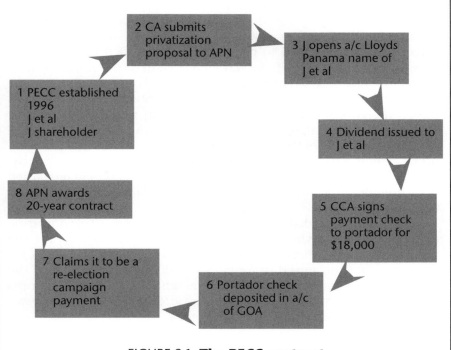

FIGURE 2.1 **The PECC contract**

judgment of $84,536.50 plus expenses and interest from PECC for services performed.

As a result of the lawsuit, PECC paid Overman de Panama $50,000, which Warwick wire transferred to Overman Associates' bank account in Virginia Beach. He then caused the funds to be distributed among Overman Associates' shareholders, personally receiving $33,350. In July 2003, after the Panamanian government resumed making payments to PECC under the lighthouse and buoy contracts, PECC issued "dividend" payments, including a check for $32,400 payable to Warmspell, which was deposited into an account belonging to Torrijos and his relatives.

The false statement allegations

Jumet was also charged with falsely stating that the payment of the $18,000 dividend check endorsed by President Balladares was a donation for his re-election campaign, when he knew that Balladares was not seeking re-election and the check was given as a corrupt payment for permitting PECC to receive contracts from the Panamanian government.

The longest sentence for FCPA offenses

Jumet subsequently pleaded guilty to conspiring to make corrupt payments to foreign government officials for the purpose of securing business for PECC, and to making a false statement. As part of his plea agreement, Jumet agreed to cooperate with the DOJ in its ongoing investigation. In April 2010, he was sentenced to 87 months in prison.

Assistant Attorney General Lanny Breuer commented that the sentencing was an example of how those who intentionally bribed and misled the government for their personal gain would be prosecuted to the maximum extent. It was an extremely long sentence given the relatively low value of the bribes involved, and indicates that the additional offense of making a false statement was taken very seriously. Individuals who get caught up in such arrangements should be warned that attempts to avoid conviction by making false statements could backfire.

John Warwick pleaded guilty to a one-count indictment of conspiring to make corrupt payments to foreign government officials for the purpose of securing business, in violation of the FPCA. As part of his plea agreement he agreed to forfeit $331,000, which represented the proceeds of this crime. In June 2010 he was sentenced to only 37 months in prison and two years of supervised release following his term. He was not charged with making a false statement.

3

BRITISH BRIBERY LEGISLATION: HOW THE UK BRIBERY ACT CAME ABOUT

UK legislation against bribery has its origins deep in the 19th century. Courts and plaintiffs had been wrestling with concepts of corruption, of public service and of obligation and duty to employers since the middle of the century. But after a long period when the courts used common law to prosecute allegations of bribery, they finally created coherent statutes with the 1889 Public Bodies Corrupt Practices Act and then with the Prevention of Corruption Act, 1916. The latter was prompted by bribery involving sales to the government of trousers for soldiers.

The origins of today's Bribery Act can be traced to a dramatic scandal involving a British architect. John Poulson's arrest in 1973 led to the biggest bribery trial of the century, lasting 52 days and costing an estimated £1.25 million (£11.4 million in today's values). The institutionalized corruption it revealed, leading all the way to the top levels of industry, town planning, and government, set in train a succession of consultations, protocols, and laws that eventually made the 2010 Act inevitable. That it took so long was down to the reluctance of vested interests to change the status quo, and to the magnitude of the problem that the Poulson trial revealed. Poulson's contacts ran deep: the investigators had some 27,000 files and 300 suspects, but decided to concentrate only on the principals, where they were confident of being able to bringing a successful prosecution.

"John Garlick Llewelyn Poulson, architect and criminal," begins his entry in the *Oxford Dictionary of National Biography*, to which we can add self-made man, bon viveur, con artist, megalomaniac, and bully. Born in Knottingley, near Pontefract, in 1910, he attended and then dropped out of Leeds School of Art, before being articled to a local architectural firm in 1927. Five years later, his father helped him set up his own practice in Pontefract, which remained his base throughout his career. When his previous employer heard the news, he remarked: "Have you heard that Poulson's starting on his own? Christ, he couldn't design a brick shithouse."

Despite having no formal training in architecture, Poulson's practice thrived. He became a licentiate member of the Royal Institute of British Architects in 1942, and by the late 1950s had one of the United Kingdom's largest practices, which was one of Europe's largest by the mid-1960s. This he achieved by building not exactly brick shithouses but a succession of

55

undistinguished boxes as the new public buildings and civic centers of northern cities. Poulson's talent was not for architecture but for business. He built his empire by ruthlessly cultivating contacts and bribing everyone he dealt with.

After he obtained a medical exemption from military service, the Second World War was the making of Poulson. He expanded his practice, treating his employees ruthlessly according to their later accounts, and built up contacts with local councillors, business owners, and politicians, noticing that they had "small personal incomes but large public budgets." When these contacts later became MPs, civic leaders, and heads of corporations and newly nationalized industries, Poulson was perfectly placed to profit from the post-war building boom.

Poulson could turn any meeting into a business opportunity. He succeeded through his "capacity to develop a personal contact into a paying business proposition by the simple expedient of satisfying the individual's personal needs or pleasures under the guise of friendship and generosity, and in a form that seemed innocuous or of little consequence."[1] A chance meeting with the commercial manager of the North-Eastern Gas Board on a train in 1952 resulted in Poulson designing the Gas Board headquarters in Leeds, gas showrooms in Pontefract, a training center, and a clutch of office buildings. The commercial manager was treated to a holiday and building work on his home to the value of £1,798 (£25,000). Another meeting on a train, with a principal regional manager at the Ministry of Health, brought Poulson a new friend who helped him win the contract to design the new Leeds Hospital.

Poulson kept meticulous records of all his transactions, including bribe payments, which was to be his undoing at his trial. Correspondence between Poulson and his associate T. Dan Smith, leader of Newcastle City Council, in January 1964 reveals how the men schemed to exert their influence: "We are going to be interviewed here for a Town Centre Development and your friend, Singleton, ought to make sure he is on the Committee" (Bolton); "Mr Tetlow is very well in here, but, of course, your side controls the Council and every little helps" (Liverpool); "A meeting with the Leader of the Party is very desirable" (Bradford).[2] In 1964, Poulson also appointed Reginald Maudling, chancellor in Macmillan's government and to become home secretary under prime minister Edward Heath in 1970, as chairman of one of his companies, the start of years of mutually beneficial association.

By the end of the decade, Poulson had overreached himself. After spending what he later estimated to be £500,000 (£4.6 million) on bribes, while maintaining an extravagant personal lifestyle, he was bankrupt. Proceedings against him began in 1969, and when lawyers questioned him on where exactly his money had gone, the truth began to emerge. *Private Eye* was the first major publication to uncover the extent of his shady dealings, in an article entitled "The Slicker of Wakefield" on April 24, 1970. The magazine commented that there were some "praying that whatever happens to the Poulson business empire its affairs will be conducted with the minimum of publicity, and that, if Mr Poulson goes down, he goes down alone."

Poulson did not go down alone. He served a seven-year term, and the list of other convictions demonstrates the extent of his influence. Included were a magistrate, an estates surveyor for British Rail, the secretary to the South-West Metropolitan Board, a principal regional officer at the Ministry of Health, the chairman and a chief engineer of the National Coal Board, the mayor of Southport and several ex-lord mayors. The affair even brought down a home secretary; Reginald Maudling resigned after it was revealed he had accepted gifts, consultancy fees, and board positions in return for parliamentary favors. Being investigated by the police, when he was ultimately responsible for the police service as home secretary, made his position untenable.

Part of Poulson's defense was that the lavish gifts he gave his clients were "entertainment." Leaving aside how to explain the bogus consultancies, sinecure directorships, and vast sums of money he gave away, he had a point when he said during his trial: "Someone is going to have to sit down and work out just what is entertaining and what is corruption so everyone will know what they stand."[3] Though his payments clearly amounted to more than "meat and drink and that of small value,"[4] legislation had still not defined exactly what constitutes the offense of bribery.

Prosecuting QC John Cobb, speaking after Poulson's trial, summed Poulson up as "an ambitious, ruthless and friendless man whose object in life was to get as much money and work as he could by bribery and corruption."[5] The Poulson affair illustrates not only the greed that underpins corruption everywhere, but also the consequences of that corruption: "by advocating town centre renewal, without controlling the way it was to be achieved, Whitehall played into the developer's hands and created the kind of business climate in which John Poulson could flourish," but also a climate in which many traditional town centers would be changed forever.[6]

Alan Doig describes Poulson's ability to delude himself that private interests and public responsibilities could and were diferentiated, even though those interests were paid from his company resources:

> Gifts and benefits were, as Poulson was later to argue, given to people as private individuals, unsolicited and without expectation of any return. Should any of these people in their official capacity do anything to the benefit of Poulson or his organisation, Poulson considered that they had done so as a result of their friendship or because they saw him as the best man for the job, and not because of what he had given them.[7]

Such deceitfulness feeds corruption and is ultimately the cause of so many personal and professional downfalls.

THE REDCLIFFE-MAUD COMMITTEE

In October 1973, prime minister Edward Heath, formed a committee under Lord Redcliffe-Maud to consider the potential conflicts of interest that might affect councillors and other office holders. The committee also looked at how individuals qualified for council membership. In its *Report* the committee found that local government was, for the most part, honest, and that personal honesty, transparency, and party probity were the only ways for it to remain so.[8]

The *Report* recommended that there be: oral disclosures of interest at each and any relevant time; a publicly available register of interests and allowances; restricted service on interests-related committees; limited use of hospitality and official facilities; mechanisms to review procedure and investigate complaints; encouragement of the media's involvement; the extension of the 1916 Act to include councillors and discretionary authority powers; the right of the director of public prosecutions to inspect financial records before bringing charges; retirement restrictions; and a national code of conduct.

THE SALMON COMMISSION

In 1975, a royal commission was set up under Baron Salmon to consider standards of conduct regarding conflicts of interest and the risk of corruption at central and local government level, as well as in the public sector. It also set out to recommend safeguards which would ensure the highest probity in public life.

The commission recommended:[9]

- extending the provisions of the 1916 Act regarding the court's powers to order forfeiture of corrupt gifts
- introducing a new offense of corruptly misusing official information
- giving the police access to financial records, and the power to set up formal procedures to receive and investigate corruption allegations
- widening requirements on oral disclosure and the register of interests at local government level
- imposing stricter requirements in the public sector regarding disclosure, the acceptance of gifts and hospitality, and complaints procedures
- increasing Ombudsman powers
- making council committee minutes available to the public
- introducing more codes of conduct
- that political parties suspend councillors charged with corruption – and ensure that no councillor held too many offices or held them too long
- including MPs and bribery within the criminal law.

In its *Report*, the commission also considered the causes of corruption. At local level, it was suggested that a combination of a grudging electorate, poor training, inadequate rewards for councillors, increased power, one-party rule, and the passivity of official investigation, amongst other factors, contributed to the problem. Looking at the public sector, the *Report* suggested that bribery was not being detected effectively, and that the private sector should be discouraged from offering bribes to financially burdened councillors. As with the Redcliffe-Maud Report, there was only limited concern about the problem of corruption. The director of public prosecutions said, "There have been, during the ten year period under review, only six concluded prosecutions for offences of corruption and dishonesty ... the indications are that the incidence of corruption in the public service is comparatively limited."[10]

Once again, perhaps unsurprisingly, there was a lack of political will to implement real change, and so the *Salmon Report*'s findings were not acted upon by the government that had commissioned it.

THE NOLAN REPORT 1995

Twenty years after the Salmon Commission, it once again took a political scandal to provoke a new phase of official action against corruption. The press was full of reports of "sleaze" in the summer of 1995, including allegations of "cash for questions" – payments to MPs in exchange for questions favorable to the payer's interests being asked in parliament. On October 25, 1994 prime minister John Major announced the formation of the Committee on Standards in Public Life (the Nolan Committee, chaired by Lord Nolan), a standing committee that continues to this day.

The Nolan Committee's terms of reference were

To examine current concerns about standards of conduct of all holders of public office, including arrangements relating to financial and commercial activities, and make recommendations as to any changes in present arrangements which might be required to ensure the highest standards of probity in public life.[11]

The terms of reference also expanded and clarified the definition of "public life" to include not only ministers, MPs, and senior civil servants, but members of the European Parliament, and the members and officials of quangos, local authorities, the National Health Service (NHS) and "other bodies discharging publicly funded functions."

The *Nolan Report* began by setting out seven general principles of public life – selflessness, integrity, objectivity, accountability, openness, honesty and leadership.[12] These are often referred to as the Nolan Principles, and are still included as an annex to the Ministerial Code. The report noted that its purpose was to buttress, and if necessary restore, standards in public life. Its recommendations "laid more emphasis on formulating good standards of practice than reform of the criminal law."[13]

The report's main recommendations were that the bribery statutes should be consolidated in a single Act, that the public/private distinction and the presumption of corruption should be scrapped, and (echoing the Salmon Commission) that the law concerning receipt of a bribe by an MP be clarified. The offense of bribery should be brought under the criminal law and its definition extended to include the actions of agents, and to include acting corruptly in the "hope" or "expectation" of a bribe, even when no such bribe had been agreed.[14] MPs' business interests should be further restricted, with more detailed disclosure. "Parliament should review the merits of allowing MPs to hold consultancies."[15] The "law of Parliament relating to which Members' interests are acceptable and which are not should be reaffirmed,"[16] and a parliamentary commissioner for standards should be appointed.

Ultimately, the report recommended self-policing: "The House of Commons should remain responsible for enforcing its own rules governing Members' financial interests, but better arrangements are needed."[17] The report made similar recommendations for civil servants and quangos: tighter controls, greater scrutiny, the appointment of independent commissioners, and better arrangements for confidential investigation of concerns about propriety.[18]

The government's response stated that it "reaffirms its commitment to consolidate the laws on corruption, and welcomes the opportunity to clarify the law relating to the bribery of, or receipt of a bribe by, a Member of Parliament alongside that consolidation," subject to review by Parliament.[19] However, the Parliamentary Joint Committee examining the bill had severe reservations about the draft bill as presented. It felt the law of corruption was not sufficiently defined, and the definition of the agent/principal relationship was too vague and "could be interpreted in a manner that was inconsistent with the UK's international obligations."[20]

As the *Nolan Report* recommended, the government asked the Law Commission to undertake a review of bribery law as it applies to MPs, which it published in 1998. The Committee on Standards in Public Life has continued to function, conducting enquiries and producing a total of 12 reports, the latest of which at the time of writing, on MPs' allowances, was published in November 2009.[21]

The 1995 Nolan Report's Seven Principles of Public Life

- Selflessness – Holders of public office should act solely in terms of the public interest. They should not do so in order to gain financial or other benefits for themselves, their family, or their friends.
- Integrity – Holders of public office should not place themselves under any financial or other obligation to outside individuals or organizations

that might seek to influence them in the performance of their official duties.

- Objectivity – In carrying out public business, including making public appointments, awarding contracts, or recommending individuals for rewards and benefits, holders of public office should make choices on merit.
- Accountability – Holders of public office are accountable for their decisions and actions to the public and must submit themselves to whatever scrutiny is appropriate to their office.
- Openness – Holders of public office should be as open as possible about all the decisions and actions they take. They should give reasons for their decisions and restrict information only when the wider public interest clearly demands.
- Honesty – Holders of public office have a duty to declare any private interests relating to their public duties and to take steps to resolve any conflicts arising in a way that protects the public interest.
- Leadership – Holders of public office should promote and support these principles by leadership and example.

THE LAW COMMISSION REPORT 1998

A recent prompt for the Bribery Act was the Law Commission report called "Legislating the criminal code: corruption."[22] Published in 1998, this found four main problems with the UK law of bribery. First, there were too many sources – from a number of common law offenses to at least 11 statutes dealing with the subject. As demonstrated above, much of the legislation had been drafted in response to pressing political scandals, and so it had sprung up in a haphazard fashion. Second, the distinction between public and non-public bodies in the Prevention of Corruption Acts was problematic. Third, it was not clear to whom the legislation applied. And fourth, the reversed burden of proof introduced under Section 2 of the 1916 Act was potentially incompatible with sections 34 and 35 of the Criminal Justice and Public Order Act 1994. The report made eight major recommendations:

- That corruption be codified in a single bill.
- That the distinction between public and non-public bodies, and the Section 2 presumption of corruption in the 1916 Act, be removed from the new bill.
- That the existing law be extended so that a person acting corruptly in the hope or expectation of a bribe – even one that had not been agreed – would be committing an offense.
- That bribery be split into five different offenses – corruptly conferring or corruptly offering to confer an advantage, corruptly obtaining or

corruptly seeking to obtain an advantage, and performing the function of an agent corruptly.

- That relevant fiduciary relationships (a relationship where one party is the agent and the other is their principal) be listed in the new statute.
- That acting corruptly be defined as acting "primarily in return for the conferring of an advantage," subject to certain defenses.
- That the offense created by the Bill be classed as a Group A under Part 1 of the Criminal Justice Act 1993, so that acts of bribery occurring outside England and Wales would come under the jurisdiction of the English and Welsh courts.
- That procurement of a breach of duty by threats or deception should not be included in the new law.

The report was well received, and the government stated its intention to present such a bill to Parliament. It set up an interdepartmental working group to consider the draft bill.

THE OECD CONVENTION

Although deliberations on the Organisation for Economic Co-operation and Development (OECD) Convention on Combating Bribery of Foreign Public Officials in International Business Transactions (the Convention) began earlier in the 1990s, the Convention – to which the United Kingdom is a signatory – came into force on February 15, 1999.[23] The Convention obliges its Parties to establish bribery of a foreign public official as an offense under their domestic law. According to Article 1 of the Convention:

1. Each Party shall take such measures as may be necessary to establish that it is a criminal offence under its law for any person intentionally to offer, promise or give any undue pecuniary or other advantage, whether directly or through intermediaries, to a foreign public official, for that official or for a third party, in order that the official act or refrain from acting in relation to the performance of official duties, in order to obtain or retain business or other improper advantage in the conduct of international business.
2. Each Party shall take any measures necessary to establish that complicity in, including incitement, aiding and abetting, or authorisation of an act of bribery of a foreign public official shall be a criminal offence. Attempt and conspiracy to bribe a foreign public official shall be criminal offences to the same extent as attempt and conspiracy to bribe a public official of that Party.

The Convention only targets those offering or paying bribes, not those in receipt of them. The OECD has no authority to enforce the Convention, but monitors Parties' implementation of it.

In order to ensure its compliance with the Convention, the UK government included certain provisions – intended to be temporary – in the Anti-Terrorism, Crime and Security Act 2002. These extended bribery laws to include cases where the persons offering or receiving bribes were not linked to the United Kingdom, and where the act of bribing took place outside the United Kingdom (part 12, section 108 of the Act). In addition, the jurisdiction of the UK courts was extended to allow prosecutions for acts that were not carried out in the United Kingdom, but that would have been criminal offenses if carried out within the United Kingdom (Section 109).

THE DRAFT CORRUPTION BILL 2003

In 2003, the draft Corruption Bill,[24] based on the draft bill appended to the Law Commission's 1998 report, was presented to Parliament. Although the government had supported the Commission's recommendations, the bill was not well received by any significant groups other than the senior judges making up the Rose Committee.

JOINT COMMITTEE ON THE DRAFT CORRUPTION BILL

In March 2003, following the initial criticism of the draft Corruption Bill, a Joint Committee was appointed to reconsider it.[25] Although it was accepted that reform was necessary, the committee had concerns about the limitations of the bill. For example:

- it did not deal with all kinds of corrupt conduct
- there was not a sufficiently clear definition of corruption
- it could be interpreted inconsistently with the UK's existing international obligations
- the bill focused too much on the agent/principal relationship, limiting its scope
- it allowed a too wide waiver of Parliamentary privilege in corruption cases.

The committee also received feedback that the bill's approach was wrong, and that it had been poorly drafted. The final conclusion of the committee was that the focus on the agent/principal relationship in the bill should be reassessed.

The government considered the committee's recommendations, but did not agree that the agent/principal approach should be scrapped. According to the government, removing this focus would mean that certain complex corruption scenarios were not covered by the new law, and it would also make the operation of the law more difficult.[26] In the absence of consensus on the draft bill, as has happened so many times over the history of bribery legislation, it was not introduced for Parliament's consideration.

THE BRIBERY CONSULTATION PAPER 2005

In December 2005, the Home Office made another attempt to move bribery legislation along, consulting to find a "way forward" from the criticism which had sunk the 2003 draft bill. The consultation[27] asked respondents about familiar areas: definitions, separation of private and public-sector offenses, and pre-legislative scrutiny. The responses, once again, showed support for the general idea of reform, but insufficient consensus on how this should be done. The government once again referred the matter back to the Law Commission.

THE TRANSPARENCY INTERNATIONAL CORRUPTION BILL 2006

In May 2006, Transparency International sponsored a Corruption Bill. It was introduced by Hugh Bayley MP under the ten-minute rule, but was dropped from the parliamentary program in June 2006 after the Africa All-Party Parliamentary Group published recommendations that the government should lead the charge against international corruption – and the government agreed to implement most of the recommendations. Lord Chidgey, mindful of the importance of the Transparency International Bill, updated and amended it to present to the House of Lords in November as a private member's bill. Although the bill was not accepted, it put the government under pressure to act.

LAW COMMISSION CONSULTATION 2007

In November 2007 the Law Commission published its detailed consultation on bribery. *Reforming Bribery: A Consultation Paper*[28] focused on potential bribery offenses, rather than a broader idea of corruption.

The consultation set out to:

review the various elements of the law on bribery with a view to modernisation, consolidation and reform; and to produce a draft Bill. The review will cover the full range of structural options including a single general offence covering both public and private sectors, separate offences for the public and private sectors, and an offence dealing separately with bribery of foreign public officials...
a) Provide coherent and clear offences which protect individuals and society and provide clarity for investigators and prosecutors;
b) Enable those convicted to be appropriately punished;
c) [make recommendations that] are fair and non-discriminatory in

accordance with the European Convention on Human Rights and the Human Rights Act 1998; and

d) Continue to ensure consistency with the UK's international obligations.[29]

The consultation sought to be transparent and involve as many stakeholders as possible. It received a significant number of responses, and became a good basis of consensus between the groups who had previously disagreed over proposed reforms.

THE OECD WORKING GROUP REPORT

The implementation and enforcement of the OECD Convention and related agreements is monitored by the OECD Working Group using a peer-review system. In October 2008, the Working Group reported back its evaluation of the United Kingdom's compliance with the Convention.[30]

The report was not favorable. Despite recommendations in 2003, 2005, and 2007 that the United Kingdom should update its bribery laws, the Working Group found that no real progress had been made. The law was not sufficient, and investigations into corruption and bribery at corporate and international levels had been hindered as a result. The United Kingdom did not have the corporate liability regime required by the Convention, the requirement for the attorney-general's consent to prosecute cases was slowing down the process, and the Serious Fraud Office (SFO) was not sufficiently independent, among other problems. The report reiterated that these issues should be resolved as a matter of urgency, and that the SFO should make foreign bribery cases a higher priority.

The Working Group requested that quarterly reports be made by the United Kingdom on its legislative progress, and warned that it might carry out further visits to the United Kingdom to follow up its recommendations. The Working Group also warned that, without clear and comprehensive legislation, the United Kingdom's legal framework had lost credibility, and that this could trigger increased due diligence over UK companies by their partners or development banks.

THE FINAL LAW COMMISSION REPORT
AND DRAFT BRIBERY BILL

Also in October 2008, the Law Commission published its final report following the consultation of the previous year.[31] Recommendations for reform included:

- repealing the existing common law and statute concerning bribery, and replacing them with two bribery offenses: offering and receiving bribes

- introducing a new offense of bribing foreign public officials
- creating a new offense to catch companies who negligently failed to prevent bribery by those acting on their behalf
- including a supplementary provision regarding jurisdiction, parliamentary privilege, the attorney-general and the special powers of the security services.

Appended to the report was a draft Bribery Bill, which was forwarded to the Joint Committee on the Draft Bribery Bill for pre-legislative scrutiny.

THE JOINT COMMITTEE ON THE DRAFT BRIBERY BILL

Formed in May 2009, the Joint Committee on the Draft Bribery Bill was given just over two months to consider the bill and report back. The committee sought advice from a range of sources – including the United Nations, the OECD, the US Department of Justice (DOJ), and parliamentary select committees. The committee supported the draft bill strongly, and stated that it was "an important, indeed overdue, step in reforming the United Kingdom's bribery laws, which have been a source of criticism at home and abroad for more than thirty years."[32]

The committee recommended that the need to prove negligence be removed for the offense of a company failing to prevent bribery amongst its agents. It endorsed calls for official guidance on what appropriate measures to prevent bribery would be, and suggested that provisions regarding parliamentary privilege be abandoned and picked up in separate legislation. The committee suggested that the requirement for the attorney-general's consent to prosecute not be removed, but rather transferred to the directors of various prosecuting authorities.

There was some concern about how the bill could affect the armed forces and intelligence services, and this continued into the parliamentary debates over the proposed legislation. Some suggested that discrete legislation should apply to these groups, whilst others felt that permission to bribe should only be given by parliamentary approval on a case-by-case basis. The government decided that this was not sufficient disagreement to hold up the legislation altogether, and so pushed on.

The government took on board most of the committee's recommendations. For example, it was not clear in the initial bill what standards a jury would apply in determining someone's guilt. In response to this criticism, the final bill stated that the relevant standard would be that of a reasonable person in the United Kingdom – that is, in determining what behavior was expected of a certain person, the jury would consider how a reasonable person in the United Kingdom would be expected to behave, and compare the two. It also removed the negligence requirement for the corporate offense, and acknowledged that "adequate procedures" in relation to this would be determined by the size of a company and its resources. The government did not make any moves regarding parliamentary privilege, partly, no doubt, because of the unfolding MP expenses scandal.

PASSAGE OF THE BILL

Finally, after years of abortive attempts to reform British bribery law, the Bribery Bill had its first reading in the House of Lords in November 2009. Extensive debate followed, but the bill progressed rapidly and received royal assent as the Bribery Act 2010 in April of the following year.

Case study: BAE – the catalyst for the Bribery Act?

The arms industry seems to loom large in any discussion of bribery and corruption. Whether the subject is US arms sales to developing countries in South America, French sales to African countries, or British arms sales to allies in the Gulf, the details of the business are rarely clear cut and certainly never transparent. Reasons for this include the size of the business, the presence of governments, and most importantly the fact that such sales are inevitably conducted in a secretive way. Security can never be treated openly, as it involves national protection, but it can serve as the cloak for activities that would not bear scrutiny in the light of day. Competition between arms providers adds a further layer of sensitivity to an already volatile mix.

The arms deal that has provided the greatest feast for critics of the business, for politicians, and for the investigative journalistic community, over the last 30 years has been the sale of fighter jets to Saudi Arabia by the British company BAE. This complex and lucrative operation – it is said to have netted the company US$43 billion – involved many of the highest-profile government and private-sector leaders in both countries. It also had important national defense implications, given the region involved. Disclosure of details was perhaps inevitable as relations between the two countries waxed and waned over the very long timespan of the deal.

The deal

Al Yamamah (meaning "the dove" in Arabic) took place in three stages, in 1985, 1988, and 2006. Stage one consisted of the sale of 72 Tornado fighter planes (48 ground attack version and 24 air defense), 30 BAE Hawk trainer jets, and 30 Pilatus PC-9 trainer jets to the Saudi government. Stage two saw 48 further Tornados sold, as well as 60 Hawks and 80 helicopters. And stage three, also known as Al Salam ("peace"), involved the purchase by the Saudi government of 72 top-of-the-range

---

BAE-built Eurofighter Typhoon jets. Al Salam also included a £2.5 billion contract to upgrade some 80 existing Tornados in the Royal Saudi Air Force fleet.

Al Yamamah was the largest export of weapons in British history. According to the *Independent*'s Steve Boggan, the cumulative sale of 100 fighter jets was the biggest arms deal ever struck between two nations.[33] In August 2006, Mike Turner, then CEO of BAE, said that his company had already earned $43 billion from Al Yamamah over 20 years, and it expected to earn another $40 billion from the deal in years to come.[34]

How are arms deals done?

A BBC website article of 2007 raised some salient points when it asked, in 2007 (with specific reference to the controversial Tanzania purchase of radar equipment), "How are arms deals done?"[35] The findings illuminate the complexity of determining whether an action is fraudulent or not.

A country seeking armaments puts out a "request for proposal" (RFP), inviting tenders from arms dealers around the world. Usually the deal is agreed between a government and an arms company. Al Yamamah was unusual in being a government-to-government agreement. On occasion, contracts can take a long time to decide; India spent 20 years, for instance, before buying Hawk jets from BAE in 2001.

Product and price are prime considerations for the buying party, but contractors often offer "offset" arrangements as inducements. The Al Yamamah deal was a prime example of this, as the buyer paid with oil, rather than liquid cash. To get business done, defense companies often pay handsomely for "introduction fees" to the highest echelons of decision makers in the buying country. As the BBC article states, "It has been argued that in the 1980s and 1990s, defence companies could not win contracts without the use of some form of bribery and corruption."[36]

Commissions paid in deals of this kind are not illegal in any sense, according to BAE. Furthermore, as the company said in relation to Al Yamamah, they were made "with the full knowledge of both governments." And as one BAE spokesman told the *Financial Times*, "Most defence companies around the world pay commission to agents from time to time. They may look like large numbers to most people but the contracts were very large."[37]

Prince Bandar, a noted Saudi prince repeatedly linked to Al Yamamah, concurred with this view when he said on American television, "We did not invent corruption, nor did those dissidents, who are so genius, discover it. This happened since Adam and Eve." He continued. "I mean, this is human nature. But we are not as bad as you think."[38]

Police interest

The Serious Fraud Office began its enquiry into Al Yamamah in 2001, and this was stepped up in 2003, when SFO director Robert Wardle put together an 18-strong team to investigate the case. The matter had already been examined by the National Audit Office, but its report was not published. Yet, despite its considerable powers and resources, the police agency was unable to bring charges against individuals or entities before 2006, when the British prime minister of the time, Tony Blair, cited security reasons for closing down the investigation. The SFO was required to return documents.

Blair said that Riyadh had threatened to suspend cooperation in the "war against terrorism" if the inquiry went ahead. Prime minister Blair claimed that this consideration was paramount. "Leaving aside the effect on thousands of British jobs and billions of pounds for British industry," he said, "our relationship with Saudi Arabia is vitally important for our country in terms of counter-terrorism, in terms of the broader Middle East and in terms of helping in respect of Israel and Palestine."[39] Robert Wardle, a former director of the SFO, cited the need to "safeguard national and international security."[40]

The closure of the investigation led the OECD, early the following year, to voice "serious concerns" about the dropping of the probe, and 12 days later, MPs in Parliament warned that Britain's reputation for fighting corruption might have suffered "severe damage" as a result.[41] While British lawyers were blocked, a report from the Swiss money-laundering authority prompted the Swiss federal prosecutor's office to announce in May 2007 the launch of a criminal investigation into BAE.[42]

Impact on bribery legislation

The affair, which became known as the Al Yamamah affair, because of the name given to the Saudi deal, was significant as far as the development of UK bribery legislation is concerned for two reasons. First, the closure of the case (which some saw as premature and politically motivated) was seized upon by many in the UK media and non-governmental organization (NGO) community as evidence of Britain's corrupt political community. Much material also leaked into the press indicating that the deal was fraught with complications and dubious if unproven practices. The publicity added to the impetus for a new piece of bribery and corruption legislation. This in due course gave rise to the UK Bribery Act. Second, the company sought to deal with the residual ethical issues and allegations by hiring a top UK judge, Lord Woolf, to examine BAE's processes and make a series of proposals to guide decision making when contracts are complex and sensitive.

The US context

The DOJ also carried out an investigation, which it pursued under the terms of the Foreign Corrupt Practices Act (FCPA). The fact that BAE then had and still has a US subsidiary was significant to the case, as part of the bribe money was alleged to have passed through a US bank.

The company was ultimately (in February 2010) required to pay fines of $400 million (£257m) after it admitted "defrauding the US." Reuters reported it as follows:

> BAE Systems Plc, Europe's biggest military contractor, pleaded guilty in U.S. court to conspiring to make false statements in connection with foreign arms contracts and will pay a $400 million fine. BAE had announced last month it would resolve a long-standing inquiry by the U.S. Department of Justice into questionable payments it made to secure arms contracts in Saudi Arabia, the Czech Republic, and other countries.
>
> The Justice Department said BAE had violated commitments it made to the U.S. government in 2000, when it was seeking to expand into the United States, to comply with the anti-bribery provisions of the U.S. Foreign Corrupt Practices Act (FCPA). The act makes it illegal to pay bribes to foreign officials in order to secure or retain business. U.S. District Judge John Bates said the company's conduct involved "deception, duplicity and knowing violations of law, I think it's fair to say, on an enormous scale." As part of its plea, BAE will retain a corporate monitor for up to three years and implement a program to ensure its compliance with the FCPA.... BAE last month also agreed to pay $50 million to settle a parallel action by Britain's Serious Fraud Office (SFO).[43]

Prosecutions: Tanzania

At the end of 2010 BAE was brought to court, facing allegations that it had made illicit payments of £8 million over three years to a "shady middleman." The case involved a Tanzanian radar deal, signed in 2002 and worth £28 million. Judge Bean fined BAE £500,000 and rejected as "naïve in the extreme" the idea that anyone could believe their claim that Sailesh Vihlani, a local intermediary, was merely a lobbyist. After all, his takings amounted to nearly a third of the total deal.[44] BAE had paid "whatever was necessary to whomever it was necessary" to get the Tanzanian contract, stated Justice Bean. He added that the payments seemed to be disguised so that BAE "would have no fingerprints on the money." "They just wanted the job done – hear no evil, see no evil," he said.[45]

The matter became controversial. MP Clare Short (secretary of state for international development from 1997 to 2003) told the BBC in October 2009, "I was really shocked by the behaviour of British Aerospace and the collusion of all these government departments in such a gross and disgraceful project." She argued that Tanzania, one of the world's poorest countries, did not need and could not afford this particular system because the country had no military aircraft. There was also no provision in the deal to transform the system for civil use. The secretary of state was particularly angry that the air traffic control system ate up most of a £35 million aid package that was originally earmarked to help improve children's education. But she faced opposition in cabinet from the top. She told the BBC, "Tony [Blair] was absolutely dedicated to all arms sales proposals. Whenever British Aerospace wanted anything, he supported them 100 per cent."[46] Foreign Minister Robin Cook confirmed the point that the government was particularly close to the company. He stated that , "I came to learn that the chairman of BAE (then Sir Dick Evans) appeared to have the key to the garden door to No 10. Certainly I never knew No 10 to come up with any decision that would be incommoding to BAE."[47]

The inadequacies of legislation prevailing at the time were evident to Gavin Cunningham, the director for the forensic accounting and investigations division of BTG Global Risk Partners. He had previously been the principal investigator at the Serious Fraud Office:

The penalty imposed by the judge of £500,000 plus costs bears no comparison to the $400m (£258m) penalty imposed by the US authorities on BAE, and partly reflects the problem in bringing a charge under the Companies Act. The agreement by BAE to pay £30m for the benefit of the people of Tanzania is effectively a civil arrangement and not part of the criminal penalty. The difficulties the judge had in accepting the basis of plea is self evident from his judgement which expresses astonishment at how anyone could be so naïve to think that the monies were legitimate lobbying expenses. I expect the new Bribery Act to sharpen the teeth of the SFO.[48]

The Woolf Report

BAE was anticipating the legal actions then active in the United Kingdom and the United States when it appointed Lord Harry Woolf, the former British lord chief justice, to produce a wide-ranging report on its handling of its sensitive arms contracts, and make recommendations. The three specific stated aims of this report were 1) to define the ethical business conduct standards expected of a global company; 2) to identify where BAE met these standards; 3) to recommend action to improve matters.[49]

The Woolf Committee report was published in May 2008, and made

23 recommendations, all of which BAE committed to adhere to over a three-year period.[50] The first five recommendations were:

- the board of directors of BAE to aspire to be a "leader in standards of ethical business conduct"
- BAE to be "open about the actions it has undertaken to investigate allegations"
- BAE to develop and implement "a global code of ethical business contact"
- the board to be increasingly proactive in ensuring ethical standards on the agenda of all meetings
- oversight by a Corporate Responsibility Committee (CRC) while BAE's Audit Committee performs its task of managing financial risk.

Other recommendations included: the CRC and Audit Committee should meet once a year; senior executives were to have "both a personal and collective responsibility to demonstrate the highest standards, tied to the "variable element of their remuneration"; and a senior executive should be appointed to oversee ethical conduct across the company, who should report to the CEO. In addition, the Woolf Committee insisted that BAE set up a clear and transparent process for selecting, appointing, and managing advisers; key ethical policies and procedures should be closely reviewed where necessary; and decision making within BAE should be subject to formal processes.

As to more specific advice, Woolf ordered that offset arrangements in export contracts would come under tight scrutiny; the company should "continue to forbid facilitation payments as a matter of global policy"; and central registers should monitor gifts, hospitality, and donations on a country-by-country basis. The report further required that BAE's acquisitions, joint ventures, and contractors, and its lobbying of government, adhere to the new global code. And it recommended that there should be regular reports on the activities of BAE's internal security division. Besides providing ethical training and enforcing discipline, BAE was expected to be "as open and transparent as possible in communicating all of its activities"; and the company should publish an "independent external audit of ethical business conduct" within three years.

Commenting on the report, Dick Olver, chairman of BAE Systems said that implementing it "is of fundamental importance to how we do business now and in the future, and it will derive benefits for our shareholders, employees and customers."[51] Not all observers were entirely happy with this outcome. "Critics condemned the Woolf Report as a whitewash because it looked only at current conduct, not alleged past misdemeanours," wrote BBC News business reporter Russell Hotten in February 2010.[52] Yet for all its shortcomings, the report set standards for the industry, addressed gray areas in the existing law, and arguably paved the way for the much-needed UK Bribery Act. "The strictness of the act can be seen as an indirect consequence of the BAE case and the damage done to the UK's international reputation by the government's handling of it," said Eoin O'Shea, head of the anti-corruption group at law firm Lawrence Graham. "The act will force British businesses to be proactive in tackling bribery."

4

THE UK BRIBERY ACT — BRITAIN'S NEW LEGAL LANDSCAPE

The UK Bribery Act came into force three months after guidance from the Ministry of Justice was published. The Act creates four main offenses. It criminalizes both demand-side (the act of demanding, asking for, or agreeing to accept a bribe) and supply-side (giving, promising to give, or offering a bribe) bribery. It creates a separate offense of bribery of a foreign public official, and a new corporate offense of failure to prevent bribery. This last offense criminalizes a corporate that fails to prevent bribe paying by those who perform services on its behalf. It is an absolute defense to this "failure to prevent" offense if the corporate can demonstrate that it had adequate procedures in place to prevent bribery.

Any business that carries out business or part of its business in the United Kingdom can be prosecuted under the Act. UK authorities have stated that it is likely the courts will take a broad interpretation of what constitutes part of a company's business. Facilitation payments are not mentioned in the Act, and there is no change to the extent to which they remain illegal. Overly lavish hospitality also remains illegal. A key feature of the Act is its extraterritorial jurisdiction; it is a crime for a corporate entity that is subject to the Act to pay a bribe anywhere in the world. The Act also marks a departure from the US Foreign Corrupt Practices Act (FCPA) because it applies to both private and public sectors. The director's guidance notes that the Bribery Act's scope is not limited to commercial bribery and may extend to attempts to "influence decisions by public officials on matters such as planning consent, school admission procedures, or driving tests."[1]

The Act raises the maximum prison sentence for bribery by an individual from seven to ten years, and the corporate offense (Section 7) carries the possibility of an unlimited fine. In some circumstances senior directors can be held personally liable under the Act.

The Act is drafted in such a way that it includes cases in which an offer, promise, or request for a bribe can only be inferred from the circumstances. An interview held over an open bag of cash could be held to represent an implied offer without there being any evidence that a formal offer was made. The director's guidance also points out that, except that where the allegation is that an advantage was given or received, there is no requirement that a transaction has been completed; the Act focuses on conduct, not results.[2]

SECTION 1: ACTIVE BRIBERY

Section 1 deals with active (supply-side) bribery. It applies to bribery relating to any function of a public nature, connected with a business, performed in the course of a person's employment, or performed on behalf of a company or another body of persons. As mentioned above, bribery in both the public and private sectors is covered.[3] A person is guilty under this section if they offer, promise, or give a financial or other advantage, and they intend the advantage to influence the official to improperly perform a relevant function or activity, of if they believe that the acceptance of the advantage would itself amount to improper performance of a relevant function or activity. The test in determining the guilt of the defendant is subjective; the intentions of the defendant and knowledge that they possessed at the time are key here.

Improper performance is determined by a two-step test. The first step of the test is to consider whether there was an expectation that the official was supposed to perform the function impartially, in good faith, or from a position of trust. The second step of the test is to determine whether the official failed to perform the relevant function or activity in breach of this expectation. The test of what is expected is a test of what a reasonable person in the United Kingdom would expect in relation to the performance of the relevant activity.

Offenses of bribing another person focus on conduct (offering, promising, or giving a financial or other advantage), and also require what the director's guidance calls a "wrongfulness element." This wrongfulness element is committed where the advantage is intended to induce (or reward) improper performance of a relevant function or activity, or where a person knows or believes that the acceptance of the advantage which has been offered, promised, or given, in itself constitutes the improper performance of a relevant function or activity.[4] Prosecutors will consider any evidence of actual intention or knowledge or belief, or whether such intention or knowledge or belief can be inferred from the circumstances. The value of the advantage will be crucial to this process.

An offense is committed if the bribery or omission was committed in the United Kingdom or if the act or omission was committed by an individual with a close connection to the United Kingdom.

SECTION 2: RECEIPT OF BRIBES

This section of the Act criminalizes taking, requesting, or agreeing to receive a bribe with the intention that a relevant function or activity be improperly performed as a result (the function does not actually have to be improperly performed).

The Act also criminalizes the act of agreeing to receive or requesting a financial or other advantage where this in itself constitutes the improper performance of a relevant function or activity. It criminalizes taking a bribe as a reward for the improper performance of a relevant function or activity by that person or another. It is important to note that an official could be guilty of an offense, despite not knowing that their performance of a relevant function or activity was improper. Business law firm Bond Pearce point out:

> a corporate entity can be held liable for an offence under section 2 if it is incorporated in the UK or the act or omission which forms part of the offence takes place in the UK. However, the "adequate procedures" defence will not be available to offences committed by a corporate entity under sections 1, 2 or 6.[5]

SECTION 6: BRIBERY OF A FOREIGN PUBLIC OFFICIAL

This offense deals with the bribing of a foreign public official. This provision reflects the OECD Convention on Combating Bribery of Foreign Public Officials in International Business Transactions.

A foreign public official is defined in the Ministry of Justice guidance[6] as including:

- officials, whether elected or appointed who hold a legislative, administrative or judicial position of any kind in a country or territory outside the United Kingdom
- any person who performs public functions in any branch of the national, local or municipal government of such a country or territory or who exercises a public function for any public agency or public enterprise of such a country or territory (for example professionals working for public health agencies and officers exercising public functions in state owned enterprises
- officials or agents of a public international organization, such as the United Nations or World Bank.

The offense requires intention to influence the official in his official capacity and intention to obtain some advantage. Bond Pearce explain that for this offense, "there is a further requirement that the person must directly or through a third party offer, promise or give an advantage to the foreign public official or to another person at the official's request or with the official's assent or acquiescence."[7] No offense will be committed where the local law explicitly permits an offer or promise of a gift. However, if there is no local law which does so, the UK Act applies. As with Section 2, intention is the key here. Bond Pearce continue that "The specific wording of this offence means that intention to influence the official will be sufficient. There is no requirement to show that the person offering or promising the bribe knew that the foreign public official would be improperly performing his function."

With regard to tenders for publicly funded contracts, it is important to repeat that any local written law which permits or requires the foreign public official to be influenced would supersede the Bribery Act. In the absence of such local law, the Bribery Act applies. The Ministry of Justice provides an example:

> Where local planning law permits community investment or requires a foreign public official to minimise the cost of public procurement administration through cost sharing with contractors, a prospective contractor's offer of free training is very unlikely to engage section 6. In circumstances where the additional investment would amount to an advantage to a foreign public official and the local law is silent as to whether the official is permitted or required to be influenced by it, prosecutors will consider the public interest in prosecuting. This will provide an appropriate backstop in circumstances where the evidence suggests that the offer of additional investment is a legitimate part of a tender exercise.[8]

SECTION 7: THE CORPORATE OFFENSE OF FAILING TO PREVENT BRIBERY

This is a strict liability offense. A corporate entity is guilty under Section 7 where an associated individual or entity intends to obtain or retain business for the commercial organization or to obtain or retain an advantage in the conduct of business for the commercial organization. Bond Pearce explain that this offense exposes business in new ways:

> It should also be noted that the section 7 offence only covers active bribery i.e. a person performing services for or on behalf of the company would have to have committed an act or omission forming part of the offences covered by sections 1 or 6 of the Act. However, this does not mean that a corporate entity can avoid potential liability under section 1 or section 6 if it has adequate procedures in place.
>
> The corporate offence under section 7 is a separate offence, so for instance there may be insufficient evidence to prove a corporate entity is itself guilty of a section 1 or section 6 offence, but if one of its employees commits an act which would constitute an offence under section 1 or section 6, the corporate entity may be prosecuted under section 7 and would then only avoid liability if it could show it had "adequate

procedures" in place. The Act clarifies that an "associated" person for the purposes of section 7 will be a person who performs services on behalf of the commercial organisation. Accordingly, this could be an employee, agent (including a contractor) or subsidiary of the commercial organisation.[9]

An associated person could be a contractor to the extent that they are performing services for or on behalf of an organization, or a supplier if they are performing services for a commercial organizations rather than just selling goods to them.[10] However, justice secretary Ken Clarke states that an associated person will only engage criminal liability for a company where they actually represent the organization, and any bribery they commit is intended to benefit it.[11]

Where the corporate offense is concerned, the director's guidance explains that:

A "relevant commercial organisation" will be liable to prosecution if a person associated with it bribes another person intending to obtain or retain business or an advantage in the conduct of business for that organisation, but only if the associated person is or would be guilty of an offence under section 1 or 6 (section 2 "passive bribery" is not relevant to a section 7 offence).

Section 7 does not require a prosecution for the predicate offences under section 1 or 6, but there needs to be sufficient evidence to prove the commission of such an offence to the normal criminal standard. For this purpose it is not necessary for the associated person to have a close connection with the United Kingdom (section 7(3)(b)).

The jurisdiction for this offence is wide (see section 12 of the Act). Provided that the commercial organisation is incorporated or formed in the United Kingdom, or that the organisation carries out its business or part of its business in the United Kingdom, courts in the United Kingdom will have jurisdiction, irrespective of where in the world the acts or omissions which form part of the offence may be committed.

The offence is not a substantive bribery offence. It does not involve vicarious liability and it does not replace or remove direct corporate liability for bribery. If it can be proved that someone representing the corporate "directing mind" bribes or receives a bribe or encourages or assists someone else to do so then it may be appropriate to charge the organisation with a section 1 or 6 offence in the alternative or in addition to any offence under section 7 (or a section 2 offence if the offence relates to being bribed).[12]

While debarment from EU contracts is a discretionary outcome if convicted of a failure to prevent bribery, justice secretary Ken Clarke's statement to the House of Commons explained that debarment was not inevitable:

> The Government have also decided that a conviction of a commercial organisation under section 7 of the Act in respect of a failure to prevent bribery will attract discretionary rather than mandatory exclusion from public procurement under the United Kingdom's implementation of the EU Procurement Directive (Directive 2004/18).[13]

As it currently stands, the court itself will not issue a judgment stating that an organization is debarred. Instead, under the rules it will simply find a corporate guilty of a Section 7 offense. The authority offering a job for tender will then stipulate whether or not it will entertain tenders from corporates guilty of a Section 7 failure to prevent offense. Barry Vitou points out that:

> Notwithstanding the shift to non-mandatory debarment for a Section 7 Failure to Prevent Bribery Offence it remains to be seen how many public tender requests stipulate that they do NOT debar companies who have been convicted of this offence. The change may turn out to be of no consequence in practice.[14]

Section 12 provides that the courts will have jurisdiction not only over Sections 1, 2, or 6 offenses committed in the United Kingdom, but also over offenses committed outside the United Kingdom "where the person committing them has a close connection with the United Kingdom by virtue of being a British national or ordinarily resident in the United Kingdom, a body incorporated in the United Kingdom or a Scottish partnership." However with regard to Section 7, a close connection with the United Kingdom is not required; a relevant commercial organization can be liable for conduct amounting to an offense under Sections 1 or 6 on the part of any person. Furthermore, Section 7 applies anywhere in the world, so long as the relevant commercial organization carries on a business or part of a business in the United Kingdom.[15]

With regard to the definition of carrying on a business or part of a business in any part of the United Kingdom, the Ministry of Justice makes it clear that this is something for the courts to determine. Where the issue of whether an organization is carrying on a business in the United Kingdom is concerned, many factors will be considered, and it has been made clear in the official guidance that merely being listed on the London Stock Exchange or having a UK-incorporated subsidiary would not necessarily be sufficient. Monty Raphael, of lawyers Peters & Peters, points out that "What will worry anti-corruption campaigners and the OECD is the wiggle room unethical businesses will have to structure corporate activities to take themselves outside the ambit of the legislation and still maintain their right to raise money on the London capital markets."[16]

This clarification in the guidance has been interpreted by some as one of a number of concessions to business, and has attracted criticism from transparency campaigners who accuse the Ministry of Justice of effectively writing a manual on how to avoid the provisions of the Act. George Boden of Global Witness argues that "the government has caved in to an aggressive business and media lobby, and, at the last minute, effectively licensed UK companies to continue bribing through the back door by use of offshore subsidiaries."[17]

Transparency International criticizes what it sees as a possible loophole that companies can use to avoid prosecution for bribery:

> A non-UK parent company A with a large UK subsidiary B could pay bribes through subsidiary C based in a third country. If UK subsidiary B did not directly benefit from the bribes, the non-UK parent company A would not be caught by the Bribery Act – even if its other subsidiary C was competing unfairly with honest UK companies.[18]

The extent of these criticisms is rejected by some in the legal profession, who point out that the formal guidance replaces the draft form which was of little practical use to companies. They also point out that companies that are listed on the London Stock Exchange usually have other connections in the United Kingdom which are likely to satisfy the court's requirement for carrying on a business. It is also important to note that historically the UK courts have indicated a very low threshold in the context of what constitutes carrying on business in the United Kingdom, and the Serious Fraud Office (SFO) has indicated that, for example, an internet retailer with operations outside the United Kingdom but with a web presence and which ships products to the United Kingdom may well be interpreted by the courts as carrying on business.[19] Ultimately, it will be for the courts to decide what the Act means in practice.

As noted above, it is an absolute defense for the corporate to demonstrate that it had adequate procedures in place to prevent bribery on its behalf. Companies should take note that the general public interest considerations for active bribery are also applicable to the failure to prevent an offense. In the absence of case law or prescriptive guidance for businesses of all sizes and sectors, it is impossible to state definitively what procedures will be deemed to be adequate by the courts. Despite this fact, it should be noted that prosecutors must take account of the Ministry of Justice guidance which identifies six principles which are likely to underpin such anti-bribery procedures: proportionate procedures, top-level commitment, risk assessment, due diligence, communication (including training), and monitoring and review.

Case study: Lord Goldsmith on the significance of the UK Bribery Act and the Guidance for company managers

Lord Goldsmith was British attorney-general between 2001 and 2007. He was the longest serving Labour attorney-general. In 2007, the SFO called off its investigation into alleged corruption involving the Al Yamamah contract between BAE and Saudi Arabia. Lord Goldsmith argued that it might "compromise national security."[20]

Significance of the new Act: puts company at risk

"The single most important point of the new law is the corporate offence of failing to prevent bribery. That is a sea-change. Until the new act came in, as far as the company was concerned, the company could be guilty of bribery, but you had to demonstrate knowledge among 'the controlling mind' of the company, and that means the most senior people. If it is a very small organization, then that is not a problem, it is the person who gets his hands dirty, but also the man who is ultimately in charge. It is not the case in larger corporations. So although you could prosecute individuals for bribery, it would be difficult to prosecute the company. The company would have the 'hear no evil, see no evil, speak no evil' defence.

"The new corporate offence completely changes it, it makes it an offence of strict liability. If somebody who is an 'associate,' that is, someone for whom you are responsible, commits a relevant act of bribery, the company itself is liable for failing to prevent it unless it can demonstrate it had in place adequate procedures. The single most important message for the corporate manager is that you need to get in place your adequate procedures now. That is your defence against sales directors and others going 'rogue' on you and landing the company in the dock. The company is at risk. If there is a relevant act of bribery, and there aren't adequate procedures in place to prevent it, then the company will be liable."

Government rows back on extraterritoriality

"Until the *Guidance*, it was possible to speculate that among the people being prosecuted would be foreign companies, because the SFO was keen to demonstrate that there was a level playing field by prosecuting foreign companies too. But the new guidance tries to row back on the extent of extraterritorial jurisdiction in a way that might make it much more difficult for the SFO to achieve that objective.

"The *Guidance* view on extraterritoriality is a matter of law, and the courts could take a different view if a prosecutor decided to prosecute.

The prosecutor could decide to prosecute someone saying they were carrying on business in the United Kingdom. They say they weren't and the only thing they did was that they had a listing in the United Kingdom. The prosecutor might challenge that that was the only thing they did. But it would be open to the court to say, 'even if that was all you did, actually as a matter of law, that constitutes carrying on business in the United Kingdom.' The prosecutors are unlikely to seek to exercise their jurisdiction in ways that the Ministry of Justice have said that they shouldn't.

"It is clear that the government was concerned about reports of anxiety among business as to how tough the new act was going to be, and has tried in a number of ways to soften its impact. One of these was the extraterritorial impact. The other way they have softened it is by their sending a very strong message about corporate entertaining, that Wimbledon, the Grand Prix and the test matches are safe. There is no suggestion that you can only put your clients in the cheap seats either. One of the major concerns is that business thought it would have to change its behaviour and not be able to engage in corporate entertaining. There will still be limits to that. So you cannot fly a man, his wife and four children to stay at a five-star hotel for two weeks, and all you want is for him to see your factory and what an excellent thing it is. That is a disguised bribe.

"The director of the SFO was saying before the *Guidance* was published that he would proceed against foreign companies. The most important thing the *Guidance* says is that you are not carrying on business in the United Kingdom if you have an independent subsidiary which is doing business. The problem is not what people are doing in the United Kingdom – on the whole the United Kingdom is not a place where you can bribe public officials and most commercial contracts don't follow brown paper envelopes – the real issue is, can we prosecute in this country for payments in countries where we know that corruption is endemic and where it's hard to do business without making big payments to local ministers or others? If you can escape the reach of the SFO or the CPS, because your only presence in the United Kingdom is a subsidiary and you are not doing business through the subsidiary, you can say that is not for you, SFO, what I do in these countries is not for you."

Clarifying the role of subsidiaries

"The argument would be that if the only part of the foreign group that does business here is the subsidiary, then the subsidiary would be vulnerable, not the parent. Only if your subsidiary paid the bribe in the foreign country, then that would put the parent at risk. This will need to be tested. Are you doing business through your subsidiary if main board directors serve on the subsidiary's board and you give it directions. How far do you have to go ... these are open questions. If the subsidiary is in the UK and doing nothing wrong in the UK, then the real problem is not that, the real problem is that the parent is winning business overseas by a corrupt practice. Can the foreign company insulate itself from the ambit of the Bribery Act by carefully constructing subsidiaries?

"The *Guidance* may be right as a matter of law, but it is rowing back and somewhat undermining the SFO's hope to level the playing field by proceeding against foreign companies. The government had a very wide consultation and it is perfectly likely that they received responses from overseas companies saying that it was very unfair that they could find themselves policed by the British authorities for what they are doing in Asia or Africa, when it didn't flow from doing business in the United Kingdom. This doesn't take account of the problem British companies will have that they would like to see their companies subject to an equally tough law."

Resources to police the Act

"There has always been a problem that economic crime is not very highly prioritized in this country. That is because the police do most of the investigating and they don't regard economic crime as a top priority. They are concerned about terrorism, murder, personal violence and bank robbery, but if the Economic Crime Agency is not properly resourced, there won't be enough emphasis on this either.

"The Bribery Act is expensive. It is likely to be multi-jurisdictional. There is likely to be some domestic bribery. There has always been a degree of domestic corruption in the public contracts area and there have been a number of high-profile cases in public works.

"The Bribery Act was intended by the last government to be a tough act, to be tougher in some respects than the FCPA, for example, the inclusion of facilitation payments.

"Business had two legitimate arguments. One was that if there wasn't a level playing field, their foreign competitors would be able to scoop up the business that they were trying to get. UK PLC would be disadvantaged. That was a significant argument which I thought was a legitimate concern. I thought that was largely met by the SFO saying that, because we have this extraterritorial reach, as long as someone is doing a bit of business in the United Kingdom, we can prosecute them for what they are doing in Indonesia or Africa, even though they are a foreign incorporated company. That is the way that British industry can be satisfied that there is a level playing field.

"The second issue was the degree of uncertainty about what the adequate procedures [were] and issues like corporate entertaining. The first guidance that came out was very weak in relation to those areas and answered very little.

"Because the government has been rowing back on what the extraterritorial jurisdiction [covers, this] may limit the SFO's ability to equalize the playing field by prosecuting foreign companies."

The FCPA and the Bribery Act

"The FCPA depends on roots for jurisdiction, but if American citizens or residents are involved, they can be proceeded against, if they are complicit in payments. The FCPA is narrower because it is directed towards corruption of corrupt foreign public officials. There are ways of getting at private payments as well, but that is through books and records disclosures, accounting. We can do that much less easily in this [country] as there is no requirement to disclose payments to agents. Accounting in the US is easier to prove, and companies find it easier to reach an agreed settlement. If you are convicted of bribery, you may find yourself prohibited [from] tendering for public contracts. The United Kingdom has false accounting in the Companies Act. This is not as refined an instrument because there is not the requirement to disclose particular payments."

Penalties

"We are moving towards tougher penalties and the argument is strong, that the cost to the public, to consumers, of economic crime is enormous. It is a mistake to think that economic crime is victimless. It does in fact cost everyone money, and there is no reason why people who cheat the system should not receive a pretty tough penalty. If you were guilty of a blue-collar fraud, you would often go to prison, but if you took 50 times that through white-collar crime, you wouldn't go to prison. You can't treat these things as less serious because they are done by someone of a different social class."

Case study: corporate hospitality, the civil law of bribery, address commissions, and facilitation payments – the Fiona litigation

Corporate hospitality is an area that has aroused considerable concern with regard to potential liability under the Bribery Act. Lord Tunnicliffe, government spokesperson for the Ministry of Justice, recognized that companies are expected to engage in corporate hospitality for legitimate commercial purposes. He went on, however, to remind companies that lavish corporate hospitality could also be used as a bribe to secure advantages, and the offenses must therefore be capable of penalizing those who used it for such purposes. Lord Tunnicliffe's letter stated: "the general bribery offences are based on an improper performance test. Corporate hospitality would therefore trigger the offence only where it was proved that the person offering the hospitality intended the recipient to be influenced to act improperly."[21] Obviously lavish or extraordinary hospitality may lead a jury to reach such a conclusion, but as the director of the SFO told the Joint Committee, "most routine and inexpensive hospitality would be unlikely to lead to a reasonable expectation of improper conduct."[22]

The definition of a bribe under the UK Bribery Act

Under the UK Bribery Act, a bribe is defined as the offer, promise, or giving of any financial or other advantage which is intended to induce or reward the improper performance of a public function or business activity (or is done in the knowledge or belief that acceptance of the advantage itself constitutes the improper performance of a public function or business activity). "Improper performance" covers any act or omission that breaches an expectation of good faith or impartiality, or an expectation arising from a position of trust. This is an objective test based on what a reasonable person in the United Kingdom would expect in relation to the performance of the relevant activity.

Bribery and civil law: luxury holidays are a bribe

In the Fiona Trust litigation, Mr Justice Andrew Smith noted, in the context of a civil case of bribery, that the law recognized that some gifts or benefits were too small to create even a real possibility of a conflict of interest, and so were too small to be treated as a bribe, and that it was a question of fact depending on the circumstances of each case where the line was to be drawn between "a little present" and a bribe. He noted that because this was a question of fact and not of law, there was little guidance from legal authorities, but the test was, as he understood it, whether it was sufficient to create a real possibility of a conflict between interest and duty. Some examples of benefits that featured in the case in the context of bribery were expensive family holidays and the use of a credit card provided by Yuri Nikitin, a Russian ship owner, to Dimitri Skarga, the former director general of Sovcomflot, a large state-controlled Russian operator of tankers and other commercial ships.

Accustomed to receiving generous hospitality

Skarga argued, unsuccessfully, that the benefits were not of sufficient value to be regarded as bribes, as they did not give rise to a real risk of a conflict (still less an actual conflict) between the interests of the recipient as an agent receiving a bribe and his duties to his principal, or other companies in the group to whom he owed the duties of an agent or other fiduciary duties.[23] Mr Justice Andrew Smith accepted that, in the circumstances of this case, in deciding whether family holidays in an expensive resort would amount to a bribe, it was appropriate to consider the fact that the recipient was accustomed to receiving generous hospitality in the course of his work and so was less likely to be impressed. It was also, in his view, relevant to consider the fact that the recipient sometimes made small contributions towards the costs. He concluded, nevertheless, that the benefit of the series of holidays and the credit card that was provided for him were sufficient to give rise to a potential conflict of interest and so to be regarded in English law as bribes.

"Address commissions" and charter parties

One type of payment that featured heavily in this case were the obscurely named "address commissions." Such payments can feature in both charter parties (ship hire contracts) and contracts for the building and selling of ships. They normally represent a form of cashback, rebate, or discount on the purchase price. In the case of Comshipco Schiffahrt-sagentur GmbH v Commissioner for South African Revenue, heard in the Supreme Court of Appeal of the Republic of South Africa in 2001:

> Historically, vessels were addressed to the master of the vessel or an agent at the port of loading or discharging and an amount of money was provided by the owner to the master or to the agent for whatever services were required in respect of the ship in a port, for example services required for getting the ship in and out of the port and for the loading and the discharging of the cargo. That is the origin of the expression "address commission." At present, according to the evidence, when a ship is chartered, it is the charterer who has to render the service of providing the cargo for the vessel and who has to ensure that the vessel gets into the port, loads and gets out quickly. In most cases the charterer requires an "address commission" to be paid by the person from whom he charters the ship in respect of the provision of such services. It is a commission payable for the provision of services in respect of a ship. However, the address commission is not actually paid to the charterer; it is deducted from the hire at the time the hire is paid.[24]

Abusive practices

In the shipping industry, such payments have been pressed into service for criminal or quasi-criminal activities such as fraud, bribery, tax avoidance/evasion, and money laundering. In the Fiona Trust case these commissions were used *inter alia* in breach of a fiduciary duty, as can be seen from the following example cited in the judgment.

A breach of fiduciary duty?

Clarkson (a London shipbroker) negotiated prices that included address commissions which they intended should not be received by, or disclosed to, the buyers (Sovcomflot), who would normally be the recipients of such cashbacks. The prosecution alleged that Clarkson, through an employee, had agreed with a businessman, Yuri Nikitin, to pay the commissions to his [Nikitin's] offshore companies while hiding this from the sellers.[25]

Legitimate payment of introductory commissions?

Nikitin and Clarkson argued that a broker was entitled to make payments of commission to third parties, including parties, like Nikitin, who were allegedly acting as shipping consultants by introducing the relevant business to the broker, out of the total commission charged by the broker, without the knowledge or consent of his principal. They argued, further, that the payment of such "introductory commissions" was consistent with ordinary market practice, a practice which did not require brokers to inform their principal of such arrangements even though the principal was funding them. Expert evidence called on behalf of Nikitin suggested, however, that there was some limitation to this market practice in that the broker would not be entitled to make such payments if he believed that his principal, if asked, would not agree to them. Such a limitation, however, according to Nikitin, did not come into play in this case.

Payments were not of the usual kind

The judge disagreed. He did agree that a broker acting for a seller was not generally in breach of duty to his principal if he paid a third party a commission of a usual kind for introducing him to a transaction and he did not disclose the payment to his principal. This, he explained, was because in normal circumstances he was entitled to assume that the principal had consented to his making a payment of this kind without specifically informing the principal of it, and to have recognized that the commission which the principal had agreed to pay the broker might cover such outgoings. On the other hand, if the broker knew that the principal would object to the payment or thought that the principal might do so, this would not be the case. The issue was whether a particular payment by way of an introductory commission was of a "usual kind" in the circumstances of the case. In this case, the court concluded that the introductory commissions were not of a usual kind and that the brokers were indeed in breach of duty in paying them. The brokers settled the case out of court. It has been reported that, at its request, the SFO has been sent copies of documents relating to the transactions involved in the case. The SFO declined to comment.

Address commissions and the Bribery Act

With regard to the possible impact of the Bribery Act 2010 on ship-broking trade practices, it has been suggested that address commissions should not come under scrutiny, provided that such payments are properly recorded in the terms of the charter party and the payment was properly made to the owner and recorded in the owner's company books. In such circumstances, it has been proposed, such payments should be acceptable. On the other hand, they could be a problem if they were directed to be paid into the offshore account of a separate entity from parties to the transaction and there was no explanation why such a payment had been made.

Following instructions

There have been cases where brokers have encountered problems because they followed instructions to include, collect and then pay commissions to parties not directly involved in the contract. The broker may, for example, have been dealing with a senior employee of the principal, such as a chartering manager, who may have given instructions that a commission is to be paid to a third party's offshore account only to discover later that the now-dismissed chartering manager was bribing some overseas government official and the broker has found itself under suspicion for having assisted in the corruption. In order to avoid potential liability, appropriate systems and controls must be in place regarding the prevention of bribery.

PART III

CORPORATE RESPONSE

5

THE GEOGRAPHIC FACTOR

Geography has some bearing on the scope, scale, and form of bribery and corruption. The economic or political situation of a country will directly influence its tolerance of corruption. So countries in a state of severe flux (such as Iraq: see below) are likely to exercise weaker control over standards of business ethics than those countries whose politics are stable. Likewise, countries whose public officials are poorly paid may overlook (if not actively encourage) practices frowned upon in developed countries' institutions. Such countries present a higher risk to the foreign company, but no risk is insuperable, if accurately calculated, and companies will not be deterred. So we see that research conducted for Transparency International (TI) shows that a large number of businesses in the City of London engage in activities or operate in environments that expose them to high risk of corruption and bribery. The report identifies four important areas where all businesses are vulnerable:

- operating in countries where corruption is perceived to be high
- interacting with public officials
- providing services to high-risk sectors
- using agents, subsidiaries, or entering into joint ventures.[1]

From both a business and a law enforcement perspective, risk management strategies to address bribery must be sensitive to geography. The Organisation of Economic Co-operation and Development (OECD) advises that "heightened risks" in particular countries "create a need for heightened care in ensuring that the company complies with law and observes relevant international instruments."[2] Stable developed democracies generally tend to be relatively free of corruption, while conflict-torn and poverty-stricken countries are unsurprisingly at the other end of most indexes. Some regions are also of special concern. Companies can also be more exposed to the threat of corruption when operating in countries where bribery is widely perceived to be a component of business etiquette or inseparable from culture and history.[3] One development consultant who wished to remain anonymous repeated the opinion that "You can rent an Afghan but you can't buy him."

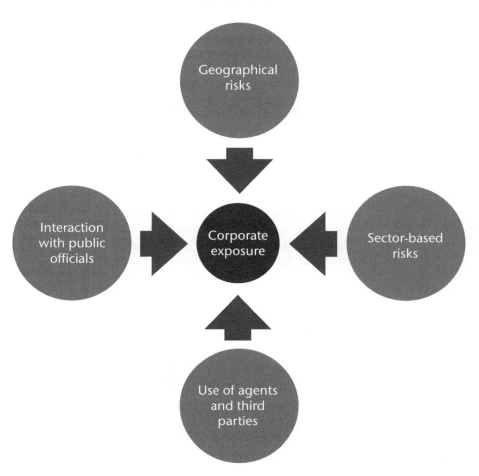

FIGURE 5.1 **Factors in corporate exposure to bribery**

Source: Pinsent Masons/Barry Vitou.

Just as certain geographical regions can increase a company's risk of exposure to corruption, so can certain sectors of business. Exposure is more likely in sectors where vendors believe that "they must survive in a business environment where greasing the palm of officials is the norm rather than the exception."[4] This "sectoral factor" may be more relevant to a multinational corporation than the geographical location of its core business. Even when most of a company's business is in environments where corruption is not a major concern, its subsidiary activities may create significant exposure. While some companies in the City operate exclusively in sectors associated with a high risk of corruption, TI's research also shows that "many businesses in sectors that are generally considered to be low-risk also engage in high-risk activities occasionally."

In addition to these geographic and sectoral factors, most businesses are exposed in some way to corruption by the nature of the global economy. A company's culture of corruption may have emerged not from a conscious decision at board level to pay bribes, but as a reaction of lower-level employees to difficulties they encounter when trying to perform routine activities. Even the routine process of registering a company can in certain countries mean exposure to corrupt practices. Private joint-stock companies operating in China during the 1990s had to pay high bribes just to be officially registered and further bribes to continue operating.[5] A company's routine business activities may rely on ancillaries around the world. Companies use subsidiaries, intermediaries, and locally based arms-length agents, who have to deal with public officials in order to obtain permits, licenses, and other forms of government approval to operate. Companies are also connected to, and to a greater or lesser degree dependent on, global supply chains. All of this must be considered when carrying out any kind of bribery audit. It is important for companies to understand that business does not exist in a vacuum; it is inseparable from society, and shapes and is shaped by it. Companies must ensure that foreign employees are well informed and communicate what they know to their head office; changes in the political or economic environment in a country in which a company operates can rapidly affect the likelihood of being exposed to corruption and bribery.

In light of the current global financial crisis, the forensic departments of the United Kingdom's Big Four accountancy firms are paying increasing attention to these dynamics. KPMG has tracked fraud for some 20 years in its monthly Fraud Barometer; the level of fraud is considered an indicator of corruption. Hitesh Patel, a partner in the company's forensic department, has been analyzing the effects of current changes:

> The full impact of the credit crunch on fraud is yet to be seen and the figures we see now show only part of the picture .... As companies look to increase top-line growth and reduce operational costs in the current stressed economic environment, supply chain and accounting related frauds are likely to be an issue .... The drive to secure new business means that bribery and corruption offences by employees may become an issue for companies – this is an area of focus for the authorities.[6]

In Europe, the impact of the economic downturn has been greatest on those countries with large deficits, such as Greece, Portugal, Italy, and Ireland (and to a lesser extent the United Kingdom), which are now proposing austerity measures. The effect has also been felt in the developing world, where the contraction of national economies places pressure both on companies with interests there, and on public officials who live with the threat of redundancy or reduced pay packets, and may be increasingly likely to demand bribes.

As the economic environment becomes more competitive, companies may be willing to pay bribes up to the point where the cost matches the profits. Consequently "domestic governments are willing to overlook or indirectly subsidise the bribes (through export credits) in order to help their firms land contracts."[7] Global economic recession affects both the demand and supply sides of the bribery equation. Offering financial inducements to acquire or retain business is likely to become more tempting as companies compete for a declining number of contracts. As D. I. Whatmore explains in an interview with the authors,, "If business is getting less and less plentiful, there are less contracts out there, then your desperation to win them probably increases – supply and demand isn't it. If you are fighting for work your tolerance for risk probably goes up."[8]

Companies are more likely to be exposed to demands for bribes in states in which the economy has deteriorated. Research shows that bribery flourishes during times of recession, but it is unlikely that the UK government will turn a blind eye in the present financial and regulatory climate. In a document outlining its foreign bribery strategy, the government states that "the fight against bribery cannot be an optional extra luxury to be dispensed with in testing economic times."[9]

The recession is placing severe pressure on law enforcement budgets, which will inevitably affect the capacity of organizations like the Serious Fraud Office (SFO). The United Kingdom's foreign bribery strategy has four aims; the time-consuming, resource-intensive and expensive options of strengthening legislation and enforcing the laws against foreign bribery, and the relatively cheaper options taking a more preventative approach: encouraging ethical businesses and reducing the demand for bribes through international cooperation.

International law enforcement strategy has recently focused on how bribery moves from one business sector to another as a developing country's political and economic circumstances change. Businesses in all sectors that operate in developing countries should keep an eye on how this process occurs. It is unclear at this stage whether and to what extent corruption may evolve during the current economic crisis, but proactive boards would do well do monitor changes in relative rankings and be able to demonstrate that they have considered such factors in their risk management strategies.

Like the state, corporations need to base their decisions on accurate, up-to-date and tailor-made reports from experienced people in the field. Having advance knowledge of a country's political situation can help companies make predictions about likely changes in corrupt practices, and take appropriate action to manage the risk. Understanding the unique dynamics in a business's sphere of operations is critical to adopting counter-measures – and being able to demonstrate that the threat of bribery is taken seriously.

CORPORATE EXPOSURE: THE GEOGRAPHICAL FACTOR

Some regions are widely reported by businesspeople to be synonymous with corruption, but in the search for more than just anecdotal evidence, attempts have been made to measure corruption and come up with a ranking so countries can be compared. The best known of these is TI's annual Corruption Perceptions Index, in which Somalia, Myanmar, and Afghanistan took the bottom three places in 2010. Information has also been compiled on the countries that are most frequently the subject of international enforcement actions. According to Trace International, in 2010 these were Iraq, Nigeria, and China, where there were numerous alleged bribe payments to officials.[10] It is clear from police strategy that companies operating in places deemed by law enforcement to be high-risk jurisdictions are more likely to attract attention from the UK anti-corruption authorities after the Bribery Act is in force. This is particularly the case where a high-risk business sector is concerned; Angola's oil and gas industry and Nigeria's financial services have recently featured prominently in policy strategy.

The risk of being exposed to corruption in certain countries is so high that the boards of major companies including BAE Systems and Balfour Beatty have considered drawing up corruption blacklists to identify countries where they will not do business, so as to avoid being tainted by corruption.[11] TI argues that after the implementation of the UK Bribery Act, City firms should "pass up business opportunities where the risk of corruption is high."[12] Lord Woolf, chair of the independent ethical standards committee set up by BAE Systems, articulated the dilemma faced by businesses: either they are "an ethical company, which involves refusing to get involved in some contracts, or [they do not] become a fully ethical company reaching the gold standard .... There are contracts that are not worth having, and that will do long-term damage to the company, and the company has to accept that."[13]

Rejecting the temptations of short-term profits in return for long-term improvements in operating environments requires businesses to adopt a broader view of self-interest. It is clear that new legislation and developments in enforcement mean that businesses will have to consider the legal as well as moral implications of being associated with countries where the risk of bribery is high, even if the company's role is limited to remaining silent about instances of wrongdoing.[14] Operating in high-risk environments, unless carefully monitored, could leave companies and directors vulnerable to legal action, says Barry Vitou:

> The SFO's position under the Bribery Act – which is yet to be tested in court – is that if a business is operating in a jurisdiction which is at the bottom end of the TI Corruption Perceptions Index and it does not put in place adequate procedures, that its directing mind has been wilfully blind to the corruption risks.

In turn the SFO take the view that that would be enough to successfully prosecute a corporate for corruption (as a result of the "consent or connivance" of its senior officers in failing to put in place adequate procedures) and enable them to prosecute directors personally.[15]

WEAK GOVERNANCE ZONES

A common characteristic of high bribery risk jurisdictions is inadequate or nonexistent governance. The OECD identifies four characteristics of "weak governance zones" associated with high levels of corruption:

- absence of workable systems for promoting public and private sector ethics
- excessive discretionary powers for public officials at all levels of government
- absence of rule-based frameworks for investment protection
- lack of adequate tendering procedures and of financial and managerial controls in all parts of the public sector.[16]

This lack of governance traps these zones in a cycle in which "broader failures in political, economic and civic institutions ... create the conditions for endemic violence, crime and corruption that block economic and social development."[17] Weak governance zones are fertile ground for contemporary organized criminal groups, which increasingly resemble multinational corporations, with operations that cross the boundaries of multiple states. These "third wave" criminal organizations are distinguished from their predecessors by this multinational footprint, and by extensive infiltration of government and increasingly sophisticated business structures, complete with directors, lawyers, financiers, and accountants.

Criminal groups have flourished in regions where the state is unable or unwilling to carry out its responsibilities effectively. The criminal organizations are richer and more powerful than many governments, and use bribery as a tool to hollow out the state and convert government officials to their cause:

> Third wave criminal groups have ridden the rapid growth of the transnational criminal economy, which already has a UN-estimated gross world product of $2.5 trillion a year (this criminal economy grows in parallel with globalization). They are heavily involved in drugs, kidnapping, protection rackets, and smuggling of all types. To protect their activities, these gangs target governments with bribery and intimidation. Given that most of their activities are beyond the reach of any one government to influence, they have become very effective at subverting states through elimination of the state's monopoly on violence and the distortion of legitimate market activity.[18]

The OECD has estimated that 15 percent of the world's population live in weak governance zones.[19]

CASE STUDIES FOR REGIONAL CORRUPTION
CASE STUDY 1: INDONESIA AND CONSTRUCTION

Over 17,500 islands make up the complex archipelago of Indonesia; the world's fourth largest population, diverse languages, several religious traditions, and a difficult terrain all make the country a complex and interesting place. It is in a strategically important location, on the Malacca Strait, which channels almost all sea traffic between the Far East and Europe. Administered by the Dutch from 1602 until the Japanese invasion during the Second World War, Indonesia subsequently gained its independence in 1949. General Suharto took power by coup in 1965 and remained in power until 1998, since when democracy has grown in strength.[20]

Economy

Indonesia is the second largest exporter of liquefied gas (behind Qatar), and occupies the same rank as a producer of palm oil. Its main industries are textiles, footwear, cork, timber, and tourism. It has made a strong recovery from the 1997 financial crisis. Its real gross domestic product (GDP) has been expanding at 5–6 percent per annum (p.a.) since 2002 and debt levels have fallen to below 35 percent of GDP, with poverty returning to pre-crisis levels. But in 2007 nearly half the population was poor or had a consumption level less than a third above the poverty line.

In 2007 an Investment Law was introduced to encourage investment in the region, and there has been some progress in developing certain markets. However the non-banking financial market remains underdeveloped, and this also fell during the 2008 financial crisis. The rupiah and bond issues suffered problems during this period. Furthermore, the country's GDP is dependent on exports to a large extent, so as demand lessens, this will correspondingly fall also. The 6 percent growth of recent years is considered by many to now be a more unrealistic expectation.

The Suharto era

It is estimated that President Suharto stole between US$15 and $35 billion from the Indonesian economy,[21] much of it coming from World Bank loans, and that at least 20–30 percent of these loans were siphoned off to members of his regime. A 2004 Global Corruption report puts him as the number one embezzler in the parade of all-time corrupt politicians.[22]

Suharto did, however, deliver a high ratio of economic growth and reduce poverty significantly. His survival as such a corrupt dictator was ensured by his determination that the corruption he ruled over was not overly detrimental to investment and general economic activity. However, such a system naturally encouraged weak institutions, the depletion of the country's resources, and a rampant culture of bribery in business.

Escaping the legacy of Suharto

To some extent governmental bodies still control corruption through the issuing of approval to conduct business in the region, and a national survey taken in recent years showed that there had certainly been a system of corruption in place that was well known and part of normal business.[23] In 2001 however the Partnership for Governmental Reform was set up with the help of the international community, and this brought together the major elements of the Indonesian government, legislature, civil service, business, and so on. In this way the country is trying to shake off an embedded tradition of corrupt business practices and to install a transparent and accountable government system. The country has a relatively open investment climate for foreign business, and this is being improved so as to attract even more foreign investment. Similarly there is a definite public mood calling for a clampdown on corruption, and there have been prosecutions of corrupt officials and the seizing of their assets.

Nevertheless and despite this definite trend of deregulation, red tape and bureaucracy is still a hurdle for foreign investment. The legal sphere is complex and hard to negotiate, and causes many firms to avoid the legal system if they possibly can. Companies are advised to settle legal disputes outside Indonesia, as the judiciary can be irregular and opaque in its operation.

Institutional capacity

Much of the governmental structure is fragmented in terms of its authority, which impedes decision making and can engender corrupt practices. As the split of responsibilities between government offices is difficult to discern it can be problematic to identify to whom or where to ask questions during project implementation. Civil servants do not have the necessary level of training for the new responsibilities that are being demanded of them by decentralization, and local-level services are adversely impacted as a consequence.

Indeed, the civil service as a whole still remains only half-modernized since Suharto's regime, with the top-down processes that were efficient during his regime yet to be replaced with a more appropriate model. Weaknesses remain in the training model and the posting system, a lack of penalization for corruption and poor performance, and an opaque compensation system that is not in any way meritocratic.[24]

The fight against corruption is an important one for the modern-day administration, with several new institutions being created to deal with freedom of information, whistleblower protection, and money laundering. Prosecutions have been instigated against senior ministers, business leaders, judges, and so on, and the president has given the go-ahead for hundreds more similar investigations.[25]

Risks of corruption

Bribery, if it occurs, is likely to take place during the licensing process, as the amount of bribes is proportional to the number of business licenses that a project requires to be in compliance with regulations.[26] Small to medium-sized enterprises therefore have more trouble than larger companies as they have to pay a larger proportion of their income to facilitate the necessary paperwork and so forth. There is still a concern about the irregularities of payments and the influence of personal contacts on possible concessions for fees. The Indonesian tax and customs administration is still considered to be a persistent enclave of corruption by the business community.[27]

Construction in Indonesia

The construction industry in Indonesia is ranked as one of the most corrupt in the country, but it also accounts for approximately one-third of gross capital formation.[28] Large payments are commonly made to influence contract decisions, to alter the course of bids, or to avoid proper regulation. Members of government are often involved in the industry as clients, owner of companies, and regulators. But corruption reaches further than merely bribe making and taking, with poor-quality construction, poor returns, and under-funded maintenance making their impact felt.

Construction is always vulnerable to corruption by the nature of its business process: plans needing approval, competitive tenders for projects, governmental oversight and regulation (health and safety, zoning, and so on), the need for fuel and power to do the work, subcontracting labor, the logistics of procuring the necessary materials, inflation of costs during the construction, and completion bonuses making the need to finish the job more urgent. In fact, a 2006 survey in the United Kingdom showed that 51 percent of construction professionals sampled by the Chartered Institute of Building felt that corrupt practices were common.[29]

Because corruption is so much of a problem in the construction industry, many say that they would not consider investing in this sector. One director of a large construction firm stated that, because all contracts require approval by the main board, they would only consider becoming involved in a project which had already been agreed and funded by an outside agency such as the World Bank, the UK Department for International Development (DFID), or USAID.[30] Even though the World Bank has the legal right to audit any project it funds, it exercises this prerogative in less than 1 percent of cases, so this does not act as a sufficient deterrent for anyone who wants to exploit the system in a corrupt fashion.

Another figure said that any foreign government that supplies budgetary support or funding to construction projects by paying for a company's services is likely to risk an incidence of corruption.[31] It is more than likely that there will be delays in output in order to secure bribes. If, however, the project was funded directly by the donor such problems would be less likely to come up. A number of observers believe that Suharto's regime has left its legacy in corruption, and that such practices are now culturally ingrained in the fabric of Indonesian society.[32] While such concerns might not necessarily prevent a company from operating in the country, they would at least cause some thought and perhaps increase the need for more thorough due diligence checks. Similarly foreign companies have low confidence in the nature of the bidding and tender process, with many reports of inquirers seeking insider information on bids and competitors.[33] The import and tax situation is also regularly corrupted, with tax being paid multiple times or goods being cleared on the basis of bribes made to the relevant authorities without having to go through the proper, official channels.[34]

"Commitment" or "success" fees are also common currency in the industry for most if not all projects. The figure is decided at the contracting stage, some observers reporting fees as low as 4 percent and others as high as 20 percent.[35] These figures tend to be dependent on the make-up of the labor force, with local firms demanding a higher "success" remuneration under pressure from the local authorities. Foreign labor elicits a lower level of fee. The largest and initial fee goes to the relevant figure on the bidding committee, then subsequent monthly fees end up in the pocket of the project manager. Most typically firms only pay off one or two individuals, but there have been cases reported of multiple pay-offs being made to other government officials, or security guards and suchlike.[36]

Facilitation payments that smooth the processing of invoices are also common practice. These tend to be small sums, around 0.5–2 percent of the invoice total, and are often put into the accounts as "lunch money."[37] Companies have been known to hold back these payments until the project is complete, thus mitigating the possibilities of extra follow-up bribes being invoked, but also to make sure that the services promised to the project are delivered at the agreed time.

Holiday payments are often demanded by officials involved in the project management, and gifts may be expected on occasions such as Christmas, children's weddings, and religious holidays. Companies have even been known to pay for travel arrangements, a child's tuition, hospital bills, and towards the officials' re-election campaigns.[38]

Favorable project audits are also available by bribe from the government's Internal Audit Agency, internal ministry auditors, and the Audit Board of Indonesia.[39] In many cases auditors deliberately identify as many regulatory infractions as possible, then use these infractions to determine the cost of a bribe. Once the bribes are paid, the infractions no longer appear in the final report. Typical bribes in this area are estimated by observers to be in the region of US$1000–10,000.[40]

CASE STUDY 2: IRAQ AND RECONSTRUCTION

In Iraq, like many Gulf states, there is a strong top-down ethos of authority, which leads to a tendency for decisions to travel upwards to higher levels of decision making. This makes it difficult to secure meaningful authority from a junior or middle-ranking official. Officials also tend to be weak in character and in a certain sense "yes men" so as not to imperil their position, and this further impacts on the efficiency of organizations.[41]

The division between ministries and offices is often unclear, there is intra-ministry fighting and squabbling over jurisdiction, and while this makes things somewhat difficult to deal with, it also offers the opportunity to go to several different parts of the bureaucracy with a view to securing the authority that one is looking for.

As is common in the region, business is navigated by developing personal contacts and building relationships of trust and respect. Larger firms will more than likely be linked to the government and bureaucracy through their family or business contacts. Smaller firms tend to struggle in such a situation without the resources and knowledge to play within such a system.

Corruption is a significant problem, but progress is being made with the institution of a strong anti-corruption strategy in line with UN conventions. Similarly, laws are being proposed in the parliament to help tackle the matter. There have been high-profile convictions: a deputy transport minister, a former trade minister and other senior officials have been or are due to be tried for corruption offenses. The courts received 445 corruption cases in the first nine months of 2009 alone.[42]

Post-war reconstruction

The vacuum of stability and structure that exists within Iraq's post-war reconstruction undermines systems and controls of administrative infrastructure which might counter the proliferation of corruption. Similarly, the rapid influx of foreign money, resources, equipment, and people exacerbates the risk of corruption and bribery. The new administration in such a situation will most likely be the conquering force along with other peace-keeping agents. These people will lack government experience and have little or no local knowledge through which they can lever the situation.

The chaos of wartime also erodes a population's ethical imperatives, so their own survival and the survival of their closest relatives becomes their absolute priority. The desire to secure more and more certainty in the form of money or position, in case chaos and uncertainty again impinge upon their lives, leads to an increased willingness to break rules and engage in corrupt practice in order to secure their own welfare. Similarly however, the breakdown of networks that war engenders leads to a destratification of markets, and there is considerable scope for the exploitation of such opportunities. Foreign firms may wish to move boldly and aggressively into the space left to secure control over positions that will only increase in value as stability begins to reassert itself over the country. Firms will want to buy up as many contracts, monopoly-supplier statuses and other benefits as possible, and to acquire land, stock, contracts, and so on as quickly as they can. In such a chaotic environment there is no shortage of people willing to take advantage of the frontier feeling, and so without an effective system of checks and balances, and with the collapse of effective law enforcement, many entrepreneurs are tempted to bend and break the rules for their own advantage. With more bribes being demanded by the population to secure their safety and more bribes being offered by business to secure whatever it is they want, a culture of corruption quickly mushrooms across the landscape.

The situation in Iraq

The second Gulf War obliterated Iraq's power structures. Consequently day-to-day administration devolved to local authorities which had less ability than the previous regime to maintain regular and widespread law and order. Organized crime was able to flourish in a way that had not been possible under Saddam Hussein.[43]

External contractors found themselves mired in a wildly chaotic situation, and under pressure from the US government to spend huge sums of money and begin the work of rebuilding the country almost instantly. The chaos of the country led to great opportunities for unscrupulous firms and contractors to take part in a wide range of corrupt and exploitative practices: over-charging, failing to deliver work for which they had already been paid, and so on.

Incentives for bribery and corruption were obvious. The huge volumes of foreign cash that had suddenly appeared in the country compounded these problems. The Coalition Provisional Authority in particular had enormous amounts of cash to dispense, and was particularly prone to bribery from unscrupulous officials in the newly constituted Iraqi ministries.[44]

One significant problem was that, after combat, when reconstruction was supposed to be proceeding there was simply no legislation, licensing regulation, or bureaucratic framework in place that could regulate the necessary work. The ministries could not agree on each other's powers of jurisdiction, and so often several different types of permit from completely different ministries which were not necessarily recognized by other bodies were issued. Similarly at the local level, authorities that were forced to pick up the slack caused by the dismantling and ineffectiveness of the high-level powers found themselves operating in a context with little oversight and with no infrastructure to help them, and corrupt practices quite naturally came to fill the political space.[45]

Many of the new national politicians were returning expatriates or exiles, so they had few connections within Iraq and little effective local knowledge. What they did have however were relationships with foreign business contractors who made efforts to exercise their influence through them.

Recently Iraq has been returning to stability, reducing the insurgency and the violence that has crippled the country, and the extent of corruption is also changing.[46] As the bureaucracy is reformed, the systems and procedures for obtaining licenses and permits should begin to emerge in a stable fashion. Bribery is no longer a necessary way of surviving within a chaotic and lawless society, but has become a function of operating within a formal system. As the formality of the legal processes develop they will become easier to use, and this should help to mitigate the problems of corruption. However, to a certain extent bribing has become common currency, and it will take time to bring down its prevalence within the system.[47]

CASE STUDY 3: ANGOLA – THE OIL AND GAS SECTOR

Since 2002, after 41 years of upheaval and conflict, Angola has been engaged in a program of post-war economic development driven by rapid growth in oil extraction. In 2008 Angola overtook Nigeria as foremost sub-Saharan oil producer, supplying it at a rate of 1.8 million barrels per day, and it has seen double digit growth in its economy for the last five years.[48] The majority of the oil is to be found in the Cabinda province, where a long-running insurgency fighting for self-determination persists.

The government of Angola's aim to make the country the third regional power in sub-Saharan Africa is a long way from becoming a reality. Angola's infrastructure continues to lag behind its economic expansion. Roads, ports, and airports suffer from a chronic lack of under-investment. Ships often sit outside Luanda port for weeks at a time because of the lack of loading and unloading capacity, and importers often prefer to unload in Namibia or the Congo and bring their goods into Angola by road rather than directly through Luanda.[49] The corruption in the country contributes to the lack of investment in infrastructure, and the problems are exacerbated by the fact that Luanda was built for a population of half a million but is now home to over 6 million people.

Despite the government's claims that they wish for a different model of economic development to that of the similarly oil-rich Nigeria, with the benefits of the oil industry being funneled towards the national benefit rather than spent on individual enrichment, the extremely large number of individuals who have become millionaires in the last seven years makes these claims questionable.[50]

The emergence from war and conflict to a peace-time economy and the boom of the oil industry have turned Angola into something of a frontier state for foreign investors. The paucity of previous investment in the Angolan infrastructure has further generated significant, attractive opportunities for foreign companies to fill.

Many UK firms are at present working in Angola, particularly in the natural resources sector, but although there is certainly money to be made, it is a complex market to negotiate, and corruption is rife in almost all spheres of life.[51]

The corruption environment

One consequence of Angola's protracted civil war is that there is practically no middle class to speak of, although a growing number of teachers and civil servants are beginning to emerge, and so it remains a highly unequal society, a problem compounded by the wealth generated by the natural resources industry. Seventy percent of Angolans live on less than US$2 per day, and at the other end of the income spectrum there is a small stratum of extremely rich individuals, not only by African standards but by Western standards.[52] Reports suggest that the proportion of Angolan millionaires could be as high as 15–20 percent of the population. The GDP per capita is US$7000, a high figure in the context of sub-Saharan Africa.[53] This is three times as large as the GDP of Nigeria and comparable with Serbia and Columbia. The high wages of salaried staff, typically $2500 per month, reflect the particularly high costs of living in the capital.[54]

Where the Marxist state used to provide assistance and provision for those who relied upon it, there is now very little provision. Property rights are hardly protected and the oil industry pays very little tax on revenue. As a consequence public services are either basic or nonexistent. The economy is awash with a huge amount of cash. This availability along with the opacity of transactions and the desire for enrichment continues to fuel a culture of corruption.

The economy is entirely based on the revenue generated by oil and minerals. Oil makes up 95 percent of exports, and the remaining 5 percent comes from diamond exports.[55] Sonangol, the monolithically powerful, state-owned oil company, controls many aspects of the economic sphere beyond those related to oil and gas, including the insurance and provision of oil contracts. In theory, Sonangol's revenue should be received and distributed by the central government; however in practice the transparency of Sonangol's accounting and of the natural resources industry in general is very poor. A Global Witness report in 2004 estimated the sum "lost" to the Angolan Treasury by failure to pay tax between 1997–2001 at around US$1.7 billion annually.[56]

Bribery hotspots

Corruption abounds within all spheres of Angolan life.[57] Bribes are paid even by the general population as a matter of course. Paying "gasosa" is necessary, in fact, to get anything done. Bribery, however, is not considered to be corruption. Rather it is viewed locally as a mechanism that necessarily emerged within a chaotic and under-developed economic system. There are stories from expatriates of nearly empty planes taking off, or people being refused tables in an empty restaurant, because the requisite bribe was not met.[58] That such allegations are common currency gives an indication of the culture.

The service sector

There is such a short supply of hotel rooms that they must be booked at least three months in advance, and cost around $500 per night.[59] Even a confirmed reservation is no guarantee that a room will actually be made available. The same kind of process is found in many aspects of everyday life.[60]

Customs

Corruption reigns in the port of Luanda because of its poor capacity, chaotic organization, and a lack of trained staff.[61] Those in the know can thus charge a premium on top of their actual wages. In the case of two cars imported to Luanda at the same time and on the same ship, for example, one took five months to clear customs and one took just two weeks.[62]

Police

The situation regarding bribes to the police has improved in recent years. Some officers refuse any money that is offered. However, motorists are still halted for spurious reasons, a bribe is demanded, and if the motorist refuses to pay, a ticket is issued. The person to whom the fine is payable is also likely to make it clear that they expect a bribe.[63]

The business world in Angola

Due diligence

Carrying out due diligence on business partners is extremely difficult in Angola, as accessing the proper information depends almost entirely on connections which are notoriously hard to obtain. Letters to banks or companies are routinely ignored, and record systems have remained in a state of chaos since the war ended.[64] One particular firm wished to break into the gaming and gambling sector but found its efforts repeatedly blocked. Later its staff obtained information indicating that the industry was monopolized by one company with connections to the president's daughter.[65]

Formal channels are not much utilized by Angolan businesses, and so operating is dependent on relationships being established and maintained. Angolans remain wary until a trustworthy relationship has been established. A legacy of the previous Marxist regime is that a disjuncture has developed between the mindset of centralized governmental control and the emergence of a system of capitalist enterprise. Without the proper connections and relationships a firm will find it difficult to even land a place on a tender shortlist, without even considering the possibility of ultimately winning a contract.[66]

The majority of political and ministerial decisions appear to be made over drinks in the evening rather than during official office hours, and even those with cooperative connections and influence can find it extremely difficult to make an appointment with a government official. Phone calls and letters are routinely ignored, though observers have found that going to a minister's office on spec can sometimes lead to a meeting. Most ministers have an interest in registered companies, and while many such companies appear dormant, if an opportunity arises to make money they are often brought to life.[67] That politicians expect to be cut in on business opportunities in this way is not considered a corrupt practice or conflict of interest but instead a normal way to do business. To become a partner of a company in which a minister has an interest makes it much more likely that an organization will win a bid.[68] Angolan companies enjoy preferential treatment by law in government tenders.

It is possible for a foreign company to survive in Angolan business without having to bribe directly but it is likely that their joint-venture local partner will not.[69] The requirements are often made explicit in negotiations. For example a partner might seek to agree both their proportion of the profits and a further figure that must be laid on the table in order to cover bribes that are seen to be necessary to get the job done.[70]

Political corruption

A vast and complex system of patronage has been built up in Angola by tradition and circumstance, and this has resulted in a pernicious climate of grand corruption on an extensive scale.[71] A fear of a return to the chaos of civil war has nurtured an atmosphere of "take as much as you can while you still have the chance."

Although the traditionally wealthy elite of Angola managed to retain their wealth, status, and influence throughout the period of the civil war, the majority of the country's wealth has been created during the last five years. New elites have emerged as a result of the war. For example, those prominent in the Popular Movement for the Liberation of Angola (MPLA) have been rewarded for their loyalty with shares of the wealth generated by the country's oil. However, even though many have benefited in recent years, the president has called for them to limit their share of personal enrichment and to "do it for Angola."[72]

High-level corruption in the upper echelons of the senior government runs within a subtle and sophisticated system. The vast wealth these elites enjoy means that an offer of a straight financial bribe could be seen as insulting. Instead they are looking for investment opportunities in the West, and to find foreign partners with other interests in which they might potentially invest.[73] This high-level corruption is based on a system of favors for which return might be sought in the long rather than the short term.

Opaque ownership structures and the commercial elite

This blurred distinction between the political and commercial elites – sometimes the same people wield political power and control commercial interests – breeds an opacity within Angolan business. The most powerful organization in Angola is the state-owned Sonangol, and the majority of business is tied up by a few key families. These families maintain the balance of interests in Angola, and a complex network of patronage rewards that maintenance, leaving the elites free to pursue their interests insofar as they make sure to keep the status quo. The extreme difficulties involved in determining ownership and interest in this situation result in many foreign firms falling foul of these opaque networks.[74]

The canny encouragement by the Angolan government of foreign direct investment (FDI) has led to the implementation of a local content require-ment for foreign firms wishing to invest and operate in Angola, but these requirements are similarly opaque and more or less depend on the whim of the government in their assessment of whatever they feel Angola needs at a particular time.[75] Because the elite overlaps to a large extent with business interests, this content requirement does not represent a bribe as much as it regulates and mediates the foreign firms' potential for relationships with the ruling classes.

The High Authority Against Corruption

Anti-corruption legislation and its enforcement are essentially absent in Angola. While there is certain nominative legislation in force, the facts that members of the government are not required to maintain transparency in their affairs and are not compelled to disclose their assets mean that the public is unable to exert much control over the matter. Compounding this fact are certain state secret and national security laws that allow the government not only to censor news and to jail anyone disclosing infor-mation that might be damaging to Angolan self-interest, but even to pros-ecute multinational organizations that discuss the nature of their Angolan deals and investments.

Similarly, there are no independent state organizations with the power to investigate and prosecute anti-corruption cases. The High Authority Against Corruption, put together in 1995, was intended to achieve such an effect within the Angolan public sphere, but 15 years after its inception it has not yet begun to function properly.

The vacuum that is left both legally and institutionally in this sense means there is no effective anti-corruption enforcement. Law enforcement and judicial institutions are also highly politicized, compounding these problems.[76]

Prospects

Despite the problems of transparency that await them and the rampant culture of bribery, investors are still willing to try and break into Angolan markets. This is welcomed by the Angolan elites, who recognize that some effort to clean up the country's reputation for corruption is necessary to further develop these relations with foreign business and enterprise. There are those in Angola who are looking to the future, including the president, and plans have been drawn up to launch an Angolan stock exchange.[77] These facts are indicative of a certain amount of long-term planning. However, it will be a long road as corruption is so deeply and systematically integrated within Angolan business and culture.

Emerging sectors

Angola is an extremely pragmatic state, and actively courts investment from a number of sources; the message seems to be "as long as there is something in it for Angola." Thus it has encouraged Portuguese firms to retain their colonial connections, and South Africans to generate pan-African investment. Western business is welcome, as is Cuban and Chinese business, a legacy of Angola's Marxist past. In fact, the Chinese presence in Angola is quite prevalent, particularly in the commercial and construction sectors. Despite Sonangol's grip on the oil industry there are still many opportunities to be had within the industry, particularly in construction and engineering. Brazilian and Portuguese banks provide the services to enable Angolan high-net worth individuals to hide their wealth offshore according to lobbying organizations such as Global Witness.[78] The logic behind targeting the banks that allow corrupt officials to remain clients, and the lawyers who create the corporate vehicles that allow embezzlement to occur, is that curtailing these activities will dramatically reduce the relative ease with which elites can currently enjoy their ill-gotten gains in other countries, and the opportunities for these elites to contribute to the capital flight which retards the development of so many African countries. As one investigator of corruption in Africa put it, "you don't take off in a plane unless you have somewhere to land it."[79]

The boom in business also implies a need for education and training. As a result of the war much of the population is illiterate, but many are employed as police officers and public servants, so there is a demand for technical training and English-language skills, with the aim that Angola will ultimately become self-sufficient as an international player.

The business sector context – oil and gas

The oil and gas industry is significantly exposed to the influence of corruption; it is an extremely complex industry. Delays and problems in the production process tend to cost large sums. The culture of competitive bidding for territory encourages bribery of the supervisors and officials in charge of the bidding process. National influence is a key component of the industry, so political power is a significant aspect. The sector is heavily taxed, and there is ample opportunity for part of the large profits to be siphoned off to corrupt officials. There is significant motivation for the theft of reserves which can then be recalculated as future reserves rather than current inventory. Oil is easily misappropriated or resold within the supply chain, as it is a valuable commodity.

Anyone wishing to work in the Angolan oil industry is required to partner with Sonangol. Conflict of interest is simply not an issue in the vocabulary of Angolan business or politics, and senior politicians are heavily involved in Sonangol and its various support and service companies. The competitive bidding process in the oil sector is extremely opaque, and the information suggests that most if not all foreign companies that work in this sector are engaged in bribery as a matter of course.[80] Even the largest oil companies take precautions to disguise their more dubious payments and cover their money trails.[81]

CASE STUDY 4: BANGLADESH AND AID

The last 15 years have seen significant economic growth for Bangladesh, averaging 5 percent a year since 1990 and climbing closer to 7 percent a year in more recent years. Similarly there has been success in poverty reduction, with a decrease of more than 1 percent a year from 1990–2000, going up to 2 percent a year from 2000–05. That said, more than 56 million people remain beneath the poverty line, subsisting on less than 50 cents per day, and even deeper within that tally lies a subset of 14 million "extreme poor" who exist on less than 30 cents per day.[82]

Corruption is rife at all levels of life, and is caused mainly by dynastic politics, a common South Asian system.[83] In Bangladesh power oscillates between the Bangladesh National Party (BNP) and the Awami League (AL). For these parties patronage plays a crucial role, and thus the parties do their utmost to support their own backers when they are in power. Expensive election campaigns leave politicians indebted to their donors, so when they take office they feel obliged to repay these debts by supplying them with exclusive contracts and employment.

The main objective of the caretaker government (2006–08) was the reduction of corruption in Bangladeshi politics in order to prime the country again for transparent democratic elections. It eliminated 35 million "ghost voters" from the country's voter register, the executive was separated from the judiciary, and other reforms were put in place. However it is feared that the Anti-Corruption Commission itself has been compromised, and is no longer effective. Many feel current anti-corruption laws are being misused as an instrument for revenge within the political sphere. The chair of the commission resigned under pressure in 2009, and observers suggest that the two major political parties are reverting to the previous patterns of corruption that have been in evidence since 1971.[84]

Bangladesh is such a disaster-prone area that it heads the UN Mortality Risk index for natural disasters.[85] It suffers regularly from floods, cyclones, tornadoes, river-bank erosion leading to landslides, storm surges, drought and earthquakes. Short-term disaster aid has been a prevalent part of the aid provided to the country. With its low levels of development, Bangladesh has also been the target of longer-term aid programs.[86]

Sector – aid

International aid organizations are highly diverse in their structure and organization, but a common thread is that they work in regions where government has to some extent failed and the country has in essence broken down. Emergency relief in particular, which depends on swift operation to be at all effective, is vulnerable to corruption. The pressure of delivery leaves it open to be strangled by corruption and interference by local power. Its operation can be deliberately delayed by those seeking bribes, and its resources can easily be channeled away from the intended targets.

The major worldwide charities are complex organizations which rely on professional staff to function properly. They incorporate the same kinds of business processes as major international companies. They often hire local residents in order to harness the advantages of local, cultural knowledge and to benefit the population, and it can be difficult to bring the corporate standards expected in the organization in line with local norms or customs. Some reports indicate that the employees of aid organizations take bribes as a matter of course in the localized situation.[87] This is sometimes excused by the claim that bribes will eventually end up going to the local people, so in a sense this is indirectly beneficial to the recipient country.[88] Furthermore, aid workers on the ground are routinely presented with situations in which a small bribe must be paid to secure access to an area in a disaster zone. In such a predicament, the worker may reason that the price demanded is worth paying, and that the benefits of providing much-needed assistance far outweigh the harms of greasing a few palms.

Several aid organizations claim, in fact, that bribery is less common in the aid sector than in commercial organizations, as there is a general perception that aid givers are trying to do good.[89] Police officers, for example, might let an aid convoy pass a checkpoint without being paid their normal bribe, as they recognize that the aid is being brought for the benefit of their villages, towns, or country as a whole. But on the other hand the sector is more vulnerable, as there is the requirement for a high level of trust between staff and officials, and this provides more scope for exploitation.

Similarly, reports tell of a division between the corporate anti-bribery message that is issued from the head of an aid organization and the attitudes and practices of the country managers in the field.[90] If a manager is willing to tolerate bribery in their operations in order to achieve the effectiveness of the operation, it is more than likely that this message will be reproduced by subordinate staff, despite the corporate message.

It is reported that aid organizations are not effective in the coordination of activities and the sharing of in-country information.[91] The lack of effective networking between regions in this way has led to a type of corruption in which an aid recipient sets up "ghost projects" which are then funded by several separate donors that are not in communication with each other, with the total funding far exceeding the amount actually expended (if any). Since aid is not a competitive sector, it is not clear why there has not developed effective information sharing between organizations operating in the same region which might mitigate such problems.

Different aid organizations – such as USAID, the UK DFID, and the World Bank – also use different formats of accounting. A common mode of accounting would increase transparency.

One leading aid organization has made it policy not to tackle the corruption it encounters at all, feeling it would damage its effectiveness.[92] In any event, it seems that charities that do enforce a hard line against corruption from the corporate headquarters find it extremely difficult to make their field workers report honestly about the corruption they have to deal with. These workers are understandably wary of being caught in contravention of the corporate policy when they feel they have had to pay bribes as a matter of operational necessity.

It is difficult to find unambiguous guidance on this issue. The UK Charity Commission, for example, demands that organizations follow the rules, but its guidance itself makes it unclear what the rules actually are.[93] For larger charities this is not a problem as they have the expertise and resources to handle the issues themselves, but for newer smaller charities this might not be the case.

Procurement is also a problem that can become a target for corruption, with aid organizations often having to adhere to difficult procurement rules. Having trustworthy local partners reduces these problems to an extent, but it is unlikely that following local rules of procurement will lead to the most cost-effective result.

Combined assessment

Corruption in Bangladesh is a serious problem, and the aid sector is not immune. The military influence compounds the problem, as senior officers take a high-profile role in extracting bribes from public projects.[94] There was a feeling that corruption eased in 2009 with the return to democratic government.[95] However, it seems that the country then gradually drifted back to its old ways and practices, particular in the political and civil service environment. Several anti-corruption measures put in place by the caretaker government were rolled back after 2009.[96] Corruption in Bangladesh is closely linked to political activity.

The aid contracting process

The tender process in Bangladesh is two-tier in nature. The first step is to secure a local partner, then there is a secondary series of transactions as the partner acts as an agent and recruits local resources in order to deliver the aid within the country. There is a great deal of evidence that large-scale corruption takes place in this process.[97]

Even if donors insist on a transparent secondary process, it is more than likely that political interference will have warped the tender list so that certain companies are allowed to fix the outcome of the bid. Bribes for information about tender lists, and bribes to discover what bids have been made, are regularly offered.[98] There is also a perception that if the "wrong" company wins a tender, political influence will be brought to bear, so the company becomes unable to deliver and the aid agency is forced to retender.[99]

Corruption and discord within the sphere of government also makes the delivery of aid difficult. Corruption is particularly evident when the local government is a partner in aid provision.[100] The Ministry of Communication has been singled out as particularly suspect.[101] That said, donor activities are not free from corruption themselves. International charities have less money at stake in Bangladesh than the larger bilateral and multilateral organizations, but they also have proportionally less official influence, and can be more vulnerable to corruption and difficulties in selecting trustworthy local partners. Similarly, they tend to have more informal processes, and that also attracts a more corrupt element to their orbit.

Delays are often common through corrupt bureaucratic processes. Systematic delays to visas, clearance of imports, permits, taxes and so on, all with the intent to extort money from charities, are regularly reported.[102]

Because of the time-sensitive nature of aid delivery, these delays significantly impact the value of the aid itself. The judiciary is reported to be a particularly vulnerable to corruption.[103] To pursue a legal case successfully a high volume of bribery is necessary, and cases can take years to resolve. These problems can stop aid projects from succeeding altogether. Local partners often detail to their parent aid organizations the amount of bribery that will be necessary before they embark on a project.[104]

CASE STUDY 5: THE GULF STATES AND LOCAL AGENTS

The impact of political instability on business relationships and processes is a growing factor for members of the Gulf Co-operation Council (GCC) – Bahrain, Kuwait, Oman, Qatar, Saudi Arabia, and the United Arab Emirates (UAE). Personal relationships have traditionally been paramount in a region experiencing great growth. This culture is characterized by a disdain for simply ticking boxes, and observers report greater integrity and less wide-scale greasing in traditional trade (rather than the massive projects such as Al Yamamah, for which see elsewhere in this book) than might be expected.[105] Whether corruption will increase as insecurity starts to impact on states and politicians as a result of the "Arab spring" revolts has yet to be seen.

Local agents and sponsors

The legislation on the issue of partners and consultants tends to be inconsistent and arcane in these countries. In order to operate locally, companies need to incorporate with a local partner. It is not a legal requirement but reportedly a practical one in order to access the market and to be able to breach the significant cultural barriers.[106]

Local cultural knowledge is paramount in this region. Friendship and trust make up a vital part of business relations, and respect and honor are prized. Hospitality is also expected. Local consultants who know the culture are generally used to facilitate business discussions and relationships, and to make contacts. They take a commission related to the size of the contract. There is little transparency or regulation in these matters.[107]

Carrying out due diligence checks on nationals close to ruling families is practically impossible. Severe offense can be caused by requesting accounts or a business history, even if it is not assumed that there is a suggestion of possible corruption: that the enquirer does not trust the potential partner is offensive in itself. Any attempt to investigate the commercial structures of the ruling families can cause similar offense, and might well damage the investigator commercially.

Corruption in Dubai used to be rife but has been dealt with in recent years with several high-profile prosecutions.[108] However, it remains difficult to determine how far down the levels of the system the drive actually reaches, particularly with regard to the sub-continental community (that is, immigrants from India, Pakistan, and Bangladesh). A large swathe of public-sector contracts are controlled by the Bani Fatima family in the UAE, and deals tend to be awarded to companies in which they have an interest.[109] Staff in outer offices are reportedly likely to require a degree of greasing in order to secure support for projects.[110] Donations are also invited, and even after approval is granted, generosity is rewarded by ensuring that implementation actually goes ahead rather than being stalled in any unforeseen way. A commission is also usually taken.

Types of agent or intermediary

The introducer

Markets are difficult to crack in the Gulf without a personal connection to a potential client or partner. This is true in all industrial sectors. This requirement has seen the emergence of agents whose only purpose is to facilitate introductions between companies and possible clients. These introducers require fees for their introductions, and these carry a high risk of being seen as bribes by UK and other Western authorities. Companies have been penalized for making such payments.[111]

The local representative office

It is common for companies to use a third-party company as a representative. Such a company will have greater local knowledge of bureaucracy, working practices, standards, and so forth, and indeed of which contracts are on the horizon.

The channel for bribes to win contracts

In many instances the best route to contracts is not a commercial consultant but a more informal agent: someone with kinship and friendship ties to prospective clients. These characters are useful as the contracts might be high-profile and political in their nature, and so their negotiation requires a level of discretion. The commission to this kind of agent needs to be paid in secret,[112] and the transaction might be very opaque, involving foreign bank accounts, for example. High-value gifts and benefits might also make up the remuneration.

The mandatory partner

The notion of having a mandatory local partner as part of a successful bid can also be classed in this category. That a partner must be involved is generally not spelled out in the tender process, but will be insisted on at the final stage of the bid procedure, when the preferred bidder has already invested in the process and is less likely to resist the requirement.

The permit fixer

This intermediary acts between a foreign firm and the local bureaucratic structures that issue permits and other such authorizing documents. Many types of permit are essential to the smooth functioning of business, and although their issue should be routine, in practice it often requires bribery.[113]

CASE STUDY 6: SHELL AND THE US FOREIGN CORRUPT PRACTICES ACT (FCPA) IN NIGERIA

Nigeria is a dynamic and burgeoning economy, the largest in the African continent north of South Africa. It has a strong banking system with a firm regulator, considerable oil resources – the country supplies no less than 10 percent of US demand – and a growing consumer market.[114] The promise of such an economy is undermined by its reputation for corruptibility. The pull of the market attracts Western companies, but they have to combat a compliance deficit. This deficit carries with it a cost to operators in the Nigerian market, under pressure from demands for facilitation payments and even outright bribes. The task for the Western company in such a market is to negotiate its way between compliance with its domestic laws, such as the FCPA and the UK Bribery Act, on the one hand, and the commercial requirements of the market on the other. This requires complicated maneuvers, as the experience of Shell in the country demonstrates.

The compliance deficit is demonstrated by Nigeria's low ranking in international tables.[115] For example the country ranks 14th on *Foreign Policy*'s Failed States Index.[116] Its score has fallen steadily since 2008, and Nigeria is now on higher alert than Yemen, Burma, and Sierra Leone. Transparency International's Corruption Perceptions Index 2010,[117] which measures perceptions of corruption in the pubic sector, has Nigeria close to the bottom, tied with Azerbaijan, Honduras, and Zimbabwe, among others, at 134th out of 178.

Bribes are most likely to be required in the procurement of goods and services, and in dealings with the courts. A joint United Nations and Nigerian Economic and Financial Crimes Commission (EFCC) report indicated that the police were ranked the most corrupt public institution, [118] and a 2010 Human Rights Watch report confirmed that "there's institutionalized corruption at every level."[119]

The Nigerian government signed up in 2003 to the Extractive Industries Transparency Initiative, a global standard supported by a coalition of businesses, governments, and civil society organizations. It seeks to improve accountability and transparency in the oil and gas sector by setting up a methodology whereby companies publish what they pay and the government discloses what it receives.[120] In 2004 it launched the Nigerian

Extractive Industries Initiative, and this was signed into law in 2007.[121] The governing body is the National Stakeholders Working Group, on which sit representatives of extractive industries.[122] At present the oil industry is represented on the working group by the group managing director of the Nigerian National Petroleum Company, Austin Oniwon.

There is growing support for the FCPA among Nigerian businesses. Desperate to escape the stereotype that all Nigerians are corrupt, they have increasingly supported foreign efforts to prosecute corruption on their soil. The FCPA blog, written by senior lawyer Richard L. Cassin, observed in December 2008 that "the law is gaining fans":[123]

> They think of the FCPA as a tool that can help clean up the place. And it's working. Suppliers in Nigeria who want to grow internationally, for example, are learning that compliance makes good business sense. It's a mini-revolution.[124]

The two national agencies charged with anti-corruption work in Nigeria are the EFCC and the Independent Corrupt Practices and Other Related Offences Commission. The former is most relevant to FCPA enforcement, and was mandated by the EFCC Establishment Act 2004 to enforce all other related legislation. It has a responsibility to "to prevent, investigate, prosecute and penalise economic and financial crimes."[125]

Shell has a long history of doing business in Nigeria. The country's first commercial oil export was from Shell's Oloibiri field. With the Nigerian National Petroleum Company (NNPC), Total, and Agip, Shell owns 30 percent of Shell Petroleum Development Company of Nigeria Limited (SPDC). SPDC is the largest oil and gas company in Nigeria, owning 90 oilfields spread over 30,000 square km.[126] It operates offshore and on land in the volatile Niger delta region.

Shell also owns the Shell Nigeria Exploration and Production Company Limited (SNEPCo).[127] Formed in 1993, SNEPCo operates offshore and deep-water oil and gas resources. In contrast to SPDC, SNEPCo is 100 percent owned by Shell but has a production-sharing contract with NNPC. In November 2005 the company started production at the Bonga deep water oil and gas project, the first of its kind in Nigeria. The site can produce 200,000 barrels of oil and 150 million standard cubic feet of gas per day. Since then SNEPCo has joined Exxonmobil as venture partner in the Erha deepwater oil and gas project.

Shell helped set up the Nigeria Liquefied Natural Gas Company (NLNG) in 1989 with a 25.6 percent interest, to open up Nigeria's natural gas resources. Most of NLNG's production is at the Bonny Island plant, which accounts for around 10 percent of the world's liquid natural gas (LNG) capacity. Other companies with interests are NNPC (49 percent), Total LNG Nigeria Limited (15 percent), and Eni (10.4 percent).[128] Shell's subsidiaries in Nigeria work together providing complementary services. SPDC supplies the bulk of the gas to the NLNG plant.

Shell Natural Gas Limited (SNG) was incorporated in 1998 with an eye to developing the Nigerian domestic market, which had traditionally relied on liquid fuels like kerosene. Shell's gas distribution systems reach over 50 clients, many of them multinationals operating in the southern states. Over time industries in the region have converted equipment to run on gas, and the sector has expanded with new entrants, but SNG is the only company in the industry which is certified to the ISO 14001 Environmental Management System standard.[129]

Shell has faced major problems in the Niger delta, as the local population has clashed with oil companies and the state. Unrest with Shell's operations in the Niger delta have been mostly directed at SPDC. They reached a peak in 2006 when SPDC shut down most of its operations in the western delta.[130] Work restarted in 2007 but the environment remains unstable, with 211 reported oil thefts from SPDC facilities in the year 2008–09.[131]

Shell's Nigerian operations contribute about 9 percent to its overall global production.[132] Recent developments in Nigeria include the new 650 MW Afam VI power plant and the Gbaran-Ubie gas project.

Shell's anti-corruption policy addresses both corruption and perceptions of corruption, which can be equally harmful to business prospects. Its main efforts are in:

- creating a conducive internal culture
- disclosure
- reporting.

The company's core business strategy documents establish an internal corporate culture that deters corruption. The General Business Principles and Code of Conduct contain a guiding commitment to "honesty, integrity and fairness in all aspects of our business." These values are communicated to its employees through regular training and induction programs, employment contracts, and various communication tools.[133]

Shell's own guidelines rule out facilitation payments, and urge its workers never to offer or accept inappropriate gifts or hospitality (G&H). The Code of Conduct 2010 says, "Facilitation payments are bribes and must not be paid."[134] As recently as 2003, however, it designated facilitation payments as permissible but discouraged. This shows Shell's internal policy has adapted to recent tightening of FCPA legislation and implementation.[135] The Code of Conduct warns that "G&H that are acceptable between private business partners may be unacceptable between a business and an official."[136] Employees must have permission from Shell to offer G&H to government officials, and the value of G&H must not exceed a set of prescribed limits. These limits are set by country. There is a special telephone helpline on which any concerns about conduct can be reported, in line with the repeated encouragement to "Tell Shell."

Shell has led the industry in publishing what it pays to the Nigerian government and public officials, through the NEITI. In 2003, SPDC was the first company to disclose how much it paid the Nigerian government, including royalties, taxes, and other payments.[137] Shell has served on the National Stakeholder Working Group of NEITI.

Shell provides reporting on its environmental and social performance both internally and through external reporting organizations, including Dow Jones Sustainability indexes, ftSe4good, and the Carbon Disclosure Project. Shell started voluntary reporting on environmental and social performance in 1997, with the *Shell Report*. It also supports the UN Global Compact Principle 10.[138]

Despite Shell's anticorruption policy, it was investigated for violations of the FCPA, and settled with the US Department of Justice (DOJ) in 2010.

In May 2008 Shell announced that it was being investigated by the DOJ in relation to the behavior of one of its contractors, a Swiss logistics firm called Panalpina Inc.[139] SNEPCo used Panalpina for logistics at the Bonga offshore plant. DOJ interest in Shell was part of a larger investigation, led by US and Nigerian agencies, into a number of companies engaged in offshore drilling and related services. They include Transocean, Tidewater Inc., GlobalSantaFe Corp., Noble Corp., and Shell and two of its subsidiaries, SNEPCo and the Shell International Exploration and Production Company (SIPC).

Panalpina was accused of spending millions of dollars bribing Nigerian officials to speed up the customs process and avoid duties, in violation of the FCPA.[140] Furthermore, payments were made to extend drilling contracts and secure other illicit perks. Panalpina pleaded guilty to three counts of conspiring to violate the US Sherman Act, and paid a fine of £11.3 million in a settlement with the SEC in October 2010.[141] It was fined an additional $70.5 million by the DOJ.[142]

In a statement of apology released in December 2010, Shell admitted "lapses" whereby payments were made to "expedite delivery of material to the project."[143] Presented in these terms, other businesses in Nigeria may fear that minor oversights could slip under their compliance officer's radar, landing them with millions of pounds of fines and reputation damage. However, in this case the sums of money involved were substantial, and the prosecution rested on the fact that Panalpina employees in the United States were routinely and systematically covering up the illegal payments and processing them as legitimate business expenses. SNEPCo subsequently "approved or condoned" the bribes made on its behalf. Specifically the DOJ was looking at $2 million given by SNEPCo to Panalpina, which it knew would all or in part be used to fund bribes, leading to profits of around $14 million. As a result, SNEPCo was forced to pay a $30 million fine.

A separate case was brought by SEC against SIPC relating to FCPA charges, for which SIEP agreed to pay $18.1 million. Robert Khuzami, director of the SEC's Division of Enforcement, described it in the following strong terms, "These companies resorted to lucrative arrangements behind the scenes to obtain phony paperwork and special favors, and they landed themselves squarely in investigators' crosshairs."[144] With a few exceptions, the companies faced charges from both the DOJ and the US Securities and Exchange Commission (SEC). The SEC proceedings against SIPC were administrative rather than criminal.

The consequences for Panalpina were disastrous. In addition to the $81.8 million settlement, in September 2007 the company suspended all local freight forwarding and logistics services for oil and gas clients.[145] Compliance concerns forced it to withdraw from the entire Nigerian domestic market a year later.[146] In July 2009, an investment fund that owned about 5 percent of Panalpina World Transport (Holding) Ltd sued to recover damages incurred by the withdrawal from Nigeria. Deccan Value Advisors Fund was not able to do this directly through FCPA, as there is no right of private action under the act. Instead it used the Securities Act, and brought charges of fraud and negligent misrepresentation. This followed a fall in Panalpina's first half net profits of 78 percent in 2009.[147]

Similarly, Noble Inc, another American firm investigated by the DOJ in relation to the Panalpina bribes, was unable to renew or obtain five out of seven operating permits for its Nigerian drilling rigs.[148] The FCPA investigation severely limited the business prospects of the company, as Noble was unable to authorize payments which could have been seen as corrupt to Nigerian officials. Commentators suspected this was a result of an explicit warning from the DOJ that companies should pull out of the Nigerian oil industry or risk further FCPA cases.[149]

However, the FCPA does not prohibit doing business in Nigeria's oil market, as shown by the positive example of Global Industries, an offshore gas and oil services provider.[150] Also a Panalpina customer, Global Industries suspected problems with the logistics firm even before the DOJ commenced investigations. It responded immediately with board-level action. The board of directors authorized a thorough internal investigation of its operations in the region, jointly conducted with outside FCPA counsel. It turned over the results of the report to the government, and self-disclosed to the SEC and DOJ. In contrast, SNEPCo did not voluntarily disclose to the DOJ at any stage during the Panalpina investigation, and as a result received the second lowest "discount" of the applicable fine range of any company included in the settlements. It was discounted only 12.3 percent off the guidelines range. This goes some way to explaining the severity of the fine SNEPCo faced, compared with Pride, Transocean, and

Tidalwater Marine International, which received discounts of 55 percent, 20 percent, and 30 percent respectively.[151]

The lessons from the Global Industries case reaffirm Principle IV, Due Diligence, of the UK Ministry of Justice guidance on anti-corruption and anti-corruption best practice.[152] It suggests that companies may wish to enquire about the internal anti-corruption policies of their partners and contractors. Companies looking to work in Nigeria may feel daunted by the level of due diligence required and the possible costs of getting caught out. It is true that an adequate compliance program demands time and resources – the Global Industries internal investigation took two and a half years.[153] But the investment will pay off. Not only do internal checks and reporting reduce the likelihood of the company finding itself in front of the DOJ on FCPA charges, but where charges are brought, the DOJ has been more sympathetic where there is strong historical evidence that a company has enforced a sound compliance program.[154]

The conviction of Snamprogetti Netherlands BV and its Italian parent company ENI SpA in July 2010 provides a case study to compare with Shell's experience. This concerned a TSKJ-Nigeria Joint Venture involving four Japanese, US, and French companies. Snamprogetti employees authorized the joint venture to hire two agents to pay bribes to "Top-level executive branch officials" to help win contracts for a Bonny Island LNG plant. TSKJ was charged by DOJ with one count of conspiracy and one count of aiding and abetting violations of the FCPA. The DOJ charged that payments totaling over $170 million were made to companies from Gibraltar and Japan, part of which was intended to be used as a bribe. Between 1995 and 2004 TSKJ won contracts worth more than US$6 billion.[155] The SEC also brought charges: both companies violated anti-bribery, record-keeping, and internal controls provisions of the Securities Act 1934.[156]

This case is similar to the Shell prosecution as it concerns payments made to Nigerian government officials. However, the Shell payments were intended partly to speed up a legal activity, already in progress, and partly to illegally avoid paying customs. The Snamprogetti payments were intended to influence the allocation of contracts and business, which firmly counts as a bribe. With uncertainty around the SFO's precise tolerance level of facilitation payments in the UK Bribery Act, it is important to note that the FCPA will prosecute companies within its jurisdiction for payments related to accelerating legal business activities.

Furthermore, both companies faced charges from the SEC and the DOJ, with both agencies ordering substantial costs or fines. Therefore, it is not simply a case of keeping track of the FCPA, organizations must also conform to the Securities Act 1934, and the Sherman Act, which dates back to 1890. US prosecutors are happy to employ domestically applicable anti-trust legislation to bring convictions. Companies should stay abreast of developments in all applicable areas of business law.

Shell took steps to tighten its anti-corruption policy after the prosecution. After an internal investigation, those staff who were found to be in breach of their policy were disciplined or dismissed.[157] A new *Anti-Bribery and Corruption Manual* was issued and an oversight committee formed. The Anti-Bribery and Corruption Committee (ABC) identifies risks of corruption and oversees the implementation of the new manual and related training programs. The manual and training focus on "more detailed due diligence of suppliers, contractors and in particular, government officials." In high-risk areas – presumably Nigeria is included in this category – anti-bribery and corruption reviews are to take place annually from 2011.[158]

In terms of the outlook for doing business in Nigeria in future, the possible tightening of the FCPA is a double-edged sword. It brings more work for compliance officers, and over time will make the Nigerian market a more competitive one. The basic activities of business – profit generation, procurement, service provision, maintenance, complying with red tape – will be easier in a more transparent environment. The last round of changes to the FCPA, the Sarbanes–Oxley governance reforms of 2002, led to a higher number of prosecutions for violation of anti-bribery laws. Companies should stay vigilant to changes in the FCPA and the UK Bribery Act. If concerns are raised about specific contractors or contracts, they should act immediately. Cooperation with the DOJ or national equivalent will pay off in the long run in lower costs and fines.

6

THE SECTORAL FACTOR

Bribery has a demand and supply nexus, much as any other part of the economy. There is a reasonable consensus about the identities of those who demand bribes; they are most often public officials and politicians in powerful positions (especially but not exclusively in emerging markets) who have contracts to allocate or favors to grant. There is less agreement about who is prepared to pay a bribe and why. The supply side is now facing further scrutiny from the doyen of the industry, Transparency International. Its Bribe Payers Index (BPI) consistently indicates that public works contracts, construction, arms and defense are particularly high risk sectors,[1] while other research singles out the extractive industries as most associated with both supply and demand for bribery.[2]

Professor Robert Sullivan of University College, London points out that the nature of specific sectors makes a huge difference to the potential for businesses to reach common ground and agreement on self-regulation:

> In certain areas like oil it might be possible to make some progress if you can coordinate all the central players and give them a common interest .... But when you get cut-throat competition, like in arms and aerospace and the oil industry, where they are selling all the same products to the same group of customers, then you may be able to get players to contract under the same set of rules, but when there is such competition that they offer all manner of inducements, it is very difficult.[3]

Companies in the oil and gas sectors have the most stringent anti-bribery policies, and this can be taken as evidence that these sectors are at a particularly high risk of exposure.[4] But the risk is not limited to particular sectors. Businesses cannot ignore the issue of bribery by limiting their involvement in sectors in which bribery is commonplace. Experts In Responsible Investment Solutions (EIRIS) found that about a third of all the companies listed on the FTSE All-World Index have a high exposure to risks linked to bribery and corruption, and approximately 50 percent of US companies "with an intermediate risk of bribery issues in their businesses have inadequate compliance policies and controls to prevent bribery."[5]

Trace International investigated levels of international enforcement activity by industry. Table 6.1 gives a breakdown of the six highest-risk sectors, measured by their proportion of overall international enforcement activity from 1977 to 2010.

TELECOMS

The telecommunications market is estimated to be worth trillions of dollars, and is expanding rapidly in the developing world where existing landline coverage is poor.[6] This creates many opportunities for financial misconduct. Richard Alderman, director of the SFO, is paying special attention to this sector:

> In developing countries mobiles give the chance for people to leap a generation, so what are these companies doing? It's worth masses of money, so how are they getting into it? I am quite interested in what the mobile phone operators are up to, because people tend to focus on the usual main risks ... but there are loads of others.[7]

As providers of mobile communications technology and infrastructure struggle for footholds in the new markets of developing countries, opportunities for foreign firms to secure large contracts with state-run telecoms companies are prime opportunities for corruption at the highest level. The recent case of Alcatel-Lucent illustrates the vulnerability of telecoms contracts, and the extent to which bribery of officials can extend all the way to the top. In addition to other corrupt payments made to Honduras, Taiwan, and Malaysia, French telecoms company Alcatel-Lucent bribed Costa Rican officials (including former President Miguel Angel Rodriguez) to the tune of $9.5 million between 2000 and 2004.[8] Alcatel's subsidiaries are reported to have channeled the bribes through phoney consulting contracts.

TABLE 6.1 **The six highest-risk sectors by proportion of overall international enforcement activity, 1977 to 2010**

Sector	%
Extractive industries	19.9
Aerospace/defence/security	14.3
Manufacturer/service provider	12.1
Healthcare	11.1
Engineering/construction	10.7
Transportation/communications	7.8

Source: Trace International, Global Enforcement Report 2010, Annapolis, USA: Trace International, p. 8, <www.traceinternational.org/compendiumGlobalEnforcementReport9.20.10.pdf> (accessed May 29, 2011).

The media reported that in the case of the most lucrative contract:

Alcatel's bribes in Costa Rica were used to obtain a contract with the Costa Rican Electricity Institute (ICE), the state-run telecommunications company. ICE awarded Alcatel a $149 million mobile telephone contract in August 2001 for 400,000 GSM cell phone lines. During that time, Alcatel allegedly paid bribes to several Costa Rican officials, including former ICE board member José Antonio Lobo and his wife, US citizen Jean Gallup. Lobo admitted to receiving payments. Lobo also testified that ex-President Rodríguez accepted 40 percent of the bribe payments.[9]

Alcatel has recently agreed to resolve the allegations and settle the US Justice Department investigation in return for $137 million (£88.7 million), $92 million as a penalty for the criminal suit and the rest in civil damages to the US Securities and Exchange Commission. The significant sums involved illustrate that there is a realistic prospect of substantial financial penalties for foreign bribery, and that such penalties are likely to reflect the extent to which a suspected company complies with investigators. The US Department of Justice (DOJ) stated that the fine was influenced by "limited and inadequate cooperation by the company for a substantial period of time."[10] However, some consideration was also given to remedial actions taken by Alcatel, including stopping its use of third-party sales agents when conducting business worldwide.

FOOD

Bribery in the fishing industry is commonly used to persuade the authorities in developing countries to look the other way while trawlers exceed their quotas by overfishing in sovereign waters. In certain seas, such as off the coast of Somalia, bribery is commonplace. The *Japan Times* reported that the head of a Japanese fishing company claimed that bribes paid to Russian officials were a "necessary expense" in the industry.[11] As well as the destructive effect that this kind of behavior has on the environment, primarily in the developing world, bribery in the food industry can have an indirect impact on raising consumer prices in the developed world. In one US case the *New York Times* reported that a food company "greased the palms of a handful of corporate buyers in exchange for lucrative contracts and confidential information on bids submitted by competitors. This most likely drove up ingredient prices for the big food companies."[12]

CONSTRUCTION

In the United Kingdom, corruption in construction has been the subject of recent settlements and law enforcement attention. The industry was the focus of the Serious Fraud Office's (SFO's) first civil settlement after receiving powers to recover the proceeds of crime in 2008. The SFO reached a £2.25 million settlement with the British building company Balfour Beatty, for alleged unlawful accounting in connection with "payment irregularities," which it self-reported, in the construction of the recreated Alexandria Library in Egypt, a prestigious UNESCO project.[13] This case was a significant event in the United Kingdom's enforcement of anti-corruption laws, because it also marked the first time a company had reached this kind of civil settlement as part of a foreign bribery investigation.

Despite widespread recognition that construction is a high-risk sector there have been complaints among UK construction firms competing for contracts overseas that local embassies are failing to provide assistance when they face demands for bribes.

D. I. Whatmore relates his experience of the sector and preventive engagement with contractors in preparation for the 2012 London Olympics:

> The construction industry has historically had a problem with corruption and the need to pay bribes, especially abroad. It has often had to pay bribes to get contracts. It is often standard practice for businesses when competing abroad. They sometimes have to pay a bribe to get the bid on the table. There has been a very high tolerance level within the construction industry for that kind of behaviour. It has almost been seen as a necessary requirement – if we won't do it, we won't stand a chance of winning.[14]

Whatmore spent six months working with the Olympic Delivery Authority (ODA), advising them on corruption around the building of the Olympics. He says:

> In any big building project there is the opportunity for corruption around the awarding of the contract, and fraud around the payment of the contract. This could amount to up to 10 per cent of the overall cost. We did a lot of awareness training with their staff, and part of that was asking: "You're in the construction industry, how often have you been offered a bribe?" and many had. And there have been surveys done that show the huge amount of people in those kind of sectors that are open to bribes, or have been offered a bribe, or consider it reasonably normal to be offered a bribe. Our work with the ODA was groundbreaking in that it was the first time we had engaged with the construction industry to actively prevent corruption and fraud and was well received by them.[15]

The industry's reputation is further blighted by the attempts of construction companies to bypass financial rules and procure favorable loans through the offering of corrupt payments. Indian federal investigators have reportedly linked executives in 21 of India's top banks, including the state-run Central Bank of India, to alleged bribes paid by Money Matters Financial Services in return for corporate loans. A director at India's Central Bureau of Investigation stated that:

> Officers in the top and middle management of various public sector banks and financial institutions were receiving illegal gratification from the private financial services company which was acting as a mediator and facilitator for corporate loans and other facilities from financial institutions.[16]

Reuters reports that a large proportion of the companies involved in this "bribes for loans" scandal are major players in India's booming infrastructure and construction industry.[17] Hostility to Indian bribery entered the global media with the arrest of Indian anti-graft campaigner Anna Hazare in mid-August 2011.

International accountancy firm KPMG states that in its experience with clients, construction is extremely vulnerable to corruption in general and bribery payments in particular.[18] It identifies three contributory factors:

- operations taking place in jurisdictions where corruption is a perceived business risk and may be perceived (by some) as a business norm
- interactions with public officials and a request for "facilitation payments" to be made to expedite decision-making processes
- using in-country agents, subsidiaries, or entering into joint ventures with contractors (alongside commission-based incentive structures) where the activities of these third parties may be less visible and controls harder to enforce.

KPMG also identified contemporary trends in fraudulent behavior in the construction industry, including:

- irregularities in relationships between sub-contractors and clients, for example "kickbacks" being paid in an attempt to secure work
- companies colluding to act in an anti-competitive manner when bidding for contracts
- bribery of local officials in order to influence the outcome of contract tenders, achieve approval or planning permission.[19]

A senior British police officer, who wished to remain anonymous, explained that the supply chains involved in construction are particularly high risk:

> If you are a business and you want to work overseas, and you want to win that contract and you want to get things done, you either do it legitimately by paying the price that things are to get your work done

– or to win contracts or to gain influence you pay them an enhanced sum. There is a whole range of corruption in the way that the payment mechanism works. Once they've won the contract, how do they get their goods and equipment to a port or border when they're working in a corrupt country? How do they facilitate the movement of their goods? They do it by paying bribes and fees at certain places. Let's think of a scenario. You win a contract to build a significant project, a bridge or dam, but you don't own all the assets to build the thing, so you need certain engineering equipment, you need certain people. So you need to sub-contract those elements, or buy some of that information.[20]

HEALTHCARE

Healthcare is identified as being extremely vulnerable to corruption and bribery,[21] and is a sector where the immediate detrimental effects of bribery on economic efficiency are overshadowed by their devastating impact on global health, in particular in developing countries. The payment of small-scale bribes to healthcare providers is associated with a lower quality of care,[22] and a culture of bribery in developing countries undoubtedly costs lives. Researchers undertaking an African multi-country study reported that:

> participants in many sites spoke openly about various forms of informal income generation engaged in by health workers. This took the form, for example, of insisting on "tips" before people received treatment, and alternative prescribing methods or alternative charging structures for treatment and prescriptions.[23]

Transparency International has identified three of the United Nations Millennium Development Goals that have particularly suffered as a result of corruption: "reduced child mortality, improved maternal health, and the fight against HIV/AIDS, malaria and other diseases."[24]

Bribery in the healthcare industry is by no means confined to small sums or to developing economies. All components of the pharmaceutical supply chain are prime targets. A senior employee of DPI, a subsidiary of US healthcare firm Johnson & Johnson, was jailed for one year in the United Kingdom for his part in paying bribes worth £4.5 million over the course of nearly four years to corrupt medical professionals in the Greek state health-care system. The bribery is alleged to have increased the price of contracts by 20 per cent. The SFO summary of the case states that:

> Robert John Dougall was appointed Director of Marketing at DPI in 1999. From 2000 he was given additional responsibility for business development in Greece. DPI sold orthopaedic products in various markets – this case involved the corrupt obtaining and retaining of

business in the Greek orthopaedic market by providing inducements/ rewards to surgeons who would purchase DPI's products.[25]

The fact that Robert Dougall received a custodial sentence despite SFO pleas for leniency should be of interest to those involved in the healthcare sector.

SPORT

Participants in sporting competitions at all levels have long been associated with bribery, in addition to the threat posed by involvement with unscrupulous bookmakers. The huge sums of money in sport today, from footballers' transfer fees to fiercely contested sponsorship contracts, the buying and selling of sports teams and the construction of stadiums, present numerous opportunities not only for lucrative business deals, but also for corruption.

Because bribes typically take a long time to be detected, investigated, and prosecuted, the negative effects of bribery scandals can resonate for decades after the events are alleged to have occurred. The selection of the host nations of the 2018 and 2022 World Cups in late 2010 was overshadowed (and arguably influenced by) a BBC *Panorama* documentary, broadcast just days before the announcement, accusing senior FIFA officials of taking bribes amounting to £64.2 million. Some involved with the UK bid went so far as to call the BBC's editors "unpatriotic" for choosing to air the program at such a sensitive time, and interpreted the allegations as an attempt to scupper the British entry. At any rate, despite the presence of David Cameron, Prince William, and David Beckham in Zurich just before the vote was taken, England's bid was unsuccessful, and Junji Ogura, the head of Japan's World Cup bid, claimed the bribery allegations definitely had an impact on the England bid.[26]

Numerous commentators alluded, without making any accusations, to the poor corruption record of the country that beat England to host the 2018 World Cup – Russia. However, Russian president Dmitry Medvedev has expressed his intention to create an anti-corruption monitoring body to oversee all major sporting events. Those tendering for contracts at such events would do well to pay attention to the president's intentions. Whatever their previous records on corruption may have been, governments of countries hosting major sporting events pay relatively more attention to financial misconduct, at least in connection with the event itself. With huge sums of money at stake and blanket coverage by the world's media, they cannot afford not to.

Just not cricket

Cricket may reportedly be declining in popularity in England, Australia, and the West Indies, but it has become a multi-billion dollar industry in the South Asian subcontinent, with the explosion in popularity of the Indian Premier League (IPL). The hugely lucrative media rights and advertising contracts are obvious targets for corrupt deals.

However, the problem is not just confined to Indian cricket. The sport's image worldwide has been tarnished by a series of betting scandals since the 1990s, resulting in the setting up of the International Cricket Council's Anti-Corruption and Security Unit in 2000.[27]

In one incident, a journalist from the *News of the World*, claiming to represent a betting syndicate, paid £150,000 to the players' agent Mazhar Majeed, who said he could ensure that the bowlers delivered no-balls at specified times during a match, and correctly predicted the exact timing of three no-balls in the following day's play. The players received five-year bans at an ICC disciplinary hearing in February 2011, and the day before the hearing, the Crown Prosecution Service announced that the three cricketers and Majeed would face criminal charges for corruption.[28]

Cricket's image has been so damaged by this latest scandal that in February 2011 the MCC considered the introduction of lie detector tests. The negative effects of corruption are widespread, affecting the reputation of the sport and of Pakistan itself, A resident of Mohammad Amir's home town of Gujjar Khan in Punjab province told the BBC: "I've been following the news and I feel very ashamed because it involves Pakistani players and it reflects badly on the country. We have floods and terrorism, cricket was our good news, but now this is terrible."[29] Cricket's governing bodies, commercial sponsors, and paying fans alike all want a sport that's seen to be free of corruption, where they can depend, in England captain Andrew Strauss's words, on "having 22 guys on the pitch that the supporters are absolutely 100 per cent certain are playing the game for the right reasons."[30]

DEFENSE

International law enforcement strategy takes a particular interest in corruption in the defense industry, and it features prominently in the UK government's *Foreign Bribery Strategy*, published in 2010.[31] This encourages all UK aerospace and defense companies to participate in the Common Industry Standards – an anti-corruption code of conduct of the Aerospace and Defence Industries Association of Europe.[32]

The BAE Systems cases (see page 67) are illustrative of the sensitive territory that surrounds defense procurement. In investigations connected with the sector, there emerges a key prerequisite: political will at the highest levels of government to investigate.[33] Where national security is concerned, this will is often lacking, and European countries seldom fully disclose the terms of weapons sales."[34] Where a case threatens to undermine national security by risking international cooperation in ongoing counter-terrorist investigations, political expediency may trump the demands of justice.

It was reported that the independent investigation into the BAE case involving a multi-billion pound contract to supply Eurofighter Typhoon aircraft to Saudi Arabia was constrained by "security obligations," which meant that Lord Woolf, chair of the ethics committee investigating BAE, was denied access to relevant documentation.[35]

The dropping of politically sensitive corruption investigations in the defense sector, together with the increased use of privately negotiated settlements and non-prosecutorial agreements between governments and businesses, has contributed to the scarcity of successful convictions in the countries with the most robust enforcement regimes. This has led critics to argue that new legislation such as the UK Bribery Act will not have much effect if the mentality of enforcers remains as it currently is, and that new legislation merely contributes to the "global façade of enforcement" embodied by the US Foreign Corrupt Practices Act.[36]

EXTRACTIVE INDUSTRIES

Extractive industries – those concerning the discovery and extraction of natural resources such as oil, gas, and minerals – are sectors with extremely high risks of all types of corruption. Interest groups such as Global Witness and Oxfam are dedicated to tackling the "resource curse," the theory that the population of developing countries with natural resource wealth are kept in poverty by a corrupt relationship between political elites and business interests, which prevents the economic benefits of their extractive industries from trickling down to the people. Critics have argued that though there is a demonstrable correlation between resource wealth and underdevelopment, the causation is the other way round – countries with corrupt or poor governance have driven away foreign investment and are left with nothing but extractive industries. Whether chicken or egg, it makes little difference to a company operating in such a high-risk environment, which must always be vigilant to avoid exposure.

It is worth reemphasizing the case of Swiss freight forwarder Panalpina, its client Royal Dutch Shell, and five oil service companies, who agreed to pay $236.5 million (£146 million) to settle charges of bribery (see page 118). Panalpina admitted in federal court in Houston to paying bribes totaling US$49 million (£30.3 million) to government officials and contractors in Nigeria and six other countries between 2002 and 2007. Panalpina admitted that "Prior to 2007 a culture of corruption within Panalpina emanated from senior level management in Switzerland who tolerated bribery as business as usual," and that "Dozens of employees throughout the Panalpina organization were involved in various schemes to pay bribes to foreign officials."[37] The company also stated that it had been specifically requested by Shell Nigeria to carry out the transactions and to provide invoices with false line entries to "hide the nature of the payments to avoid suspicion if anyone audited the invoices." Most of the bribes had been to customs officials to expedite the passage of documents and equipment, but Panalpina had taken advantage of its position to avoid customs charges and smuggle contraband including medicines and explosives. At the same time, Shell separately admitted to paying $2 million (£1.2 million) in bribes to Nigerian subcontractors on its deepwater Bonga Project.[38] Panalpina's share price dropped over 4 per cent as the case became public.[39]

The industry's long-term reputation for systemic corruption prompted the setting up in 2002 of the Extractive Industries Transparency Initiative (EITI), an independent worldwide body made up of governments, civil society groups, and 50 of the world's largest oil, gas, and mining companies. EITI "promotes transparency on the revenue side .... so as to facilitate more effective use of extractive industry revenues in weak governance host countries."[40] On March 2, 2011, EITI announced that six new countries – Central African Republic, Kyrgyz Republic, Niger, Nigeria, Norway, and Yemen – had achieved EITI compliance, joining the previous five, Azerbaijan, Ghana, Liberia, Mongolia, and Timor-Leste. In addition, Guatemala and Trinidad & Tobago joined the other 22 candidate countries awaiting validation, bringing the total number of EITI implementing countries up to 35.[41] EITI is also active, along with numerous NGOs and interest groups, in the Publish What You Pay campaign, which calls on governments to disclose how much they receive for oil concessions and companies to reveal what they pay for them. Participation in such voluntary drives for transparency in the high-risk extractive sector may help companies to demonstrate commitment to the spirit as well as the letter of anti-corruption legislation.

SUBSECTOR TO WATCH: RARE EARTH ELEMENTS

Rare earth elements (REEs) comprise 17 metals that are used in petroleum refinement and are vital to a wide range of modern and emerging technologies: laptop computers, lasers, masers, camera lenses, X-ray and MRI machines, aerospace components, and a range of green technologies including wind turbines, fuel cells, catalytic converters, and the batteries in the Toyota Prius. This sector will be increasingly important in the future, and is being very closely observed, particularly because China controls about 97 percent of world production, and has demonstrated that it will use its position in the global supply chain as a tool of foreign policy. In September 2010, China suspended rare earth elements shipments to Japan (its biggest REE customer) after the Chinese navy arrested a Japanese fishing boat in disputed waters – though the Chinese government denied this was the reason, citing environmental concerns. In October, the *New York Times* reported that China had partially expanded its embargo to the

United States and Europe, in response to President Obama's criticisms of the China's policy of subsidizing clean energy exports.[42]

Whether it is in China's interests to do so or not, the threat of cutting off supply is a powerful bargaining tool, as surely as it is for Russia's gas supply to Eastern Europe. Shipments resumed in November 2010, but Japan's realization of how dependent it is on China prompted it to seek new agreements with Vietnam, Mongolia, and Australia, and step up its research into alternatives to REEs. In December Hitachi announced its new plant to recover rare earth magnets from computer hard drives will come on stream in 2013.[43]

Despite the name, rare earth elements are plentiful; the world relies on China simply because it is cheap. China stepped up production to drive the price down and corner the market, and now that it has begun to limit supplies – citing environmental reasons – prices are rising. In late 2010 China announced a 35 per cent reduction in REE exports for the first half of 2011, and over the previous five years it has more than halved its export quotas, causing prices for some rare earths to more than quadruple in 2010.

There are huge REE deposits in Australia, Canada, South Africa, the United States and elsewhere, and in some cases it is only a matter of reopening old mines as soon as the price rises enough to make extraction worthwhile. In California, Molycorp Minerals raised $500 million to reopen its Mountain Pass mine, the world's biggest supplier of REEs before competition from China forced its closure in 2002.[44]

Demand for REEs is rising, but their supply may also be limited by environmental concerns. REEs are extracted by open-cast mining that leaves radioactive spoil; it was not just Chinese competition that closed the mine, but the discovery that it had concealed more than 60 ruptures of a waste water pipe that spilled hundreds of thousands of gallons of radioactive waste water, resulting in $1.2 million in fines and a clean-up order. Even China, whose environmental record in mining and industry has not been exemplary, is worried about REEs. But that simply contributes further to the sector's "oil rush" mentality. In the medium term, until other mines come on stream or new technologies emerge, the REE market is likely to be highly volatile, and gaps between supply and demand mean the price is likely to increase over the next decade. Such instability in the supply chain, coupled with rising demand, will increase the sector's susceptibility to corruption.[45]

Exposure to bribery is likely in this sector, not only by importers whose business may depend on circumventing future import restrictions, but by the multinationals aiming to extract these elements, who will be vulnerable to the sector's many opportunities to demand bribes – and not just in systemically corrupt China. As one commentator has observed:

Regardless of jurisdiction, a company needs to secure the lease (usually

132

from the central government) and obtain a considerable variety of permits, not the least of which is for handling and storing the toxic – and in the case of REEs, radioactive – waste from the mine. Even if the governments involved want to streamline things, vested interests such as the environmental lobby and indigenous groups appear at every stage of the permit process to fight, lobby and sue to delay work. And depending on the local government, successfully mining a deposit could involve a considerable amount of political uncertainty, bribe paying or harassment.[46]

There are clearly many reasons why REEs will be a key sector of interest for anti-corruption authorities over the next decade, and mining companies and those directly involved in extracting REEs will be well prepared for the toxic bribery environment they are likely to encounter. Businesses lower down the REE supply chain – there is a long and growing list – must make sure to be equally prepared to monitor their corruption compliance all the way back down the chain, from computer vendor to parts manufacturer, component supplier and the mine where they were dug out of the ground.

7

THIRD PARTY RISK AND CORPORATE EXPOSURE: HOW CAN THE COMPANY GET INVOLVED, AND WHY?

A company is vulnerable to corruption at arms' length, conducted by agents, couriers, shippers, or any one of numerous businesses in a long chain of suppliers. This can occur even if it does not operate in a high-risk area.

Exposure to demands for facilitation payments can occur at any time, through routine interaction with public officials and participation in supply chains. Companies may feel obliged to provide first-class hospitality to promote their corporate brand or to match the amount spent by competitors. If this hospitality is deemed overly lavish, or in the jargon "disproportionate," the company may be at risk of prosecution. And companies that routinely rely on local fixers to maintain a presence in a region can be exposed by the corrupt activities of their associates if they lack adequate preventive procedures. The UK Bribery Act tackles these problems head-on, and has caused much alarm in all these areas.

SUPPLY CHAINS

Corporations can be exposed to bribery through those who prey on the mechanisms and infrastructure of the global economy. Whenever goods or people move through the pinch points of borders, ports, transit areas, and checkpoints, they are attractive sitting targets for badly paid officials, as well as for organized criminals and terrorist groups, where bribery is a thinly veiled form of extortion backed up by the threat of violence.

Transparency International's briefing on the UK Bribery Act notes that: "There are particular risks for companies with overseas supply chains as this could cover bribery by their suppliers or contractors wherever they are based, whether in the UK or abroad."[1] Global trade is increasingly dependent on just-in-time supply chains. They can be extremely efficient when every link in the chain runs smoothly, but these networks, with nodes spread across many countries, present numerous opportunities for bribery and corruption. The more links in a supply chain there are, and the more territories it traverses, the greater the number of opportunities for

134

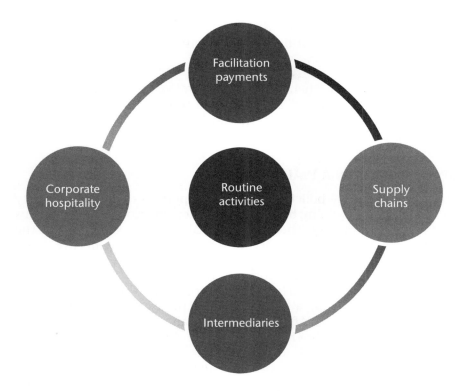

FIGURE 7.1 **Risky routine business activities**

Source: Pinsent Masons/Barry Vitou.

unscrupulous individuals to commit bribery. The increasing complexity of cross-border trade flows and logistical operations of multinational corporations, combined with a depressed global economy, present a heightened potential for corruption.

In the view of a compliance officer at Coca-Cola, "the supply chain generally has the highest risk for corruption."[2] He gives three reasons:

- supply chains have more touch points with the centers of corruption (more temptation, more opportunity)
- supply chains are often small and medium-sized local businesses that may be awash in a corrupt culture
- small and medium-sized businesses have less leverage than multinationals to resist corruption and influence institutions.

Each choke point in the supply chain presents a permanent opportunity for parasitic officials to prey on all those who pass through. In India, low-level corruption in the supply chain and transport system, such as traffic police demanding bribes from drivers, has spawned a local initiative to tackle the demand side of bribery by public officials. A social entrepreneur, Shaffi Mather, explains:

> We provide a service where people who don't want to pay bribes call us, like they'd call a plumber .... And we will take on the responsibility of fighting that demand, while at the same time getting whatever they are legally entitled to.[3]

SUPPLY CHAINS IN A WAR ZONE

Countries may pursue policies deemed so important to national security that the necessity of doing business somewhere overcomes any concerns about cultures of bribery. There are national security exemptions in the UK Bribery Act for both military commanders and intelligence agencies, and the common law "public authority defense" is relevant to the application of the US Foreign Corrupt Practices Act (FCPA) (see the case study on Giffen, page 47). The strategic necessity to maintain a steady supply of resources into a theater of operations can contribute to a culture of corruption; in Afghanistan, for example, this may mean that corruption in the supply chain is tolerated. Businesses that operate in war zones may likewise be forced to engage with systemically corrupt regimes and risk becoming corrupt themselves. The imperative to maintain the Northern Distribution Network, the main supply military supply route to Afghanistan from Uzbekistan, has forced the United States to collude with an Uzbek regime that is widely rumored to be characterized by rampant corruption. Kyrgyzstan occupies another strategic point for US forces engaged in the Afghanistan war effort, as the country houses the Manas airbase which is used to refuel US military aircraft. To ensure the government of Kyrgyzstan allows the United States to retain the base, against much popular pressure to remove it and revert to its historic Russian allegiance, US agencies have been very widely rumored to have used intermediate companies to bribe officials of the previous regime.

In conflict zones the price of honesty may be much higher than a delayed shipment or a lost contract. Where security is weak or nonexistent, refusing to pay bribes may result in the destruction of goods and a complete breakdown of operations. A US congressional report on extortion and corruption along the US supply chain in Afghanistan found that:

> Trucking companies that pay the highway warlords for security are provided protection; trucking companies that do not pay believe they are more likely to find themselves under attack. As a result, almost everyone pays. In interviews and documents ... contractors frequently

referred to such payments as "extortion," "bribes," "special security," and/or "protection payments."[4]

The same report identifies millions of dollars in bribes paid by the US government's private contractors as significant sources of funding for the Taliban. Whether corrupt officials are collecting directly for the Taliban or are forced to pay them protection money, when a company pays a bribe it has no way of knowing where its money may end up or what it may unwittingly be funding.

Businesses in sectors that are particularly vulnerable to supply chain corruption are organizing themselves in an effort to leverage their collective expertise in response to the UK Bribery Act and increased enforcement of the US FCPA. One example of this was the "Compliance the global supply chain" conference which took place in April 2011 in Texas. This was described as "the first event in the Anti-Bribery and Corruption Series, aimed at the oil and gas, mining chemical, and engineering industries." It featured senior officials including heads of compliance, chief procurement officers, and legal counsel across sectors such as oil and oil service companies, freight and shipping, security, and large multinationals. The event was billed as an industry-wide bid to "address the differences between the UK Anti-Bribery Act [sic] and the FCPA, giving you the information you need to adapt your existing policies whilst allowing you to continue doing business in high-risk regions of the world."[5]

INTERMEDIARIES

Businesses can be exposed to the risk of being associated with bribery because they have done insufficient due diligence on their intermediaries' activities. While the use of intermediaries to conduct dubious dealings at arms' length has long been a standard operating procedure, intermediaries are often used for legitimate activities. Without intermediaries it would be hard for many companies to engage with local power structures, understand the local culture and follow local customs, gain and maintain access to elites, and navigate the bureaucratic labyrinth that characterizes the government regulations of many developing – and developed – countries. Intermediaries are defined here as agents, consultants, lobbyists, or other external service providers, including individuals or companies that assist in gaining or retaining business or provide marketing advice.[6]

While intermediaries are not directly employed by the company, they act on its behalf, and the company is not absolved from prosecution under the UK Bribery Act because bribery is a strict liability offense. According to the Lectric Law Library, "strict liability" means "Liability even when there is no proof of negligence. Often applicable in product liability cases against manufacturers, who are legally responsible for injuries caused by defects in their products, even if they were not negligent."

Under the Act, companies may be liable for bribery carried out by intermediaries, despite being ignorant of it, if they do not have adequate procedures in place:

> Indirect bribery is expressly prohibited. The Act prohibits all corrupt payments, regardless of whether they are paid directly by the company, or on its behalf by a third party. If the bribe is paid by someone else on the company's behalf or in furtherance of its business activities (which could include a supplier), the company may be guilty of an offence – even if the bribe is paid without its knowledge.[7]

The practical implication of this is that when a business has even minor activities carried out by an intermediary on its behalf, the third party must be made aware of and be committed to the anti-bribery policies of the principal, and be warned that the company has a zero-tolerance culture.

Under the FCPA, deliberate disregard (amounting to wilful cultivated ignorance) can satisfy the requirement for "knowledge" of bribery, and the fact that under the UK Bribery Act ignorance can never be a defense should be a sobering thought for those who employ intermediaries. Robert Amaee, former head of the Serious Fraud Office's (SFO's) Anti-Corruption and Proceeds of Crime Unit, says these kinds of third-party arrangements will be under close scrutiny from regulators from now on:

> Many of the companies I speak to have identified their relationships with intermediaries – agents, distributors, contractors – as their number one area of focus when it comes to ensuring readiness for the Bribery Act .... The SFO is taking this very seriously and I will tell you that they are closely monitoring and collecting information on intermediaries oper- ating on behalf of British companies in certain high-risk jurisdictions. In the end it comes down to two simple questions. The board should ask: "Where are we doing business?" and "How are we doing that business?" And if the board does not like the answers, it should be prepared to take the business elsewhere.[8]

Intermediaries should be subject to due diligence, as with all parts of a business's operating structure, and should be monitored to determine their behavior.

Case study: BAE and Tanzania

In December 2010, BAE Systems ended a longstanding investigation into its sale of radar and air traffic control systems to Tanzania. The

---

case, which BAE managed to settle without admitting to bribery or corruption,[9] is a prime example of how a company can find itself in trouble through the use of intermediaries.

Mr Justice Bean called BAE "naive in the extreme" to think that its Tanzanian agent was paid millions merely as a lobbyist rather than a payer of bribes. The *Telegraph* reported that:

> The SFO's deal with BAE involved the company paying a £30m fine after pleading guilty to failing to keep proper accounting records. The accounting records relate to $12.4m paid to a "marketing agent" in Tanzania, Shailesh Vithlani, to facilitate an air traffic control deal with the country. The evidence put before the court established a trail of payments made via offshore companies to Mr Vithlani. Roughly 97pc of the $12.4m fee was paid to a British Virgin Islands company described by BAE as a "covert" company. The balance was paid to a company called Merlin registered in Tanzania and described by BAE as "overt." Both companies were controlled by Mr Vithlani. The court heard covert agents were hired by BAE in a number of circumstances; when it was illegal to employ them overtly; because of tax implications arising from the agent making undeclared payments to third parties; or to avoid "embarrassment and press interest" due to large fees being paid.[10]

For supporting sources which contain description, discussion, and analysis of the evidence put before the court see note 11.

CORPORATE HOSPITALITY

One of the greatest concerns of compliance officers is the dividing line between legitimate and illegitimate corporate hospitality under the UK Bribery Act. Many firms spend millions on hospitality and expenses for clients, and may not intend (or obtain) any advantage from such activity. UK justice secretary Kenneth Clarke has asserted that there are unlikely to be many prosecutions for overly lavish hospitality under the new law, and that "reasonable hospitality to meet, network and improve relationships with customers is a normal part of business." He explained that "no one is going to try and stop businesses getting to know their clients by taking them to events like Wimbledon, Twickenham or the Grand Prix."[12]

The vagueness of the draft form of the guidance caused fear in the private and public sectors. Before the formal Ministry of Justice guidance, there were fears that the entire edifice of corporate hospitality could be under threat from the provisions of the Bribery Act. Katja Hall, the director of employment policy of the Confederation of British Industry (CBI), raised concerns that "there is a risk that some parts of the Act's implementation could have a negative effect on investment in the UK."[13] In one extraordinary case, it was reported that a UK parish council had informed players at its bowls club that their £20 annual gifts to council officials must cease to avoid potential liability under the new law.[14] The potential implications of Section 6 of the UK Bribery Act, covering hospitality, were emphasized by Transparency International, which argued that:

> A company that gives modest hospitality, gifts or travel expenses to a Foreign Public Official could be committing an offence under the Act by providing an advantage to an FPO if the gifts are intended to influence the FPO, and to obtain or retain business or a business advantage.[15]

Professor Sullivan of University College, London explained that this issue is still somewhat of a gray area and that companies cannot necessarily get round the law by relying on forms of hospitality that have no resale value:

> The law says "other advantage," and by and large that advantage is not defined. Clearly if the advantage has an exchange value which is of some significance that may be a problem, but that is not the issue with corporate hospitality. Forms of enjoyment which may be very expensive at the time may not have anything of value behind them. Some of that is quite dodgy – it really is focused on winning hearts and minds.[16]

However, in its guidance, the Ministry of Justice seeks to reassure businesses that the corporate hospitality industry is not under threat from the Act:

> In order to proceed with a case under section 1 based on an allegation that hospitality was intended as a bribe, the prosecution would need to show that the hospitality was intended to induce conduct that amounts to a breach of an expectation that a person will act in good faith, impartially, or in accordance with a position of trust. This would be judged by what a reasonable person in the UK thought. So, for example, an invitation to foreign clients to attend a Six Nations match at Twickenham as part of a public relations exercise designed to cement good relations or enhance knowledge in the organisation's field is extremely unlikely to engage section 1 as there is unlikely to be evidence of an intention to induce improper performance of a relevant function.[17]

A lawyer explains that there is no hard and fast rule, such as a numerical limit above which law enforcement will act. Rather, the issue is that "the higher the establishment, the more lavish the hospitality, the greater the tendency there is to influence ... there are degrees and nuances to the whole thing."[18] With regard to the prosecutorial requirements for Section 6, once a financial or other advantage has been established to have been offered, promised or given, the prosecution must be able to show a connection between the advantage and the intention to influence and secure business or a business advantage. The Ministry of Justice states that consideration of all the evidence and circumstances will include:

> matters such as the type and level of advantage offered, the manner and form in which the advantage is provided, and the level of influence the particular foreign public official has over awarding the business. In this circumstantial context, the more lavish the hospitality or the higher the expenditure in relation to travel, accommodation or other similar business expenditure provided to a foreign public official, then, generally, the greater the inference that it is intended to influence the official to grant business or a business advantage in return.[19]

The guidance suggest that businesses may review their policies on hospitality and promotional and other expenditure as part of the selection and implementation of bribery prevention procedures to ensure that they are seen to be acting both competitively and fairly.

In its explanatory guidance on the Bribery Act, legal firm McDermott Will & Emery emphasizes that a company could face prosecution for offering bribes to a public official in the form of lavish hospitality, without there being any explicit intention to improperly influence him:

> To commit the offence of bribing a foreign official, it is not necessary for the person offering the advantage to intend that the official act improperly. It suffices that he intends to influence him and that there is no applicable written local law permitting the official to be so influenced. By way of example, a corporate bidding for a state contract to build an energy plant in a foreign country invites a foreign official on a trip to the United Kingdom to show him examples of previous work carried out by the corporate. His flights and hotel are paid for by the corporate. There is no intention that the official act improperly, but it is intended to influence the official to award a contract to the corporate.[20]

Tom Beezer, an expert in multijurisdictional law with law firm Bond Pearce, provides two contrasting examples to distinguish between proportionate and illegitimately lavish hospitality:

> It will not be taking someone for lunch down the road but more excessive hospitality like picking a client up in a private jet, wining and dining them with champagne and caviar en route to a sporting event overseas while spending a week in a six-star hotel.[21]

McDermott Will & Emery suggests that the status of those involved is likely to influence considerations of whether the hospitality is excessive and illegal under the Act:

> If the flight was economy class, the hotel a modest hotel and only basic expenses are reimbursed, it would appear difficult to fault the hospitality under the Bribery Act. If the flight is first class, the hotel a five-star and generous expenses are paid, the perception of the "reasonable person" may be different. It may also differ depending on the status of the official (perhaps the more high-ranking, the more appropriate that that official be accommodated in the manner to which he is accustomed, in the eyes of the reasonable person.[22]

There is a distinction between lavish and legitimate hospitality, but this is a relative judgment and clarification has not been forthcoming. Furthermore, if the hospitality or expenditure is a cost that would otherwise by borne by the relevant foreign government, the Ministry of Justice suggests that in such cases the hospitality may not even amount to a financial or other advantage, and levels of expenditure on hospitality will not be considered to be equal across sectors. Investigators are aware that different standards apply to different industries. The norms applying in a particular sector will be relevant to considerations of all the evidence and circumstances. If the hospitality is not extravagant for a particular industry, it is unlikely that it will raise the inference that its provision was intended to have a direct impact on decision making. The joint prosecution guidance of the director of the SFO and the director of prosecutions explains that:

> The more lavish the hospitality or expenditure (beyond what may be reasonable standards in the particular circumstances) the greater the inference that it is intended to encourage or reward improper performance or influence an official. Lavishness is just one factor that may be taken into account in determining whether an offence has been committed. The full circumstances of each case would need to be considered. Other factors might include that the hospitality or expenditure was not clearly connected with legitimate business activity or was concealed.[23]

The Ministry of Justice provides some examples in order to illustrate some of these points:

> The provision by a UK mining company of reasonable travel and accommodation to allow foreign public officials to visit their distant mining operations so that those officials may be satisfied of the high standard and safety of the company's installations and operating systems are circumstances that fall outside the intended scope of the offence.

Flights and accommodation to allow foreign public officials to meet with senior executives of a UK commercial organisation in New York as a matter of genuine mutual convenience, and some reasonable hospitality for the individual and his or her partner, such as fine dining and attendance at a baseball match are facts that are, in themselves, unlikely to raise the necessary inferences. However, if the choice of New York as the most convenient venue was in doubt because the organisation's senior executives could easily have seen the official with all the relevant documentation when they had visited the relevant country the previous week then the necessary inference might be raised.

Similarly, supplementing information provided to a foreign public official on a commercial organisation's background, track record and expertise in providing private health care with an offer of ordinary travel and lodgings to enable a visit to a hospital run by the commercial organisation is unlikely to engage section 6. On the other hand, the provision by that same commercial organisation of a five-star holiday for the foreign public official which is unrelated to a demonstration of the organisation's services is, all things being equal, far more likely to raise the necessary inference.[24]

Lord Tunnicliffe, the government spokesperson for the Ministry of Justice, answering a request for clarification on where the line would be drawn on corporate hospitality, stated that what is acceptable is in the first instance determined by prosecutors:

> We share the Joint Committee's conclusion that, for the purposes of the Clause 6 offence, it is sufficient to rely on prosecutors to differentiate between legitimate and illegitimate corporate hospitality .... We recognise that corporate hospitality is an accepted part of modern business practice and the Government is not seeking to penalise expenditure on corporate hospitality for legitimate commercial purposes.[25]

Despite the emphasis by lawyers that corrupt intention is not a prerequisite for hospitality to be deemed illegal, the SFO's Vivian Robinson says that prosecutors are nevertheless likely to consider intention as a relevant factor:

> There are circumstances that are so extreme that we would be perfectly justified in saying "Well hang on, a jury would say that is bribery, that is not just ordinary business relations." You are piling it on in such a way as to gain some sort of advantage in business. And again it is about our discretion – we would look at the lavishness of the hospitality, we would ask ourselves whether the only influence from the factual circumstances was that this was intended to be a bribe.[26]

It is important to note that the general public interest considerations for active bribery are also applicable to hospitality.

Transparency International, in dealing with concerns over corporate hospitality, advises companies that they should ensure that, in addition to instituting adequate policies and procedures, their hospitality and expenses conform to its four basic principles: transparency, proportionality, reasonableness, and being bona fide.[27] If the procedural requirements and principles are satisfied, Transparency International expects that hospitality expenditures are unlikely to be considered illegal, under either the general offenses or Section 6. It is impossible to say to what extent a prolonged recession or changing political environment may influence future perceptions of what the authorities would deem a prosecution in the public interest, or exactly what UK juries would consider legitimate hospitality.

FACILITATION PAYMENTS

While a bribe is paid to obtain or retain business, a facilitation payment is defined as a payment made to an official to ensure that they perform a routine function which they are already obligated to perform. The SFO's Vivian Robinson explains that:

> A facilitation payment is a provision of services. It is to facilitate an already existing arrangement. If you pay money to someone to enter into an arrangement or a contract that is clearly a bribe in everybody's eyes. But if the arrangement has already been entered into, and a company already has a contract and in order to carry out that existing arrangement it is necessary to pay a minor official a payment to facilitate the carrying out of that particular function which is already in place it is a bribe of a different sort. It is bribe which goes not to the contract itself, but to the carrying out of what has already been agreed.[28]

Many contractors working in areas that necessitate repeated contact with public officials believe that "greasing the wheels" through making these payments to government officials is the only way to ensure that these officials perform their routine activity (or expedite processes), and ultimately the only way for the contractor to perform its contracted duties.

Facilitation payments tend to be particularly prevalent in countries with stifling bureaucratic apparatus and a history of colonialism. These systems create opportunities for low-paid officials to exploit their positions by demanding facilitation payments for performing routine functions.[29] Political analysts point out that the civil service in Nigeria (which they identify as probably the world's most corrupt country) is "massively overstaffed, with many illiterates requiring documents to be processed."[30] However, while businesses can easily dismiss such payments as supplementing the

144

incomes of lowly paid officials in poverty-stricken countries, this is not always where the money ends up. Vivian Robinson explains that:

> There are lots of cases in which facilitation payments to minor officials are symptomatic of something corrupt – they are part of schemes whereby officials at a much higher level get the benefit. That is why they are insidious. If they are paid on a routine basis by companies who put up no resistance and cannot show that they are unwilling participants of this, [they] send out a message that they are open to corruption on a much broader basis.[31]

At the international level, there appears to be a trend towards decreasing tolerance of facilitation payments. Both the Inter-American Convention and the UN Convention Against Corruption prohibit facilitating payments. Sections VI and VII of the OECD's Recommendation for Further Combating Bribery of Foreign Public Officials in International Business Transactions (issued on 9 December 2009) cite the "corrosive effect of small facilitation payments, particularly on sustainable economic development and the rule of law" as the basis for its recommendation that all signatories should:

i) undertake to periodically review their policies and approach on small facilitation payments in order to effectively combat the phenomenon;

ii) encourage companies to prohibit or discourage the use of small facilitation payments in internal company controls, ethics and compliance programmes or measures, recognising that such payments are generally illegal in the countries where they are made, and must in all cases be accurately accounted for in such companies' books and financial records.

Furthermore, this guidance urges "all countries to raise awareness of their public officials on their domestic bribery and solicitation laws with a view to stopping the solicitation and acceptance of small facilitation payments."[32] Under the previous anti-corruption standard of the FCPA, there is an exemption for legitimate payments for routine action by public officials, but the continued zero-tolerance stance of the UK Bribery Act means that the issue is sure to be a contentious area.

When a company has core business in countries that necessitates frequent contact with lowly paid semi-literate public officials it is hard to see how its employees can avoid being exposed to demands for such payments. Lord Woolf points out that:

> it is almost impossible to carry on business in those countries without being put in a position where it is almost impossible not to do things ....

It is certainly true of facilitation payments. There are countries where you will have to use advisers and the advisers will find it very difficult to operate.[33]

The Bribery Act has caused concern among businesses who fear they might be liable to prosecution for minor payments. McDermott Will & Emery state that the "corporate should review and, if necessary, modify their existing policies on ... facilitation payments accordingly."[34]

Transparency International argues that the positive impact of the UK Bribery Act on the reputation of the City of London will outweigh any negative impact on global competitiveness caused by the prohibition of facilitation payments, and suggests that its research demonstrates the new legislation is unlikely to be significantly detrimental in this regard. Vivian Robinson supported this position, and stated that in the long term companies that have eliminated such payments have not been permanently disadvantaged:

> Quite a number of companies do have zero tolerance and we are hearing anecdotally that after a period of initial pain their competitiveness hasn't really been affected. If a country wants to have serious players operating in their country rather than some cheapskate organisation they will understand that they can only do so if they are not at risk of disadvantage by paying these facilitation payments.[35]

However, the fact that the same Transparency International research recommends that the UK government lobby the OECD Working Group on Bribery to enact a ban on facilitation payments "to ensure a level playing field"[36] suggests that the potential consequences for British business have not gone unrecognized.

CONSTRAINTS ON THE FCPA EXEMPTION

As previously mentioned, the previous standard of the US FCPA provided a theoretical defense to payments made to expedite routine governmental actions. However this exemption is by no means the get-out clause for businesses as it is sometimes portrayed. One issue with the FCPA exemption is that it has changed since the act came into force in 1977.

Gregory Husisian of the international law firm Foley and Lardner explains that the original language of the FCPA focused on the function that the official performed and the status of the foreign official. If the official was low-ranking and the function administrative (requiring no discretion), this theoretically would have satisfied the requirement for the exemption. Uncertainty over how low-ranking an official had to be, and exactly what was a discretionary function, was the driver for amendments in 1988 which sought to clarify the situation with regard to the exemption for facilitation payments. Under the post-1988 FCPA the distinctions between ranks of officials and discretionary and nondiscretionary acts were removed, and all payments made to a secure the performance of a routine function can be theoretically exempt. The FCPA exemption thus covers facilitating payments that are not given with corrupt intent but merely to obtain something to which the payer is entitled in any event.

Husisian states that:

> FCPA practitioners used to say that if you were paying a person to do the job that he was "supposed to do" (hooking up your cable, processing paperwork, etc.) then this was okay. But the DOJ now takes the position that deciding the order to process paperwork is a "discretionary act" and hence can be a payment to obtain or retain business.[37]

The result of this uncertainty, says Husisian, is that the FCPA exemption is of limited use to companies:

> Despite this FCPA exemption there is a trend in US compliance programmes to eliminate such payments completely and take a zero tolerance approach. This is partly because of the difficulty for compliance officers in distinguishing between a payment made to facilitate a service and one made to obtain or retain business. Another reason for the decreased tolerance of US business to such payments is that even if the defence of facilitation payment can be successfully made under US law, the payment would almost certainly be illegal in the local jurisdiction in which it was made.[38]

The fact that other jurisdictions make no distinction between facilitation payments and bribes means that the defense is of limited use to companies, and will be of even less use when the UK Bribery Act comes into force. Barry Vitou explains that, with the passing of this Act, companies that are registered on the US stock exchange but have a UK nexus and do business elsewhere will have three problems – the FCPA, the UK Bribery Act, and the law of the local jurisdiction. A further problem is that for publicly traded companies, the Securities and Exchange Commission requires that all facilitation payments be fully recorded. Vitou points out that:

> Under the FCPA exemption for facilitation payments, a company cannot take advantage of the defence unless such payments are properly recorded in their books and records. However if a company does record them in order to gain an exemption in the US, as a UK company they have just admitted an offence under UK law.[39]

When authorities take an interest

The uncertainty over the exemption for facilitation payments in the United States may have influenced the United Kingdom's approach to the Bribery Act, which ignores the concept. Vivian Robinson explains that:

> The government decided not make any provision in relation to facilitation payments because of the difficulty of drawing the line and instead they said that the best way of dealing with this position is to leave it to the discretion of the prosecutors. They are basically saying that we are still going to make these payments unlawful, but we are going to leave it to the good sense and discretion of the people whose job it is to enforce this Act, and they will take action in the most appropriate cases.[40]

Under the present UK system even minor facilitation payments made to recover property are illegal, but it seems that they are largely ignored by prosecutors. Theoretically under UK law any such payments are illegal if there is not an imminent threat. Professor Sullivan emphasized the lack of exception made for these payments under the UK Bribery Act, and made the point that payment to secure the return of property in a high-risk area would still be illegal under its provisions:

> There was a dreadful case where someone was employed by a particular agency to provide security vehicles to diplomatic and other personnel in Afghanistan, and local officials impounded his vehicles, as being not registered, which was the case because the same officials had refused to register them. So they impounded these vehicles and then insisted on payments – and this guy's gone through hell in an Afghan prison. Now there would be jurisdiction under the 2010 Bribery Act in that case because he is an English national so he has a close connection ... and in terms of the payment of these officials it's an open and shut case, but the nature of facilitation payments is only to get what is yours back again so you can use it![41]

However, it is interesting to note that the application may be very different from the letter of the law. Robinson indicates that small non-systemic payments, or those made to avoid destruction or damage to goods, would likely in practice be ignored by UK authorities:

> Somebody came to see us the other day. They were very concerned. They said, "the nature of our industry is such that we do need to operate in foreign countries and in these countries there are sometimes threats of physical safety or the safety of our property if we do not make a payment, and so in order for us to operate in those countries in this particular

industry we make those payments, are we likely in those circumstances to find ourselves as prosecutors looking at it?" No, of course not! We wouldn't think of taking procedures against anybody who made a facilitation payment because they were under some threat either to body or to property.[42]

Another SFO official stated that "We certainly don't condone facilitation payments and never will. But whether we prosecute depends on whether it falls within our criteria. Is it significantly serious?"[43] The director's guidance on the Bribery Act outlines a number of factors which tend towards and against prosecution in the context of facilitation payments.[44]

Factors tending in favor of prosecution

- large or repeated payments are more likely to attract a significant sentence (Code 4.16a)
- facilitation payments that are planned for or accepted as part of a standard way of conducting business may indicate the offence was premeditated (Code 4.16e)
- payments may indicate an element of active corruption of the official in the way the offence was committed (Code 4.16k)
- where a commercial organization has a clear and appropriate policy setting out procedures an individual should follow if facilitation payments are requested and these have not been correctly followed.

Factors tending against prosecution

- a single small payment likely to result in only a nominal penalty (Code 4.17a)
- the payment(s) came to light as a result of a genuinely proactive approach involving self-reporting and remedial action (additional factor (a) in the Guidance on Corporate Prosecutions)
- where a commercial organization has a clear and appropriate policy setting out procedures an individual should follow if facilitation payments are requested and these have been correctly followed
- the payer was in a vulnerable position arising from the circumstances in which the payment was demanded.

Another SFO official provides some clarification which indicates that the agency considers many factors. Vivian Robinson identifies a number of considerations:

> When we are considering public interest, and I would be saying that public interest will depend on the exercise of our discretion – the amount, the system, what efforts have the company made to reduce

149

the incidence of such payments and fourthly special sector interests. In addition to all this ... we have to ask ourselves what the likelihood is given the particular facts of the case of an English jury convicting a person for making these particular payments. There are all kinds of safeguards against our taking action in relation to the payment of facilitation payments in a given circumstance.[45]

A further factor which may determine the interest of the SFO is the unique context in which a facilitation payment is made. Vitou explains that:

What the SFO have said when pressed on these questions is that if you had a US corporate (with a UK nexus) and a UK corporate in a corrupt jurisdiction both wish to set up a factory, and both want to get phone lines installed, and they are told by local officials that a facilitation payment would ensure that these lines are installed immediately and if you don't pay then it will be 6 months. In the example the US corporate takes advantage of the US FCPA exemption while the UK corporate does not and is out of the market for 6 months. The SFO say that they in those circumstances they would look to prosecute.[46]

In the United States there is uncertainty about the point at which a facilitating payment (or payments) becomes so large as to be a bribe in the eyes of the US DOJ. Husian explains that despite the fact that the post 1988 FCPA theoretically exempts any payment made to expedite a routine governmental function, US authorities have indicated that they would be more likely to take action on a single payment that was large or a series of smaller payments that was systemic. The lack of case law in this area or further clarification from the DOJ regarding what exactly a routine activity is again increases uncertainty. Vitou says that that consequently, "There is a debate in the US about the real world applications of facilitation payments exemption. Ultimately what the DOJ say is or is not a facilitation payment is or is not."[47]

Due to the increased focus on such payments internationally, a concern for businesses is whether the tolerance of the SFO towards facilitation payments is likely to change with the new Bribery Act. Comments made by Vivian Robinson appear to indicate that there will be a grace period for businesses after the Act comes into force:

What we are really looking at in these circumstances is to say "Is there evidence that the company concerned can demonstrate to us that they have genuinely worked towards either eliminating completely or at least reducing the facilitation payments that they have been paying?" What we would not be very impressed with is if they had done nothing. We are saying "We don't expect people overnight, the day after the Act comes into force to suddenly come along and tap shoulders and say we are going to prosecute this facilitation payment because this is something which we appreciate will take time. What we are looking for is that everybody who is in a position where he is being required to make facilitation payments are doing something to reduce the incidents of making such payments, because that is a move in the right direction.[48]

How facilitation payments can be resisted

While it may be naive to suggest that facilitation payments can be eliminated globally, a combination of concerted pressure from a coordinated sector together with informal pressure exerted through the diplomatic contacts of authorities can make a real difference. Robinson provides one example:

> An ethical company came to us and said, "Look, we are having great difficulty with a country because we are being required to make facilitation payments. We don't want to do so and we have done everything we possibly can but we have hit a brick wall. Is there any way that you could help us?" We said, "I think there is." Number one, get in touch with your competitors and find out whether they also having similar difficulties and together draw this to the attention of the respective embassies of the countries that the companies came from, and the SFO was able through our own contacts to put pressure and get the payments stopped. So in other words there was a concerted effort on a sector lead initiative backed up by the contacts that we had.

This example shows that the SFO is taking a cooperative and preventive approach to reducing the incidence of facilitation payments, but that it expects companies to get together on a sector-wide scale to tackle the problem collectively. Despite considerable prosecutorial discretion in this area it may well be that the SFO takes a more aggressive approach once the Bribery Act has been in force for a period of time. Businesses should not be complacent in their approach to facilitation payments, and should take notice of the trend towards zero tolerance in compliance programs. Practical ways to control facilitation payments include implementing a zero tolerance approach, or alternatively ensuring that all requests for payments are recorded and referred to a compliance officer for review.

8

SPOTTING, STOPPING, AND COMBATING CORPORATE CORRUPTION

All companies face a risk of becoming involved in corruption. Corporate practice and policy needs to reflect and counter the dangers of involvement in corruption. This is important for stopping corruption, and can be of help to the company if bribery allegations arise. According to the UK Bribery Act and the US Foreign Corrupt Practices Act (FCPA), showing that a company has preformed due diligence and tried to prevent bribery can defend the company from charges that may be brought against it for an act of bribery carried out by an employee. As well as acting as a defense in court, trying to prevent bribery makes good business sense for a company and is the ethical thing to do. There are a number of basic steps that a company can take to prevent bribery. Often these steps will use existing features of a company's operations, such as financial and auditing controls or pre-existing disciplinary procedures.[1]

ASSESSING RISK

The Ministry of Justice guidance on preventive procedures indicates that, regardless of the size, activities, customers, or markets of a commercial organization, its risk assessment procedures usually reflect a few basic characteristics:[2]

- oversight of the risk assessment by top-level management
- appropriate resourcing – this should reflect the scale of the organization's business and the need to identify and prioritize all relevant risks.
- identification of the internal and external information sources that will enable risk to be assessed and reviewed
- due diligence enquiries
- accurate and appropriate documentation of the risk.

Exactly what policies and procedures an organization should put in place to stop corruption depends on its individual circumstances:

> The level of risk that organisations face will also vary with the type and nature of the persons associated with it. For example, a commercial organisation that properly assesses that there is no risk of bribery on the part of one of its associated persons will accordingly require nothing in the way of procedures to prevent bribery in the context of that relationship. By the same token the bribery risks associated with reliance on a third party agent representing a commercial organisation in negotiations with foreign public officials may be assessed as significant and accordingly require much more in the way of procedures to mitigate those risks.[3]

The guidance also acknowledges that geographic area of operation will be an important factor in determining risk:

> Although commercial organisations with entirely domestic operations may require bribery prevention procedures, we believe that as a general proposition they will face lower risks of bribery on their behalf by associated persons than the risks that operate in foreign markets. In any event procedures put in place to mitigate domestic bribery risks are likely to be similar if not the same as those designed to mitigate those associated with foreign markets.[4]

Companies should adapt their rules and methods depending on their size, type, and the sectors and areas in which they operate. For this reason effective anti-bribery controls should be developed on the basis of a thorough risk assessment.[5] A risk assessment will help a company be aware of the dangers so that it will know what it faces, and it is hoped, will know how to deal with problems when they arise.

The Ministry of Justice gives a few basic examples of ways in which the risk of bribery can be addressed from the perspective of small businesses:

> There are simple practical steps you can take to assess and mitigate risks. These are mostly obvious, and are similar to (or even the same as) those you probably take anyway (for example, to make sure you can trust the people you work with). For example, you might use simple internet searches to find out about the levels of corruption or bribery in the particular country you propose to do business in. You could consult UK diplomatic posts or UK Trade and Investment for advice. You could also consult business representative bodies here and in the relevant country for up to date local knowledge. We set out some contacts below including

a Government-sponsored Business Anti-Corruption Portal aimed at small and medium sized businesses involved in overseas trade.[6]

Kenneth Clarke states that "small companies ought not to fear that they will suddenly need an army of lawyers in order to manage bribery risks. They can rely heavily on simply telling staff, verbally."[7] In addition to the main Bribery Act guidance, the Ministry of Justice has published "quick-start" advice which is specifically tailored to the needs of small business owners, and which all small businesses would be wise to review. This quick-start advice seeks to reassure small businesses about the implications of the Act:

> There is no need for extensive written documentation or policies .... In larger organisations it will be important to ensure that management in charge of the day to day business is fully aware and committed to the objective of preventing bribery. In micro-businesses it may be enough for simple oral reminders to key staff about the organisation's anti-bribery policies.[8]

As well as depending on external factors, risks can arise from inside the company.[9] For example parts of the company that are involved in bidding or making deals with other companies, or any part of the company that relies on intermediaries, is at a higher risk. There is more risk involved when more money is involved. Parts of the company involved with political issues are likely to be at risk. Furthermore if a company's pay scheme gives large bonuses for making deals, this can encourage bribery.[10] A risk assessment will pinpoint the parts of the company that are most in danger of becoming involved in corruption,[11] so that a company knows where to target anti-bribery measures.

There are a number of ways of researching the risks. Companies can use company information, such as audit reports, employee complaints, and internal investigations, to give an idea of the high-risk areas.[12] For example if staff are researching the risks involved in a particular country, employees who worked there can be used to give an accurate account of the climate of corruption.

There are also a number of public resources.[13] Companies can consult embassies, chambers of commerce, and non-governmental organizations (NGOs). Transparency International can be helpful for assessing external risks as it has around 90 locally established national chapters that collect more in depth data locally on bribery. Trace International is a useful non-profit membership association that pools resources and information on bribery cases and local laws and customs to help multinational companies develop anti-bribery compliance policies. It also offers due diligence reports on intermediaries, and anti-bribery training. Other trustworthy companies can also be contacted for advice and information. For more general information there is the UN Global Compact, a policy platform and a practical framework for companies aiming towards ethical business practices, as well as a host of other NGOs and business groups willing to provide useful information. Some companies may consider asking an external consultant to make the analysis for them.[14]

An analysis of the risks should be repeated at various intervals.[15] Risks can change. New laws can be passed and the expected standards of compliance can increase.[16] Entering new markets, changing governments, or company changes in business structure and business strategy can all affect the risks of becoming involved in corruption, and all need to be considered when reanalyzing the risks that a company faces.

COMMON ELEMENTS

The Ministry of Justice guidance suggests that anti-bribery procedures should embrace six principles: proportionate procedures, top-level commitment, risk assessment, due diligence, communication (including training), and monitoring and review. Hypothetical scenarios are reproduced from the guidance at the end of this chapter to illustrate how the Ministry imagines such principles could be applied.

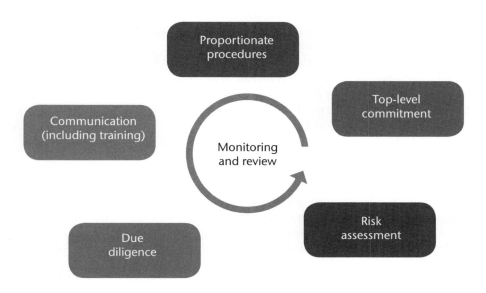

FIGURE 8.1 **Principles of corporate response**

Source: Pinsent Masons/Barry Vitou.

In addition to these principles, the guidance anticipates that preventive policies are likely to include certain common elements.[17] These include:

- an organization's commitment to bribery prevention
- its general approach to mitigation of specific bribery risks, such as those arising from the conduct of intermediaries and agents, or those associated with hospitality and promotional expenditure, facilitation payments, or political and charitable donations or contributions
- an overview of its strategy to implement its bribery prevention policies.

In addition, the guidance provides a list of procedures that bribery prevention procedures might include, depending on the risks faced:

- the involvement of the organization's top-level management (see Principle 2)
- risk assessment procedures (see Principle 3)
- due diligence on existing or prospective associated persons (see Principle 4)
- the provision of gifts, hospitality and promotional expenditure; charitable and political donations; or demands for facilitation payments
- direct and indirect employment, including recruitment, terms and conditions, disciplinary action, and remuneration
- governance of business relationships with all other associated persons including pre and post contractual agreements
- financial and commercial controls such as adequate bookkeeping, auditing, and approval of expenditure
- transparency of transactions and disclosure of information
- decision making, such as delegation of authority procedures, separation of functions, and the avoidance of conflicts of interest
- enforcement, detailing discipline processes and sanctions for breaches of the organization's anti-bribery rules
- the reporting of bribery including "speak up" or "whistleblowing" procedures
- the detail of the process by which the organization plans to implement its bribery prevention procedures: for example, how its policy will be applied to individual projects and to different parts of the organization
- the communication of the organization's policies and procedures, and training in their application (see Principle 5)
- the monitoring, review and evaluation of bribery prevention.

These elements can be incorporated into compliance in a number of ways.

CODE OF CONDUCT

After assessing the risks, the first step that a company (or other organization) might take towards tackling bribery and corruption is to introduce a code of conduct. The purpose of this is twofold. First, it will set out the rules and regulations that employees need to follow. Second, it will set out an ethical code for the company. It should include a statement of the company's business principles and ethics, and have a strong anti-corruption message, publicizing both the business benefits of and the moral reasons for stopping corruption. This is the first step towards encouraging a positive ethical philosophy within the company, and thereby reducing corruption.

Such a code of conduct should be applicable to all employees. It should become part of the contract that employees sign when they are taken on. The code of conduct should also apply to any contractors, suppliers, subsidiaries, business partners, and so on, of the company.[18]

There are a number of different ways a company could construct such codes. There could be separate codes of conduct for the company's ethical views and for its rules and regulations. Smaller companies with a very low risk of becoming involved in bribery or corruption may have shorter, less detailed rules about bribery, whereas a large international company may choose to have a number of local anti-bribery and ethical polices for each country that it does business in, depending on the risks and problems in that country.[19] The code of conduct and a company's ethical policies should be displayed publicly.[20]

A company may consider having a number of different codes of conduct or contracts for employees and for employees from other companies or business partners to sign to show their good intention.

Anti-bribery rules

The code of conduct should also clearly set out the company's rules and guidelines so that both employees and business partners know how to respond and how to act in line with a company's anti-bribery policies and what may be undertaken on the company's behalf.[21] It should explain that bribery is not to be part of the company and set out what counts as bribery. In the United Kingdom this should be based on the new UK laws, and should cover all cases of giving or accepting payments to influence a decision, including facilitation payments.

The code of conduct should state a company's policy on giving and receiving gifts and hospitality, and on giving charitable and political donations.[22] The giving of gifts needs to be strictly limited to prevent the possibility of bribery. The code of conduct should give the details of people to whom employees should turn to ask for advice if they are ever unsure of the rules. It should also provide details of who to report to if the employee has something to report as part of a confidential whistleblower policy. Employees should be asked to report anything suspicious and any red flags of corruption. They should be obliged to report any possible conflicts of interest.[23] The code of conduct should stress that any employee choosing

157

to make a report will be assured of confidentiality.[24] These important concepts (a gifts policy, a whistleblower policy, red flags, and conflicts of interest) will be explained in more detail over the next few pages.

The code of conduct should make it clear that the rules will be strictly enforced and there will be zero tolerance of any petty corruption and bribe paying.[25] Also any violation of the policy by other organizations will result in termination of business.[26] Of course, the policy and the rules should make an exception for emergency situations, for example if a facilitation payment is required for the provision of emergency medical care.[27] It should also be made clear that no one will be penalized for any delays or problems caused by not paying bribes.[28]

TRAINING

Obviously for any code of conduct and set of rules to work, the employees and business partners must know of it. Any such policy should be well publicized to employees. It should be in company handbooks or appear in company newsletters, and be communicated periodically to all current employees. It should be explained to new employees in their initial training.[29] Furthermore all employees should undergo regular anti-bribery training.

Having well trained employees who are alert to dangers of corruption and can spot warning signs at an early stage, and who know exactly what actions would violate company rules and the law, can significantly help prevent a company from becoming involved in corruption, and help a company spot corruption when it is taking place.[30]

Training should cover all types of corruption that a company might face (such as bribery, fraud, or cartels). It should explain why corruption is wrong and also bad for business, and that it is against the law. The relevant laws should be explained in detail, for the countries that the company does business in. Employees should be made fully aware of the company's policy on gifts and other anti-corruption rules, and internal controls including the company's disciplinary procedures. They should be familiarized with examples of bad conduct, and know what to do when confronted with corruption, such as requests for bribes or extortion.[31] There should also be a push to encourage ethical thinking and ethical behavior within the company.

The training should also publicize the company's whistleblowing procedures and red flags that may signify corruption is taking place, so that employees can keep a look out for anything suspicious. Employees should be encouraged to report anything possibly relevant to stopping corruption, even if they are unsure about it.[32]

Training should be tailored for the different functions and roles within an organization,[33] and for the different countries that an employee will be working in. Employees should receive extra training when there are higher risks associated with their jobs.[34]

Larger companies should also consider offering training to employees of intermediaries and business partners. A company may even decide that it is to be a requirement for business partners that they provide anti-bribery training or send their employees to the company's anti-bribery training.[35]

The anti-bribery training should consist of workshops accompanied by written material. There should also be a company member who can give advice and answer employees' questions. Anti-bribery training sessions should take place regularly (ideally at least once a year[36]) so that employees are constantly up to date and knowledgeable.[37] A company should also record and keep evidence that it carries out such training, as this may be needed to show compliance if a bribery case arises.[38]

CREATING AN ETHICAL CULTURE

The code of conduct could contain other ethical guidelines and rules,[39] such as how staff should treat fellow employees, and how the environment should be considered. Having an ethical code of conduct and providing training to encourage ethical behavior are only the first steps towards creating an ethical business culture where people are unlikely to become involved in corrupt activity.

Employment and pay

Companies may want to consider judging people on their values as well as on their skills when recruiting.[40] Furthermore employers should perform due diligence: carry out a series of background and identity checks, on potential employees to discover if there is anything that may suggest that they have been, or might become, involved in corrupt activity. This can involve investigating whether they have a criminal record involving corruption, looking at references from previous employers, and asking previous employers if there were any problems of corruption.

Similarly potential employees should check companies to which they are applying for jobs, to see whether they have a bad corruption record. As suggested earlier, an employee's contracts should contain at least a declaration of the employee's commitment to abide by the company's anti-corruption rules. There should also be mention of penalties if the employee breaks the anti-corruption rules, and the contract should give the company the right to suspend employees if they are suspected of corruption and to sack them if they are found guilty of corrupt activities. Similarly the contract should put across the company commitment to ending corruption, and give the employee the right to terminate the contract if the company is found to be corrupt.[41]

It is also important for companies to remove any incentives to corruption. If employees are paid a reasonable salary for the work they do, this will reduce the incentive to accept bribes. Often large companies have pay schemes that award large bonuses to employees who make successful deals. This can encourage employees to turn a blind eye to corruption in other companies with which they are making a deal, or even to resort to bribery to make the deal. Such systems of bonuses should be treated very carefully by an employer. One possible way of dealing with this is to introduce bonuses to employees who avoid corrupt contracts. Companies appointing an employee to a high-risk position should take all possible steps to appoint employees who are trusted, such as employees who have been with the company for some time. In some cases it may be reasonable to request that an employee in a high-risk position annually reports their assets and the assets of their close family. Employees should also be prohibited from buying shares in organizations they are currently working with.[42]

Lead from the top

It is important when creating an ethical working culture that senior management is seen to be doing the right thing. There needs to be visible commitment from senior management for anti-corruption policies and ethical behavior.[43] This can be manifest in a number of ways. The individual responsible for implementing, overseeing, and monitoring bribery policies should be from senior management. There should be an executive-level statement of commitment to combating corruption and bribery. Senior management could talk at training sessions. Senior management should be seen to support disciplinary action and to withdraw from deals with high-risk or corrupt companies.[44]

The importance of leadership is embodied by Principle 2 of the Ministry of Justice guidelines, "Top-level commitment." The ministry anticipates that this will include communication of the organization's anti-bribery policy and significant involvement in developing bribery prevention procedures. With regard to the way in which the company's leadership can communicate the anti-bribery message, the ministry suggests that effective formal statements that demonstrate top-level commitment are likely to include:

- a commitment to carry out business fairly, honestly and openly
- a commitment to zero tolerance of bribery
- the consequences of breaching the policy for employees and managers
- for other associated persons the consequences of breaching contractual provisions relating to bribery prevention (this could include a reference to avoiding doing business with others who do not commit to doing business without bribery as a "best practice" objective)

160

- articulation of the business benefits of rejecting bribery (reputational, customer, and business partner confidence)
- reference to the range of bribery prevention procedures the organization has or is putting in place, including any protection and procedures for confidential reporting of bribery (whistleblowing)
- key individuals and departments involved in the development and implementation of the organization's bribery prevention procedures
- reference to the organization's involvement in any collective action against bribery in, for example, the same business sector.[45]

In addition to commitment at the most senior level, the Ministry of Justice suggests that top-level *engagement* in the development of bribery prevention procedures is likely to reflect the following elements:

- selection and training of senior managers to lead anti-bribery work where appropriate.
- leadership on key measures such as a code of conduct.
- endorsement of all bribery prevention related publications.
- leadership in awareness raising and encouraging transparent dialogue throughout the organization so as to seek to ensure effective dissemination of anti-bribery policies and procedures to employees, subsidiaries, and associated persons, etc.
- engagement with relevant associated persons and external bodies,

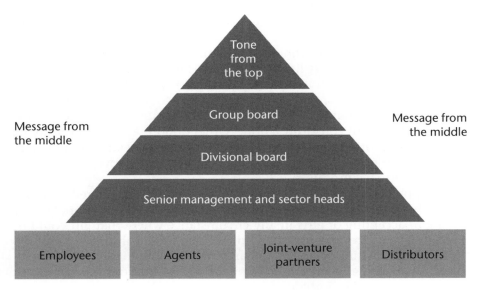

FIGURE 8.2 **Components of an ethical culture**
Source: Pinsent Masons/Barry Vitou.

such as sectoral organizations and the media, to help articulate the organization's policies.

- specific involvement in high profile and critical decision making where appropriate.
- assurance of risk assessment.
- general oversight of breaches of procedures and the provision of feedback to the board or equivalent, where appropriate.[46]

ANTI-CORRUPTION AND ANTI-BRIBERY RULES

As well as an ethical culture, both enforcement of the rules set forth in the code of conduct, and implementation of a range of anti-corruption and anti-bribery policies and internal controls are needed to ensure that a company stays on track and is able to show compliance with anti-bribery regulations.

To begin with, employees should be expressly forbidden from being involved with or condoning any corrupt activities. This includes but is not limited to offering or receiving bribes, deliberately falsifying or withholding information, putting forward misleading information, and providing substandard work or materials in breach of a contract.

Gifts

There should be a clear policy on gifts and hospitality. As mentioned, the code of conduct should explain what can be given in terms of gifts and entertainment.[47] This should also apply to donations to charities or political organizations.

The anti-bribery rules should set a limit to gift giving and receiving. This could be a monetary limit, so the rule is never to give or accept a gift above a certain value. If a monetary threshold is set, it should vary from location to location.[48] A gift with a value of £25 could be acceptable in the United Kingdom, but in Zambia that would be equivalent to a few weeks wages,[49] and might constitute a bribe. Other options are to ban the giving and receiving of gifts outright, or to set a more general non-monetary limit, such as that employees should never offer gifts above the ability of the receiver to reciprocate.[50]

The policy on gifts should forbid money ever being offered as a gift, the giving or accepting of gifts during the process of negotiation,[51] or the giving or accepting of gifts in any circumstance where that gift could be perceived by others to constitute a bribe. There should always be a prohibition on the soliciting of gifts.[52] Similarly the rules should limit what constitutes reasonable expenses and hospitality. Providing overly extravagant hospitality should be forbidden.

Gifts should never be offered or accepted in secret. Companies should have a gifts register where the details (where the gift is from, when it was given, its approximate value, and so on) are recorded.[53] This register should be inspected routinely. Similarly all spending on hospitality should be reported and recorded.

There should also be thresholds to the amount that can be given as political or charitable donations by a company or its employees. These thresholds can be higher than the threshold for gifts given to persons. There need not be a threshold to personal charitable donations, but at the same time steps should be taken to ensure that charitable donations are not used to disguise bribery. Political donations are more risky, and can sometimes be illegal. The amount and timing of political donations should be reviewed to ensure that they are not made so as to obtain or retain any business advantage.[54] Details of political and charitable donations should be made pubic.

There could be the possibility of suspending the various thresholds in exceptional circumstances: for example, if an employee is invited to a big expensive event and feels that refusing could cause offense. In these cases permission would be needed from senior management.[55]

Conflicts of interest

Another important policy relates to reporting conflicts of interest by employees. A conflict of interest arises when an individual has any personal motivation or any interest that might influence their decisions or judgments in the workplace.[56] For example there would be a conflict of interest if a person was in charge of choosing a supplier, and one of candidate organizations was run by a close family member. The knowledge that a family member would benefit from the decision could affect it, even subconsciously. It is important therefore that employees should report all conflicts of interest as soon as possible. Conflicts of interest should be reported even if an employee feels certain that the conflict will not affect their judgment,[57] as that should not be their personal decision to make. Management will then have to consider the risks and decide whether the employee should be required to stand aside while the decision is made.

Employees should also be asked to disclose if they are in a vulnerable personal situation (for example if their affairs are financially unstable)[58] as this could raise the chances of being tempted to become involved in bribery or corruption. Once again management will then have to assess the risks and decide whether the employee should continue in their present role.

Separation of duties

Companies should also enforce separation of duties. The principle here is that more than one person is required to carry out a particular process. This reduces the possibility of corruption as it means that at least two people would need to be involved, rather than just one corrupt individual. For example, money handling could be made a separate responsibility from recording the receipt of money. Another example is enforcing a rule that all checks need two signatures.[59] Any function that could lead to the abuse of power should be divided up[60] to minimize the possibility of corruption. Obviously the separation of duties can lead to extra cost and time, so companies should decide what duties to divide up, and to what extent, based on the risks they feel they face.[61]

DUE DILIGENCE

Most of the anti-corruption measures mentioned so far have been dealing with the rules and regulations that a company needs to put in place to prevent bribery by its employees. Companies are also legally responsible for any other organization that could be seen to be acting on the company's behalf. This can include subsidiaries, intermediaries, agents, distributors, joint venture partners, and so on. Furthermore there is the risk that a company will lose out as a result of corrupt activity even if it is in an organization that the company is not responsible for. For example it could lose out to competitors who are paying bribes, or have to break off a business deal if its partner in the deal was discovered to be corrupt.

Just as a company should perform due diligence on potential employees, it must also perform due diligence before entering into a deal with another company.

Companies should carry out due diligence for a number of reasons: to check that another company is not involved in any form of corruption, to check that there are no hidden costs involved with a particular business deal (for example in an acquisition process, due diligence should show if there are there any large impending costs, such as a requirement for new machinery), and to have a better knowledge of the other company to inform decisions and business strategies and maximize profit.[62] In short due diligence involves looking for any reason not to buy, merge with, rely on, or do business with another company.

Due diligence should be carried out before entering any business contract. It should be proportional to what is already expected of the risk, and the size of the contract. Ministry of Justice guidance on preventive procedures recognizes that appropriate due diligence is likely to vary between posts within a commercial organization:

> A commercial organisation's employees are presumed to be persons "associated" with the organisation for the purposes of the Bribery Act. The organisation may wish, therefore, to incorporate in its recruitment and human resources procedures an appropriate level of due diligence to mitigate the risks of bribery being undertaken by employees which

is proportionate to the risk associated with the post in question. Due diligence is unlikely to be needed in relation to lower risk posts.[63]

In a similar way to the formal guidance on preventive procedures, the Ministry of Justice's quick start guidance seeks to reassure businesses that due diligence will not be required in all cases:

> You only have to think about doing due diligence on persons who will actually perform services for you, or on your behalf. Someone who simply supplies goods to you is unlikely to do that. It is very unlikely, therefore, that you will need to consider doing due diligence on persons further down a supply chain.
>
> Where you decide to undertake due diligence, how much you need to do will depend on your risk assessment. If you assess the risk as low then all you may need to do is satisfy yourself that people performing services for you (for example, an agent) are genuine and someone you can trust to do your business without bribing. You could do this by making enquiries with business contacts, local chambers of commerce or business associations or via the internet for example.
>
> Where you think the risks are higher, then you may need to do more. You might ask your agent for a CV, financial statements or accounts, and other references. You might then follow those up to ensure they are genuine. The aim is to satisfy yourself that the person that is to represent your organisation can be trusted not to use bribery on your behalf, but this does not necessarily require sophisticated and costly techniques. Personal contact, allowing you to assess the person for yourself, can be very helpful.[64]

Due diligence should never be so thorough and expensive as to in itself make a contract not worthwhile.[65] It should be an ongoing process. Companies should regularly reassess the risks and continue to monitor their business partners.[66]

However, the guidance acknowledges that commercial organizations will not be able to directly control businesses or individuals several links down the supply chain, and may only be able to carry out proper due diligence on its closest associates:

> Where a supply chain involves several entities or a project is to be performed by a prime contractor with a series of sub-contractors, an organisation is likely only to exercise control over its relationship with its contractual counterparty. Indeed, the organisation may only know the identity of its contractual counterparty. It is likely that persons who contract with that counterparty will be performing services for the

counterparty and not for other persons in the contractual chain. The principal way in which commercial organisations may decide to approach bribery risks which arise as a result of a supply chain is by employing the types of anti-bribery procedures referred to elsewhere in this guidance (e.g. risk-based due diligence and the use of anti-bribery terms and conditions) in the relationship with their contractual counterparty, and by requesting that counterparty to adopt a similar approach with the next party in the chain.[67]

Detailed due diligence should look at the details of the particular project that is being proposed, the workings of other company (or companies) involved, and the senior staff and owners of that company. In examining these, those carrying out due diligence should look to see whether there are any red flags that could signify corruption (red flags are discussed in more detail later) and whether there are any effective anti-corruption policies in place and in use, both in the company and specific to the particular project. It is important to check the reputation of the company and its owners, and to see whether there is any history of involvement with corruption or bribery.[68]

To carry out due diligence companies can use sources external to the other company. For example they can look in the media to see whether the company has recently been involved in any bribery cases, and search government databases of blacklisted people and companies, or online databases (like http://kyc360.com/tools/free-tools?default=riskscreen).[69] Researchers should also analyze information from the company itself. They should ask the company to fill out a disclosure form. In the form they should ask questions that might show up red flags,[70] and ask about any history of corruption and about the company's finances. Researchers should look at company's records, financial statements, internal anti-bribery controls, management accounts, budgets, projections, insurance policies, and contracts with employees, suppliers, customers, and others.[71]

Due diligence and contracts

It is important that companies should act on the results of due diligence checks. If another company seems particularly suspicious or at a high risk of being involved in bribery, it is best to avoid entering into a deal with it. In other cases the results of due diligence should inform the contract signed.[72]

Generally a company should look to have anti-bribery agreements included as a part of every contract. It should inform business partners of its anti-bribery policies, and expect them to agree to conform to them.[73] A contract should also give termination rights if either side is found breaking the agreed anti-bribery policies.[74]

As suggested before, a company may also consider having a number of different contracts for employees from other companies or business partners to sign to show their good intentions. They may choose to insist on more stringent contracts in cases where they are not happy with a business partner's own anti-bribery policies. They may as mentioned insist on anti-bribery training for another company's employees, and require their business partner to allow inspections and regular auditing of their anti-corruption compliance.[75]

One useful example is the Integrity Pact developed by Transparency International for bidders for public contracts. Both the company involved and government officials should sign this, and declare that they promise to refrain from bribery and to disclose all expenses.[76]

INTERNAL CONTROLS

An internal control is a plan and method that a company puts in place to help improve efficiency, to reach its goals, to safeguard assets, and to ensure adherence to company rules.[77] Generally internal controls are systematic measures with specific aims. Often they deal with accounting, and are designed to ensure accuracy and efficiency in accounting procedures. This was where the term originated, although now it applies to actions taken throughout a company.[78] For example, a recruitment process that is designed to ensure the company hires people who have strong ethical values is a preventive internal control with the aim of reducing corruption.

Companies need to introduce further business and accounting internal controls, to prevent, deter, and catch, corruption and bribery. The exact details of these controls will depend on a number of factors, such as the precise nature of the business and the personnel involved.

The controls should include measures to limit the ease with which an employee can use company money to pay bribes, such as enforced separation of duties and countersigning of checks, and also limiting access to petty cash, and check-signing privileges.[79] There should be controls that pre-empt and prevent corruption, such as regular interviews with employees to ensure they are satisfied with their job and pay and are unlikely to risk becoming involved in corrupt activity.[80]

Primarily internal accounting controls will be designed to detect, and thereby deter, corrupt activity. Examples range from having a bid auditor who is independent of the bid team and who will ensure resources are being used in accordance with anti-corruption policies, to reviewing selected email and communications or anything suspicious.

When monitoring communications employers should be aware of the legal issues involved with data protection. The key points are that (under UK law) those involved in the communication must be made aware that the communication may be monitored. Employers are entitled to monitor work communications but not personal communications. This can be difficult as generally they are indistinguishable. There are a number of possible steps that employers can take to work around this, such as asking employees to use a particular template for personal emails. Monitoring must be a proportionate response to the risk. Employers should look to part 3 of the Employment Practices Data Protection Code for complete details of monitoring employees.[81]

Companies should have accounting controls to ensure that, at a minimum, transactions and assets are protected from unauthorized use, transactions are properly recorded, and recorded asset values are periodically compared with actual assets to check for any differences.[82] To detect corrupt activity, companies should routinely review all payments made,[83] and carry out physical inspections and independent reviews, and have technical systems of data analysis and audits.[84] A company should also have an effective whistleblower policy to help detect corruption. Data analysis, in this context, uses technology to identify anomalies and trends in a large body of transactions. Data analysis tools can be used not only to spot financial numerical trends and anomalies (although that is an obviously useful and significant part of their function), but also to spot relationships between particular individuals and organizations,[85] and hence identify signs of possible corruption. (There is more information later in the book on audits and whistleblower policy.)

This is not an exhaustive list of the types of controls a company should put in place, and there might be other useful measures that would help to combat corruption. A large company should have full-time staff (including accountants and information system architects) dedicated to implementing and reviewing internal controls. The basic steps towards introducing internal controls are to look at where there is a possible risk or weakness that a corrupt employee could exploit, identify the controls that could prevent such a risk, carry out a cost–benefit analysis, and decide, depending on how big the risk is and how cumbersome the controls are, whether to introduce the controls.[86]

It is of course hugely important to ensure that the relevant employees are trained regularly in all the internal controls and policies, so they are used effectively. It is also important to remember that one of the strongest deterrents to corruption is an effective system of capturing problems as soon as they arise. By putting these controls in place a company is helping to deter corrupt activities and bribery.[87] Often management will have the power to override internal controls. This may be important in certain circumstances, but it is an obvious security risk. Part of the job of the internal audit is to counter this risk.

WHISTLEBLOWING POLICIES AND COMMUNICATION

The importance of providing ways in which internal or external parties can raise concerns about bribery is embodied in the Ministry of Justice's fifth principle of preventive procedures – communication. The guidance stresses the importance of two-way communication, rather than a top-down one-way flow of information, and emphasizes the importance of speak-up procedures as well as whistleblowing channels:

> Another important aspect of internal communications is the establishment of a secure, confidential and accessible means for internal or external parties to raise concerns about bribery on the part of associated persons, to provide suggestions for improvement of bribery prevention procedures and controls and for requesting advice. These so called "speak up" procedures can amount to a very helpful management tool for commercial organisations with diverse operations that may be in many countries. If these procedures are to be effective there must be adequate protection for those reporting concerns.[88]

However, no matter how much procedures are improved, they will never be perfect and there will always be some risk. The most effective way of discovering corruption is through tip-offs. A company should therefore have an effective system for whistleblowers.

A whistleblower policy should include a written procedure which describes what will happen if someone reports a suspicion of corrupt activity. It should include details such as who to report to in different situations, and how the report will be handled.[89] The aims of a whistleblower policy are to allow and encourage people to report any suspicious activity. An effective policy can serve as a fraud deterrent just by its existence.[90]

Importantly all whistleblower schemes should make it clear to employees that no repercussions will be taken against any employee who comes forward. The anonymity and confidentiality of the whistleblower should be respected. Companies should try to ensure that a whistleblower suffers no harassment or retaliation for speaking up. Both the appearance and the reality of security and anonymity are necessary to encourage people to come forward.[91] It also needs to be made clear that maliciously raising a false concern against a fellow employee is wrong and will result in disciplinary action.[92]

The 1998 Public Interest Disclosure Act (PIDA) makes it illegal to carry out repercussions against whistleblowers. Specifically if someone comes forward in good faith with information and makes an internal disclosure, then they are protected by law. External disclosures to certain parties are also protected, for example to a lawyer to ask for advice or to Her Majesty's Revenue & Customs (HMRC). External disclosures of information are protected if disclosure through internal channels has been exhausted.[93]

People submitting information should have a choice about where, how, and to whom they submit it. The system should enable anyone with information to make a report. For example they should be able to pass information on to someone other than their direct boss. They should be able to pass on information by phone, email, or post, completely anonymously if they so wish. Employees passing on information should be treated with respect, listened to, and thanked, even if their concerns appear ungrounded.[94] Ideally such a service should be available at all times, and when necessary it should support foreign languages. Preferably there should be external routes for raising the concerns; people should be able to contact an independent separate company to make their complaints,[95] so as to avoid any conflicts of interest. There should also be a system to offer free confidential advice, also ideally run by a separate company.[96] Whistleblowing schemes should also allow people from other companies to make complaints. In some cases, a company might want to demonstrate its commitment to anti-bribery principles by communicating its anti-bribery policies to the wider world. This could raise awareness of avenues for reporting from external parties. The Ministry of Justice guidance notes that:

> A commercial organisation may consider it proportionate and appropriate to communicate its anti-bribery policies and commitment to them to a wider audience, such as other organisations in its sector and to sectoral organisations that would fall outside the scope of the range of its associated persons, or to the general public.[97]

It is important to obtain as much information as possible from the submitter. Well-trained listeners talking on the phone are best. Once information has come to light it is important investigate it thoroughly.[98] It should be policy to report back to the whistleblower in a fixed amount of time to let them know what has happened to the investigation.[99]

The Dodd–Frank Act in the United States (enacted July 2010) has strengthened the whistleblower's hand, arguably at the expense of internal reporting regimes. The provisions of the Dodd-Frank Wall Street Reform and Consumer Protection Act (to give it its full designation) create a financial incentive for employees to report criminal activity directly to the Federal government. Under the Act, employees are promised between a 10 percent and 30 percent share of any financial penalties over $1 million, if they provide original information about unlawful conduct by the corporate. Because this bounty could potentially amount to a substantial chunk of the monetary penalties, the Act gives employees a strong motivation to circumvent the internal reporting procedures and compliance regimes of the corporate and go directly to the Federal government.

AUDITING, MONITORING, AND ADAPTING –
INTERNAL AUDITING PROCEDURES

Internal auditing is an independent appraisal and consulting activity, established within an organization, that uses a systematic approach to examine and evaluate the organization so as to help improve effectiveness and establish its objectives.[100] The role of the internal audit is to provide assurance to management that all key risks are being managed effectively, and where they are not being managed effectively to suggest how internal controls can be improved.[101]

The audit can help prevent bribery and corruption in a number of ways. Auditors may detect evidence of bribery or corruption; they can objectively examine the controls and procedures in place in a company to see whether they are working, and they can examine the cases where controls have been overridden or circumvented by management.

Auditors first need to understand how the company carries out its business and its ethical and anti-bribery policies. They should also be aware of the risks and threats, and the relevant local laws. They should be adequately funded and specially trained. The auditor needs to be independent of the activity being audited, needs to be senior enough in the company to be influential and effect change, and needs to be able to communicate with management or the board.[102] They should have access to all relevant information including whistleblower reports.

During an internal audit, auditors should go through accounts and financial statements looking for anything suspicious or anything that may have been falsified.[103] Auditors should check that both giver and receiver in transactions recorded the same amount of goods or money being transacted at the same time.[104]

Auditors should also measure effectiveness of internal controls,[105] evaluate their design and effectiveness, reassess the risks, review employee compliance, and feed back to the board or managers.[106] Auditors should spot where there is no separation of duties.[107] When auditors examine the cases where controls have been overridden or circumvented by management, they should be professionally skeptical of information they receive, and aware of the possibility of fraud and attempts to cover up bribery.

In these ways the internal audit will be a vital tool in the fight against corruption. The auditors can, and should, be used by management to advise on difficult possibly risky decisions, such as whether to enter a risky contract. The auditors should have a say in the company's anti-corruption policies and the writing of the code of conduct.

As mentioned earlier, risks change with time as new legislation is introduced, new markets are entered, and business strategies change.[108] It is important for companies to monitor and review their anti-corruption policies. An internal audit provides a periodic review of these programs, and can help companies adapt to changes.

Audits should be carried out fairly regularly. There is no set requirement: some processes may need to be audited monthly, while others need be looked at only annually.[109]

AUDITING, MONITORING, AND ADAPTING – EXTERNAL AUDITING PROCEDURES

Companies should also have an external audit. External audits are carried out by someone who is not an employee of the organization, who should be a trained professional with a good understanding of the company, the law, and the risks, and with access to all relevant information.[110]

Smaller businesses that do not have the resources for an internal audit system should use external auditors instead,[111] as a way of assessing their organization and the success of controls and policies. For larger companies, external audits will perform a different role from an external audit. Generally they are audits of a company's financial record. They aim to provide assurance to shareholders that the company is achieving as well as it says it is achieving, and to detect any fraud.[112] External audits can therefore play a part in detecting bribery and corruption. Often a company will have an external audit carried out at least annually.[113]

A large company that has received a bad press report may consider hiring an independent external body to review its anti-bribery controls.[114] If an external body is used for this purpose, the company should consider making the results of the review public.[115]

To ensure that a commercial organization is up to date with best practice in its sector or region of operations, it may wish to seek out gold standard verification of its procedures. The Ministry of Justice notes that:

> organisations might wish to consider seeking some form of external verification or assurance of the effectiveness of anti-bribery procedures. Some organisations may be able to apply for certified compliance with one of the independently-verified anti-bribery standards maintained by industrial sector associations or multilateral bodies.[116]

It is important to note that such verification is useful but not in itself sufficient to absolve the organization of any responsibilities under the Bribery Act.

RED FLAGS

A number of red flags may indicate that corruption has taken or is taking place. It is important to keep an eye out for these, and to ensure that others watch out for them too, in both your own and related companies. The red flags vary depending on exactly the type of corruption that has taken place, but generally they take the form of an unusual pattern of events.

First, refusal by a foreign firm to agree that it will not take any action that may be in violation of anti-bribery laws or to adhere to anti-bribery polices is an obvious sign that something is wrong. Similarly an individual who chooses not to follow all the correct checks and procedures, or receives inappropriately large gifts, should be treated with suspicion.

Of course spotting the telltale signs of corruption is not always so simple. Any unusual activity by a company could be seen as a warning sign that bribery or other corrupt activities are taking place. In particular a lack of transparency in a company's expenses or accounting records and overly complicated deals are both signs that a company may be trying to hide bribes. Frequent use of large sums of petty cash and payments without the proper approval process, for example no countersigning of checks or with management overriding internal controls, may show that bribes are being paid. If a possible business partner appears to lack the qualifications or resources to perform the services offered, or has been recommended by an official of the potential governmental customer, then this is grounds for suspicion. Unusually large or small profit margins is another bribery red flag. Many payments in round amounts is another warning sign. For example companies based in the United States have to report cash payments of above $10,000, so it would constitute a red flag if a company has made a number of payments in round dollar amounts just below this threshold.[117]

Companies should also be aware of payments going offshore to an unusual address, in particular to known money-laundering countries or tax havens that often have very few regulations.[118] A company should be wary of any person or organization based in a known tax haven, and avoid paying agents in tax havens unless there is a good reason.[119]

There may also be signs that a particular individual is corrupt. The individual may be suspiciously too affluent, appear to have an excessive salary,[120] may receive inappropriate gifts or may allow payments through without proper approval processes (such as refusing to sign documents, so as to ensure their name cannot be traced back to any bribery). The employee in question might show red flags in their personality, such as an inability to relax, argumentative moods, personal extravagance, or alcohol or drug abuse, which could lead them to commit corrupt acts. If an employee's family members appear to be suspiciously too affluent, this too could be a result of bribery.

Signs of bid rigging, price fixing, or collusion are evident when one company always wins tenders or always loses, or if there seems to be a rotating pattern of contract allocation. Other red flags fly when it appears that there are too few competitors to make a bid, when some bids are much higher than expected, when the winner subcontracts the work to another bidder, and when a company acts differently in some way from how it has acted in the past in the same situation, without apparent reason.

Prices changing randomly without the costs of goods changing, or staying the same for a very long time, or changing very suddenly, are all red flags that suggest price fixing. If there are any last-minute changes to bids, or if a company submits bids that it cannot honor, these are signs of possible collusion.

When looking at red flags, it is important to keep in mind the known risks of the particular area. An unusual pattern of bids might be much more significant in Russia than in Canada, although nowhere should be assumed to be free from bribery and corruption, so precautions should always be taken.

RECOMMENDED PROCEDURES WHEN BRIBERY IS SUSPECTED IN AN ORGANIZATION (AS EITHER GIVER OR RECEIVER)

A company should have a documented protocol for investigation in the event that evidence of bribery arises.[121]

The first step is to decide to investigate. There should be prompt action at board level to decide the direction of the investigation. The board should not condone, conceal, or fail to address the corruption. A company should decide on its priorities in carrying out the investigation, which might include punishing the wrongdoer, trying to recover company's assets, and protect the company's reputation. This choice will likely effect the other decisions made.

If a company is unsure of how to proceed at any point in investigating, it should seek external legal advice. If bribery takes place in a country that is not the company's home country, legal advice will be needed for both countries. When beginning the investigation a company should check its insurance, as business insurance will in some cases cover the cost of legal expenses.

Self-reporting

The decision should be made early on whether to self-report the bribery to the authorities, and at what stage to do so. In the United Kingdom, apparent incidents of bribery should be reported to the Serious Fraud Office (SFO). The SFO is trying to encourage self-reporting of active bribery by companies. The SFO offers a number of benefits to companies that self-report. These include the possibility of the company avoiding criminal charges and only facing civil charges, the company retaining an element of control over the investigation and over publicity, and the company being able to have a say in how the offense is remedied internally. However the SFO stresses that there are no guarantees. For example in the case of Mabey & Johnson, the company self-reported and still faced criminal charges.[122]

Self-reporting itself is not enough to guarantee an organization leniency from the SFO. The SFO also expects continued cooperation with all of its investigations, both in the United Kingdom and abroad, as well as a resolution to improve and change the company to prevent any other cases of bribery, and a public statement to this effect.[123]

On the other hand the SFO warns that it is getting better at catching corruption, and should the organization not self-report, there is a reasonable chance that the SFO will learn about the corruption from some other source.[124]

The decision whether to self-report is not an easy one to make. Companies are strongly recommended to seek legal advice as soon as bribery is discovered. Companies should weigh up the risks of not reporting with the possible benefits of reporting. With the new Bribery Act not coming into force until July 2011, and a lack of past cases to make judgment from, it is not entirely clear how the SFO's push towards self-reporting will pan out, and it remains to be seen how the authorities will operate in practice. What is clear is that the SFO is trying to emulate the US system of self-reporting, and in the United States many companies have recently decided to go down this route. [125]

Companies should also be aware that the full extent of the corruption may still be unknown. They may want to consider at exactly what point they will approach the SFO, and may decide that they want to begin their own investigations first to make sure that there is a real issue and that self-reporting is really necessary.[126]

DISCOVERING AND INVESTIGATING BRIBERY

When beginning the investigation the company should set up an investigation team that includes some or all of senior management, internal or external lawyers, internal or external IT support (or both), human resources, a public relations team (to minimize reputation damage), and forensic accountants (to examine audit controls and processes). When planning the investigation they may wish to gather interim findings, then reconvene to decide how to investigate.[127]

The investigation should be carried out promptly, objectively, and discreetly. The investigation should be kept confidential for as long as possible, and admitted on a need to know basis only. The investigation should be carried out by trained professionals who know what to do and how to collect evidence. The company should also be willing to cooperate with the relevant authorities if they are involved in the investigation.

The company should decide how to deal with the suspect(s) during the process of the investigation. For example they might allow the individual to work as normal, so they are not tipped off about the investigation, or suspend them on paid leave, so there is no danger of their carrying out any more corrupt acts or destroying evidence if they somehow become aware of the investigation. Ideally the right to suspend an employee during an anti-bribery investigation should be worded into the employee's contract. Otherwise an organization cannot suspend an employee without good reason, but the risk of the suspect destroying evidence should be a sufficient reason for suspension. If suspended, the employee should be asked to return all company property. Relevant third parties, such as anyone from another company who was expecting to communicate with that employee, should be informed that the employee has been suspended.

The investigative team need to act quickly to preserve evidence before it can be destroyed. This means securing all relevant paper and electronic documents. As well as emails and financial records, companies should look at CCTV, security logs, telephone recordings, IT access records, and so on. Information needs to be collected lawfully. Companies should be aware of the legal issues involved in an investigation. In particular a good knowledge of data protection laws is necessary, because if these laws are violated they could make evidence inadmissible or be cause for criminal sanctions against the company. The company may consider requesting help from the courts in securing the evidence, such as asset freezing or obtaining search and seize warrants. When evidence is collected, each item needs to be carefully logged with details of its origin, and the information stored. Companies may need expert help with evidence collecting and storage. Evidence collected should be stored for at least 20 years. Companies should consider consulting third parties, customers, and suppliers for evidence.

If the initial discovery of the corruption was made through a tip-off or if company employees have any testimonial evidence, then the company should look to obtain legally valid witness statements detailing the evidence. These should be in writing, and signed. Companies should be aware that they may need to make an effort to protect the whistleblower and anyone giving evidence. This protection could range from police protection if they feel the people involved are in physical danger, to protecting them from any discrimination within the company if their role becomes known. The identity and details of any whistleblowers should be kept as confidential as possible.

AFTER THE INVESTIGATION

Internally

After the investigation, if clear evidence is obtained of action that is illegal and/or infringes the corporate code, disciplinary action should be taken against the guilty employee(s). This will range from a warning for minor offenses to a dismissal for serious offenses. If the employee has been directly involved in bribery, this is normally considered an offense that warrants immediate dismissal, although care should be taken to conform to legal requirements and corporate policies throughout.

After the investigation is over the company should review its policies and procedures and consider where it could have preformed better, in either deterring the bribery or spotting it sooner.

Externally

Generally a company in which staff are found to have violated anti-bribery regulations will have to deal with the relevant authorities. The 2010 UK Bribery Act allows companies to argue that they had "adequate" anti-bribery measures in place. This can act as an affirmative defense and the company can avoid any prosecution, although individuals may still be prosecuted.[128]

A guilty company will generally be given an opportunity to negotiate a civil settlement with the relevant authorities (as was the case for Balfour Beatty and AMEC), or be subject to a criminal prosecution and plea negotiation around that (as in the cases involving Innospec and BAE). The SFO points out that:

> the benefit [of self-reporting] to the corporate will be the prospect (in appropriate cases) of a civil rather than a criminal outcome as well as the opportunity to manage, with us, the issues and any publicity proactively. The corporate will be seen to have acted responsibly by the wider community in taking action to remedy what has happened in the past and to have moved on to a new and better corporate culture. Furthermore, a negotiated settlement rather than a criminal prosecution means that the [possibility of] debarment provisions under Article 45 of the EU Public Sector Procurement Directive in 2004 will not apply.[129]

The SFO stresses that driving up corporate standards and establishing a robust anti-corruption culture is key to the outcome it is set on achieving. It explains that self-referral 'leading to a civil outcome in appropriate cases is one tool for this: criminal prosecution and confiscation in other cases is another vital tool we shall be using.'[130]

When reporting to the SFO, timing is a crucial issue for a corporate and its advisers. The SFO states that:

> We appreciate that a corporate will not want to approach us unless it had decided, following advice and a degree of investigation by its professional advisers, that there is a real issue and that remedial action is necessary. There may also be earlier engagement between the advisers and us in order to obtain an early indication where appropriate (and subject to a detailed review of the facts) of our approach. We would find that helpful but we appreciate that this is for the corporate and its advisers

to consider. We would also take the view that the timing of an approach to the US Department of Justice is also relevant. If the case is also within our jurisdiction we would expect to be notified at the same time as the DoJ.[131]

The SFO states that it will seek to settle self-referral cases civilly wherever possible. This is likely to occur when it is satisfied with the answers to the following questions:

- Is the board of the corporate genuinely committed to resolving the issue and moving to a better corporate culture?
- Is the corporate prepared to work with us on the scope and handling of any additional investigation we consider to be necessary?
- At the end of the investigation (and assuming acknowledgment of a problem) will the corporate be prepared to discuss resolution of the issue on the basis, for example, of restitution through civil recovery, a programme of training and culture change, appropriate action where necessary against individuals and at least in some cases external monitoring in a proportionate manner?
- Does the corporate understand that any resolution must satisfy the public interest and must be transparent? This will almost invariably involve a public statement although the terms of this will be discussed and agreed by the corporate and us.
- Will the corporate want us, where possible, to work with regulators and criminal enforcement authorities, both in the UK and abroad, in order to reach a global settlement?[132]

The SFO will seek to impose reparations, cultural change, and improvement of anti-bribery regulations in the affected company. Often it will also request that an external compliance monitor enter the company (at the company's expense) to check that it is implementing new anti-bribery policies and complying with them. All of these issues will to some extent be up for discussion as part of plea negotiations,. However in the end the sentencing will remain at the discretion of a judge. The SFO will require a public statement from the company. It will also look to prosecute the guilty individuals: that is, those who were directly involved in the bribery or corruption.

CASE STUDIES FROM THE MINISTRY OF JUSTICE

The Ministry of Justice has provided guidance by way of 11 illustrative case studies that accompany the official guidance about procedures that businesses can put into place to prevent bribery. They serve to illuminate the six principles upon which adequate preventive procedures are likely to be based, through discussion of hypothetical scenarios. The considerations that are discussed in the cases studies are helpful, and have been reproduced here from the guidance.[133] It is important to note that the case studies are not intended to be the final word or to provide an exhaustive list of possible procedures.

Case study 1 – Principle 1: Facilitation payments

A medium-sized company ("A") has acquired a new customer in a foreign country ("B") where it operates through its agent company ("C"). Its bribery risk assessment has identified facilitation payments as a significant problem in securing reliable importation into B and transport to its new customer's manufacturing locations. These sometimes take the form of "inspection fees" required before B's import inspectors will issue a certificate of inspection and thereby facilitate the clearance of goods.

A could consider any or a combination of the following:

- communication of its policy of non-payment of facilitation payments to C and its staff
- seeking advice on the law of B relating to certificates of inspection and fees for these, to differentiate between properly payable fees and disguised requests for facilitation payments
- building realistic timescales into the planning of the project so that shipping, importation, and delivery schedules allow where feasible for resisting and testing demands for facilitation payments
- requesting that C train its staff about resisting demands for facilitation payments, the relevant local law, and provisions of the Bribery Act 2010
- proposing or including as part of any contractual arrangement certain procedures for C and its staff, which may include one or more of the following, if appropriate:
  - questioning of legitimacy of demands
  - requesting receipts and identification details of the official making the demand
  - requests to consult with superior officials
  - trying to avoid paying "inspection fees" (if not properly due) in cash and directly to an official
  - informing those demanding payments that compliance with the demand may mean that A (and possibly C) will commit an offense under UK law
  - informing those demanding payments that it will be necessary for C to inform the UK embassy of the demand
- Maintaining close liaison with C so as to keep abreast of any local developments that may provide solutions, and encouraging C to develop its own strategies based on local knowledge.
- use of any UK diplomatic channels or participation in locally active

NGOs, so as to apply pressure on the authorities of **B** to take action to stop demands for facilitation payments.

Case study 2 – Principle 1: Proportionate procedures

A small to medium-sized installation company is operating entirely within the UK domestic market. It relies to varying degrees on independent consultants to facilitate business opportunities and to assist in the preparation of both pre-qualification submissions and formal tenders in seeking new business. Such consultants work on an arms' length fee-plus-expenses basis. They are engaged by sales staff and selected because of their extensive network of business contacts and specialist information. The reason for engaging them is to enhance the company's prospects of being included in tender and pre-qualification lists and of being selected as main contractors or subcontractors. The reliance on consultants, and in particular difficulties in monitoring expenditure which sometimes involves cash transactions, has been identified by the company as a source of medium to high risk of bribery being undertaken on the company's behalf.

In seeking to mitigate these risks the company could consider any or a combination of the following:

- Communication of a policy statement committing the company to transparency and zero tolerance of bribery in pursuit of its business objectives. The statement could be communicated to the company's employees, known consultants, and external contacts, such as sectoral bodies and local chambers of commerce.
- Firming up its due diligence before engaging consultants. This could include making enquiries through business contacts, local chambers of commerce, business associations, or internet searches, and following up any business references and financial statements.
- Considering firming up the terms of the consultants' contracts so that they reflect a commitment to zero tolerance of bribery, set clear criteria for provision of bona fide hospitality on the company's behalf, and define in detail the basis of remuneration, including expenses.
- Consider making consultants' contracts subject to periodic review and renewal.
- Drawing up key points guidance on preventing bribery for its sales staff and all other staff involved in bidding for business, and when engaging consultants.
- Periodically emphasizing these policies and procedures at meetings. For example, this might form a standing item on meeting agendas every few months.
- Providing a confidential means for staff and external business contacts to air any suspicions of the use of bribery.

Case study 3 – Principles 1 and 6: Joint venture

A medium-sized company ("**D**") is interested in significant foreign mineral deposits. **D** proposes to enter into a joint venture with a local mining company ("**E**"). It is proposed that **D** and **E** would have an equal holding in the joint venture company ("**DE**"). **D** identifies the necessary interaction between **DE** and local public officials as a source of significant risks of bribery.

   D could consider negotiating for the inclusion of any or a combination of the following bribery prevention procedures into the agreement setting up **DE**:

- Parity of representation on the board of **DE**.
- That **DE** put in place measures designed to ensure compliance with all applicable bribery and corruption laws. These measures might cover such issues as:
  - gifts and hospitality
  - agreed decision-making rules
  - procurement
  - engagement of third parties, including due diligence requirements
  - conduct of relations with public officials
  - training for staff in high-risk positions
  - record keeping and accounting.
- The establishment of an audit committee with at least one representative of each of **D** and **E**, which has the power to view accounts and certain expenditure, and prepare regular reports.
- Binding commitments by **D** and **E** to comply with all applicable bribery laws in relation to the operation of **DE**, with a breach by either **D** or **E** being a breach of the agreement between them. Where such a breach is a material breach this could lead to termination or other similarly significant consequences.

Case study 4 – Principles 1 and 5: Hospitality and promotional expenditure

A firm of engineers ("**F**") maintains a program of annual events providing entertainment, quality dining and attendance at various sporting occasions, as an expression of appreciation of its long association with its business partners. Private bodies and individuals are happy to meet their own travel and accommodation costs associated with attending these events. The costs of the travel and accommodation of any foreign public officials attending are, however, met by **F**.

   F could consider any or a combination of the following:

- conducting a bribery risk assessment relating to its dealings with

181

business partners and foreign public officials, and in particular the provision of hospitality and promotional expenditure
- publication of a policy statement committing it to transparent, proportionate, reasonable, and bona fide hospitality and promotional expenditure
- the issue of internal guidance on procedures that apply to the provision of hospitality and/or promotional expenditure, providing:
  - that any procedures are designed to seek to ensure transparency and conformity with any relevant laws and codes applying to F
  - that any procedures are designed to seek to ensure transparency and conformity with the relevant laws and codes applying to foreign public officials
  - that any hospitality should reflect a desire to cement good relations and show appreciation, and that promotional expenditure should seek to improve the image of F as a commercial organization, to better present its products or services, or establish cordial relations
  - that the recipient should not be given the impression that they are under an obligation to confer any business advantage or that the recipient's independence will be affected
- criteria to be applied when deciding the appropriate levels of hospitality for both private and public business partners, clients, suppliers, and foreign public officials, and the type of hospitality that is appropriate in different sets of circumstances
- that provision of hospitality for public officials be cleared with the relevant public body so that it is clear who and what the hospitality is for
- for expenditure over certain limits, approval by an appropriately senior level of management may be a relevant consideration
- accounting (book-keeping, orders, invoices, delivery notes, etc)
- regular monitoring, review and evaluation of internal procedures and compliance with them
- appropriate training and supervision provided to staff.

Case study 5 – Principle 3: Assessing risks

A small specialist manufacturer is seeking to expand its business in one of several emerging markets, all of which offer comparable opportunities. It has no specialist risk assessment expertise, and is unsure how to go about assessing the risks of entering a new market.

The small manufacturer could consider any or a combination of the following:

- incorporating an assessment of bribery risk into research to identify the optimum market for expansion
- seeking advice from UK diplomatic services and government organizations such as UK Trade and Investment

- consulting general country assessments undertaken by local chambers of commerce, relevant NGOs, and sectoral organizations
- seeking advice from industry representatives
- following up any general or specialist advice with further independent research.

Case study 6 – Principle 4: Due diligence of agents

A medium to large-sized manufacturer of specialist equipment ("**G**") has an opportunity to enter an emerging market in a foreign country ("**H**") by way of a government contract to supply equipment to the state. Local convention requires any foreign commercial organizations to operate through a local agent. G is concerned to appoint a reputable agent and ensure that the risk of bribery being used to develop its business in the market is minimized.

G could consider any or a combination of the following:

- compiling a suitable questionnaire for potential agents requiring for example, details of ownership if not an individual; CVs and references for those involved in performing the proposed service; details of any directorships held, existing partnerships and third-party relationships, and any relevant judicial or regulatory findings
- having a clear statement of the precise nature of the services offered, costs, commissions, fees, and the preferred means of remuneration
- undertaking research, including internet searches, of the prospective agents and, if a corporate body, of every person identified as having a degree of control over its affairs
- making enquiries with the relevant authorities in **H** to verify the information received in response to the questionnaire
- following up references and clarifying any matters arising from the questionnaire or any other information received with the agents, arranging face-to-face meetings where appropriate
- requesting sight or evidence of any potential agent's own anti-bribery policies and, where a corporate body, reporting procedures and records
- being alert to key commercial questions such as:
    - Is the agent really required?
    - Does the agent have the required expertise?
    - Are they interacting with or closely connected to public officials?
    - Is what you are proposing to pay reasonable and commercial?
- renewing due diligence enquiries on a periodic basis if an agent is appointed.

Case study 7 – Principle 5: Communicating and training

A small UK manufacturer of specialist equipment ("**J**") has engaged an individual as a local agent and adviser ("**K**") to assist with winning a contract and developing its business in a foreign country where the risk of bribery is assessed as high.

J could consider any or a combination of the following:

- making employees of J engaged in bidding for business fully aware of J's anti-bribery statement, code of conduct, and where appropriate, that details of its anti-bribery policies are included in its tender
- including suitable contractual terms on bribery prevention measures in the agreement between J and K, for example: requiring K not to offer or pay bribes; giving J the ability to audit K's activities and expenditure; requiring K to report any requests for bribes by officials to J; and, in the event of suspicion arising over K's activities, giving J the right to terminate the arrangement
- making employees of J fully aware of policies and procedures applying to relevant issues such as hospitality and facilitation payments, including all financial control mechanisms, sanctions for any breaches of the rules, and instructions on how to report any suspicious conduct
- supplementing the information, where appropriate, with specially prepared training to J's staff involved with the foreign country.

Case study 8 – Principles 1, 4, and 6: Community benefits and charitable donations

A company ("L") exports a range of seed products to growers around the globe. Its representative travels to a foreign country ("M") to discuss with a local farming cooperative the possible supply of a new strain of wheat that is resistant to a disease which recently swept the region. In the meeting, the head of the cooperative tells L's representative about the problems that the relative unavailability of antiretroviral drugs cause locally in the face of a high HIV infection rate.

In a subsequent meeting with an official of M to discuss the approval of L's new wheat strain for import, the official suggests that L could pay for the necessary antiretroviral drugs, and that this will be a very positive factor in the government's consideration of the license to import the new seed strain. In a further meeting, the same official states that L should donate money to a certain charity suggested by the official, which, the official assures the employee of L, will then take the necessary steps to purchase and distribute the drugs. L identifies this as raising potential bribery risks.

L could consider any or a combination of the following:

- making reasonable efforts to conduct due diligence, including consultation with staff members and any business partners it has in country M in order to satisfy itself that the suggested arrangement is legitimate and in conformity with any relevant laws and codes applying to the foreign public official responsible for approving the product, which it could do by obtaining information on:

- **M**'s local law on community benefits as part of government procurement, and if there is no particular local law, the official status and legitimacy of the suggested arrangement
- the particular charity in question, including its legal status, its reputation in **M**, and whether it has conducted similar projects
- any connections the charity might have with the foreign official in question, if possible
- adopting an internal communication plan designed to ensure that any relationships with charitable organizations are conducted in a transparent and open manner and do not raise any expectation of the award of a contract or license
- adopting company-wide policies and procedures about the selection of charitable projects or initiatives which are informed by appropriate risk assessments
- training and support for staff in implementing the relevant policies and procedures of communication which allow issues to be reported and compliance to be monitored
- if charitable donations made in country **M** are routinely channeled through government officials or to others at the official's request, a red flag should be raised, and **L** may seek to monitor the way its contributions are ultimately applied, or investigate alternative methods of donation such as official "offset" or "community gain" arrangements with the government of **M**
- evaluation of its policies relating to charitable donations as part of its next periodic review of its anti-bribery procedures.

Case study 9 – Principle 4: Due diligence of agents

A small UK company ("**N**") relies on agents in a country ("**P**") from which it imports local high-quality perishable produce and to which it exports finished goods. The bribery risks it faces arise entirely as a result of its reliance on agents and their relationship with local businesspeople and officials. **N** is offered a new business opportunity in **P** through a new agent ("**Q**"). An agreement with **Q** needs to be concluded quickly.

N could consider any or a combination of the following:

- conducting due diligence and background checks on **Q** that are proportionate to the risk before engaging **Q**, which could include:
  - making enquiries through **N**'s business contacts, local chambers of commerce or business associations, or internet searches
  - seeking business references and a financial statement from **Q**, and reviewing **Q**'s CV to ensure **Q** has suitable experience
- considering how best to structure the relationship with **Q**, including

how **Q** should be remunerated for its services and how to seek to ensure
Q's compliance with relevant laws and codes applying to foreign public
officials
- making the contract with **Q** renewable annually or periodically
- traveling to **P** periodically to review the agency situation.

Case study 10 – Principle 2: Top-level commitment

A small to medium-sized component manufacturer is seeking contracts
in markets abroad where there is a risk of bribery. As part of its preparation, a senior manager has devoted some time to participation in the
development of a sector wide anti-bribery initiative.

The top-level management of the manufacturer could consider any or a
combination of the following:

- the making of a clear statement disseminated to its staff and key business partners of its commitment to carry out business fairly, honestly,
  and openly, referencing its key bribery prevention procedures and its
  involvement in the sectoral initiative
- establishing a code of conduct that includes suitable anti-bribery
  provisions and making it accessible to staff and third parties on its
  website
- considering an internal launch of a code of conduct, with a message of
  commitment to it from senior management
- senior management emphasizing among the workforce and other associated persons the importance of understanding and applying the code
  of conduct, and the consequences of breaching the policy or contractual
  provisions relating to bribery prevention for employees and managers
  and external associated persons
- identifying someone of a suitable level of seniority to be a point-person
  for queries and issues relating to bribery risks.

Case study 11 – Proportionate procedures

A small export company operates through agents in a number of different
foreign countries. Having identified bribery risks associated with its reliance on agents, it is considering developing proportionate and risk-based
bribery prevention procedures.

The company could consider any or a combination of the following:

- using trade fairs and trade publications to communicate periodically its
  anti-bribery message and, where appropriate, some detail of its policies
  and procedures
- oral or written communication of its bribery prevention intentions to
  all of its agents

- adopting measures designed to address bribery on its behalf by associated persons, such as:
  - requesting relevant information and conducting background searches on the internet against information received
  - making sure references are in order and followed up
  - including anti-bribery commitments in any contract renewal
  - using existing internal arrangements such as periodic staff meetings to raise awareness of "red flags" as regards agents' conduct, for example evasive answers to straightforward requests for information, overly elaborate payment arrangements involving further third parties, and ad hoc or unusual requests for expense reimbursement not properly covered by accounting procedures
- making use of any external sources of information (UKTI, sectoral organizations) on bribery risks in particular markets, and using the data to inform relationships with particular agents
- making sure staff have a confidential means to raise any concerns about bribery.

9

WHO WOULD BE A DIRECTOR?
DIRECTORS' LIABILITY

Directors found guilty of a bribery offense can expect to receive a jail term from the courts. Two recent cases under existing UK legislation emphasize the risk of the severe penalties directors run if they become involved in corruption, and provide sobering illustrations of how incidents may come to light.

THE SALES DIRECTOR AND "A SMALL PART" IN CORRUPTION

Mabey & Johnson Ltd was the first company successfully prosecuted in the UK for overseas corruption.[1] The details of the corruption appear to have come to light as a result of an internal investigation undertaken by the company solicitors. This investigation was sparked by allegations made by a former Mabey manager in litigation brought by Mabey against him. In the course of the former manager's defense he in turn made damaging allegations about Mabey. Allegations had also appeared in the media.

Mabey entered into a contract to supply 13 bridges under the UN Oil for Food Programme, a scheme introduced to alleviate hardship for the Iraqi people. The illegal kickback payments of over €420,000 secured the contract with the Iraqi government and represented 10 percent of the total contract value. This kickback was required to be paid before products could cross the Iraqi border. If it had not been paid, the goods would not have been permitted to enter the country and Mabey would not have received payment.

The kickback was characterized as "commission" payable to Mabey's local representative, Upper Gulf Agencies (UGA), and added onto the contract. Mabey did not as a result bear the cost of making this kickback payment. Richard Gledhill, a sales manager, negotiated the contract with the Iraqi government and obtained approval from Charles Forsyth and David Mabey (both directors) to make the kickback payments via UGA.

It was an offense to make funds available to the Government of Iraq without the authority of a license granted by HM Treasury, and no license had been applied for by Mabey & Johnson. Mabey & Johnson itself pleaded guilty to violating UN sanctions, It was fined £6.6 million in 2009, and submitted its internal compliance program to a Serious Fraud Office (SFO)-approved independent monitor.

Richard Alderman, the director of the SFO, said about the guilty plea:

> These are serious offences and it is significant that Mabey & Johnson has cooperated with us to get to this landmark point. This has enabled this case to be dealt with in just over a year and is a model for other companies who want to self report corruption and have it dealt with quickly and fairly by the SFO.[2]

He said after the sentence:

> This is a landmark outcome. The first conviction in this country of a company for overseas corruption and for breaking the UN Iraq sanctions and, satisfyingly, achieved quickly. The offences are serious ones but the company has played its part positively by recognising the unacceptability of those past business practices and by coming forward to report them and engage constructively with the SFO. I urge other companies who might see some parallels for them, to come and talk to us and have the matter dealt with quickly and fairly.[3]

The SFO continued to investigate the roles of Gledhill, Mabey, and Forsyth, and each was subsequently charged with breaching UN sanctions. Gledhill, the former sales manager, pleaded guilty and gave evidence for the prosecution. He received an eight-month prison sentence, suspended for two years. The crown court jury also convicted former directors Forsyth and Mabey, and each received a prison sentence. Judge Rivlin said "The bare truth of this case is that Mr Forsyth bears the most culpability."[4] He said of Mabey, "When a director of a major company plays even a small part, he can expect to receive a custodial sentence."[5] Richard Alderman expressed approval of the outcome.

THE CEO AND SUBSTANTIAL PAYMENTS TO SENIOR GOVERNMENT OFFICIALS

Julian Messent headed the Property (Americas) Division at PWS International, a London-based insurance business, now in administration, responsible for obtaining contracts for reinsurance in Central and South America.[6] Messent's contract of employment entitled him to an annual bonus, calculated as a percentage of the brokerage produced by him, less commissions paid to third parties and other expenses. Between 1999 and 2002, PWS acted as broker on behalf of Instituto Nacional de Seguros (INS), which in turn was the insurer for Instituto Costarricense de Electricidad (ICE).

INS is the Costa Rican state monopoly supplier of insurance. ICE is the Costa Rican state-run electricity and telecommunications company. ICE covered Costa Rica's electricity generation and supply infrastructure.

Messent authorized 41 corrupt payments totaling $1,982,230.77 to be paid to Costa Rican officials, their wives, and associated companies, as inducements or rewards for assisting in the appointment or retention of PWS International as broker of a lucrative reinsurance policy for INS.

Following elections in Costa Rica in 2002, officials in INS and ICE were replaced. Enquiries were made into the contract with PWS, and questions were raised about payments made under it. The UK Foreign and Commonwealth Office referred the case to the SFO in October 2005 and the case was accepted for investigation in August 2006.

In April 2010 Messent was charged. He had started plea negotiations under the attorney-general's guidelines with the SFO, and these were successfully concluded in September 2010. In October 2010 he pleaded guilty to two counts of making corrupt payments between February 1999 and June 2002, contrary to section 1(1) of the Prevention of Corruption Act 1906. He also asked for 39 similar offenses to be taken into consideration.

Judge Rivlin, when sentencing, highlighted six aggravating and six mitigating features of Messent's case.[7]

The aggravating features

- First and foremost, he was a director.
- The corruption involved bribes to government officials.
- The offenses took place over a lengthy period.
- Large sums of money were involved.
- The bribes were paid from state funds (through increased costs).
- Messent benefited significantly as a result of the bribery.

The mitigating factors

- He cooperated and pleaded guilty.
- He did not initiate the corrupt relationship between PWS, INS, and ICE.
- The cost of the PWS reinsurance was competitive. PWS made some contribution to Costa Rican charities.
- Messent was a man of previously positive good character.
- The financial consequences of the offending were serious.
- There were implications for his family, his employment, and his future employment.

Messent was sentenced to 21 months imprisonment on each count, to run concurrently.[8] He was ordered to pay £100,000 in compensation to the Republic of Costa Rica, and was disqualified from acting as a company director for five years. Richard Alderman commented afterwards that Messent's sentence reflected his early cooperation with the authorities.

THE "DIRECTOR" OF MARKETING

Robert Dougall received a custodial sentence for his part in a corrupt scheme in Greece relating to the sale of orthopaedic products.[9] The sentence was subsequently suspended on appeal, but this should not give a false sense of security as the Appeal Court judges listed no less than 14 mitigating factors. One of those listed was the fact that he was "never a statutory director." This case does not undermine the proposition that a director of a company can expect to face a custodial sentence if convicted of a bribery offense.

Prosecutions of directors have historically been exceptions rather than the rule, and without a director's involvement in bribery, the likelihood of prosecution and securing a conviction was practically impossible. In each of the cases mentioned above, the court found that the director was personally implicated in the bribery.

The SFO has said that liability for violations of the Bribery Act will be brought directly into the boardroom,[10] and while it is true that the risks to directors and senior officers have increased under the Bribery Act, the SFO statement masks some complexity in this legislation.

It is Section 14 of the Bribery Act upon which the SFO tends to rely when it makes this statement. On the face of it Section 14 is fairly straightforward, and provides a direct route to prosecution of directors. In this context it is important to note that there are a number of criteria to be met. One of these is that the corporate body is also successfully prosecuted for the same offense. In order to prove the case against the corporate, the prosecution will need to show, as it did before the passage of the Bribery Act, that the directing mind of the corporate participated in the bribery. This has historically been hard (though not impossible) to prove. The SFO believe that compliance or steps taken to try to comply with Section 7 of the Bribery Act by way of putting in place adequate procedures to prevent bribery will assist in the prosecution of corporates under Sections 1, 2, and/or 6. Clearly the tone from the top and the likelihood that boards of directors will now be more involved will help.

In particular, it is anticipated that the likelihood of liability under Section 14 will increase if, having been made aware of a bribery problem as a result of having put in place adequate procedures, the board does nothing about it, and the problem recurs. For companies that as a result contemplate that doing nothing might be the better option to avoid knowledge at board level, the SFO has also flagged the risk of not putting in place any procedures to prevent bribery in high-risk situations. This would be regarded as being tantamount to being wilfully blind to the risk, and again would create liability under Section 14 of the Act. It is a case maybe of damned if you do and damned if you don't. However, in truth, the full application of Section 14 remains to be seen and the jury is still out. Businesses should err on the side of caution and put in place adequate procedures to prevent bribery. One thing is certain: doing nothing is very risky.

Under the UK Proceeds of Crime Act 2002 (POCA), a fresh stand-alone offense is committed if someone enters into or becomes concerned in an arrangement which they know or suspect facilitates (by whatever means) the acquisition, retention, use, or control of criminal property by or on behalf of another.

For example, if as a result of due diligence on a third party (undertaken as part of having put in place adequate procedures to prevent bribery) a board of directors suspects that a contract was or is to be obtained using corrupt means, it will be at risk of committing a money-laundering offense.

Section 328 of POCA outlines the situation:[11]

328 Arrangements
(1) A person commits an offence if he enters into or becomes concerned in an arrangement which he knows or suspects facilitates (by whatever means) the acquisition, retention, use or control of criminal property by or on behalf of another person.

There is a potential defense available, that of informing the police. Under Section 328 (2):

(2) But a person does not commit such an offence if:
    (a) he makes an authorised disclosure under section 338 and (if the disclosure is made before he does the act mentioned in subsection (1)) he has the appropriate consent.[12]

Under POCA, contracts and assets (wherever they are located in the world) acquired directly or indirectly as a result of a bribe are at risk of confiscation. The amount subject to confiscation is not limited to net profits of the relevant contract but by its value. At a minimum, this means total revenues under the contract.

English courts have referred to POCA as "justifiably draconian."[13]

In summary, through "adequate procedures," the Bribery Act forces organizations to root around in the closet. If they find something, directors, who are forced to be aware of such examples as a result of compliance with the Bribery Act, face the unhappy choice of whether or not to self-report. Doing so could also force disclosure in the United States.

Richard Alderman has spoken before of this dilemma, and said this:

I could give you a number of reasons why I think [keeping quiet] would be wrong. Let me though just give you one. Which of you would like to go and visit your CEO and CFO in a police station where they are being held following arrest on money-laundering charges? Those charges will be based upon decisions by the CEO and CFO on your advice that disclosure will not be made to the SFO and that the benefit of the corruption will therefore be retained within the corporate. I can imagine some difficult discussions.[14]

PART IV

THE LAW ENFORCEMENT RESPONSE

10

FORCES FIGHTING BRIBERY

Bribery and corruption are being targeted by a growing number of agencies and institutions, as the perception grows that they threaten social stability and open markets. These agencies range from corporations through to police forces, transnational economic and political institutions, trade and industry bodies, specialist ethical agencies, and lobbying groups.

The police are at the forefront of this battle. They have received new tools (such as the UK Bribery Act), and old tools like the US Foreign Corrupt Practices Act (FCPA) have been invigorated, to boost their fight. That said, we all know that the countries where bribery takes place are unlikely to give much evidence or be much help, largely because bribery is either a way of doing business, or because local politicians (possibly in league with the bribe recipients) will seek to put a stop to investigations by foreign law enforcement agencies.

Yet bribery has risen up the scale of police priorities, alongside, and indeed in tandem with, a growing assault on economic crime. Police and other prosecution bodies link bribery and corruption with fraud, as deeply corrosive of society's values and security. The two forms of economic crime differ in that fraud is a form of theft on individuals or defined groups of individuals (or classes of individuals such as shareholders), whereas bribery is a theft from the wider society. Bribery also involves two willing parties, the giver and the receiver of the bribe, whereas fraud typically involves criminal parties either acting separately or in consort to dupe an innocent. The closest comparison to bribery in the context of a fraud is the organized gang's corruption of an inside official in a bank or a company, to help them defraud the employee's institution.

Law enforcement's role in tackling bribery is complicated by the fact that the two willing parties to a bribe are typically in different countries. This requires police cooperation across borders. Such cooperation is rarely straightforward, but the issue is doubly difficult because recipients of bribes are frequently in countries where external investigators are dealing with local corporations. They might be aligned with unreliable local politicians who have the power to slow down or stymie external investigations. In short, the obstacles against cross-border bribery investigations and prosecutions succeeding are formidable.

UK law enforcers have responded to these obstacles by seeking to raise their game. They have done this by forming specialist agencies to deal with corruption, and by building teamwork between existing organizations to focus on bribery. One such new agency is the Overseas Anti-Corruption Unit (OACU) – a multi-agency taskforce staffed by the Metropolitan Police and City of London Police, and dedicated to investigating international corruption and bribery by UK businesses in other countries.

Inter-agency collaboration in tackling international corruption and bribery is critical, says Detective Chief Inspector Steve Head of the City of London Police:

> Investigation of overseas corruption and bribery is still a relatively new, but nevertheless crucial dimension of UK policing. Our dedicated resources will make it possible for us to target international corruption and we have already secured the first UK conviction. Our work in conjunction with the Serious Fraud Office, the Metropolitan Police Service and other international law enforcement agencies has enabled us to take a global lead in this vital area of work.[1]

The conviction to which Head refers was a plea bargain in August 2008 resulting in a five-month suspended sentence for the managing director of UK security company The CBRN Team, who paid two Ugandan officials £83,000 to secure a contract worth £210,000 to cover a Commonwealth event in that country. One of the Ugandan officials served six months on remand before confessing and releasing £52,800 from his bank account to the City of London Police for restitution. American law firm Fulbright and Jaworski remarked on the potential power of British anti-corruption law in this case:

> The UK's ability to prosecute the foreign official who took the bribe sets the UK's legislation apart from the Foreign Corrupt Practices Act. Under the FCPA, only the giver of a bribe, and not the foreign official who received the bribe, may be prosecuted. For all the criticism that the UK's foreign bribery legislation has received in recent years, those laws are stronger than the FCPA.[2]

THE UK ANTI-CORRUPTION AGENCIES

The task of policing UK corruption and bribery is currently divided between various authorities, including the OACU, the Serious Fraud Office (SFO), the Serious and Organised Crime Agency (SOCA), and regulators of industry, such as the Financial Services Authority (FSA), which have responsibility for their particular sectors. The case of AON, for example, was investigated by the FSA rather than the SFO or City of London Police, says Transparency International's Robert Barrington, for two reasons: first, because it is the regulator for the insurance industry, and second, because the infringement was regarded more as a regulatory offense, rather than a criminal one.[3]

SOCA focuses on providing training programs and intelligence collection. The agency has national responsibility for receiving, analyzing, and disseminating financial intelligence submitted through the Suspicious Activity Reports (SARs) regime. Under the UK Bribery Act, lawyer Jonathan Fisher argues that businesspeople will have a legal duty to inform SOCA's Financial Intelligence Unit of every occasion where a facilitation payment is made, regardless of the size of the payment.[4] The novelty of this duty is disputed by Barry Vitou, who points out that, because facilitation payments are already illegal under UK law and money laundering legislation has been in force for a decade, any reporting obligation (if in the relevant circumstances there is one) with regard to facilitation payments, already exists.[5]

While the Bribery Act has put the focus on corruption, in fact UK law enforcement experts expect to link it with other offenses to raise the profile of the offense. These offenses include money laundering and fraud. At a conference in Belgium, SFO director Richard Alderman pointed to this bigger picture:

> We have tended to concentrate on corruption offences by themselves. What we have been doing recently though and I certainly see this developing much more in the future, is to make the important link between corruption and money laundering. We are starting to do this in cases. I expect to see far more of this work in future. I expect us to follow the money against a range of individuals and organisations so that all of those involved in corruption and the laundering of corrupt monies are dealt with by prosecution or through some other way. It seems to me that there is a very great deal of potential in this area.[6]

An SFO press release of February 16, 2011 explained the way in which it used the Proceeds of Crime Act 2002:

> The Serious Fraud Office (SFO) has taken action in the High Court today which has resulted in an Order for the company, M.W. Kellogg Limited (MWKL), to pay just over £7 million in recognition of sums it is due to receive which were generated through the criminal activity of third parties. The High Court made the Order under Part 5 of the Proceeds of Crime Act 2002. The SFO recognised that MWKL took no part in the criminal activity which generated the funds. The funds due to MWKL are share dividends payable from profits and revenues generated by contracts obtained by bribery and corruption undertaken by MWKL's

parent company and others. The agreement will lead to the payment of £7,028,077 within fourteen days in full and final settlement of the case. This sum represents the share dividends due and the interest which has accrued on these sums. The contracts were awarded to a company partly owned by MWKL on behalf of its US parent company. MWKL reported concerns to the SFO under the "self referral" scheme and fully co-operated with the subsequent investigation. The SFO, working in partnership with the US Department of Justice, reviewed the conduct of MWKL and decided that the most appropriate approach was to remove the funds which will become due to the company through the unlawful conduct. This reflects the finding that MWKL was used by the parent company and was not a willing participant in the corruption.[7]

Businesses have good reason to fear the aggressive use of this existing UK legislation. Vitou and Kovalevsky explain that:

> Under the Proceeds of Crime Act, contracts and assets (wherever located in the world) acquired directly or indirectly as a result of a bribe will be at risk of confiscation. The amount subject to confiscation is not limited to net profits of the relevant contract but by its value. At a minimum, this means total revenues under the contract.[8]

A further agency taking this approach is the Proceeds of Corruption Unit, within the Specialist and Economic Crime Directorate of the Metropolitan Police. This was set up in 2004 to investigate foreign officials who siphon off public money and transfer it through the United Kingdom. Key to the success of the crackdown on demand-side bribery is to increase the risk of prosecution for those foreign officials who demand, or are on the receiving end of, corrupt payments. A senior British police officer related a hypothetical scenario which explains how the concept of a "politically exposed person" fits into the picture of corruption:

> If you're the head of the state, and somebody comes to you and says, "We want the rights to your oil, and we will pay you, as an individual, this amount of money." That money is a trade deal in effect, that you should put back into the development of your country. But you don't, you take it out, you asset strip from your own country, and you put it into a bank account in London. The bank in London shouldn't be taking that asset-stripped money. This politically exposed person has inappropriately taken money which should belong to the state and has put it in a different country's jurisdiction. He's laundered it through a process, to ensure that the state's money is now his money.[9]

The Proceeds of Corruption Unit has had a number of high-profile successes in targeting corrupt politically exposed persons and confiscating the benefits they have generated through corruption. The unit's head, Detective Inspector Paul Whatmore, explains that they enjoy "a good relationship [with other UK agencies] in that if we uncover something that we think sits with them more than us then we refer it to them, and vice versa."[10] The increasingly collaborative approach is further evidenced by SOCA's Counter Corruption Department, which supports all UK police forces in their battle against corruption, as well as delivering an anti-corruption training course.

UK investigations have previously been divided between the SFO and City of London's OACU based on an assessment of whether the suspected offense is committed by an individual or on behalf of a corporate controlling mind. The SFO would investigate a case where a decision had been taken at a senior corporate level to pay bribes to gain influence (or, under the Bribery Act, where a company has failed to take adequate preventive measures to protect itself from the risk of bribery). The SFO relies on the expertise of its accountants and lawyers, many seconded from the private sector, to investigate high-profile cases, the investigation of which is more likely to impact on share prices. Where the corporate controlling mind of corruption cannot be demonstrated, the OACU, formed in 2006, targets individuals involved in bribery. While there is close cooperation between the agencies, their remits and associated powers differ. The SFO's investigative powers apply more to the company as a whole, whereas police powers apply more to individuals.[11]

Discussions about future reforms of the UK's enforcement architecture concerning corporate fraud previously centered on the creation of a single Economic Crime Agency (ECA). This project was to be spearheaded by the Home Office. Police and criminal justice minister Nick Herbert stated that "As the department with the role of crime fighting, it is right that the Home Office should be focused on economic crime …. There has not been that focus up until now."[12] This agency, which was proposed as a way to reduce the confusion of the existing multi-agency approach with a single unified entity, was to be created by the merger of the FSA, SFO, and Office of Fair Trading (OFT).

The Home Office responded to questions about the future arrangements of the ECA by stating that it would become part of their structure for dealing with organized crime:

We have set out a firm commitment to create a single Economic Crime Agency to rationalise the current piecemeal approach to enforcement. The Coalition commitment will be developed in close conjunction with the National Crime Agency, which will take the lead on organised crime. The Home Office and the Attorney General's Office are working to develop the ECA and its powers and we plan to have the initial elements in place in shadow form before the end of this summer, following consultation with key stake-holders ... we have already confirmed that for now the FSA's powers of prosecution will lie with the new Consumer Protection and Markets Authority rather than the Economic Crime Agency.[13]

It is important to point out that there has been some uncertainty about future of the ECA, and that the provisional title of Consumer Protection and Markets Authority has been dropped and the organization is now called the Financial Conduct Authority. This may herald a desire to split the oversight and enforcement arms. This was the focus of an industry-wide consultation whose outcome was the survival of an autonomous SFO as of June 2011.

BILATERAL RELATIONS: BRITAIN AND NIGERIA

Bilateral investigations into corruption are influenced by historical ties. The United Kingdom is connected to Nigeria through the legacy of colonialism and Nigeria's membership of the Commonwealth, and equally through a large UK population of Nigerian immigrants and British citizens of Nigerian descent. International investigations into corrupt officials have in some cases established good relations and improved channels of communication between law enforcement in specific countries. DI Whatmore commented that his unit, by "the very nature of our work links to other countries and regimes, we are very closely linked with other government departments and the Foreign Office who are aware of what we are doing .... it's pretty groundbreaking."[15] The fruits of this cooperation come in the form of a string of cases investigating Nigerian officials, which are currently being processed by the courts.

MULTILATERAL ENFORCEMENT INITIATIVES: CONSTRAINTS ON LAW ENFORCEMENT AND BARRIERS TO COOPERATION

Informing and barriers to private–public disclosure

Because bribery and attempted bribery are under-reported and difficult to detect, the effectiveness of legislation is dependent on businesses self-reporting incidences of bribery, and whistleblowers within or attached to companies. Critical to laws being enforced is the presence of "capable guardians," which one police strategy defines as the "network of those who are empowered and paid to enforce or regulate, as well as those with legal or moral obligations and those who are responsible for delivering public funds and holding the allocation of state assets to account."[16] In the context of bribery, this network includes public authorities (the police, FSA, SFO, and SOCA), and private actors (the CEOs, directors, secretaries, and boards of businesses, as well as lawyers, accountants, and auditors). Non-departmental public bodies such as the Department for International Development (DFID), the Foreign and Commonwealth Office (FCO), and the Ministry of Defence (MOD), as well as non-governmental organizations (NGOs) such as Transparency International also have a crucial role to play.

One constraint on the effectiveness of anti-corruption enforcement is therefore that it relies to a large extent on people coming forward: a resource-intensive and expensive investigation has to be justified by credible evidence that corruption is occurring.

The anti-bribery agenda has only recently been given significant global attention. Consequently, in the United Kingdom and elsewhere, a relatively small number of companies and employees have been convicted of bribery. If recent trends in investigation continue, this will change rapidly. Companies increase reporting of suspected corruption when the issue is seen as one with a substantial risk of incurring the wrath of law enforcement. A senior police officer explains the process:

> As the issue rises up, people ... become more fearful of it and therefore they start reporting more. As our influence grows in the field, we become a greater deterrent, and the greater the deterrent, the more people want to avoid being on the receiving end, so they share more. It's a natural policing process, no matter what area of crime we're looking at.[17]

Police and regulators of corruption depend on informers of various kinds. Various avenues through which corruption can be brought to the attention of the authorities include:

- whistleblowers
- suspicious activity reports (SARs)
- informants
- employees and members of the public reporting
- information from the international press
- staff from embassies of other nations reporting things they see.

There is a drive within law enforcement agencies to encourage whistle-blowers both within the ranks of a company, and from competitors (where that can be backed up with evidence). Richard Alderman states that he will be "looking for cases in which corruption has been used in order to put at a disadvantage a good ethical UK corporate. Clearly, we shall need help. We need evidence and we need to be tipped off in the first instance."[18] Part of the adequate procedures required for a company to avoid charges of failing to prevent bribery is likely to include provision and protection for those who blow the whistle on corruption. Alderman says:

I certainly ask companies to come to me when they think they are undercut by unethical competitors. That is quite difficult for them – they would be worried about retaliation – particularly if the company that they are complaining about is basically a state-owned company in another country and they have operations there. It is a big issue for these companies – and I would very much like them to tell me about instances there and be tipped off about this, and I'd like to give them the opportunity to talk to us. We don't have the jurisdiction quite yet because the Bribery Act has not come into force, but as I said, when it comes into force, I want to know – and I'm encouraging them to let us know. It's the same issue with any other complaint made to law enforcement – what's their motive, how cogent is their evidence? If a corporation came to us and said "We know that such and such a contract was obtained as the result of a bribe of £100 million to such and such a minister, and this is how we know" – then this is what we'd like to hear. If they come to us and just grumble about it without evidence, then, yes, we might look at it, but we would have to think about what we do because we would be conscious of the fact that there could be all manner of reasons why they failed to get the contract .... So that may involve a bit of digging on our part, and we are happy to do that. ... We don't close our ears to any allegations that are made to us, and we have a section here that is actually looking at that. I would like to see cases like that in court – if there are foreign corporations in our jurisdiction that have undercut one of our companies, getting them before a judge and jury would send out an incredibly powerful message about the high standards in the UK.[19]

The prospect of news of an investigation leaking into the public domain and impacting on the share price is one consideration that may deter employees from reporting misconduct within their own ranks. Where competitors are concerned, as Alderman explains, fear of retaliation is a constraint on disclosure.

THE PROBLEM OF FINITE RESOURCES

One constraint on international corruption investigations is that they are by definition multi-jurisdictional, which means they have a long lead time, generate many documents, and require extensive resources. DI Whatmore outlines some of the problems faced by his unit. Although he is referring here to the United Kingdom's investigation of foreign politically exposed persons (PEPs), the issues raised are relevant to all international corruption investigations:

By the very nature of the enquiries, they are international ... the money doesn't always stay in the UK, it will come in, go out, go to somewhere else before it comes in. It will sit in offshore trusts and corporations incorporated in offshore financial centres like Guernsey, Jersey, Cayman Islands etc, which are favourites for money launderers ... and so your enquiries lead you to all those jurisdictions as well as to the losing state, and that takes a long time, it's expensive and not straightforward – bureaucracy gets in the way. You need formal requests. Some are more able and willing to assist than others. It's a very lengthy process and it costs thousands. It's very hard to have a quick win in this kind of arena .... We have pretty good relations with most countries but it will still take time. The investigators can be very good at finding the evidence but sometimes [the problem] is just getting it released.[20]

The time taken to achieve extradition between countries is frequently a major barrier to investigating and addressing multi-jurisdictional financial misconduct by public officials. The extradition of Karl-Heinz Schreiber from Canada to Germany on charges including bribery took ten years, from 1999 to 2009.[21] The German authorities eventually charged Schreiber not with bribery but with tax evasion, for which he was convicted and sentenced to eight years in jail. The length of time taken to secure convictions in international bribery cases is a major reason for the trend towards negotiated settlements.

Such document-heavy international investigations require financial resources that are often not available (or willingly released) in sufficient quantities. This is by no means limited to developing countries, which are often associated with high levels of corruption. Transparency International's assessment of the enforcement of the OECD Convention on Combating Bribery of Foreign Public Officials in International Business Transactions shows how much work has still to be done in this area: 'With active enforcement in only seven of the 38 parties to the Convention, the Convention's goal of effectively curbing foreign bribery in international business transactions is still far from being achieved.'[22]

In the cases where a state commits resources and has the will to build enforcement architecture, dedicated units are still often arguably under-resourced in comparison with their remit. Therefore there is a gap (sometimes a chasm) between the letter and reality of the law. DI Whatmore explains this potential problem with regard to the Bribery Act:

The Bribery Act is pretty wide-ranging, with a long reach, but like all these things, it can be seen as draconian in its drafting, but it's down to whether the resources are there to enforce it, and in terms of actually conducting these investigations with finite resources, you can only do so much.[23]

In addition to the financial commitment, expertise on which cases to investigate is also at a premium. Lengthy investigations require a special kind of police expertise, which is best gained on the job. Whatmore continues that:

> it's about having the right people in there with the right skills – investigative and case management. There are lots of good investigators who don't put a good case together, and some who can put a case together but aren't the best, most tenacious investigators. You need an omnicompetent skill set.[24]

Such a skill set takes years to acquire, and the potential for large numbers of people to build up the expertise and "organizational memory" required is limited when law enforcers change career path.

The paucity of resources available to enforcement in many countries is compounded by the relative ease with which corrupt officials can stall investigations. Unsurprisingly, those corrupt public officials are often rich, with ample resources available to fight their corner, and these sums (and the legal expertise they can buy) are dwarfed by the amounts available to the world's leading companies. Whatmore points out that:

> The people we are after, who are stealing vast sums of money, can pay for the very best lawyers ... they can employ the best, most difficult kind of lawyers on the planet, because they will try every tactic to get their client off.[25]

UNCERTAINTY

One limitation of the UK Bribery Act is that, as new legislation, it has not yet been tested by the courts. This is a key constraint on the clarity with which advice can be given to industry, by either enforcers or private experts. In the words of former attorney-general Lord Goldsmith, "Over a period of time [what the Act actually means in practice] will become clearer, but that is a problem: it becomes clearer as a result of cases taking place. That means someone has been wrung through the mangle first."[26]

The uncertainty in outcomes applies to those engaged in enforcement as well as to the boards of corporations. At a speech in Washington, DC, SFO director Richard Alderman stated his intention to pursue corrupt firms using an "aggressive interpretation" of the Act, and said that one key question in making a decision whether to bring a case against a firm would be, "Can I persuade a judge and jury that you are carrying on business in the UK?"[27] This uncertainty in how the courts will respond, in addition to the possibility that foreign companies could stall any case by requesting a judicial review, tempers the extent to which the SFO can exult in its powers under the new Act.

Such uncertainty about how the legislation will be policed may cause businesses to take an adversarial approach when there is little or no information available to them on the likely penalties if they cooperate. Alderman explains that companies:

want to know before charges are brought and the criminal justice [process] starts, they want to know what they are in for – and if they don't know that with reasonable certainty, then they may not be prepared to take the risk, and they may simply say: "Fine, we are not going to reach agreement with you, you carry on with your investigation, we will fight you every inch of the way, and when it gets to court we will continue to fight it." And it's going to take years. And that's something that they can legitimately say and I'm not going to criticise them for doing that. ... BAE wanted to know what it was in for. And Innospec did, because they only had a certain amount of money and if the judges were going to give more than that, they would go bust. So Innospec needed to know how much they were in for. The Weir Group case, they had a slightly different approach – they agreed to compensation and then let it up to the judge to determine a fine, that's OK provided that fines are in the low figures, which they are in this jurisdiction. But if the judge could have fined them £100 million then that is totally different. In the States there has been an enormous amount of guidance on this, and it is possible to calculate with reasonable precision how much is going to be determined by the judge. Here they have got no picture of it whatsoever.[28]

These barriers and limitations to effective enforcement are significant, and many are years from resolution. But these problems are neither static nor insurmountable. If current trends continue, then many more companies, executives, and public officials will be convicted of corruption and bribery over the next decade.

THE POPULARITY OF NEGOTIATED SETTLEMENTS

The various problems with investigating international bribery and hurdles to the adversarial approach have led enforcers in a number of countries to seek more collaborative approaches. Resolution of investigations into financial offenses have been characterized by negotiated agreements between enforcers and businesses. In US Department of Justice (DOJ) terminology these are known as DPAs (deferred prosecution agreements) and NPAs (non-prosecution agreements). The former drops criminal charges when agreed action is taken, the latter avoids charges completely. In exchange for leniency from enforcers, the company typically agrees to take remedial action and pay a significant fine. These settlements have been increasingly popular in European countries:

During the last year, prosecutors in the US, Germany and the UK announced a number of settlements of important foreign bribery cases in which the defendants agreed to pay fines amounting to many hundreds of millions of dollars. These settlements demonstrate the ability of prosecutors to resolve cases without interminable litigation. The settlement levels provide a sharp wake-up call to international business regarding the gravity of foreign bribery.[29]

Settlements are attractive to boards because they avoid the prospect of conviction for offenses which, as well as causing damage to the company's reputation, and leading to the potential imprisonment of individuals, and larger financial penalties, can debar companies from competing for public works contracts on which their business depends. Enforcers favor such resolution because it avoids the huge cost in person power and resources of bringing a case to court. Organizations like the SFO are concerned with encouraging cooperation between business and enforcement and in driving up corporate standards (and increasingly in compensating the real victims of the wrongdoing) as much as they are with punishing transgressors. Alderman explains that the terms of the settlement will depend on the company and the seriousness of the alleged offense:

> In Mabey and Johnson we reached a certain way of doing it, Innospec was another one, Messent was another, BAE …. It's about working it out in practice. Because we're dealing with corporations it won't be a case of one size fits all, because they have got their own negotiating teams and it's a question of negotiating a sensible compromise.[30]

DISADVANTAGES AND CRITICISMS OF SETTLEMENTS

These settlements have been criticized for pre-empting proper investigation of serious allegations and letting businesses off for minor infractions. Alderman admits that "in the Innospec case, the judge didn't like the idea that we had tried to reach an agreement on everything beforehand."[31] Because these deals mean the company involved admits to lesser charges than bribery (such as false accounting), they distort figures on how many instances of bribery there have been, and may give the public a false impression of the company.

Judges in the United Kingdom have expressed concern about the terms of these settlements because the fines are typically much less than similar deals struck between corporates and the US DOJ. Lord Justice Thomas stated in the Innospec case that:

> The courts have a duty to impose penalties appropriate to the serious level of criminality that are characteristic of this offence. For example,

one of its many effects is to distort competition; the level of fines in cartel cases is now very substantial and measured in tens of millions. It is self-evident that corruption is much more serious in terms of both culpability and harm caused.[32]

In addition to the terms of the particular settlements, Lord Justice Thomas also criticized the underlying premise of the SFO's approach. In the same Innospec case he stated that "I have concluded that the director of the SFO had no power to enter into the arrangements made and no such arrangements should be made again."[33]

The criticism from the judiciary has been varied. Richard Alderman explains that the SFO has:

> not found the right formula yet, and in each case we are doing it slightly differently. Judges differ in their views about this, and they have abso- lutely belittled this stuff ... the judge in BAE, he didn't like it very much, and he said that he felt under moral pressure to keep the fine low to £500,000 to maximize the amount of money going to the people of Tanzania ... the judge in the Innospec case said that "it is no business of the Director of the SFO to direct money to the people in the country, so I'm going to cancel that and add it to the fine." He took a different view.[34]

In these settlements there is also a danger that monies that were intended for restitution to the losing population do not get further than corrupt politicians and bureaucrats. A big concern in these agreements for both business and enforcers is therefore that such money reaches those who suffer the most from corrupt deals. Alderman explains that:

> The people that really matter to me are the people who suffer. No one speaks up for them. They are poor people, who suffer from bad drugs, inadequate infrastructure. No one knows who they are. How do we get the money back to benefit them?[35]

THE WAY FORWARD

Future settlements may require changes, says Alderman:

> What is going to be needed is finding ways in which we can quite properly, and it may involve earlier judicial involvement, get the views of the court at that earlier stage. It is fraught with difficulty for all sorts of reasons. But for instance in BAE, before I had signed up to the deal, even if the deal was going to be subject to the opinion of the court, the deal was for £30 million, and the judge would determine the fine, and

any balance between the amount of the fine and the £30 million would be paid for the benefit of the people in Tanzania.

Now that was agreed at about half-ten on the Thursday night. Now if on the Friday morning, because it was announced in court in the States on the Friday afternoon, I had been able to go with BAE and see a judge, and say "This is the outline settlement" – and this is where it gets very difficult, because judges loathe getting drawn into something like that unless they have got all the evidence and all the information. The danger for them, which I absolutely agree with, is getting drawn into something without full argument and information, and that's a real problem, and I respect that very much.

But if in some way there is a benefit of total disclosure to the judge, and full argument on that Friday morning, and the judge has said "I think the settlement is right, it's appropriate," then ... I would have felt immensely reassured by that ... and I think the public would have been reassured, because it is not an unaccountable civil servant reaching an agreement in the dead of night in the City, but it's something that judges were involved in, and people trust judges – quite rightly.

To have a judge look at it ... would have meant that pressure groups and others do not have to challenge it and put their own money at stake, because they know it has been looked at independently. I would be very interested in [finding] a way that we could bring judges in earlier, but is not easy because they would be brought into a criminal case before the proceedings start and that is very difficult for them, and I don't underestimate the perfectly respectable reasons there are for saying that the judges have to be cautious about getting drawn into them. It may only be in a small number of cases, but if we can find a way, I think that would reassure everybody. ... It might require some legislation, but we need to get into that area because, as I look back on the BAE saga – it's all pretty unusual stuff, it would have been really helpful if I had been subject to a judge at that early stage rather than 11 months afterwards.[36]

This view has substantial support from many influential enforcement figures. Former attorney-general Lord Goldsmith (the government lawyer who announced the closure of the BAE case) for example says, "I don't see why it should not be possible for experience prosecutors, who can understand the public interest, together with well advised corporations to be able to reach an agreement and then say to the judge this is what we think and why."[37]

11

GLOBAL EFFORTS: BATTLING AGAINST THE CHAIN OF CORRUPTION

The battle against corruption starts with the institutional failures that enable that corruption to take root. It proceeds to the financial system which allows those who have corrupt money to launder it. It moves to the corporate sector which is alert to its dangers and wants no part of them. It ends with the police agencies who discover or are tipped off about an incident and investigate it. The all-encompassing nature of this virus means that a host of agencies are involved in the prevention, detection, and prosecution of crimes of corruption. Efforts to contest corruption and fraud take place across borders, and involve a wide range of agencies. Cooperation and information sharing are the names of this particular game, without which the chances of successfully repressing these crimes are hamstrung.

Tackling demand-side bribery is one way that the pressure can be reduced on business. It is important for companies to be conscious of the local domestic efforts to tackle corruption by public officials, particularly in regions of the world that have traditionally been associated with bribery. Detective Inspector Whatmore explains the rationale:

> If people awarding the contracts in these countries are properly policed by their own authorities to prevent them from receiving the bribes then the company doesn't have to pay the bribe in the first place .... If domestically people are well policed then the opportunity for them to ask for the bribe is reduced and therefore the companies have got less pressure on them to pay bribes.[1]

A key finding of Trace International, a non-profit membership association that helps multinational corporations pool resources to fight corruption, is that where international bribery is concerned, OECD countries comprise under a third of all the 33 bribe-recipient countries. It is apparent (but not surprising) that the main flow of international bribes is from developed countries to developing ones. The United Kingdom is second only to the United States in the enforcement of foreign or "outbound" bribery, with 22 enforcement actions from 1977 to 2009.[2]

One recent trend has been an increase in domestic enforcement to tackle "inbound" bribery (where a country's law enforcement agencies prosecute a foreign company or its representative for offering a bribe to a public official). Political pressure to crack down on international bribes has intensified in recent years, and this has to some extent translated into better enforcement in a growing number of countries. There is also better information on comparative levels of enforcement against international bribery in different countries. Trace International's *2010 Global Enforcement Report* is a step forward in that it is the first in an ongoing series of annual reports that identify and track international anti-bribery enforcement trends.

According to Sam Eastwood, a partner with lawyers Norton Rose:

> the Bribery Act is only one element in a larger anti-corruption dynamic. Russia and China, for example, have both reinforced their respective anti-corruption laws in the period prior to the Act coming into force and countries whose enforcement records have received OECD criticism show signs of increasing their enforcement efforts. Canada and Australia are two notable examples of this.[3]

The international importance of the issue is demonstrated by greater enforcement in all countries in each successive year of the first decade of the 2000s. Trace International found that most countries that have enacted laws prohibiting foreign bribery have done so since 2000, and that around half of all the formal foreign bribery enforcement actions pursued since the passing of the US Foreign Corrupt Practices Act (FCPA) in 1977 and 2009 occurred in the last decade of this period.[4] South Korea tops the list of most aggressive enforcers since 1977, followed by Italy, Argentina, and South Africa.[5] Despite increased enforcement, the momentum has yet to translate into meaningful investigations in many cases; the majority of countries analyzed by Trace International failed to pursue even one international bribery investigation in the period from 1977 to 2010.

THE EGMONT GROUP

Where corruption, money laundering, and other financial crime (such as terrorist financing) is concerned, multilateral intelligence-sharing networks and open channels of communication between law enforcement agencies in different countries are crucial to investigating and detecting cases spanning multiple jurisdictions. Following the criminal money trail around the world is a vital part of bringing a corruption case to court. Since 1995, this has been an ongoing project for members of the Egmont Group of Financial Intelligence Units (FIUs), of which the UK Serious and Organised Crime Agency (SOCA) is a member. Egmont is a forum of central national agencies which are responsible for receiving, requesting, analyzing, and disseminating disclosures of financial information to competent authorities. The group combines the expertise of units from over 100 jurisdictions, and offers advice and training to its members. Its objectives include:

- expanding and systematizing international cooperation in the reciprocal exchange of information
- increasing the effectiveness of FIUs by offering training and promoting personnel exchanges to improve the expertise and capabilities of personnel employed by FIUs
- fostering better and more secure communication among FIUs through the application of technology, such as the Egmont Secure Web (ESW)
- fostering increased coordination and support among the operational divisions of member FIUs.[6]

The increase in membership of the Egmont Group (from 69 in June 2002 to 108 in 2008) illustrates the growing interest in multilateral cooperation between law enforcement agencies. Each new member widens the net.

THE EU ANTI-CORRUPTION AGENDA AND THE STOCKHOLM PROGRAMME

The post-cold war explosion in cross-border commerce (and criminality) has prompted increased attention to corruption by the European Union, which has beaten the drum for a more coordinated response for over a decade. In 1994, the ministers of justice of Council of Europe member states agreed that corruption should be addressed at European level. Five years later, the EU Criminal Convention on Corruption required all members to pass domestic legislation criminalizing the intentional bribery of a public official or private sector employee from any other country, and GRECO (Group of States against Corruption) was set up by the Council of Europe to monitor compliance with its anti-corruption standards. GRECO now includes 48 European states and the United States.[7] Anti-corruption measures in the European Union gained further momentum in the wake of a series of US FCPA investigations, many of which involved European companies.

Helge Kvamme, PricewaterhouseCoopers head Forensic Services/ Anti-Corruption/FCPA in Norway, explains that:

In Europe, we are used to investigations and convictions against individuals, but what we see as a trend in Europe is action towards companies, because this has not been a typical element of investigations ... more and more organisations are being investigated and have been convicted [and this shows the importance of] ... implementing anti-corruption programmes.[8]

213

An increasing official focus on corruption in European businesses has been accompanied by greater public resentment of corruption in both the private and public sectors. A 2009 Eurobarometer survey found that over 75 percent of the EU citizens surveyed said they believed that corruption was a serious problem in their country, with nearly a third of them stating that they thought it was part of daily life.[9]

Fighting corruption is one of the five pillars of the Stockholm Programme, the framework for European cooperation on judicial, police, and legal matters from 2010 to 2015. Monica Macovei MEP explains that "At present, anti-corruption measures mainly concern accession countries, while after accession, there is nothing ... we need a common policy for the European Union."[10] In addition to the growing clamor from non-governmental organizations (NGOs) and academics for a robust and multilateral anti-corruption strategy, there has been mounting pressure from the public. Macovei expressed the increasingly common belief among MEPs that "Expectations of European citizens, the role of corruption in the economic crisis and its undermining effects on EU policies require action at EU level, including a monitoring mechanism."[11]

The Stockholm Programme places great emphasis on the importance of greater law enforcement cooperation generally, through the sharing of training and expertise. Principal elements of the programme's anti-corruption policy include the creation of a database of suspicious activity reports within Europol, commitments to strengthen powers of financial investigation, and combining "all available instruments in fiscal, civil and criminal law" in order to do so.[12] The programme also emphasizes the need to improve the prosecution of tax evasion and corruption in the private sector. Such proposals for a comprehensive anti-corruption policy will probably require the reform and strengthening of OLAF (the European Union's anti-fraud office), as well as strengthening links between OLAF and other countries outside the European Union.

Forward-looking companies will keep a close eye on these developments. A comprehensive EU anti-corruption strategy and policing at a Europe-wide level could have significant implications for businesses in the future.

THE WORLD BANK

The World Bank has also been instrumental in fostering cooperation between enforcement officials, most recently through the International Corruption Hunters Alliance, which met for the first time in December 2010. This is a global network of over 200 anti-corruption enforcement personnel from 134 countries, which focuses on how to combat corruption and bribery as it relates to development.

Speaking to the first meeting of the Alliance, World Bank president

Robert Zoellick remarked that the network would "help us learn how to pursue more multi-jurisdictional prosecutions."[13] The Bank's press release on the initiative explains that the Alliance's objectives include pursuing "the international enforcement of national anti-corruption and asset forfeiture laws, to yield higher-end results" and driving "for commitments and outcomes in bribery prosecutions, asset recovery, public interest litigation, legal assistance, promoting greater transparency, and monitoring of performance." Leonard McCarthy, the World Bank's vice president for integrity, stated that "While our focus remains on preventing, investigating and sanctioning fraud and corruption impacting Bank-financed projects, we embrace global opportunities to assert integrity."[14]

According to lawyer Sam Eastwood:

> The World Bank has revised its approach to sanctions, increasing the prospect of penalising contractors participating in World Bank financed projects who fail to adhere to best practice in anti-corruption compliance. New developments include negotiated settlements (often including an independent monitor with the prospect of a reduction in any debarment if the compliance program is approved by the World Bank); the creation of an integrity compliance officer role to counsel and monitor parties on implementation of compliance programs and harmonisation of the World Bank's debarment procedures with the Inter-American Development Bank group, the African Development Bank group, the Asian Development Bank group and the European Bank for Reconstruction and Development.[15]

Transparency International reported in 2010 that the number of countries it assesses as having "active enforcement" of the OECD Convention on Combating Bribery of Foreign Public Officials in International Business Transactions has increased from four to seven. With the addition of Denmark, Italy, and the United Kingdom to the list of Germany, Norway, Switzerland, and the United States, this represents about 30 per cent of world exports. Active enforcement means that a certain number of cases are investigated and brought to trial, a level of enforcement that Transparency International considers "an adequate deterrent to foreign bribery." TI also notes that "The OECD significantly strengthened its anti-corruption programme in late 2009 and early 2010 .... The OECD Council has adopted extensive new recommendations for further combating foreign bribery, addressing a range of issues which arose during the Convention's debate."[16]

In addition to greater enforcement through the OECD, there has also been increased cooperation between the World Bank and the United Nations in a joint Stolen Assets Recovery Initiative, which helps developing nations recover looted funds.

STRENGTHENING LAW ENFORCEMENT AND BUILDING INSTITUTIONS IN DEVELOPING COUNTRIES: SPOTLIGHT ON SOUTH-EAST ASIA

In South-East Asia, where there has often been a general culture of official corruption, many countries have made recent attempts to strengthen domestic anti-corruption policing. Indonesia is lauded by the some anti-corruption activists as being one of the success stories in the difficult task of tackling the corruption of public officials, in order to curb demand-side bribery.[17] Since 2003, Indonesia has jailed more than 100 high-ranking officials. Other South-East Asian countries that are arguably more challenged by corruption have made efforts to take it more seriously.

Cambodia has set up a new Anti-Corruption Unit as part of its anti-corruption strategy, which aims to respond to pressure from international donors and NGOs for its reputation. In Transparency International's most recent Corruption Perceptions Index, Cambodia came 154th out of the 178 countries surveyed, and a poll by the Political and Economic Risk Consultancy identified it as the second most corrupt country in South-East Asia. However, there is some evidence that this might change for the better. While the new unit has received criticism for its close links to the executive, it has already made a series of high-profile arrests, including the head of Cambodia's anti-drug trafficking agency.[18]

Under the provisions of Cambodia's new anti-bribery law, passed in March 2010, public officials convicted of corruption face 15-year prison sentences. The 2010 law also created an anti-corruption council that requires mandatory asset declaration for over 100,000 state officials over a five-year period. As well as a trend towards greater transparency, Cambodian law enforcement agencies have professed the intention to improve the integrity of their staff. If the head of the Anti-Corruption Unit is to be believed, all his staff face an annual polygraph test to ensure that the guardians do not go unguarded.

In Malaysia, action on corruption has been increasingly important to the government since the formation of the Malaysian Anti-Corruption Commission (MACC) in 2009.[19] This replaced a previous multi-agency effort with a unified modern structure based on leading anti-corruption agencies. Ensuring the integrity of such an agency is always vital to win domestic and international confidence in its abilities. To enhance faith in the system, five bodies independent of the government were established to monitor MACC, placing special importance on prevention. During the 15th Malaysian Law Conference in July 2010, the head of MACC stated that he would resign "if there is a case or report made against any minister and we do not investigate."[20]

The Philippines recently ran into problems trying to tackle rampant public sector corruption. In an attempt to make good on his 2010 anti-corruption campaign platform, President Aquino's first executive order was to create a "truth commission" to investigate allegations of systemic corruption by the previous government.[21] This commission was struck down by the country's Supreme Court as unconstitutional. In February 2011, Philippine army general Angelo Reyes committed suicide during Senate hearings that alleged that a number of army chiefs of staff received multi-million-dollar corrupt payments. Despite these setbacks, the Philippines has developed a National Anti-Corruption Plan of Action, a long-term strategy for improving the situation, which has already resulted in the creation of the National Tripartite Efficiency and Integrity Board, which aims to tackle corruption in the Department of Labour and Employment. Some successes have been partially attributed to the Office of the Ombudsman's project to set up regional offices to encourage reporting from members of the public.[22]

CONTRASTING APPROACHES TO ENFORCEMENT: RUSSIA AND CHINA

Media reports paint a bleak picture of the contemporary Russian political system, in which bribery alone totals an estimated $300 billion a year.[23] The rampant corruption across the country reached epidemic proportions in the decade or so after the fall of communism, and President Medvedev recently admitted that there has been no significant progress with his repeated anti-corruption drives since then. A researcher from the London School of Economics explains that:

> Corruption, the oxygen of organised crime, is a two (or more)-way process. For the majority of foreign businesses, bribe-giving is seen as essential – the only way to get things done. "We call it Russian business," smiled one visitor to Moscow I interviewed recently. Taken to their logical conclusion, what these "revelations" tell us – and embassies don't – is that most foreign operations in Russia, in some way or another, are complicit in official and private sector corruption.[24]

In response to domestic and international pressure not to give up on the issue, the future of Russian enforcement is based on Medvedev's proposed law, under which the size of the fine is proportional to the size of the corrupt payment. While Russia is planning to increase the financial risk to those engaged in bribery, China is taking a more severe approach.

The managers of foreign businesses with interests in China are not immune to lengthy prison sentences. On March 29, 2010, a senior Australian executive of mining firm Rio Tinto was sentenced to ten years in prison along with three Chinese colleagues for taking up to £6 million in bribes.[25] There have been rumors that this trial was connected to the firm's rejection of a bid by the state-owned Chinalco to increase its stake

217

in Rio Tinto. While Chinalco denies this, it is likely that doing business with state-owned companies in authoritarian countries increases the risk of being subject to politically motivated scrutiny.

According to the *Hurun Report*, released in January 2011, bribery is the main reason for the imprisonment of Chinese billionaires, with those found guilty being jailed for an average of 11 years.[26] There have also been high-profile cases where the government has considered that a lengthy prison sentence is insufficient. On December 30, 2010, a former senior Chinese official charged with investigating corruption was executed for taking the equivalent of £2.9 million ($4.7 million) in bribes over a period from 1997 to 2006.[27]

12

CURBING BRIBERY AND THE WAY FORWARD: ANTI-BRIBERY PROCESSES, FOR COMPANIES, POLICE, AND THE COURTS

The public concern about bribery is making new demands on law enforcement and the judiciary. Both are seeking new ways to respond to an issue which demands some wider interpretations of the crime itself, as well as of its seriousness and reach.

First and foremost, there is the need to understand the sort of institutions that give and receive bribes, and their motivations. This has given rise to some quite specific categorizations of motivation and structures.

Second, we seek to understand how institutions can be persuaded to prevent the incidence of bribery. This involves exhortation, audit checking, and awareness. Police and other civil society agencies are active in this area.

The third innovative aspect occurs when the previous two have failed, when bribery has taken place, and when a party has admitted to it. In these circumstances, law enforcement will use the courts to make a payment, in the form of restitution to the losing party, typically a state.

As is evident from statements made by UK authorities and police strategy, the extent to which authorities perceive that a company is committed to fighting corruption and bribery (and making efforts to reduce the incidence of facilitation payments) is likely to influence the approach of investigators.

PART ONE: WHO COMMITS BRIBERY, AND WHY

The mentality of UK law enforcement: corporate competence and consciousness

In assessing the briber's motivation, there are four degrees of culpability, each with an appropriate enforcement response, based on four states of corporate competence and consciousness.

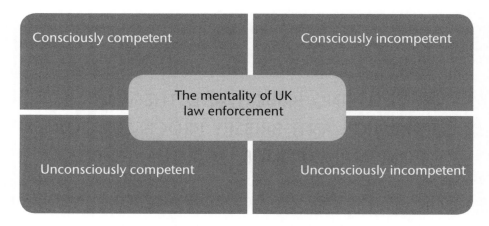

FIGURE 12.1 **How law enforcement strategy has conceptualized corporate competence**

Source: Pinsent Masons/Barry Vitou

Unconsciously incompetent

This company is negligent; ignorant of the nuances of anti-bribery law, and pays scant attention to policies, procedures, and controls to counter the threat of bribery. The defining characteristic of this category is the absence of direct criminal intent.

Consciously incompetent

This company is the most at risk from prosecution for bribery. Senior employees have taken a conscious decision to condone, engage with, or turn a blind eye to bribery. Low-level employees who engage in either receiving or paying bribes are seen as "doing their master's bidding."

Consciously competent

This company has "reasonable" policies and procedures. However, in practice, these policies and procedures are not adhered to below senior management. (Middle management and low-level employees engage in bribery, while senior executives are ignorant of these offenses.)

Unconsciously competent

This company has exemplary anti-bribery policies, procedures, and controls. The anti-bribery message is adhered to and taken seriously by all levels of the company. When a rogue operator is identified, they are reported to the appropriate authorities, and the company fully complies with the subsequent investigation to facilitate the correct application of the law.

In each case, the goal is to instigate behavioral change and drive up standards. There are various responses for law enforcement to the offense, with a level of action proportional to the company's perceived level of consciousness of the suspected bribery.

In the case of the unconsciously incompetent (negligent) company, the law enforcement response in the United Kingdom is for the Serious Fraud Office (SFO) to encourage self-referral and internal investigation, concluding in financial sanctions and remedial action. The strategy notes that this process is costly for the organization but reduces the burden and reputational harm.[1]

The company that wilfully condones bribery at the highest level (the consciously incompetent) elicits the strongest response, involving both the police and the SFO, who will deploy the full range of intelligence-gathering and investigative measures against the company, and when the preparation has been done, arrest and charge senior executives.

Where the company is consciously competent (mid and low-level employees are committing bribery without the senior employees being aware of it), law enforcement strategy suggests that the police will conduct a collaborative, rather than combative, investigation, working with the company – provided that all necessary cooperation is provided at board level, and the company also commits resources to the investigation. The expectation here is that the damage to the company will be limited to the cost of remedial action and some form of financial penalty in the form of a fine.

Finally, where the company is unconsciously competent (with exemplary anti-bribery policies), the only action taken by law enforcement is to applaud the company's efforts to root out rogue elements who commit bribery in opposition to company policy and culture.

These indications, while they should not be taken as a definitive guide, provide an insight into the mentality of law enforcement and the likely response to different kinds of offense. When a company considers how to draw up or reform its compliance program, it should bear in mind the principles upon which enforcers may be basing their decisions and strategy. It is important to note that these considerations do not extend to regulatory bodies; watchdogs vary in their approaches and may pursue companies where they discover inadequate procedures. A police officer stated that the extent of discretion in this area is unknown, and that of crucial importance is "the appetite and the ability of ... [bodies] like the FSA to say how busy they want to be in their sector and to impose fines."[2]

With regard to the Bribery Act, the "Joint prosecution guidance of the director of the Serious Fraud Office and the director of public prosecutions" (hereafter "director's guidance") outlines some general indicators for consideration when deciding whether, once the evidential test has been met, it is in public interest to prosecute.[3] There is a presumption in favor of prosecution unless the prosecutor is sure that public interest factors tending against prosecution outweigh those tending in favor. The guidance mentions four factors tending in favor of prosecution and three tending against it.[4]

Public interest factors in favor of prosecution

- A conviction for bribery is likely to attract a significant sentence.
- Offenses will often be premeditated and may include an element of corruption of the person bribed.
- Offenses may be committed in order to facilitate more serious offending.
- Those involved in bribery may be in positions of authority or trust and take advantage of that position.

Public interest factors against prosecution

- The court is likely to impose only a nominal penalty.
- The harm can be described as minor and was the result of a single incident.
- There has been a genuinely proactive approach involving self-reporting and remedial action.

The director's guidance makes similar reference to public interest factors for and against prosecution where the case concerns facilitation payments made to a foreign public official. There is a presumption in favor of prosecution unless the prosecutor is sure that public interest factors tending against prosecution outweigh those tending in favor.[5]

Factors tending in favor of prosecution

- Large or repeated payments are more likely to attract a significant sentence.
- Facilitation payments that are planned for or accepted as part of a standard way of conducting business may indicate the offense was premeditated.
- Payments may indicate an element of active corruption of the official in the way the offense was committed.
- Where a commercial organization has a clear and appropriate policy setting out procedures an individual should follow if facilitation payments are requested and these have not been followed correctly.

Factors tending against prosecution

- A single small payment likely to result in only a nominal penalty.
- The payment(s) came to light as a result of a genuinely proactive approach involving self-reporting and remedial action.

- Where a commercial organization has a clear and appropriate policy setting out procedures an individual should follow if facilitation payments are requested and these have been correctly followed.
- The payer was in a vulnerable position arising from the circumstances in which the payment was demanded.

PART TWO: THE INSTITUTIONAL IMPERATIVE, PREVENTION FOLLOWED BY CURE

Bribery and corruption will never be stopped. But it will be reduced when the state can persuade individuals, through both moral education and material enrichment, to decide that they would rather earn a reliable and sustainable wage than one that is not only unpredictable but also dubious. The need to raise awareness among those who are prone to offer, or receive bribes, is increasingly understood, by the police, non-governmental organizations (NGOs) and financial institutions.

Economic crime specialist DI Paul Whatmore of the Metropolitan Police describes his recent and ongoing role in the London 2012 Olympic Games:

> My role at the ODA [Olympic Delivery Authority] was to get them to put in place procedures for the head of anti-fraud, and also to do a lot of awareness training for their procurement staff, who were doing the evaluations deciding on who was awarded the contract. So we tried to get in there, for the first time ever for a UK police force like the Metropolitan Police, to go into a company like the ODA, to actually build the infrastructure of the Olympics, and say to them: "Look, let's talk. ... These are the types of preventative action you need with your evaluation processes. Are your conflict of interest forms being properly maintained? Do you check whether someone is conflicted? How do you protect yourself when someone is conflicted but they are the best person for the job?"
>
> A lot of [the Olympics] people were on short-term contracts seconded to businesses that were competing for contracts, but they were brought in because they've got the industry expertise. Understandable, nothing wrong in that, but how do you make sure that the contract doesn't go to the company that they have worked for? And once those contracts are awarded – hopefully they are done fairly – how do you then stop lots of money being siphoned off by overcharging? You have site inspections, but a site inspector can be bribed. If a site inspector can be bribed, what do you have in place to check that his reports are actually accurate? We said to senior management within the Met: "Look, let's not wait for five years down the line for a massive resource-intensive reactive investigation. If we get in at the front end with a bit of education and get in there

223

proactively, then we might prevent a lot of that. So it was a pretty novel approach."[6]

This preventive approach has been echoed in development strategy at the global level. The World Bank's Stephen Zimmerman emphasizes the organization's commitment to prevention of corruption:

> The Bank's efforts to tackle fraud and corruption in development projects are now further reinforced by its commitment to emphasise the deterrent effect of sanctions and the need to encourage companies to rehabilitate and prevent future misconduct.[7]

This commitment to the preventive model is being translated into practice through the World Bank's newly created Preventative Services Unit, which turns the results of investigations into practical advice on how to prevent corruption, acts as a consulting group for staff of all Bank-sponsored projects, and maintains a database on all the companies it works with. In the fiscal year 2010, the unit trained 1,200 people in preventive activities, such as identifying red flags in procurement and watching for early warning signs of corruption in new projects. The prevention approach is new, and its efficacy in pursuing the anti-corruption agenda is unknown. Judging whether a particular preventive measure or approach has worked is notoriously problematic. In the words of one senior police officer, "you can't always quantify success when you are preventing something because you don't know what you are preventing."[8]

Anecdotally at least, there is some evidence that preventive education and awareness raising has had some effect on the level of reporting. A senior police officer states that the pre-emptive approach of the City of London Police's Overseas Anti-Corruption Unit (OACU) elicited a wave of self-reporting by foreign officials:

> We need to get much smarter, [we stood] in front of them saying: "OK, here's an assessment of what's happening on the ground, this is what sectors before you experienced, here is some good anti-corruption advice, and by the way, this is what the law says. And we're having you closely watched." In this assessment, we've had over 500 responses from overseas government officials.[9]

PART THREE: PREVENTING BRIBERY THROUGH POLICY AND PROCEDURE

The OECD's recommendation of November 2009 calls on governments to expand the liability of corporations by covering such steps as failure to implement adequate compliance programs.[10] The UK Bribery Act represents one way in which this recommendation is being applied. It is particularly significant for companies because it includes a new corporate offense of "failure to prevent bribery," as well as the offense of bribery of a foreign official. The act also introduces two key offenses, one of giving bribes and one of agreeing to accept them. According to Robert Barrington, director of external affairs at Transparency International, "Companies must now realise that the risk of paying bribes to win a contract is greater than the benefits to be obtained by winning the contract."[11]

The new legislation dramatically changes the terms under which companies can be prosecuted for bribery. Under the former law, it had to be shown that a company knew about and actively instigated an act of bribery by one of its employees. Now the company need only have neglected to set up and implement systems to monitor and contain the risk of bribery. Barrington says that the bar has been significantly lowered for corporate prosecutions:

> There are rarely paper trails of instructions from headquarters, but now companies can't shy away from their role in foreign corruption, intended or unintended. Companies must be able to show that the board has a policy and set of standards relating to corruption, they must have a policy for training employees to avoid bribery and corruption, there must be working whistle-blowing policies in place.[12]

The issue of prevention has raised some questions about how the Bribery Act will eventually be applied. Under the UK interpretation of EU procurement rules, companies convicted under Section 7 of the Bribery Act (failing to prevent bribery) may be debarred from tendering for public contracts across the European Union. (Kenneth Clarke, the lord chancellor and secretary of state for Justice, has stated that such debarment is discretionary under the Bribery Act, rather than mandatory.[13])

CASE STUDY: AON, THE FSA, AND PREVENTIVE MEASURES

At the same time that recent enforcement strategies have focused on educating businesses in corruption, in the United Kingdom there are also signs of greater appetite by regulators to use an aggressive interpretation of existing regulations to deal with companies that lack adequate prevention procedures, without having to comply with all the standards of criminal prosecution. To date, the Financial Services Authority's (FSA's) largest fine for a financial crime, levied on 8 January 2009, was for lack of adequate anti-corruption measures. The FSA's summary of the case concluded that the insurance company Aon failed "to take reasonable care to establish and maintain effective systems and controls to counter the risks of bribery and corruption associated with making payments to overseas firms and individuals."[14]

DI Whatmore describes the case:

> Aon Ltd were recently fined by the FSA for £5.25 million and they weren't actually shown to have made any facilitation payments or paid a bribe. They had some pretty lavish hospitality thrown around, none of it that you'd actually say was a bribe, or illegal, in terms of what the Bribery Act will say is illegal, but the FSA have fined them £5.25 million because they didn't have the procedures in place to reduce their vulnerability, so it might have been a bribe. So it's even more draconian really than the Bribery Act. At least with the Bribery Act you have got to show that a bribe has been paid, whether it be called a facilitation payment, whether it be under the guise of hospitality, it's still got to have been shown to be a bribe for the company to be guilty of not preventing it. But under the regulation, which won't change with the Bribery Act, the regulators, such as the FSA for the financial services industry, are already fining companies for not stopping things like lavish hospitality, for them being open to potentially being bribed.[15]

In the case of Aon, it had:

> failed to give its staff, particularly those within the aviation and energy divisions, adequate training or written guidance in respect of specific bribery and corruption risks. Although Aon Ltd staff received training on the code of conduct and were require to declare annually that they had read and understood the code, they were not provided with focused training on the anti-bribery statements.[16]

The failure of the company's whistleblowing system meant that staff complaints about the practices went unheard, says Robert Barrington: "There was a cultural problem."[17] The case prompted the FSA to conduct a review into the way overseas third parties were being used by commercial insurance companies to pay illicit inducements. If this case is followed by others of similar magnitude, companies without substantive preventive measures could find themselves in trouble with the FSA.

PART FOUR: RESTITUTION OF THE LOSSES TO THE VICTIM

On the principle that a country as a whole loses when a corrupt politician takes a bribe, a practice is being increasingly applied by global courts and law enforcement officials of making the briber pay restitution to the deprived country.

The concept of restitution has already been to some extent incorporated into the UK criminal justice system. Since 2007, where a criminal penalty involves a fine, the perpetrator must also pay a flat rate "victim's surcharge" of £15, which is paid into a fund to help improve services for victims of crime. This measure has been introduced with the acknowledgment that more needs to be done to assist those who are affected in many different ways by all types of crime.

Former attorney-general Lord Goldsmith criticizes the current system in the UK because it treats complex and interrelated issues as separate and unrelated. He says the key questions to consider are:

> What does the criminal penalty need to be? What is the compensation that will be paid to the people affected? Are people going to be disqualified? What we have at the moment is a massive machine which deals with these things separately and I think that is unacceptable.[18]

The principle of restitutive settlement has recently also found favor with prosecutors in Nigeria. Dr Simeon Igbinedion of the Department of Jurisprudence and International Law at the University of Lagos explained that financial misconduct by three multinational corporations (Halliburton, Siemens, and Julius Berger Nigeria plc) gave rise to large fines with restitutive components, levied by the Nigerian Attorney General and Minister for Justice.[19]

A variety of ways to ensure restitution have been agreed in corruption cases in the United Kingdom. Alderman cites the case of Julian Messent of insurance company PRS, found guilty in October 2010 of paying bribes in Costa Rica to gain business:

> Messent, the insurance broker who was involved with bribing Costa Rican [officials], agreed to pay £100,000 back to the government. So there was some restitution there. Meaningful restitution is not going to come from individuals. It is going to come from corporates. We tend to use the formula "UK corporates that have committed offences," because we can't say that BAE committed corruption, it committed offences. It's also a wider point, it's about the standards that we expect our corporate to adopt when they do business in other countries. The rationale is just as great for health and safety as for corruption. And in those circumstances where the local community has suffered, the local community ought to get the benefit ... we are saying: "Look, you as a corporate have been party to this deception in the country, therefore whatever you pay back we are transferring."[20]

Such an approach has advantages for law enforcement and for business. The success of the global anti-corruption project depends to some extent on public support, which in turn is likely to be bolstered by evidence that successful resolutions benefit those who suffer the most because of corrupt deals. For law enforcement, restitution provides a way to compensate victims for their losses. And restitution is also welcomed by many businesses because it gives corporate social responsibility departments the chance of a PR coup; a fine for financial misconduct can be spun into the company's commitment to transparency and ethical business.

Alderman says that restitution:

> is an ethical principle. If the courts were to rule specifically against me on that, and, as result of argument and full discussion – because there hasn't really been an awful lot of argument on these issues – said that it was inappropriate for me do this, then I can't do it again. Then it becomes a matter for Parliament, and for Parliament to think: "Well that's the law, but is that really what we want? Is that really in the public interest?" I think I will have done my bit by bringing the issue firmly into the public domain and then raising it in such a way that it is up to parliament.[21]

Restitution on a global scale

Restitution is increasingly reaching across national divides. Consideration is being given not only to particular populations who have suffered from a specific instance of corruption, but to the concept of a global population of future victims. For the first time in the resolution of an investigation of a World Bank-financed project, restitution of US$350,000 is to be paid to Indonesia for the loss suffered through Italian engineering firm Lotti's misconduct in a public works programme in the water sector.[22]

This settlement is important in the context of future global anti-corruption enforcement strategy for a number of other reasons. It represents an increasingly cooperative approach between the five multi-lateral development banks – Lotti has been cross-debarred by the other four. It signals an approach based on incentivizing firms to drive up their corporate standards, and includes for the first time debarment with conditional discharge, where a company can be released from debarment upon demonstrating "compliance with certain remedial, corrective and preventive measures such as implementation of an acceptable corporate compliance program and cooperation with the World Bank's ... investigations." Stephen Zimmerman, director of operations of the World Bank's Department of Institutional Integrity, stated that the Lotti settlement "moves us closer to answering a longstanding call by victim countries to return illicit gains [and] is a major step in mobilising the commitment of all concerned jurisdictions to step up global enforcement efforts."

While the Lotti settlement marks the first time that restitution has been written into the resolution of an investigation of a World Bank-financed project, it is not the first time the bank has made restitution a core component of a settlement. The comprehensive settlement agreed in December 2009 between the World Bank and Siemens AG included an agreement for the company to pay $100 million over 15 years to non-profit organisations worldwide that promote business integrity and fight corruption.[23] An important difference with the Lotti case is that the beneficiaries of this $100 million are victims of corruption across the world, rather than the specific population that lost out through misconduct.

In a statement, Siemens said:

> Projects that will be supported by this initial tranche include assisting the Brazilian organisation Instituto Ethos in ensuring the transparent award of the infrastructure contracts for the [FIFA] World Cup 2014 and the Olympic Games 2016 in Brazil. In Europe, the newly founded International Anti-Corruption Academy is receiving funding for research and teaching. This Vienna-based international organisation was set up to train anti-corruption experts from all over the world. Other initiatives will be supported in the following countries: Angola, Brazil, China, Egypt, Hungary, India, Indonesia, Italy, Mexico, Nigeria, the Philippines, Russia, the Slovak Republic, South Africa, the Czech Republic, the US and Vietnam and various Middle Eastern states.[24]

Problems with restitution and the future of negotiated settlements

The SFO's approach has led to questions from other law enforcement agencies about how money allocated to victims can be prevented from falling into the hands of corrupt public officials. One police officer voices his concern:

> In the BAE case the fine was only £500,000, but the agreement is for BAE to pay about £30 million or something to Tanzania. I am engaging with [the SFO] because I want to know under what legal processes they are actually doing this, because it sits outside of any kind of criminal confiscation act. Although they did plead guilty, it is not a criminal confiscation .... I am interested to know under what procedures they do that – what strings are attached to it, and what will Tanzania do with it when they get their hands on the money? ... It could get stolen or misappropriated once it is given back.[25]

Alderman responds to such concerns:

> The legal system does not contemplate this at all. It does in the case of fraud. The victims of corruption, of poor infrastructure or things like that, they are not victims in the sense of fraud, but I want to find a way of channelling money back to them. There is nothing in the criminal justice system that gives me any support or any legal framework, so we step out of the criminal justice system in order to do that.[26]

Despite the lack of an existing legal framework, Alderman is determined to do something about this issue, and is seeking partners and methods to ensure such agreements are not undermined by further financial misconduct:

> If you have got £20 billion from an African country that needs to be returned, it's the government that is claiming it, and ... our government needs to negotiate with [them] and find ways of doing that. What we are trying to do in the SFO in our cases, it's not that we want to ignore the governments, but we want to find ways in which the money demonstrably goes to the victims of the corruption.
>
> So in BAE, it is the people of Tanzania. What we did during the middle of last year, and BAE have got their own views and their own contacts, but we tried to come up with a scheme with the government of Tanzania to direct the money towards poor children in poor parts of Tanzania. BAE have got some concerns about that, because we have to go through the government but they don't. So I think there is quite an interesting issue about how this money goes back to the real victims – not to the government, not to the bureaucrats, which is what everybody is worried about, but so that it works to the benefit of the poorer members of their society .... I can't go to Tanzania with a suitcase full of money and hand it out to villages. We actually need a respected international institution, whether it is the World Bank, the Red Cross or the Global Fund to do that sort of thing. If it goes through the government, everybody will be deeply suspicious. And even if it is not pinched by corrupt politicians, how many millions go in bureaucracy? We want it to go to the real victims.
>
> Victims of corruption in other countries don't have a legally enforceable right to any form of recompense. We could operate on the basis that any money we get back from corporates from the criminal justice system just goes back to the treasury. The problem I have with that is that the victims of these other countries lose twice. They lose out because of the corrupt contract which means that they have inadequate infrastructure. Secondly, when there was money to punish the companies, who gets the benefit of it? The UK exchequer. So they lose out twice. I'm very concerned about that. I would like to find a way in which we can try to channel money back to the real victims in a way that is auditable, transparent, and that members of the public, NGOs and others have confidence in and they think "Yes, this is a really good thing," and we can be sure that the money ends up benefiting poor people, not rich politicians. It is very much work in progress. In our next case, whatever that is, we will no doubt try another way of doing it.[27]

Alderman notes the considerable hurdles to the successful negotiation and implementation of these settlements, and is committed to pursuing it until forced to do otherwise:

> It isn't easy, we can't say: "We will give it to village A," because Village B will then object. We are in the realms of sensible, commonsense practical administration. Say if a hospital is built – I would like for these amounts of money to make a difference to the victims. We will continue in the SFO in pursuing [settlements] until we get to the stage where we are told absolutely that we can't. I think the judges are not telling us that, they are saying that they don't like it, it's a private deal, but there is only so much that I can push on these things. If the judge is resolute that is inappropriate for the SFO to be doing it then I would have to listen to that.[28]

The future of restitution is an issue that may be clarified through statements from judges and potentially through legislation. For such an approach to work, the key components are earlier judicial involvement in settlements, and an increased role for independent NGOs in administering restitution to the affected population.

CONCLUSION: BRIBERY AND CORRUPTION, THE UNFINISHED BUSINESS

The principles of bribery law are not complicated, the lawyers say. The difficult part is the interpretation. Gray areas of definition abound, and these will need clarifying by the judiciary and by courts.

The key definition required by corporates and their advisers in the United Kingdom is that of "adequate procedures." Here the very term raises critical issues, given that the procedures will only be tested and scrutinized by the police and the courts, at the very moment when bribery is alleged. The issue then is whether the procedures were "inadequate" or whether adequate procedures were implemented, but a rogue individual slipped through the corporate net. That in turn will raise questions about the quality of the "net" that was designed to ensure compliance across the whole corporate body. It will be observed that the corporate's only defense to a charge of bribery is that the procedures were adequate and in place and implemented, but the rogue bypassed them.

As this book demonstrates repeatedly, organizations are now under great pressure to establish the nature and the scale of their exposure to bribery and corruption, for it is only through regular and penetrating analysis of this that an organization can determine what procedures are adequate to cover the risk. Given that the risk of bribery and corruption is dynamic, with country and market exposure in constant flux, such assessment needs to be factored in to corporate strategy now as a routine part of any decision-making process. The company's capacity to show a credible assessment of its risk will be a key part of the "adequate procedures" test, should it be demanded by the authorities.

Another gray area likely to require judicial clarification is the concept of "proportionality." Companies will be under pressure to determine a formal procedure to show that the value and scale of an offer to a client or customer is proportionate to the business it undertakes (or hopes to undertake) with the customer. This is of particular importance to companies in the hospitality sector.

But value is not the only criterion in determining what is fair and legal. The process in which one builds up relationships with clients is also critical. One concept used by the law revolves round exerting "influence." Competing for business is an integral part of the market system in which

232

all companies participate, and a key element in the process of winning or retaining business is one company's ability to exert greater influence than another. But the new law appears to be saying that there are legal ways of exerting influence and illegal ones. Bribes are clearly viewed by the authorities as rigging the marketplace, an aspect of cartelization.

Another issue raised by the law – although admittedly it has been a factor as long as companies have exported to unstable countries – is how to conduct business in a country where buying influence through corruption is a higher than average risk. Three routes present themselves.

The first involves the corporate closing its eyes to the risk, believing either that a government official or private client will not behave according to form, or that the local sales executive will do whatever they have to do to win the business, even if it contravenes the law.

The second has the corporate responding to a request for a bribe by saying that its national law has changed, and it can no longer agree to it.

Finally, the company might examine the risks, using its own history or the research of others, decide that the risk is too great, and simply exit the market.

The assessment of each route will involve the cost to the business of the loss of a client or market, and the possible cost (in reputational as well as financial terms) of a successful bribery prosecution. The law enforcement authorities would clearly like to believe that companies – which have primarily their self-interest at stake – will take the message from the passing of the Bribery Act, that the odds of a bribery prosecution are stacking up in the authorities' favor. The interpretation by law enforcement and police of the Bribery Act will demonstrate how far those odds have moved. Some concerns about the resources allocated to the Serious Fraud Office (SFO) to police the Act have led to questions about the commitment of the UK government. This contrasts with a push by the US Department of Justice to toughen up implementation of the Foreign Corrupt Practices Act.

Given tight resources, the authorities can be expected to pay greatest attention to companies operating in countries at greatest risk of exposure to corruption, namely those with unstable or politically insecure regimes. Companies seeking to introduce the necessary procedures will need considerable insight into the range of behaviors and customs applying in countries where they operate.

These include aspects around political stability. So in countries with unpredictable factors (like the whim of a dictator or an incipient civil war) public servants are more likely to make demands for a payment, as they will view the tenure of their power base as temporary, and will want to maximize the fruits so long as they have it. Countries in Central Asia, like Kazakhstan and Kyrgyzstan, in Africa, Angola for instance, and Asia, such as Indonesia, pose these sorts of problem. Corruptibility is vulnerable to the shifting sands of political flux. So events in the Middle East can be expected to start to undermine relatively stable and non-corrupt business environments. For example, it has been observed recently that theft has become commonplace on the streets of Cairo.[1]

The new Bribery Act will undoubtedly lead to greater scrutiny of company behavior and of internal practices, but the authorities policing the act can also expect scrutiny. There can be little question that the SFO's decision to cease the investigation of the Al Yamamah contract weakened the credibility of Britain's anti-bribery credentials. It remains a moot point how the authorities would deal with a large and very public case, were it to arise, where a company from an important BRIC country (Brazil, Russia, India or China) is mired in a bribery scandal involving a British company. These countries feature rather prominently in most bribery indexes, and this is by no means an academic suggestion.

Fears about the reach of the Bribery Act have undoubtedly been exaggerated. The degree of deliberate abuse is much less than many suspect; the intentions of the regulators to behave in a draconian manner are wildly misunderstood. Discussion of the Act, and of the underlying issue, is better focused on corporate and enforcement behavior, and on the responsibility of large global institutions and agencies to the wider society and to their marketplaces. If the UK legislation achieves these – not modest – goals, it will have been a notable success.

APPENDIX 1
CASE STUDY: PHONE HACKING
AND CORRUPTION

Allegations about criminal activity at a UK newspaper, the *News of the World* (*NotW*), precipitated a crisis in public and private life and sent shockwaves through the UK establishment in the summer of 2011. As reports emerged of the telephones of murder and terrorism victims, dead servicemen, and high-profile individuals being hacked, so did allegations that journalists bribed police officers to obtain confidential information.

The furore over allegations of these illegal journalistic practices provides an example of the ways in which corruption can threaten both private and public interests. While the affair expands far beyond reports of corruption, the allegations of bribery can be seen to facilitate other illegal activities and to threaten organizations and individuals. Viewing the scandal through this lens provides some insight into the substantial and diverse risks surrounding direct involvement in, or indirect association with, corrupt practices.

The extent of illegal activity at the *NotW* is as yet unknown, as is the extent of illegal activity at other newspapers which might have used bribery to obtain information. The long-term implications are uncertain, but the impact on individual and organizational reputation is already apparent. Transparency International remarks that this scandal "has shone the spotlight on the media, the police, politicians, regulatory scrutiny and the ethical integrity of a major UK company" and illustrated that "there is systemic complacency about corruption in the UK, even if the problem is not endemic."[1]

REPUTATION

The revelations about corrupt practices in the NotW have resulted in damage to its parent company: News Corporation shares fell 17.4 percent in the wake of the allegations, while the *NotW*'s reputation was so badly damaged that, in an attempt at corporate damage control, the entire paper was scrapped as advertisers fled and the publication drowned in a storm of negative publicity. In addition to the drubbing that News Corporation's share price took, the affair has, at least temporarily, derailed the organisation's $14 billion bid for 61 percent of the satellite broadcaster BSkyB.[2]

The allegations have tarnished the reputations of senior employees in the Murdoch empire as well as police and politicians. There has also been considerable collateral damage. Previous employees of the *NotW*, many of whom will have had nothing to do with hacking phones or paying bribes, have not only lost their jobs but have had their reputations sullied by association with the title. This has resulted in law firm Silverman Sherliker launching a NotW action group with the aim of instigating a class action against the newspaper for stigma damages and the long-term impact on the careers of former employees.[3]

Other News Corporation assets and employees quickly became targets in the backlash. On Tuesday, July 19, 2011, all of News International's servers were taken offline in response to relentless attacks by a hacker collective know as Lulzsec. This group also claims to have obtained email and passwords of senior News International executives and journalists. Attacks on Rupert Murdoch have been physical as well as virtual. A hacking attack on the Sun newspaper's website led visitors to be redirected to a spoof page reporting the death of the News Corporation CEO.[4] On the same day, while giving evidence to a House of Commons Select Committee, Rupert Murdoch was attacked by a member of the public with shaving foam.

REPUTATION OF THE POLICE

Evidence of a corrupt network or relationships between journalists, private investigators, and law enforcement is not confined to the ongoing controversy engulfing the Murdoch empire. Several years before these latest allegations, an internal police report noted that private investigators "have for a number of years been involved in the long-term penetration of police and intelligence sources .... They have ensured that they have live sources within the Metropolitan police service and have sought to recruit sources within other police forces." The report noted that "Their thirst for knowledge is driven by profit to be accrued from the media."[5]

In the context of the most recent reports currently being investigated by the Metropolitan Police Service, Lord MacDonald, the former director of public prosecutions, told the Home Affairs Select Committee that evidence of bribery of police office was "blindingly obvious" from a cursory examination of *NotW*'s internal emails collated in 2007.[6] A number of Metropolitan Police officers in sensitive positions were allegedly bribed a total of at least £100,000 in return for confidential details about current criminal investigations, the reporting of which might have compromised them.[7] If these reports are true, they represent clear evidence of a corrupt nexus between the UK media and law enforcement which has threatened the course of justice. Former assistant commissioner John Yates told the Home Affairs Select Committee that "I confidently predict as a result of the News International disclosures, a very small number of police officers will go to prison as a result of corruption."[8]

The widely criticized police response to previous reports of phone-hacking and payments to police has already claimed high-profile scalps in law enforcement with the resignation of the Metropolitan Police Service's commissioner Sir Paul Stephenson and assistant commissioner John Yates. Those tasked with overseeing the investigation into allegations of police corruption readily admit that trust in the Metropolitan Police Service has been damaged. Deborah Glass, the deputy chair of the Independent Police Complaints Commission, stated that "I share the public concerns expressed so powerfully about police officers being bribed by newspapers .... Public confidence has been understandably shaken by these allegations."[9]

This controversy over police corruption has been magnified by claims that officers took bribes to reveal the real-time physical location of high-profile individuals through "pinging" their mobile phones. According to the *New York Times*, a former *NotW* journalist reported that this service cost £300 per trace.[10] If true, this corrupt practice would represent a gross invasion of privacy and might breach the UK's Regulation of Investigatory Powers Act 2000 (RIPA), which regulates the surveillance of serious criminal and terror suspects, and is supposed to ensure that techniques like "pinging" are reserved for such investigations.

HOSPITALITY

There have also been questions over hospitality provided to police officers, in light of revelations that former assistant commissioner of the Metropolitan Police Service Andy Hayman, the officer in charge of the previous investigation into phone hacking, dined frequently with News International executives at the company's expense while it was under investigation. The fact that Hayman subsequently went on to work for News International is just one example of the notably close relationship and revolving door between sections of the UK media and the upper ranks of law enforcement, a relationship that has been the subject of further discussion since the news that Sir Paul Stephenson accepted numerous offers of hospitality, including a £12,000 spa break at a company with links to News International.[11]

Both Andy Hayman and Sir Paul Stephenson have denied any impropriety, and there is no doubt that these instances of hospitality would have caused more controversy if they had not been declared. The case is an interesting example of when legitimate business-related hospitality could be perceived to be moving towards a corrupt relationship. John Yates and other senior officers dined a number of times with News

International's editors, and Commissioner Stephenson dined with the company's executives 18 times during the police investigation.[12] While "perks" with no resale value such as fine dining and spa breaks are not likely to be considered in the same light as payments for information, stories about the frequency with which senior police accepted hospitality compound the damage to the reputation of the Metropolitan Police Service, and contribute to negative public perceptions and suspicion of the existence of a culture within the British establishment conducive to the blunting of moral sensibilities. Transparency International has attacked the complacency of elites which "has allowed a culture of impunity to develop, in which corruption is not seriously analyzed or investigated, and individuals have behaved unethically in the belief that they would not or should not be held to account."[13]

CORPORATE AND INDIVIDUAL LIABILITY?

The recent revelations that a newspaper owned by News Corp. may have authorized its reporters to "hack" into cell phones could have even greater implications than the closing of the *NotW*. The implications of this case are far-reaching in terms of possible law enforcement action and the potential expansion of anti-corruption and fraud theories to new areas of corporate conduct. It is understood that the US Department of Justice is consulting with the UK's Serious Fraud Office on how best to proceed with investigations into the alleged bribery, and that both are conducting preliminary investigations into News International.[14] The additional factor of political pressure to investigate in both countries will also have an unknown impact, since most FCPA investigations generally take place internally, with disclosure to the public only occurring at the end of the investigation. Consequently the Murdoch empire will be in the unusual position of having to conduct its internal investigation at the same time that it is under attack from two sides of the Atlantic.

The potential scale of the investigation is staggering. In addition to the sheer number of alleged payments involved, the complications include the likelihood that the US and UK authorities will want a full accounting of conduct all across the entire News Corp. enterprise, including conduct with regard to any type of interactions with government officials – even if it has nothing to do with the alleged phone hacking. Further, because of the allegedly widespread nature of the conduct, a whole host of related laws could be implicated, including not only violations of the US FCPA anti-bribery provisions, but also the books and records provisions of US securities laws, wire and mail fraud statutes, the US Travel Act (which could be used to reach instances of bribery to private individuals), and other US laws. Under US law, there can be liability even if none of the conduct relating to the alleged corrupt payment occurred within the United States.

Further, as the announcement of a £6.9 million penalty on insurance broker Willis Ltd (for failing to ensure payments it made to third parties were not used to support corrupt purposes) underscores, the UK Financial Services Authority (FSA) is not necessarily going to be a bystander either.

Gregory Husisian, who is a senior counsel with Foley & Lardner LLP and the author of a forthcoming treatise that extensively covers the FCPA and FCPA compliance, gave his opinions on the possible implications of the affair:

> It is highly likely that the U.S. Government will investigate. We have seen in other cases that the Department of Justice will cooperate and share information with the Serious Fraud Office, and it would not be surprising if the DOJ and the SEC worked out a cooperative agreement to have the SFO take the initial lead on this case, since so much of the conduct happened in the United Kingdom. But regardless of which agency goes first, the U.S. Government will want to stake out its position that it also will enforce the FCPA, even in situations where the foreign authorities also are investigating the conduct at issue (much like happened with Siemens). News Corp. is a U.S. issuer, and the bookkeeping and internal controls violations of a U.S. issuer are separate from potential violations of UK bribery laws. If the public allegations turn out to be true, large fines from both governments are highly likely. A further worry for management has to be the issue of personal liability – since the payments allegedly were widespread, one has to wonder whether the SEC would be looking at the situation as one where the corporate controls were so lax that there is the possibility of personal liability, as happened with some senior officials in the Nature's Sunshine investigation.[15]

This last point raised by Husisian is particularly important, because it refers to the possibility that the US Securities and Exchange Commission (SEC) could go after News Corp. senior management for FCPA violations, potentially even in a situation where these individuals are not alleged to have any knowledge of the financial misconduct. The theory would be that these senior officials were in a position to put in place controls to halt the conduct, yet did so little that they had no effective means of knowing about or stopping what is alleged to be widespread corporate misconduct.

The issue is all the more relevant when we consider the growing appetite of law enforcement agencies for taking an increasingly wide interpretation of the FCPA, and the recent propensity of anti-corruption authorities, particularly in the United States, to target individuals rather than, or in addition to, organizations.

Because of the high profile and negative publicity surrounding the affair, News Corporation and its employees (as "issuers" and "domestic concerns" under the FCPA) may well take the route of self-disclosing and working with the DOJ and SEC to attempt to minimize any penalty. Although they cannot be given credit for "voluntary" self-disclosure (since the conduct presumably was reported in the news before any talks occurred with the agencies), there nonetheless is the possibility of gaining mitigating credit for substantial cooperation with investigators. The fact that News Corporation has hired Mark Mendelsohn, former head of the DOJ's criminal fraud division (which is in charge of DOJ FCPA enforcement) gives weight to this possibility. During his term at the DOJ, Mark Mendelsohn oversaw the largest penalties in the history of the anti-corruption enforcement; now he may have the opportunity to be negotiating them from the other side as well – and on two sides of the Atlantic Ocean.

On the UK front, it must be remembered that the Bribery Act will be irrelevant to the investigation into the reports of payments to police officers (Operation Elvedon) because the alleged corruption predates the coming into force of the new legislation.

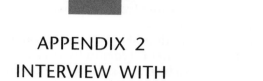

APPENDIX 2
INTERVIEW WITH
RICHARD ALDERMAN, JUNE 27, 2011

The authors held this interview with Richard Alderman shortly before the Bribery Act came into force.

You have spoken about hoping that companies will develop a culture of compliance with the Act. Do you feel that this is being accomplished?
Many companies are well prepared – not least because this is not new to them. They have been working with the FCPA [the US Foreign Corrupt Practices Act] for years. This is something added to that. I have spoken to lots of big companies, sector-wide groupings, lawyers, and many other professionals. My very strong impression is that many companies are well up to this.

They are not only ensuring that they have anti-corruption culture in their own company, they also making sure that those who want to bid for work from them are also implementing an anti-bribery culture. I find that a really interesting and welcome development because that is commercially as well as ethically driven – and therefore more likely to be successful.

Could you elaborate on that?
If you want to do business and you want to bid for a contract from a big company, they may ask you, have you been subject of an investigation regarding corruption? If you have, then you have to disclose it. Clearly that factor will weigh with a big company because they will think: Do we want to do business with these people? They might still decide to take on that company, and let them do business for them – but they are on warning and they might want to insist that there is a much better ethical standard in that company.

So it is in the commercial interests of companies wanting to do business with others, to ensure that they have that proper anti-corruption culture. I see this moving through the economy. It is interesting and very powerful. It is the industry policing itself and I find that is a good way in which an anti-corruption culture can be built up.

You have spoken about self-policing. Could you explain how that will work?

Big companies do not want to find themselves getting into a criminal case because they have failed to prevent bribery which was carried out by somebody who is providing services for them. And if they know or are aware that that company was involved in bribery beforehand, then they have some explaining to do.

This is not just a question of reputation, though that is very important. It is also whether they will find themselves in a criminal court. I don't want that, so I want them to be really rigorous about this and to make sure that an anti-corruption culture is followed in the companies they do business with. So it is ethical but also commercial – in order to protect themselves and make sure they are doing business with the right people.

Does the Serious Fraud Office (SFO) have the power to give a company that comes to you an opinion about a bribery risk?
Yes, we do the same thing. The Department of Justice (DoJ) has an opinion procedure and you can go to them; they will give you a "formal binding opinion," which is then published. We have something similar, though it is rarely used. I don't even think the DoJ procedure is used that much. I have been told that there would be many demands for this, before acquisitions. But I am now no longer sure that the demand is prior the acquisitions, because these acquisitions tend to be made under enormous pressure of time. Sometimes the commercial imperative is to close the deal. If that is so, I am not going to second-guess that.

I would suggest very strongly that if there are corruption issues, the *acquiring* company needs to get in straight away and start sorting it out, and tell us what they are doing. I don't want to find out that reports come to us of what that target company has been up to, and we start an investigation. I would rather suggest to senior management of acquiring companies that if there is a problem I very much want it sorted out, but do tell us what you are doing. And if you prefer to do it after the acquisition, then that is fine by me.

We might wish to consider the position of *individuals* in the target company, and their role. But by and large, if a good company is trying to sort out a bad company, and bring about an anti-corruption culture, that is a good result for society.

I was interested in situations where an unanticipated risk might have been incurred.
That is right, the issues for the company's circumstances, prior to the acquisition, is: Can they make full disclosure when they don't actually know the full detail of what they are likely to uncover? So I recognize the source of that. And if they prefer to come to me afterwards, so be it! But they have the option.

You have said that passive investors in a company where bribery is uncovered are not liable to prosecution under the Act. How would you define

passivity in this case? Is it always clear from public statements that some of these people are as passive as they might claim to be?
If people are shareholders in a company and that company, with its employees, gets involved in bribery, then the company obviously has some criminal issues to talk with us about. But what about the shareholders? Are the company employers providing "services to the shareholders"? Well, normally they are not. Employees provide services to a company, not to its shareholders.

So shareholders normally will not be criminally liable for bribery by a company about which they know nothing. So passive investors, in that sense, are not going to be the subject of criminal action under the Bribery Act.

The caveat I put, though, was to see whether there was any money laundering, or whether or not you enjoyed through dividends or whatever, any of the proceeds of crime. We might want to start tracing that. I tell people, especially major shareholders: Society expects you to do your bit in ensuring proper governance in the companies you are involved in.

People's expectations about behavior and culture are so very different from what they were, say, 20 years ago. They want the big institutions to have a role in the companies they are investing in – to tell them, we expect you to do this, that, and the other. For instance, care for the environment is a no-brainer. I think bribery and corruption is the same.

So we tell investors: Society expects you to play a role here. The may be more we can do in legal terms. We might see more on that in the course of the year. But I said society wants you to do more in terms of the companies you invest in. We will be developing this over the next year or so.

So do you expect investors to get more curious and interventionist in the management of companies where they invest?
Well, making sure that major shareholders will have regular meetings with companies, and they will talk about all sorts of things. Bribery is something that could actually bring down that company. So it seems perfectly right for investing institutions to ask the management: What are you doing? Are you sure you have good procedures now, in terms of the Bribery Act? That is a perfectly legitimate question.

But they would only become a "relevant person" in the event of a prosecution, IF the employee of a company were part of the scheme?
The "failing to prevent bribery" offense applies where an associated person commits bribery, and you have failed to prevent that bribery. A person is, broadly, associated with you if they performed services "on your behalf." So the question is: The employee certainly performed services for that company – but not for the pension fund that holds that company in its portfolio.

So the pension fund is not guilty of failing to prevent bribery, because the bribery is not carried out by an associated person. In the normal type of case the big pension funds won't be on the boards. They won't be involved in running the companies. So I don't think the employees in those cases are providing services to the pension fund.

So if the pension fund is enjoying the dividends, then that could be construed as money laundering?
There are questions that we will be asking about these money flows. I don't think pension funds should be in a position where these questions are asked. Pensioners would be very unhappy to find that their fund had got itself into this difficulty, and I would encourage fund managers to look at what society expects from them.

Given that people are now geared up to implement the Act, is it not time for you to mount some cases? Wouldn't that show people, this is what we meant?
The quickest way of clearing up gray areas is not through the criminal justice system but through clarification from the SFO. If you expect clarification through the justice system, you may have to wait years for a result! Companies do not want to wait for years. They want to know what the position is now, and I very much respect that.

If gray areas are identified then I am encouraging corporate advisors to talk to us, to tell us what this area is. They come to us as well and say, we are concerned at the specific, specialized area of our own industry. So what is the SFO's view on this? We work together on the problem.

What is the likely timescale of prosecutions?
The Bribery Act applies broadly to new bribes that are paid after 1 July. There are some technical transitional provisions that we have to respect. But by and large we will be looking for new bribes paid after 1 July. We have to find those. We then have to investigate, and if there is to be a prosecution, bring it before the criminal courts. It is something that will not see action in criminal courts for some years because of the length of time all of this takes. We won't see such cases for a few years. Although there will be enforcement activity by us before then.

I certainly made no secret of the fact that one of priorities is going after the foreign companies within our jurisdiction that are doing their best to do down ethical UK companies. That is difficult. We are not looking for low-hanging fruit. We are looking for the difficult cases.

We don't want to find that people will think: Oh, those were the easy cases, or "They just knocked off a few small companies because they were easy." That is NOT what we want to do. We want to go for the difficult cases, the most difficult to bring before the criminal courts of this country. When people see them, we want them to think: Yes, these are exactly the sort of cases we want the SFO to bring before the courts.

If we brought a handful of small companies to court over facilitation payments, people would think: What on earth are they up to? That is not what we want to do. We want to go for the big bribes paid by the really corrupt companies. Now finding that is really difficult, but that is what we want to do.

Presumably these are bribes paid by foreign companies, where British companies are going to be the losers, and they will be major companies, bribes, contracts, and they will really show that "we mean business"?
Yes, that is right. It means we can support the UK companies – because if a UK company has lost out, and has had to lay off employees in these difficult economic circumstances, it will make a big impact on families and communities. If we bring a case like that to the criminal courts, the jury will think, yes, this is the sort of case we expect to see from the SFO.

Did the guidance procedures not appear to provide some let-out for foreign companies operating in the UK – more restricted definitions, for instance?
There is some very fine detail about some very specialized circumstances, where the Ministry of Justice said this might have to go before the courts. In most cases those points are not likely to be relevant. If you have a company engaged with the United Kingdom then they are within our jurisdiction. They recognize that.

I say to them: Please don't take a highly technical interpretation of the Bribery Act and persuade yourself that you are NOT within UK jurisdiction, and that you are free to go on bribing. The only safe way is to assume that, if you have that exposure, you need to build up the anti-corruption culture.

The two instances that seem to have some discussion are the question about the mere listing on the UK stock exchange. I questioned how often that happens, because the vast majority of these listings are by foreign companies. They instruct bankers, lawyers; they have places of business here. They are within our jurisdiction because more than a mere listing is involved.

The mere fact of a listing does not bring you within the jurisdiction; that is fine. But when you get more involved with bankers and lawyers in the United Kingdom that takes you beyond a listing. My view is that you are then carrying on business in the United Kingdom. Many people I speak to share that view.

I take the point, I have no difficulty with what the guidance says on that, and I accept that a mere listing, as the Ministry of Justice says, is not enough. What we are looking for is what more there is. If there is more, then we will take the view [that they are] carrying on business over here.

You referred earlier to small companies being understandably less geared up – but also being less at risk because of their lower international profiles. Is that so?
Really small companies are unlikely to be doing international business. But everyone wants them to be successful, and the more that is the case, the more they will explore contracts abroad. My concern is: I do not want

them to think that we expect them to have the same bureaucracy that is essential in running a large company.

If you have an organization of half a dozen people, then all that is necessary is that the head of the organization, the CEO or chairman, says to people around a table: Let's be absolutely clear, we do not do bribes. If it is said [then they] all believe it. That is great; tone from the top, everyone is fine with it. We do not expect to see lots of documents for that level of company.

The bigger the company, the more natural it is for them to have more bureaucracy. But it is tailored to the size of the company. So I am looking for something proportionate. I am, though, worried about where they are looking for advice. I am extremely anxious, and have been for some time, to reach out to the small company sector.

I want to say: I understand you have issues with this. There are concerns and you don't have the level of backup to be expected from large companies. I also want to reassure small companies that they are the backbone of this economy and we want them to succeed. They are dealing with very difficult circumstances and when they deal with people abroad, they have limited backup. I want to make sure that we do not get in the way of what they need to do. I want to be as light touch as possible.

The question is, how do we help them? It has to be through trusted intermediaries, like journalists, magazines, and the organizations they subscribe to, providing them with help and reassurance. There are some things they need to do. It could be as simple as agreeing: We don't do bribes. But they have a really difficult job running a small business, they are multi-tasked. I am trying to find ways to reach them. If people have ideas about how to reach them, I am always interested. It is a sector that worries me.

Couldn't they easily be an informal intermediary, an agent or conduit of a bribe, without being part of the large corporation which has all the procedures?
Well, they could, and of course if they need to check out somebody, if they are looking for help in another country, a big corporate can get associates to do rigorous, thorough searches on: Who are these people, what are their risks?

But if you are a small company you can't do that. Some things you can do, but there is a limit. If you are small, provided you have done some sensible things – Google them, etc. – we are not going to expect you to spend millions of pounds which you have not got, doing due diligence, when your basic searches are not throwing up red flags.

If they do throw up a red flag, then you are on notice. But if not, if it looks all right, we cannot expect much more.

Do you have plans to boost the size of the team for policing the Bribery Act, now that the Act is in force; and now that the SFO has its future assured? [There had been some debate at the time that the UK Government's review

of prosecution agencies might result in the disbandment of the SFO, with its powers dispersed among other agencies. This did not happen.]
We now have a fairly flexible workforce, compared with when I arrived at the SFO when it was based in about seven divisions. We allocated people to each one. Now we have moved away from that with a number of specialists and also a pool of people with high-level specialisms who can be moved around, depending on demand. So when there is big demand in a particular area, as there was earlier this year, we could do that.

If you are going after big corporations it is going to take a lot of diligence and skilful work?
The question is, which bits do you really want to go for, because all of these cases are incredibly complicated. Money has been routed through vast numbers of jurisdictions and there is a raft of complicated offshore structures. So the question is: How do you dismantle them, where do you get your information from, what is it that you want to get before the criminal courts? I do not want a 12–15 months trial in front of a jury. I want the key criminality extracted and a three or four-month trial before a jury, max.

Business Integrity and Corruption

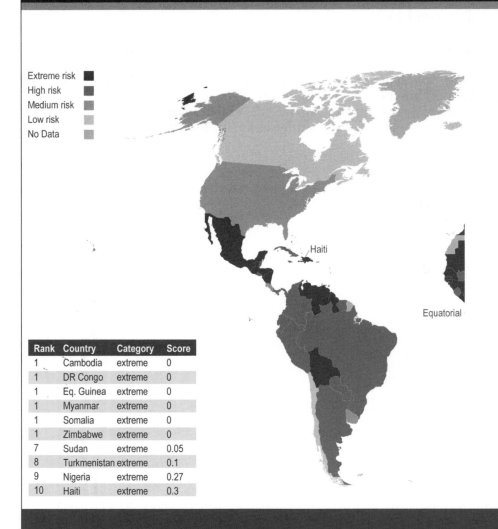

Extreme risk
High risk
Medium risk
Low risk
No Data

Haiti

Equatorial

Rank	Country	Category	Score
1	Cambodia	extreme	0
1	DR Congo	extreme	0
1	Eq. Guinea	extreme	0
1	Myanmar	extreme	0
1	Somalia	extreme	0
1	Zimbabwe	extreme	0
7	Sudan	extreme	0.05
8	Turkmenistan	extreme	0.1
9	Nigeria	extreme	0.27
10	Haiti	extreme	0.3

INTEGRITY AND CORRUPTION INDEX 2011

Index 2011   maplecroft

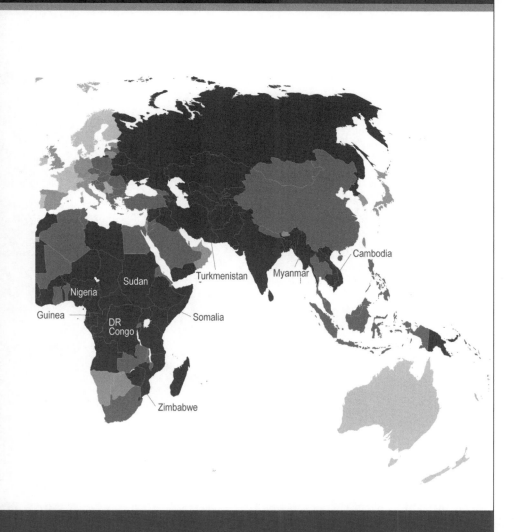

| t: +44 (0) 1225 420 000 | www.maplecroft.com | info@maplecroft.com | humanrights@maplecroft.com

NOTES

PREFACE

1   Ministry of Justice, *The Bribery Act 2010: Guidance about procedures which relevant commercial organisations can put into place to prevent persons associated with them from bribing*, London: Ministry of Justice, p. 2 <www.justice.gov.uk/guidance/docs/bribery-act-2010-guidance.pdf> (accessed May 28, 2011).

2   John Emerich Edward Dalberg Acton, first Baron Acton (1834–1902). The historian and moralist, who was otherwise known simply as Lord Acton, expressed this opinion in a letter to Bishop Mandell Creighton in 1887: "Power tends to corrupt, and absolute power corrupts absolutely. Great men are almost always bad men."

INTRODUCTION

1   Rajib N Sanyal and Subarna K Samanta, "Determinants of bribery in international business," *Thunderbird International Business Review*, Vol. 46, No. 2, 2004, pp. 133–4; Carolyn Warner, ch. 30, "Globalization and corruption," in *The Blackwell Companion to Globalization,* ed George Ritzer, Blackwell, 2007.

2   Speech by Eric Holder: "Attorney General Holder delivers remarks at the Organization for Economic Co-Operation and Development, Paris, France 31/05/2010" <www.justice.gov/ag/speeches/2010/ag-speech-100531.html> (accessed May 2, 2011).

3   Global Witness, <www.globalwitness.org/about-us> (accessed May 2, 2011).

4   Global Witness, <www.globalwitness.org/our-campaigns> (accessed June 6, 2011).

5   BBC World Service, *The World Today: New Year's Revolutions*, December 30, 2010.

6   Speech by Robert Amaee, "Remarks to World Bribery and Corruption Compliance Forum, October 14, 2010" <www.sfo.gov.uk/about-us/our-views/other-speeches/speeches-2010/world-bribery-and-corruption-compliance-forum.aspx> (accessed 2 May 2011).

7   McDermott Will & Emery, "The Bribery Act 2010: raising the bar above the US Foreign Corrupt Practices Act, 2010" <mwe.com/info/news/wp0910b.pdf> (accessed May 2, 2011).

8   Dmitry Medvedev, Statement to Anti-Corruption Council Meeting, Moscow, January 13, 2011.

9   EU Procurement Directive 2004/18, 2004.

10   Lee Young-keun, interviewed in Song Sang-Ho, "ASEAN News: Korea to lead global anti-corruption efforts," *Korea Herald*, November 14, 2010 <www. aseanbusinessforum.com/news/allDetail.php?id=15478&sec=1> (accessed May 2, 2011).

11   Angel Gurría, "Remarks to World Bank and IMF Annual Meeting, Panel on Countering Corruption in International Business and Development Activities," Washington, DC, USA, October 21, 2007 <www.oecd.org/document/26/0,3746 ,en_21571361_39316778_39526682_1_1_1_1,00.html> (accessed 2 May 2011).

12   OECD, Convention on Combating Bribery of Foreign Public Officials in International Business Transactions, 2010, p. 13.

13   Mark Snyderman, "Combating bribery in the supply chain: multinational companies and the UN Global Compact" <www.13iacc.org/files/Snyderman_ slides_for_IACC_supply_chain_panel.ppt> (accessed June 8, 2011).

14   UN Global Compact: The 10 Principles <www.unglobalcompact.org/ aboutthegc/thetenprinciples/index.html> (accessed 2 May 2011).

15   Tom Beezer, "Corporate hospitality could fall foul of the Bribery Act, " Bond Pearce, July 7, 2010 <www.bondpearce.com/.../Corporate_hospitality_foul_of_ Bribery_Act/> (accessed June 8, 2011).

16   Financial Services Authority, *Smaller Wholesale Insurance Intermediaries Newsletter*, Issue 2, June 2010 <www.fsa.gov.uk/pubs/newsletters/gi_jul10.pdf> (accessed May 2, 2011).

17   Financial Services Authority, *Smaller Wholesale Insurance Intermediaries Newsletter*, Issue 2, June 2010, p. 2 <www.fsa.gov.uk/pubs/newsletters/gi_jul10. pdf> (accessed May 2, 2011).

18   Liz David-Barrett, "Avoiding corruption risks in the City: the Bribery Act 2010," report prepared for the City of London Corporation by Transparency International, May 2010 <217.154.230.218/NR/rdonlyres/26DD8F2B-17D9-42B7-AB51-20F1D8542892/0/AvoidingCorruptionRisksintheCity_final.pdf> (accessed May 3, 2011).

19   David Frost quoted in Richard Tyler, "Bona fide corporate freebies 'must survive Bribery Act,'" *Telegraph*, November 8, 2010 <www.telegraph.co.uk/finance/ yourbusiness/8118495/Bona-fide-corporate-freebies-must-survive-Bribery-Act. html> (accessed May 3, 2011).

20   Johann Graf Lambsdorff, "Deterrence and constrained enforcement – alternative regimes to deal with bribery," University of Passau discussion paper no. V-60-10, <www.uni-passau.de>.

21   "Bribes let tomato vendor sell tainted food," *New York Times*, February 24, 2010, <www.nytimes.com/2010/02/25/business/25tomatoes.html> (accessed May 3, 2011).

22   Geetanee Napal, "Is bribery a culturally acceptable practice in Mauritius?" *Business Ethics*, Vol.14, No. 3, September 2005, pp. 231–49.

23   Thomas W Dunfee and Danielle E Warren, "Is *guanxi* ethical? A normative analysis of doing business in China," *Journal of Business Ethics*, Vol. 32, 2001, p. 192.

24   Sheila Puffer and Daniel McCarthy, "One culture's favor is another's bribe," News@Northeastern, Northeastern University, October 22, 2010 <www. northeastern.edu/news/stories/2010/10/favors.html> (accessed May 3, 2011).

25   Christopher Hope, "BAE faces losses over corruption blacklist," *Telegraph*, May

11, 2008 <www.telegraph.co.uk/finance/newsbysector/industry/2789756/BAE-faces-losses-over-corruption-blacklist.html> (accessed May 3, 2011).

26   E. C. Moore Jr, "Causes of demand for international bribery," *Electronic Journal of Business Ethics and Organization Studies*, Vol. 12, No. 2, 2007, p. 19.

27   Wai-Man Liu and Xiaokai Yang, "Good capitalism versus bad capitalism: effects of political monopoly of the ruling elite on the extent of the market, income distribution, and development," Monash University Department of Economics Discussion Papers, No. 08/01, May 2001; Güzin Bayar, "The role of intermediaries in corruption," *Public Choice*, Vol. 122, No. 3, March 2005, pp. 277–98.

28   Dan Roberts, "Bribery is bad for business," *Telegraph*, April 13, 2008 <www.telegraph.co.uk/comment/columnists/danroberts/3557215/Bribery-is-bad-for-business.html> (accessed May 3, 2011).

29   David Voreacos and Laurel Brubaker Calkins, "Shell bribes among 'culture of corruption,' Panalpina admits," Bloomberg, October 5, 2010 <www.bloomberg.com/news/2010-11-05/shell-bribes-among-culture-of-corruption-panalpina-admits.html?cmpid=msnmoney> (accessed May 3, 2011).

30   Authors' correspondence with Sam Eastwood, July 2011.

31   HM Government, UK *Foreign Bribery Strategy*, CM 7791, January 2010, section 3.1.

32   World Bank, press release no: 129/2007/INT, <http://web.worldbank.org/WBSIT E/EXTERNAL/NEWS/0,,contentMDK:21116129~pagePK:64257043~piP K:437376~theSitePK:4607,00.html> (accessed May 3, 2011).

33   Carolyn Warner, "Globalization and corruption," p. 596.

1 THE THREATS

1   Email correspondence between authors and Barry Vitou, Pinsent Masons, Spring 2011.

2   Quoted in Michael Binyon, "Eversheds offers guidance on new bribery law," *The Times*, January 2, 2011 <business.timesonline.co.uk/tol/business/law/article6973414.ece> (accessed May 3, 2011).

3   Angel Gurría, Remarks at World Bank and IMF Annual Meeting Panel on Countering Corruption in International Business and Development Activities, 2007 <www.oecd.org/document/26/0,3746,en_21571361_39316778_39526682_1_1_1_1,00.html> (accessed May 3, 2011).

4   Serious Fraud Office, "Innospec Limited prosecuted for corruption by the SFO," March 18, 2010, <www.sfo.gov.uk/press-room/latest-press-releases/press-releases-2010/innospec-limited-prosecuted-for-corruption-by-the-sfo.aspx> (accessed March 18, 2011).

5   Foreign Policy Centre/Transparency International (UK), seminar briefing "Countering corruption: the role for corporate security," May 1, 2003 <fpc.org.uk/fsblob/139.pdf> (accessed May 3, 2011).

6   Martin Gainsborough, "National integrity system country study," Transparency International, 2006, p. 11 <www.transparency.org/policy_research/nis/nis_reports_by_country> (accessed May 3, 2011).

7   Rajib Sanyal and Subarna Samanta, "Correlates of bribe giving in international business," *International Journal of Commerce and Management*, Vol. 14, No. 2, 2004.

8   James A. Tackett, "Bribery and corruption," *Journal of Corporate Accounting and Finance*, Vol. 21, No. 4, 2010, p. 5.

9   BBC News, "Monsanto fined $1.5 million for bribery," January 7, 2005 <news.bbc.co.uk/1/hi/business/4153635.stm> (accessed May 3, 2011).

10   David Voreacos and Laurel Brubaker Calkins, "Shell bribes among 'culture of corruption', Panalpina admits," Bloomberg, October 5, 2010 <www.bloomberg.com/news/2010-11-05/shell-bribes-among-culture-of-corruption-panalpina-admits.html> (accessed May 3, 2011).

11   Former MD of Thorn's defence system division John Hoakes, quoted in *Guardian*, November 14, 1994, and in Carolyn Warner, ch. 30, "Globalization and corruption," in *The Blackwell Companion to Globalization*, ed. George Ritzer, Blackwell, 2007, p. 608.

12   Author interview.

13   Anne Speckhard and Khapta Akhmedova, "The new Chechen jihad: militant Wahhabism as a radical movement and a source of suicide terrorism in post-war Chechen society," *Democracy and Security*, Vol. 2, No. 1, pp. 103–55, January–June 2006.

14   Ishan Tharoor, "How Somalia's fishermen became pirates," *Time*, April 18, 2009 <www.time.com/time/world/article/0,8599,1892376,00.html> (accessed May 3, 2011).

15   Robert Amaee, speech at World Bribery and Corruption Compliance Forum, November 14, 2010 <www.sfo.gov.uk/about-us/our-views/other-speeches/speeches-2010/world-bribery-and-corruption-compliance-forum.aspx> (accessed May 3, 2011).

16   Bryan W. Husted, "Wealth, culture, and corruption," *Journal of International Business Studies*, Vol. 30, No. 2, 1999, pp. 356–9.

17   Huguette Labelle, "Response to global crises must prioritise zero tolerance for corruption," Transparency International <www.ti.or.id/.../response-to-global-crises-must-prioritise-zero-tolerance-for-corruption> (accessed June 8, 2011).

18   Ke Li, Russell Smyth, and Shuntian Yao, "Institutionalized corruption and privilege in China's socialist market economy: a general equilibrium analysis," *Pacific Economic Review*, Vol. 10, No. 3, pp. 342, October 2005 <papers.ssrn.com/sol3/papers.cfm?abstract_id=817469> (accessed May 3, 2011).

19   John Robb, *Brave New War: The next stage of terrorism and the end of globalization*, Wiley, 2007, p. 86.

2   THE GLOBAL LEGAL CONTEXT

1   Wesley A. Cragg and William Woof, "The US Foreign Corrupt Practices Act and its implications for the control of corruption in political life," <http://home.iscte.pt/~ansmd/CC-Cragg.pdf> (accessed May 27, 2011).

2   Watergate Chronology <http://watergate.info/> (accessed June 8, 2011).

3   Linda Chapman Thompson, Remarks Before the Minority Corporate Counsel 2008 CLE Expo, March 27, 2008 <www.sec.gov/news/speech/2008/spch032708lct.htm> (accessed June 8, 2011).

4   Frontline World, "Corruption in the crosshairs: a brief history of anti-bribery legislation," April 7, 2009 <www.pbs.org/frontlineworld/stories/bribe/2009/04/timeline.html> (accessed May 27, 2011).

5   Cragg and Woof, "The US Foreign Corrupt Practices Act."

6   Cragg and Woof, "The US Foreign Corrupt Practices Act."

7   Memo from Elliot L. Richardson to the US President, June 8, 1976, available on <www.pbs.org/frontlineworld/stories/bribe/images/pdf/richardson_memo_1. pdf> (accessed May 27, 2011).

8   Cragg and Woof, "The US Foreign Corrupt Practices Act"; FCPA Professor, "S 1700 ... a bad bill," October 29, 2009 <http://fcpaprofessor.blogspot.com/ 2009/10/s-1700-bad-bill.html> (accessed May 27, 2011).

9   Frontier World, "Corruption in the crosshairs," April 7, 2009 <www.pbs.org/ frontlineworld/stories/bribe/2009/04/timeline.html> (accessed May 27, 2011).

10 Margaret M. Gatti, Clive R. G. Ogrady, and O. Forrest Morgan, "Foreign Corrupt Practices Act," Amicus Attorney, 1997 <http://library.findlaw.com/1997/ Jan/1/126234.html> (accessed May 27, 2011).

11 Frontline World, "Spotlight: history of the FCPA," February 13, 2009 <www. pbs.org/frontlineworld/stories/bribe/2009/02/history-of-the-fcpa.html> (accessed May 27, 2011).

12 1 billion is defined here as 1,000,000,000.

13 Michael V. Seitzinger, "Foreign Corrupt Practices Act CRS Report to Congress," March 3, 1999 <www.fas.org/irp/crs/Crsfcpa.htm> (accessed May 27, 2011).

14 Multinational Monitor, "ISC: Corporate bribe factory," February 1980 <http:// multinationalmonitor.org/hyper/issues/1980/02/riley.html> (accessed May 27, 2011).

15 Enotes, "Foreign Corrupt Practices Act of 1977," Encyclopedia of Business and Finance <www.enotes.com/business-finance-encyclopedia/foreign-corrupt-practices-act> (accessed May 27, 2011).

16 Statement of Donald L. Scantlebury before various Senate committees on the impact of the FCPA on business, May 20, 1981, available on <http://archive. gao.gov/f0102/115367.pdf> (accessed May 27, 2011).

17 Frontier World, "Corruption in the crosshairs."

18 Frontline World, "Spotlight: history of the FCPA."

19 Seitzinger, "Foreign Corrupt Practices Act CRS Report to Congress"; Lectric Law Library, Excerpt from U.S. Commerce Dept. material dated May 10, 1994, <www.lectlaw.com/files/bur21.htm> (accessed May 27, 2011).

20 Cragg and Woof, "The US Foreign Corrupt Practices Act."

21 Report from Senator Jesse Helms accompanying the Convention on Combating Bribery of Foreign Public Officials in International Business Transactions, July 16, 1998, available on <www.fas.org/irp/congress/1998_rpt/e105-19.htm> (accessed May 27, 2011).

22 US Department of Commerce (USDC) and Department of Justice (DOJ), Lay persons' guide to the FCPA, <www.justice.gov/criminal/fraud/fcpa/docs/ lay-persons-guide.pdf> (accessed May 27, 2011).

23 Stanley R. Soya and David Handler, "The International Anti-Bribery and Fair Competition Act of 1998 amends the Foreign Corrupt Practices Act," 1998 <http://library.findlaw.com/1998/Dec/1/130472.html> (accessed May 27, 2011).

24 Soya and Handler, "The International Anti-Bribery and Fair Competition Act of 1998 amends the Foreign Corrupt Practices Act,"; Seitzinger, "Foreign Corrupt Practices Act CRS Report to Congress."

25 Steven Andersen, "Big sting: January sting sets FCPA precedent," InsideCounsel

<www.insidecounsel.com/Issues/2010/March-2010/Pages/Big-Sting.aspx> (accessed May 27, 2011).

26 Frontier World, "Corruption in the crosshairs."

27 Richard Levick, "Record-breaking FCPA sentence highlights the benefits of cooperation," April 20, 2010 <www.bulletproofblog.com/2010/04/20/record-breaking-fcpa-sentence-highlights-the-benefits-of-cooperation/> (accessed May 27, 2011).

28 "The FCPA explained" <www.fcpaenforcement.com/explained/explained. asp> (accessed May 27, 2011); USDC and DOJ, *Lay persons' guide to the FCPA.*

29 USDC and DOJ, *Lay persons' guide to the FCPA.*

30 Edward G. Hinkelman, Myron Manley, James L. Nolan, Karla C. Shippey, Wendy Bidwell, and Alexandra Woznick, *Importers manual USA*, World Trade Press, p. 98 <http://books.google.co.uk/books?id=SVoVKSXBTzwC&lpg=PA 98&ots=vGeuPskOOR&dq=FCPA%20%22about%20to%20violate%22%20 civil%20action%20SEC&pg=PA98#v=snippet&q=%22about%20to%20vio-late%22&f=false> (accessed May 27, 2011).

31 USDC and DOJ, *Lay persons' guide to the FCPA.*

32 American Bar Association, "FCPA prosecutions: the critical role of the accounting and recordkeeping provisions" <www.abanet.org/buslaw/blt/ content/articl+es/2010/08/0001.shtml> (accessed June 8, 2011).

33 American Bar Association, "FCPA prosecutions."

34 Sheppard Mullin, "The Foreign Corrupt Practices Act: What our clients need to know and why they need to know it," October 11, 2008 <www. governmentcontractslawblog.com/uploads/file/GC08.PPT> (accessed May 27, 2011); Roi Bak, "Foreign Corrupt Practices Act: Legal analysis – antibribery provisions," <www.israelbar.org.il/uploadFiles/Foreign_Corrupt_Practices_ Act.pdf> (accessed May 27, 2011).

35 Paul J. Martinek, "FCPA's other side: accounting enforcement," ComplianceWeek, April 4, 2006 <www.complianceweek.com/article/2413/ fcpa-s-other-side-accounting-enforcement> (accessed May 27, 2011).

36 American Bar Association, "FCPA prosecutions."

37 Shearman & Sterling, "FCPA digest," March 2010 <www.shearman.com/files/ upload/FCPA-Digest-Spring-2010.pdf> (accessed May 27, 2011).

38 Edward J. Fishman and Jeffrey B. Maletta, "FCPA enforcement activity and severity of penalties relating to business activities in China likely to increase dramatically as global trade with China surges to record levels," K&L Gates, February 2007 <www.klgates.com/newsstand/Detail.aspx?publication=3580> (accessed May 27, 2011).

39 Stephen Fishbein and Danforth Newcomb, "Compliance advisers reduce FCPA risk," Law.Com, May 26, 2010 <www.law.com/jsp/cc/PubArticleCC. jsp?id=1202458742540://> (accessed May 27, 2011).

40 Mike Koehler, "What did the Willbros compliance monitor find?" Corporate Compliance Insights, January 6, 2010 <www.corporatecomplianceinsights. com/2010/what-did-the-willbros-compliance-monitor-find/> (accessed May 27, 2011).

41 Shearman & Sterling, "FCPA digest."

42 Shearman & Sterling, "FCPA digest."

43 Reported in the *New York Times*, April 27, 2007.

44 Sue Reisinger, "Why are more companies self-reporting overseas bribes?"

Law.Com, July 16, 2007 <www.law.com/jsp/cc/PubArticleCCjsp?id=118423 11962> (accessed May 27, 2011).

45 Reisinger, "Why are more companies self-reporting overseas bribes?"

46 Wilmer Cutler Pickering Hale and Dorr, "Foreign Corrupt Practices Act Update," January 5, 2005 <www.wilmerhale.com/files/Publication/2169810a-9c0a-46ad-93c27fcb1ff1aa12/Presentation/PublicationAttachment/de152104-ecd5-418e-9eff-80de37b356c4/FCPupdate_Jan2005.pdf> (accessed May 27, 2011).

47 US Securities and Exchange Commission, Litigation Release no. 19078, February 14, 2005 <www.sec.gov/litigation/litreleases/lr19078.htm> (accessed May 27, 2011).

48 OECD, "Country reports on the implementation of the OECD Anti-Bribery Convention," <www.oecd.org/document/24/0,3343,en_2649_34859_193314 4_1_1_1_1,00.html> (accessed May 27, 2011).

49 UK Anti-Corruption Forum, *Newsletter* No. 15, August 2009 <www.anti corruptionforum.org.uk/acf/upload/newsletters/2009-08.pdf> (accessed June 8, 2011).

50 Michael T. Gass, Stephen G. Huggard, and Katherine Barr Hollingsworth, Edwards Angell Palmer & Dodge, "Corporate FCPA compliance programs: a necessity in today's aggressive enforcement environment," 2006 <www.eapdlaw.com/files/News/605faaa2-2fc3-49eb-ba811b005ec9675c/ Presentation/NewsAttachment/1394a9e9-8fbf-44e6-bf17-9ed992347ce5/ Client%20Advisory_Corporate%20FCPA%20Compliance%20Programs.pdf (accessed May 27, 2011).

51 Corporate Compliance Insights, "Deloitte FCPA survey finds 75% of participants concerned about anti-bribery violations," May 20, 2009 <www. corporatecomplianceinsights.com/2009/deloitte-fcpa-survey-results/> (accessed May 27, 2011).

52 Transparency International, "Emerging economic giants show high levels of corporate bribery overseas," 2008 <www.transparency.org/news_room/latest_ news/press_releases/2008/bpi_2008_en> (accessed May 27, 2011).

53 Deloitte, "Look before you leap", February 15, 2010 <www.deloitte. com/assets/Dcom-UnitedStates/Local%20Assets/Documents/us_fas_ LookBeforeYouLeap_021510.pdf> (accessed 1 January, 2011).

54 Law et al News, "FCPA should be enforced more thoughtfully – Dr Andrew Spalding Brady," October 20, 2009 <www.lawetalnews.com/NewsDetail. asp?newsid=81> (accessed May 27, 2011).

55 Shearman & Sterling, "FCPA digest"; Cragg and Woof, "The US Foreign Corrupt Practices Act."

56 Jason Leopold, "KBR says obeying US laws puts company at a competitive disadvantage," The Public Record, March 21, 2009 <http://pubrecord.org/ nation/486/kbr-says-obeying-us-laws-puts-company-at-a-competitive-disadvantage/> (accessed May 27, 2011).

57 Tyler Bridges, "FCPA: execs see benefits, challenges," Latin Business Chronicle, June 28, 2010 <www.latinbusinesschronicle.com/app/article.aspx?id=4312> (accessed May 27, 2011).

58 Thomas Chai-San Chow, "Practical compliance with the Foreign Corrupt Practices Act (FCPA)," 2009 <www.avvo.com/legal-guides/ugc/practical-compliance-with-the-foreign-corrupt-practices-act-fcpa> (accessed May 27, 2011).

59 Bridges, "FCPA: execs see benefits, challenges."

60 Shearman & Sterling, "FCPA digest."

61 Shearman & Sterling, "FCPA digest."

62 Steptoe & Johnson, "International Law Advisory: Late 2006 FCPA enforcement explosion reaches across industries and around the globe, focusing on countries in lower ranks in the Transparency International 2006 Corruption Perceptions Index," November 6, 2006 <www.steptoe.com/publications-3949.html#3> (accessed May 27, 2011).

63 FCPA Blog, "Mandarins gone wild," December 7, 2008 <http://fcpablog. squarespace.com/blog/tag/china?currentPage=15> (accessed May 27, 2011).

64 Claudius Sokenu, "United States: FCPA insights: post Akzo-Nobel and Flowserve – is the jurisdictional scope of the Foreign Corrupt Practices Act all-encompassing?" Mondaq, May 6, 2008 <www.mondaq.com/unitedstates/ article.asp?articleid=59764> (accessed May 27, 2011).

65 Steptoe & Johnson, "International Law Advisory."

66 Shearman & Sterling, "FCPA digest."

67 FCPA Blog, "Mandarins gone wild."

68 Sokenu, "United States: FCPA insights."

69 Steptoe & Johnson, "International Law Advisory."

70 US DOJ, "Former senior officer of Schnitzer Steel Industries Inc. subsidiary pleads guilty to foreign bribes," press release, June 29, 2007 <www.justice.gov/ opa/pr/2007/June/07_crm_474.html> (accessed May 27, 2011).

71 US Securities & Exchange Commission v. York International Corp., US District Court for the District of Columbia, Case: 1 :07-cv-01750, 2007 <www.sec.gov/ litigation/complaints/2007/comp20319.pdf> (accessed May 27, 2011).

72 Roger M. Witten, Kimberly A. Parker, and Jay Holtmeier, "FCPA developments include increased enforcement related to UN Oil-for-Food Program and reinstatement of charges in *Kozeny* case," WilmerHale, October 24, 2007 <www.wilmerhale.com/publications/whPubsDetail.aspx?publication=8087> (accessed May 27, 2011).

73 FCPA Blog, "Guilty plea by shot-show defendant," April 29, 2011 <www. fcpablog.com/blog/tag/richard-bistrong> (accessed May 27, 2011).

74 Diana B. Henriques, "Supplier accused of bribes for UN contracts," *New York Times*, January 22, 2010 <www.nytimes.com/2010/01/23/business/23sting. html?_r=1> (accessed May 27, 2011).

75 James T. Parkinson and Elisa F. Kantor, "FCPA sting operation: 22 arrested in US; search warrants executed simultaneously in US and UK," Mayer Brown, January 21, 2010 <www.mayerbrown.com/publications/article.asp?id=8461&nid=6> (accessed May 27, 2011).

76 McGuire Woods, "Catch 22: Lessons from DOJ's massive undercover FCPA sting," January 22, 2010 <www.mcguirewoods.com/news-resources/item. asp?item=4481> (accessed May 27, 2011).

77 FCPA Blog, "Guilty plea by shot-show defendant."

78 Miller Chevalier, "Historic FCPA sting nets 22 individuals," January 20, 2010 <www.millerchevalier.com/Publications/MillerChevalierPublications?find=2 4405> (accessed May 27, 2011).

79 See 'The Trace Compendium,' Armor Holdings/Bistrong for an account of the US Government settlement with Armor Holdings.

80 DOJ press release, July 13, 2011; SEC press release, July 13, 2011; Complaint: SEC vs Armor Holdings Inc (July 13, 2011).

81 US DOJ, "Former Willbros International consultant pleads guilty to $6 million foreign bribery scheme," press release, November 12, 2009 <www.justice.gov/opa/pr/2009/November/09-crm-1220.html> (accessed May 27, 2011).

82 Amy Miller, "'He shut it down': GC smashes bribery ring at own company," February 12, 2010 <www.law.com/jsp/cc/PubArticleCC. jsp?id=1202443205137&hubType=Top%20Story&He_Shut_It_Down_GC_Smashes_Bribery_Ring_at_Own_Company> (accessed May 27, 2011).

83 Abiodun Oluwarotimi, "Nigeria: court halts deportation of US fugitive," All Africa.Com, August 19, 2010 <http://allafrica.com/stories/201008200974. html> (accessed May 27, 2011); Abiodun Oluwarotimi, "Nigeria: $6m scam: court halts deportation of US fugitive," All Africa.Com, August 20, 2010 <http://allafrica.com/stories/201008200687.html> (accessed May 27, 2011).

84 United States versus James H. Giffen, et al, case filed on April 2, 2003, in the Southern District of New York <www.justice.gov/criminal/fraud/fcpa/cases/giffen-etal.html> (accessed May 27, 2011).

85 United States versus James H. Giffen; Practising Law Institute, "The Foreign Corrupt Practices Act 2009: coping with heightened enforcement risks," PLI Order No. 18499 New York City, April 29, 2009, Chicago, May 29, 2009 San Francisco, June 26, 2009, Introduction, Donald Zarin Holland & Knight LLP, 1737 PLI/Corp 95.

86 David Glovin, "Seven year Kazakhstan bribery case ends with 'sputtering' misdemeanor plea," Bloomberg, August 6, 2010 <www.bloomberg.com/news/2010-08-06/oil-consultant-giffen-to-plead-guilty-to-misdemeanor-after-bribery-charges.html> (accessed May 27, 2011).

87 Larry Neumeister, "NY judge: Kazakh bribe defendant is cold war hero," ABC News, November 19, 2010 <http://abcnews.go.com/US/wireStory?id=12196186> (accessed May 27, 2011).

88 United States versus James H. Giffen.

89 United States versus James H. Giffen.

90 Justia, 473 F.3d 30: United States of American, Apellant, v. James H Giffen, Defendant-appellee <http://law.justia.com/cases/federal/appellate-courts/F3/473/30/589178/> (accessed May 27, 2011).

91 Mike Koehler, "The Giffen gaffe – the final chapter," FCPA Professor, November 22, 2010 <fcpaprofessor.blogspot.com>.

92 Quoted by Mike Koehler, "The Giffen gaffe."

93 David Glovin, "Oil dealer Giffen avoids prison in onetime bribe case," Bloomberg Businessweek, November 19, 2010 <www.businessweek.com/.../2010...19/oil-dealer-giffen-avoids-prison-in-onetime-bribe-case.html> (accessed June 8, 2011).

94 Steve LeVine, "James Giffen update," FCPA Professor, August 6, 2010 <fcpaprofessor.blogspot.com> (accessed June 8, 2011).

95 LeVine, "James Giffen update."

96 FCPA Blog, "Longest FCPA prison sentence," April 19, 2010 <www.fcpablog. com/blog/2010/4/19/longest-fcpa-prison-sentence.html> (accessed May 27, 2011).

97 US DOJ, "Virginia resident sentenced to 87 months in prison for bribing

foreign government officials," press release, April 19, 2010 <www.justice.gov/opa/pr/2010/April/10-crm-442.html> (accessed May 27, 2011).

98 United States v. Charles Paul Edward Jumet, Court Docket Number: 09-CR-397-HEH, filed on November 10, 2009, in the Eastern District of Virginia <www.justice.gov/criminal/fraud/fcpa/cases/jumetc.html> (accessed May 27, 2011).

3 BRITISH BRIBERY LEGISLATION

1   A. Doig, *Corruption and Misconduct in Contemporary British Politics*. London: Penguin, 1984, p. 127.
2   Doig, *Corruption and Misconduct*, pp. 130–2.
3   Doig, *Corruption and Misconduct*, p. 357.
4   Doig, *Corruption and Misconduct*, p.127.
5   Owen Luder, *Oxford Biography* index entry for John Poulson, <www.oxforddnb. com/index/101053151/> (accessed June 8, 2011).
6   R. Fitzwalter and D. Taylor *Web of Corruption: The Story of John Poulson and T. Dan Smith*, Manchester: Granada, 1981, p. 52.
7   Doig, *Corruption and Misconduct*, p. 127.
8   The Prime Minister's Committee on Local Government Rules of Conduct, *Conduct in Local Government: Report (the Redcliffe-Maud Report)*, Cmnd 4040, London: HMSO, May 1977.
9   Royal Commission on Standards of Conduct in Public Life, *Report 1974–76 (the Salmon Report)*, Cmnd 6524, London: HMSO, 1976.
10 Doig, *Corruption and Misconduct*, pp. 148–9.
11 Committee on Standards in Public Life, *Standards in Public Life: First Report of the Committee on Standards in Public Life (the Nolan Report)*, Cmnd 2850, London: HMSO, 1995.
12 *Nolan Report*.
13 Law Commission, "Legislating the criminal code: corruption" <www.justice.gov.uk/lawcommission/docs/lc248_Legislating_the_Criminal_Code_Corruption.pdf>, p. 28 (accessed May 28, 2011).
14 *Nolan Report*.
15 *Nolan Report,* para 2.59.
16 *Nolan Report*, para 2.70.
17 *Nolan Report*, paras 2.90–2.102.
18 *Nolan Report*, para 3.53.
19 House of Lords Debate, Defamation Bill 596, March 8, 1996, *Hansard,* Vol. 570, cc. 576–610, <http://hansard.millbanksystems.com/lords/1996/mar/08/defamation-bill-hl> (accessed June 14, 2011).
20 Joint Committee on the Draft Corruption Bill, Session 2002–2003, HL Paper 157, HC 705 (2003), quoted in Law Commission, *Reforming Bribery*, HC928, London: Law Commission, November 2008, para 2.37.
21 Committee on Standards in Public Life, *MPs' Expenses and Allowances*, Cmnd 7724, London: The Stationery Office, November 2009 <www.public-standards.gov.uk/Library/MP_expenses_main_report.pdf> (accessed May 28, 2011).
22 Law Commission, "Legislating the criminal code: corruption."
23 OECD, Convention on Combating Bribery of Foreign Public Officials in

International Business Transactions, Paris: OECD. <www.oecd.org/documen
t/20/0,3343,en_2649_34859_2017813_1_1_1_1,00.html> (accessed May 28,
2011).

24 Home Office, *Corruption: Draft Legislation*, Cmnd 5777, London: HMSO, March
2003.

25 "The government reply to the Report from the Joint Committee on the Draft
Corruption Bill, Session 2002–2003," HL paper 157, HC 705, Cmnd 6086,
London: The Stationery Office, July 2003 <www.archive2.official-documents.
co.uk/document/cm60/6086/6086.pdf> (accessed May 28, 2011).

26 "Government reply to the Report from the Joint Committee on the Draft
Corruption Bill," CM 6086, London: The Stationery Office, December 18, 2003.

27 HM Government, *Bribery: Reform of the Prevention of Corruption Acts and SFO
Powers in Cases of Bribery of Foreign Officials: a consultation paper*, London: The
Stationery Office, December 2005.

28 Law Commission, *Reforming Bribery: A Consultation Paper*, No 185, London:
Law Commission, November 2007.

29 Law Commission, "Reforming bribery," LC313, London: Law Commission,
October 2008.

30 OECD: Working Group on Bribery, October 2008, Annual Report, <www.oecd.
org/dataoecd/21/24/44033641.pdf> (accessed June 14, 2011).

31 Law Commission, "Reforming bribery," LC313.

32 *Joint Committee on the Draft Bribery Bill First Report*, HC 430-I, HL 115-I- HC
430-I, London: The Stationery Office, 2009.

33 Steve Boggan, "The Mark Thatcher affair," *Independent*, October 10, 1994.

34 Dominic O'Connell, "BAE cashes in on £40bn Arab jet deal", *Sunday Times*,
August 22, 2006.

35 BBC News, "Q&A: How are arms deals done?" February 5, 2010 <http://news.
bbc.co.uk/1/hi/business/8284853.stm>(accessed May 28, 2011).

36 BBC, "Q&A: How are arms deals done?"

37 BBC, "Q&A: How are arms deals done?"

38 YouTube from Wn.Com, "Bandar Bin Sultan, Saudi money is mine and I do
what I want with it" (video) <http://wn.com/bandar_bin_sultan_saudi_
money_is_mine_and_i_do_what_i_want_with_it> (accessed May 28, 2011).

39 BBC, "Blair defends Saudi probe ruling," December 15, 2006 <http://news.bbc.
co.uk/1/hi/uk_politics/6182125.stm> (accessed June 14, 2011).

40 Sean O'Neill, "BAE Systems 'paid actresses to entertain Saudi prince,'" *The
Times*, April 2, 2007 <http://www.timesonline.co.uk/tol/news/uk/article1599
694.ece> (accessed June 14, 2011).

41 BBC News, "Timeline: BAE corruption probe", February 5, 2010 <http://news.
bbc.co.uk/1/hi/business/8501655.stm> (accessed May 28, 2011).

42 "Swiss investigate BAE corruption claims," *Observer*, May 13, 2007 <www.
guardian.co.uk/world/2007/may/13/bae.armstrade> (accessed May 28, 2011).

43 Reuters, "BAE pleads guilty to US conspiracy charge," March 1, 2010. <http://
www.reuters.com/article/2010/03/01/bae-plea-idUSN0110271820100301>
(accessed June 14, 2011)

44 Rob Evans and David Leigh, "Judge 'astonished' by corruption demals as he
fines BAE £500,000," *Guardian*, December 21, 2010 <www.guardian.co.uk/
world/2010/dec/21/bae-fined-illicit-payments-middleman> (accessed May 28,
2011).

45 Rob Evans and David Leigh, "Judge questions BAE deal over payments for Tanzania contract," *Guardian*, December 20, 2010 <www.guardian.co.uk/business/2010/dec/20/judge-bae-deal-tanzania-contract> (accessed May 28, 2011).

46 Andrew Hosken, "BAE: the Tanzanian connection," October 1, 2009 <http://news.bbc.co.uk/today/hi/today/newsid_8284000/8284510.stm> (accessed June 14, 2011).

47 Robin Cook quoted in Tim Web, *Bribing for Britain, Campaign against the arms trade*, p. 16 <www.caat.org.uk/resources/publications/corruption/Goodwin5_web.pdf> (accessed June 14, 2011).

48 "BAE systems fined for Tanzanian radar sale: reaction," *Telegraph*, December 21, 2010 <www.telegraph.co.uk/finance/newsbysector/industry/defence/ 8217 190/BAE-Systems-fined-for-Tanzania-radar-sale-reaction.html> (accessed June 14, 2011).

49 "Ethical business conduct in BAE systems plc – the way forward," May 2008 <http://ir.baesystems.com/investors/storage/woolf_report_2008.pdf> (accessed June 14, 2011).

50 "Ethical business conduct in BAE Systems plc – the way forward: Executive summary" <http://ir.baesystems.com/investors/storage/woolf_report_recom mendations.pdf> (accessed May 28, 2011).

51 Dick Olver, "Woolf Committee Report" <http://ir.baesystems.com/investors/woolf/> (accessed June 14, 2011).

52 Russell Hotten, "BAE hopes its SFO settlement marks a new chapter", BBC, February 5, 2010 <www.bbc.co.uk/2/hi/business/8500742.stm> (accessed June 8, 2011).

4 THE UK BRIBERY ACT

1   Serious Fraud Office, "Bribery Act 2010: Joint prosecution guidance of the director of the Serious Fraud Office and the director of prosecutions," London: Serious Fraud Office, p. 4 <www.sfo.gov.uk/media/167348/bribery act joint prosecution guidance.pdf> (accessed May 28, 2011).

2   "Joint prosecution guidance," p. 6.

3   Ministry of Justice, *The Bribery Act 2010: Guidance about procedures which relevant commercial organisations can put into place to prevent persons associated with them from bribing*, London: Ministry of Justice, p. 10 <www.justice.gov.uk/guidance/docs/bribery-act-2010-guidance.pdf> (accessed May 28, 2011).

4   "Joint prosecution guidance," p. 6.

5   Bond Pearce, *Bribery and Anti-Corruption: Key Issues on the Bribery Act 2010*, Bristol: Bond Pearce, p. 2 <www.docstoc.com/docs/71072992/Bribery-and-anti-corruption-key-issues-on-the-Bribery-Act-2010-May-> (accessed May 28, 2011).

6   Ministry of Justice, *The Bribery Act 2010: Guidance*, p. 11.

7   Bond Pearce, *Bribery and Anti-Corruption,* p. 3.

8   Ministry of Justice, *The Bribery Act 2010: Guidance*, p. 12.

9   Bond Pearce, *Bribery and Anti-Corruption,* p. 3.

10 "Joint prosecution guidance," p. 16.

11 "Bribery Act in force from July 1: Ken Clarke's Statement in full" <thebriberyact. com/.../bribery-act-in-force-from-july-1-ken-clarkes-statement-in-full/> (accessed June 8, 2011).

12 "Joint prosecution guidance," pp. 10–11.

13 Barry Vitou and Richard Kovalevsky, "Important: debarment not mandatory for conviction of failure to prevent bribery offence," The Bribery Act.Com, March 31, 2011 <http://thebriberyact.com/2011/03/31/important-debarment-not-mandatory-for-conviction-of-failure-to-prevent-bribery-offence/> (accessed May 28, 2011).

14 Email correspondence between authors and Barry Vitou, Spring 2011.

15 Ministry of Justice, *The Bribery Act 2010: Guidance*, p. 9.

16 Jane Croft and Elizabeth Rigby, "Fraud chief vows tough stance on Bribery Act," *Financial Times*, March 30, 2011 <www.ft.com/cms/s/0/a7c5d7b2-5b07-11e0-a290-00144feab49a.html> (accessed June 8, 2011).

17 Global Witness, "Government bows to pressure from business to allow bribery through the back door" <www.globalwitness.org/.../government-bows-pressure-business-allow-bribery-through-back-door> (accessed June 8, 2011).

18 Transparency International 2011, "Government guidance deplorable and will weaken the Bribery Act," press release, March 30, 2011.

19 Barry Vitou and Richard Kovalevsky, "A lot more than just the Bribery Act guidance – our essential roundup of the year so far," April 1, 2011 <http://thebriberyact.com/2011/04/01/newsletter-a-lot-more-than-just-bribery-act-guidance-our-essential-round-up-of-the-year-so-far/> (accessed May 28, 2011).

20 The following section is a verbatim account of an interview that took place between the author and Lord Goldsmith on April 18, 2011.

21 Letter from Lord Tunnicliffe to Lord Henley, January 14, 2010 <www.justice.gov.uk/publications/docs/letter-lord-henley-corporate-hospitality.pdf> (accessed May 28, 2011).

22 Joint Committee on the Draft Bribery Bill, Draft Bribery Bill <www.publications.parliament.uk/pa/jt200809/jtselect/jtbribe/115/11510.htm> (accessed May 28, 2011). The material that follows is drawn from Fiona Trust and Holding Corporation Oars v. Privalov Oars (2010) EWHC 3199 (COMM), <www.bailii.org/cgi-bin/markup.cgi?doc=/ew/cases/EWHC/Comm/2010/3199.html&query=fiona+and+trust&method=boolean> (accessed May 28, 2011).

23 Ince & Co, "The Fiona Trust litigation and the Bribery Act 2010" <www.incelaw.com/documents/pdf/Strands/Commercial-Disputes/the-fiona-trust-litigation-and-the-bribery-act-2010.pdf> (accessed May 28, 2011).

24 South Africa Supreme Court of Appeal, Comshipco Shiffahrtsagentur GmbH v Commissioner for South African Revenue Service (472/98) [2001] ZASCA 24 (19 March 2001) <www.saflii.org/za/cases/ZASCA/2001/24.html> (accessed May 28, 2011).

25 England and Wales High Court (Commercial Court) Decisions, various parties, [2010] EWHC 3199 (Comm) <www.bailii.org/cgibin/markup.cgi?doc=/ew/cases/EWHC/Comm/2010/3199.html&query=fiona+and+trust&method=boolean> (accessed May 28, 2011); Ince & Co, "The Fiona Trust litigation and the Bribery Act 2010."

5 THE GEOGRAPHIC FACTOR

1   Liz David-Barrett, "Avoiding corruption risks in the City: the Bribery Act 2010," report for City of London Corporation by Transparency International, 2010.

2   OECD, "Risk awareness tool for multinational enterprises in weak governance zones," 2006, p. 12, <www.oecd.org/document/5/0,3746,en_2649_34889_368 99994_1_1_1_1,00.html> (accessed May 28, 2011).

3   Christopher Booth, Michael Segon, and Tim O'Shannassy, "Managerial perspectives of bribery and corruption in Vietnam," *International Review of Business Research Papers*, Vol. 6, No 1, 2010, pp. 574–89.

4   James A. Tackett, "Bribery and corruption," *Journal of Corporate Accounting and Finance*, Vol. 21, No. 4, May/June 2010, pp. 5–9.

5   Ke Li, Russell Smyth, and Shuntian Yao, "Institutionalized corruption and privilege in China's socialist market economy: a general equilibrium analysis," *Pacific Economic Review*, Vol. 10, No. 3, October 2005, p. 343.

6   Hitesh Patel, partner at KPMG Forensic, in Katie Allen, "Recession pushes white-collar crime to new highs," *Guardian*, December 31, 2010 <www.guardian. co.uk>.

7   Carolyn Warner, "Globalization and corruption," ch. 30 in *The Blackwell Companion to Globalization*, ed. George Ritzer, Oxford: Blackwell, 2007.

8   Interview with DI Whatmore, Metropolitan Police Service, Spring 2011.

9   UK Ministry of Justice, *UK Foreign Bribery Strategy*, CM7791, London: The Stationery Office, January 2010 <www.justice.gov.uk/uk-foreign-bribery-strategy.pdf>(accessed February 2, 2011).

10 Trace International, *Global Enforcement Report 2010*, p. 2 <www.traceinter national.org>.

11 Christopher Hope, "BAE faces losses over corruption blacklist," *Telegraph*, May 11, 2008 <www.telegraph.co.uk>.

12 Liz David-Barrett, "Avoiding corruption risks in the City."

13 Russell Hotten. "BAE is not afraid of the big bad Woolf Report," *Telegraph*, May 11, 2008 <www.telegraph.co.uk/finance/newsbysector/industry/2789757/ BAE-is-not-afraid-of-the-big-bad-Woolf-Report.html> (accessed May 29, 2011).

14 OECD, "Risk awareness tool for multinational enterprises in weak governance zones," p. 26.

15 Email correspondence between authors and Barry Vitou, Spring 2011

16 OECD, "Risk awareness tool for multinational enterprises in weak governance zones," p. 25.

17 OECD, "Risk awareness tool for multinational enterprises in weak governance zones," p. 9.

18 John Robb, *Brave New War: The next stage of terrorism and the end of globalization*, Chichester: Wiley, 2007, p. 92.

19 OECD, "OECD offer guidance for multinationals in weak governance zones" <www.oecd.org/document/6/0,2340,en_2649_34529562_36887622_1_1_1_3 4529562,00.html> (accessed June 9, 2011).

20 City of London Police, "Overseas corruption assessment for The UK Bribery Strategy Group", draft report, January 15, 2010, pp. 88–9.

21 Marianne Kearney and Thomas Bell, "General Suharto divides Indonesia in death," *Telegraph*, January 27, 2008 <www.telegraph.co.uk/news/world

news/1576745/General-Suharto-divides-Indonesia-in-death.html> (accessed May 28, 2011); Fiona Robertson-Snape, "Corruption, collusion and nepotism in Indonesia," *Third World Quarterly,* Vol. 20, Issue 3, 1999, pp. 589–602.

22 Transparency International, *Global Corruption Report 2004* <www.transparency.org/publications/gcr/gcr_2004#download> (accessed May 28, 2011); BBC News, "Suharto tops corruption rankings," March 25, 2004 <http://news.bbc.co.uk/1/hi/3567745.stm> (accessed May 28, 2011).

23 Transparency International, *Measuring Corruption in Indonesia: Perception Index 2008 and Bribery Index,* <www.ti.or.id/media/documents/2010/11/09/i/p/ipk-english_final.pdf> (accessed May 28, 2011).

24 M. C. Ricklefs, *A History of Modern Indonesia since c.1200,* 3rd edn, Stanford, Calif.: Stanford University Press, 2001.

25 Ross H. McLeod, "Soeharto's Indonesia: a better class of corruption," *Agenda,* Vol. 7, No. 2, 2000, pp. 99–112.

26 Author's interview with local businessman, October 25, 2008, Jakarta.

27 Author's interview with local businessman, October 25, 2008, Jakarta.

28 Emerging Markets Direct, Report on Indonesia's construction industry, May 5, 2010.

29 Chartered Institute of Building (CIB), *Corruption in the UK Construction Industry,* 2006.

30 CIB, *Corruption in the UK Construction Industry.*

31 Author interview with local businessman, October 25, 2008, Jakarta

32 J. Vernon Henderson, Brown University, and Ari Kuncoro, Brown University and University of Indonesia, *Corruption in Indonesia,* April 2006.

33 Author interview with local businessman, October 26, 2008, Jakarta.

34 Henderson and Kuncoro, *Corruption in Indonesia.*

35 Henderson and Kuncoro, *Corruption in Indonesia.*

36 Henderson and Kuncoro, *Corruption in Indonesia.*

37 Author interview with local businessman, October 24, 2008.

38 *Jakarta Globe,* March 9, 2010.

39 Author interview with local civic administrator, October 25, 2008.

40 Henderson and Kuncoro, *Corruption in Indonesia.*

41 Report by Abbas Kadhim, assistant professor of national security affairs, Naval Postgraduate School, Monterey, California, in *Arab Bulletin,* Carnegie Endowment for International Peace, March 3, 2010.

42 Kadhim, *Arab Bulletin.*

43 CBS News, "Iraq: state of corruption," February 11, 2009.

44 CBS News, "Iraq: state of corruption."

45 *Independent on Sunday,* May 29, 2009.

46 Author interview with international agency representative, January 7, 2010.

47 Author interview with international agency representative, January 7, 2010.

48 Economywatch.com on Angola economy, accessed 11 June, 2011.

49 *Angola Infrastructure,* market research report, bharatbook.com <www.bharatbook.com/detail.asp?id=125545&rt=Angola-Infrastructure-Report.html> (accessed May 10, 2011).

50 Assis Malaquias, "Making war and lots of money: the political economy of protracted conflict in Angola," *Review of African Political Economy,* Vol. 28, Issue 90, 2001, pp. 521–36.

51 Malaquias, "Making war and lots of money."

52   <www.allafrica.com>, 5 August 2010 (accessed 11 June 2011).
53   *Doing business in Angola*, 2010.
54   *Doing business in Angola*, 2010.
55   CIA country report.
56   BBC News, October, 18 2002.
57   Global Witness, *Global Corruption Report 2004, Special Focus: Political Corruption*, Transparency International, February 2004.
58   Global Witness, *Global Corruption Report 2004*.
59   Author's interview with local businessman, February 19, 2008.
60   HumanRights Watch, "Transparency and accountability in Angola: an update," report, April 13, 2010.
61   Interview with local businessman, February 19, 2008.
62   HumanRights Watch, "Transparency and accountability in Angola."
63   Interview with local businessman, February 19, 2008.
64   City of London Police, "Overseas corruption assessment for the UK Bribery Strategy Group", draft report, January 15, 2010, pp. 63–71.
65   City of London Police, "Overseas corruption assessment," pp. 63–71.
66   AfricaFiles, "Corruption prerequisite for government contracts," September 24, 2009 <www.africafiles.org/article.asp>.
67   AfricaFiles, "Corruption prerequisite for government contracts."
68   AfricaFiles, "Corruption prerequisite for government contracts."
69   AfricaFiles, "Corruption prerequisite for government contracts."
70   AfricaFiles, "Corruption prerequisite for government contracts."
71   HumanRights Watch, "Transparency and accountability in Angola."
72   "Angola's president calls for crackdown on corruption," BBC News, November 21, 2009.
73   AfricaFiles, "Corruption prerequisite for government contracts."
74   AfricaFiles, "Legal doubts over Thales Angola deal; ABB reaches settlement with SEC in July 2004," <www.africafiles.org>. The SEC alleged: "ABB's subsidiaries made corrupt payments to Angolan government officials during a period beginning before, and continuing after, ABB became a reporting company in the United States. The payments were made to Sonangol engineers who had responsibility for the technical evaluation of bid submitted to Sonangol, and were issued in the context of three separate training trips sponsored by ABB from 2000 to 2002 <www.sec.gov/litigation/complaints/comp18775.pdf> (accessed June 14, 2011).
75   Filomeno Vieira Lopes, *Conciliation Resources, the Challenges of Democratisation* (in Angola) (2004).
76   Lopes, *Conciliation Resources*.
77   Report concerning Investec in "How we made it in Africa," November 15, 2010.
78   Global Witness, report on Angola, December 2, 2010.
79   Author interview with investigator, February 19, 2008.
80   HumanRights Watch, "Transparency and Accountability in Angola"; Center for Public Integrity, "Greasing the skids of corruption, making a killing, the business of war," report, November 4, 2002.
81   Author interview with investigator, February 2008.
82   Centre for Policy Dialogue (CPD), "State of the Bangladesh economy in FY2010–11," paper prepared under the programme Independent Review of Bangladesh's Development (IRBD), January 4, 2011.

83 Transparency International, "Bangladesh," report, October 28, 2010.
84 Transparency International, "Bangladesh."
85 UN International Strategy for Disaster Reduction (UNISDR), *Mortality Risk Index*, June 15, 2009; Jonathan Lynn, "Bangladesh and China top U.N. disaster risk index," Reuters, June 15, 2009 <www.reuters.com/article/2009/06/15/us-disasters-idUSTRE55E4ZM20090615> (accessed May 29, 2011).
86 <www.discoverybangladesh.com> (accessed June 11 2011).
87 "Bangladesh's chain of corruption," September 22, 2009 <www.upiasia.com>.
88 Local aid worker, in interview with author, March 2009.
89 Local aid worker, in interview with author, March 2009.
90 Local aid worker, in interview with author, March 2009.
91 Almas Zakiuddin, "Corruption in Bangladesh, an analytical and sociological study," report, Transparency International – Bangladesh.
92 Local aid worker, in interview with author, March 2009.
93 <www.charitycommission.gov.uk> (accessed June 2011).
94 Zakiuddin, "Corruption in Bangladesh."
95 Zakiuddin, "Corruption in Bangladesh."
96 Author interview with local businessman, March 2009.
97 Md.Rafiqul Islam Suzan, " Public procurement and corruption in Bangladesh, confronting the challenges and opportunities," *Journal of Public Administration and Policy Research*, August 2010.
98 Suzan, " Public procurement and corruption in Bangladesh."
99 Suzan, " Public procurement and corruption in Bangladesh."
100 Local aid worker, in interview with author, March 2009.
101 Suzan, " Public procurement and corruption in Bangladesh."
102 Local aid worker, in interview with author, March 2009.
103 Transparency International, "Bangladesh."
104 Local aid worker, in interview with author, March 2009.
105 Author interview with local businessman, Nassib Ghobril, Sarada Investment House, July 23, 2007.
106 Trip Van Noppen, "Bleeding Gulf is evidence of corruption in oil drilling oversight," Earthjustice.com, May 19, 2010 <http://earthjustice.org/blog/2010-may/bleeding-gulf-evidence-corruption-oil-drilling-oversight> (accessed June 16, 2011).
107 "Corruption fight pledged," *Gulf Daily News*, December 9, 2004.
108 Alharbi Ali Khalaf, "An overview of the Saudi Arabian criminal justice procedures against corruption in the public sector."
109 "Corruption high in Dubai state firms," December 31, 2009 <www.Maktoob.com>.
110 "Corruption watchdog lauds UAE," The National (Dubai), 2010 <www.thenational.ae/>.
111 Martin Hvit, "Ease of doing business in the gulf countries" <http://static.sdu.dk/mediafiles//Files/Om_SDU/Centre/C_Mellemoest/Videncenter/Nyheder/2009/090630MH.pdf> (accessed June 14, 2011).
112 Martin Hvit, "Ease of doing business in the gulf countries."
113 Jadaliyya, "The modernization of bribery: the arms trade in the Arab Gulf," December 10, 2010 <www.jadaliyya.com/pages/index/413/the-modernization-of-bribery_the-arms-trade-in-the> (accessed June 14, 2011).
114 City of London Police, "Overseas corruption assessment for the UK Bribery Strategy Group", draft report, January 15, 2010, pp. 95–103.

115 Jibrin Abubakar, "Nigeria's economy and the Failed States Index," *Daily Trust*, October 11, 2010 <http://dailytrust.dailytrust.com/index.php?option=com_content&view=article&id=4245:nigerias-economy-and-failed-state-index&catid=3:business&Itemid=3> (accessed May 29, 2011).

116 Fund for Peace, "Failed States Index Scores 2010" <www.fundforpeace.org/web/index.php?option=com_content&task=view&id=452&Itemid=908> (accessed February 2, 2011).

117 Transparency International, "Corruption Perceptions Index 2010 results" <www.transparency.org/policy_research/surveys_indices/cpi/2010/results> (accessed May 29, 2011).

118 Nigerian National Bureau of Statistics (NBS) and Economic and Financial Crimes Commission (EFCC), *NBS/EFCC Business Survey on Crime & Corruption and Awareness of EFCC in Nigeria, 2007 Summary Report*, December 2009 <www.nigerianstat.gov.ng/ext/latest_release/NBS_EFCC%20Survey.pdf> (accessed May 29, 2011).

119 Human Rights Watch, "Everyone's in on the game," August 17, 2010 <www.hrw.org/en/reports/2010/08/17/everyone-s-game-0> (accessed May 29, 2011).

120 Extractive Industries Transparency Initiative, "What is the EITI?" <http://eiti.org/eiti> (accessed May 29, 2011).

121 Nigerian Extractive Industries Transparency Initiative (NEITI) Act 2007 <www.neiti.org.ng/files-pdf/neitiact.pdf> (accessed May 29, 2011).

122 NEITI Act 2007.

123 Richad L Cassin, "Postscript from Nigeria," FCPA Blog <www.fcpablog.com/blog/2008/12/2/postscript-from-nigeria.html> (accessed June 14, 2011).

124 Cassin, "Postscript from Nigeria."

125 EFCC, "The Establishment Act," December 21, 2007 <www.efccnigeria.org/index.php?option=com_content&task=view&id=12&Itemid=30> (accessed May 29, 2011).

126 Shell in Nigeria, *Shell Interests in Nigeria Briefing Paper*, May 2010 <www-static.shell.com/static/nga/downloads/pdfs/briefing_notes/shell_interests.pdf> (accessed May 29, 2011).

127 *Shell Interests in Nigeria Briefing Paper.*

128 *Shell Interests in Nigeria Briefing Paper.*

129 *Shell Interests in Nigeria Briefing Paper.*

130 Shell in Nigeria, *Operating Environment: May 2010* <www-static.shell.com/static/nga/downloads/pdfs/briefing_notes/operating_env.pdf> (accessed June 14, 2011).

131 *Operating Environment: May 2010.*

132 Royal Dutch Shell plc, *Sustainability Review 2009* <http://sustainabilityreport.shell.com/2009/servicepages/downloads/files/sd_review_shell_sr09.pdf> (accessed May 29, 2011).

133 Article 13, "Shell: integrating transparency and anti-corruption throughout its business in Nigeria," <www.article13.com/UNGC/Shell%20anti-corruption%20case%20study.pdf> (accessed May 29, 2011).

134 Royal Dutch Shell plc, "Code of conduct," <www-static.shell.com/static/aboutshell/downloads/who_we_are/code_of_conduct/code_of_conduct_english_2010.pdf> (accessed May 29, 2011).

135 Royal Dutch Shell plc, *Dealing with bribery and corruption* <www.shell.com/static/envirosoc-en/downloads/management_primers/dealingwithbriberyprimer_final.pdf> (accessed May 29, 2011).

136 Shell plc,"Code of conduct."

137 Royal Dutch Shell plc, "Payments to governments," www.shell.com/home/content/environment_society/society/business/payments_to_governments/> (accessed May 29, 2011).

138 Shell, *Sustainability Review 2009*.

139 Tom Bergin, "US quizzes Shell in foreign corruption probe," Reuters, March 17, 2008 <www.reuters.com/article/2008/03/17/shell-bribery-idUSL1775263320080317> (accessed May 29, 2011).

140 Steptoe & Johnson, "Resolution of Panalpina and related cases yields significant penalties, new enforcement theories," November 29, 2010 <www.steptoe.com/publications-newsletter-27.html#_ftn7> (accessed May 29, 2011).

141 Panalpina Inc., "Panalpina enters into plea agreement in US antitrust case," January 10, 2010 www.panalpina.com/www/global/en/media_news/news/news_archiv_2/10_10_01_-_anti-trust.html> (accessed June 8, 2011)

142 FCPA Blog, "Seven companies settle for $236.5 million (updated)," November 4, 2010 <www.fcpablog.com/blog/2010/11/4/seven-companies-settle-for-2365-million-updated.html> (accessed May 29, 2011).

143 "Shell Nigeria Exploration and Production Company: Public affirmation of corporate governance," December 17, 2010 <www.shell.com/static/nga/downloads/pdfs/apology_letter.pdf> (accessed May 29, 2011).

144 Rowena Mason and Richard Blackden, "Shell to pay $48m Nigerian bribe fine," *Telegraph*, November 4, 2010 <www.telegraph.co.uk/finance/newsbysector/energy/oilandgas/8111277/Shell-to-pay-48m-Nigerian-bribe-fine.html> (accessed May 29, 2011).

145 FCPA Blog, "Panalpina quits Nigeria," August 18, 2008 <www.fcpablog.com/blog/2008/8/19/panalpina-quits-nigeria.html> (accessed May 29, 2011).

146 Panalpina Inc., "Panalpina with market share gains and significantly increased profitability," March 9, 2011 <www.panalpina.com/www/global/en/media_news/news/news_archiv_2/11_03_09.html> (accessed May 29, 2011).

147 Cargo News Asia, "Panalpina profit plunges 78%," August 5, 2009 <www.cargonewsasia.com/secured/article.aspx?article=20228> (accessed May 29, 2011).

148 Anna Driver, "Nigeria a legal trouble spot for oil service firms," August 26, 2007 <www.reuters.com/article/ousiv/idUSN2646957520070826?pageNumber=2> (accessed May 29, 2011).

149 FCPA Blog, "An exoduc from Nigeria?" August 27, 2007 <www.fcpablog.com/blog/2007/8/27/an-exodus-from-nigeria.html> (accessed May 29, 2011).

150 FCPA Professor, "The payments ... would not constitute facilitation payments for routine governmental actions within the meaning of the FCPA," November 10, 2010 <fcpaprofessor.blogspot.com/.../payments-would-not-constitute.html> (accessed June 8. 2011).

151 Steptoe & Johnson, "Resolution of Panalpina and related cases yields significant penalties, new enforcement theories."

152 UK Ministry of Justice, *Consultation on guidance about commercial organisations preventing bribery (section 9 of the Bribery Act 2010)*, London: Ministry of Justice, p. 3 <www.justice.gov.uk/consultations/docs/bribery-act-guidance-consultation1.pdf> (accessed May 29, 2011).

153 FCPA Blog, "Corruption and enforcement: by the book," December 6, 2010 <www.fcpablog.com/blog/2010/12/6/compliance-and-enforcement-by-the-book.html> (accessed May 29, 2011).

154 FCPA Blog, "Corruption and enforcement: by the book."

155 US DOJ, "Snamprogetti Netherlands B.V. resolves Foreign Corrupt Practices Act investigation and agrees to pay $240 million criminal penalty," press release, July 7, 2010 <www.justice.gov/opa/pr/2010/July/10-crm-780.html> (accessed May 29, 2011).

156 FCPA Blog, "Snamprogetti, ENI in $365 million settlement," July 7, 2010 <www.fcpablog.com/blog/2010/7/7/snamprogetti-eni-in-365-million-settlement.html> (accessed May 29, 2011).

157 FCPA Blog, "Snamprogetti, ENI in $365 million settlement."

158 FCPA Blog, "Snamprogetti, ENI in $365 million settlement."

6 THE SECTORAL FACTOR

1 Foreign Policy Centre/Transparency International (UK), "Countering corruption: the role for corporate security," seminar briefing, May 1, 2003, p. 1 <fpc.org.uk>; PricewaterhouseCoopers, "Corruption prevention in the engineering and construction industry," 2010, p. 2 <www.pwc.com>.

2 E. C. Moore Jr., "Causes of demand for international bribery," *Electronic Journal of Business Ethics and Organization Studies*, Vol. 12, No. 2, 2007, p. 19 <ejbo.jyu.fi>; Global Witness, "Country for sale: welcome to Cambodia: how Cambodia's elite has captured the country's extractive industries," report, 2009 <www.globalwitness.org>.

3 Interview by author with Robert Sullivan, University College London, Spring 2011.

4 Sachi Suzuki, "Reduced risk, enhanced reputation? An analysis of corporate responses to bribery," EIRIS, 2010, <www.eiris.org>.

5 Jackson Lewis, "What increased Foreign Corrupt Practices Act enforcement means for companies", April 5, 2011 <www.jacksonlewis.com/resources.php?NewsID=3639> (accessed May 29, 2011).

6 Market Trends: Global Telecommunications Market Take, Worldwide, October 2010 <http://www.gartner.com/DisplayDocument?id=1457815> (accessed June 9, 2011).

7 Interview by authors with Richard Alderman, Serious Fraud Office, Spring 2011.

8 Samuel Rubenfeld, "Former Costa Rican president sentenced over Alcatel bribery scandal," *Wall Street Journal*, April 28, 2011 <http://blogs.wsj.com/corruption-currents/2011/04/28/former-costa-rican-president-sentenced-to-prison-over-alcatel-bribery/> (accessed June 9, 2011).

9 Adam Williams, "Alcatel reaches settlement in Cost Rica bribery scandal," Tico Times, March 12, 2011 <www.ticotimes.net>.

10 Kara Scannell, "Alcatel-Lucent fined over bribery allegations," *Financial Times*, December 27, 2010 <www.ft.com>.

11 *Japan Times*, December 28, 2010.

12 William Neuman, "Bribes let tomato vendor sell tainted food," *New York Times*, February 24, 2010 <www.nytimes.com>.

13 David Leigh and Rob Evans, "Balfour Beatty agrees to pay £2.25m over allegations of bribery in Egypt," *Guardian*, October 7, 2008.

14 Interview by authors with DI Whatmore, Scotland Yard, Spring 2011.

15 Interview by authors with DI Whatmore.
16 Rohini Singh, "RBI joins bribes-for-loans scam probe," Economic Times, December 27, 2010 <http://articles.economictimes.indiatimes.com/2010-12-27/news/27602762_1_loans-public-sector-banks-financial-institutions> (accessed June 9, 2011).
17 Krittivas Mukherjee and Devidutta Tripathy, "India probes 21 companies in bribes-for-loans scandal," Reuters, November 26, 2010 <uk.reuters.com>; Kaustubh Kulkarni and Sowmya Kamath, "Top India banks, fin firm execs held on bribery charges," Reuters, November 24, 2010 <uk.reuters.com>.
18 Fiona McDermott, "UK Bribery Act 2010 – a blessing in disguise?" construction industry briefing, KPMG <www.kpmg.com>.
19 Fiona McDermott, "UK Bribery Act 2010 – a blessing in disguise?"
20 Interview by author with senior British police officer, Spring 2011.
21 Carin Nordberg, updated by Taryn Vian, "Corruption in the health sector," *U4* Issue 2008:10, U4 Anti-Corruption Research Centre <www.u4.no>.
22 Jennifer Hunt, "Bribery in health care in Uganda," *Journal of Health Economics*, Vol. 29, No. 5, June 2010, pp. 699–707.
23 Sharon Fonn, Anne Mtonga, Hope Nkoloma, Grace Bantebya-Kyomuhendo, Leopoldina da Silva, Esther Kazilimani, Sara Davis, and Ramata Dia, "Health providers' opinions on provider-client relations: results of a multi-country study to test 'Health Workers for Change'," *Health Policy and Planning*, Vol. 16, No. 1, 2001, pp. 19–23.
24 Transparency International, *Global Corruption Report 2006: Corruption and Health*, 2006 <www.transparency.org>.
25 SFO, "British executive jailed for part in Greek healthcare corruption," press release, April 14, 2010 <www.sfo.gov.uk>.
26 David Bond, "England 2018 bid sunk by media, says Japan's Ogura," *BBC News*, December 3, 2010 <www.bbc.co.uk>.
27 Paul Condon, "Report on corruption in international cricket in 2000," Anti-Corruption and Security Unit, International Cricket Council, April 2001 <http://icc-cricket.yahoo.net/anti_corruption/condon-report.php> (accessed June 9, 2011).
28 BBC News, "Pakistan cricket trio face corruption charges," February 4, 2011 <www.bbc.co.uk/news/uk-12365517> (accessed June 9, 2011).
29 Rania Abouzeid, "Pakistan cricket scandal brings disbelief in Mohammad Amir's home town," *Guardian*, August 30, 2010 <www.guardian.co.uk/sport/2010/aug/30/pakistan-betting-cricket-mohammad-amir> (accessed June 9, 2011).
30 BBC Sport, "Cricket may use lie detector tests to fight corruption," October 15, 2010 <http://news.bbc.co.uk/sport1/hi/cricket/9289145.stm> (accessed June 9, 2011).
31 UK Department of Justice, *UK Foreign Bribery Strategy*, Cm 7791, London: Department of Justice, January 2010 <www.justice.gov.uk/publications/docs/uk-foreign-bribery-strategy.pdf>.
32 *UK Foreign Bribery Strategy*, p. 3.
33 John Hatchard, "Combating transnational corporate corruption: some further lessons from Lesotho," *Journal of Commonwealth Law and Legal Education*, Vol. 7, No. 2, October 2009, pp. 155–63.
34 Carolyn Warner, "Export led corruption: the European Union, oil, arms and infrastructure projects," Department of Political Science, Arizona State

University <http://iis-db.stanford.edu/evnts/3821/Carolyn_Warner_paper_May_20041.p.pdf> (accessed June 9, 2011).

35   Russell Hotten, "BAE is not afraid of the big bad Woolf Report," *Telegraph*, May 11, 2008 <www.telegraph.co.uk>.

36   Butler University business law professor Mike Koehler ("the FCPA Professor"), in Joe Palazzolo, "Professor says FCPA enforcement is a façade," *Wall Street Journal* blog, October 10, 2010 <blogs.wsj.com>.

37   David Voreacos and Laurel Brubaker Calkins, "Shell bribes among 'culture of corruption,' Panalpina admits," *Business Week*, November 5, 2010 <www.businessweek.com/news/2010-11-05/shell-bribes-among-culture-of-corruption-panalpina-admits.html> (accessed June 9, 2011).

38   Voreacos and Calkins, "Shell bribes among 'culture of corruption.'"

39   Voreacos and Calkins, "Shell bribes among 'culture of corruption.'"

40   EITI, "The EITI principles and criteria" <http://eiti.org/eiti/principles> (accessed May 29, 2011).

41   EITI Fact Sheet, October 25, 2010 <www.eiti.org>.

42   Keith Bradsher, "China said to widen its embargo of minerals," *New York Times*, October 19, 2010 <www.nytimes.com/2010/10/20/business/global/20rare.html> (accessed June 9, 2011).

43   *New York Times*, "Japan recycles minerals from used electronics," October 4, 2010 <www.nytimes.com/2010/10/05/business/global/05recycle.html?pagewanted=2> (accessed June 9, 2011).

44   Cathy Proctor, "Molycorp gets ok for rare earth processing plant", *Denver Business Journal*, December 13, 2010 </www.bizjournals.com/denver/news/2010/12/13/molycorp.html> (accessed June 9, 2011).

45   Keith Bradsher, "Challenging China in rare earth mining," *New York Times*, April 21, 2010; Matthew Hill, "China REE quota reductions not unexpected – analyst," *Mining Weekly*, December 29, 2010 <www.miningweekly.com>; Andrew Restuccia, "Troubled mine holds hope for US rare earth industry," *Washington Independent,* October 25, 2010.

46   John Mauldin, "China and the future of rare earth elements," *Commodities Now*, October 16, 2010 <www.commodities-now.com>.

7   THIRD PARTY RISK AND CORPORATE EXPOSURE

1   Transparency International, "2010 Bribery Act: how are supply chains affected?" briefing note, December 2010 <www.ashurst.com/doc.aspx?id_Resource=4930> (accessed June 9, 2011).

2   Mark Snyderman, "Combating bribery in the supply chain: multinational companies and the UN Global Compact," Coca-Cola, August 10, 2008.

3   Fellows Friday with Shaffi Mather, TED Blog, October 15, 2010 <http://blog.ted.com/2010/10/15/fellows-friday-with-shaffi-mather/> (accessed June 9, 2011).

4   Warlord, Inc, Report of the Majority Staff, Subcommittee on National Security and Foreign Affairs, Committee on Oversight & Government Reform, US House of Representatives, June 2010, p. 3 <oversight.house.gov>.

5   Compliance in the Global Supply Chain, conference website, 2011 <www.compliance-supplychain.com>.

6   Business and Industry Advisory Committee to the OECD, "BIAC experiences

with challenges to anti-bribery associated with hiring intermediaries," May 4, 2009, p. 1 <www.biac.org>.

7   Transparency International UK, *UK Bribery Act Adequate Procedures: Guidance on good practice procedures for corporate anti-bribery programmes,* July 2010 <http://www.transparency.org.uk/attachments/138_adequate-procedures.pdf> (accessed June 9, 2011).

8   Speech by Robert Amaee, "Remarks to World Bribery and Corruption Compliance Forum, October 14, 2010" <www.sfo.gov.uk/about-us/our-views/other-speeches/speeches-2010/world-bribery-and-corruption-compliance-forum.aspx> (accessed 2 May 2011).

9   Rob Evans and David Leigh, "Judge 'astonished' by corruption denials as he fines BAE £500,000," *Guardian,* December 21, 2010 <www.guardian.co.uk/world/2010/dec/21/bae-fined-illicit-payments-middleman> (accessed May 29, 2011).

10 Jonathan Russell, "BAE pays fine to settle Tanzania corruption probe," *Telegraph,* December 21, 2010 <www.telegraph.co.uk>.

11 R. v. BAE Systems plc, Southwark Crown Court, Case No: S2010565 <www.bailii.org/cgi-bin/markup.cgi?doc=/ew/cases/Misc/2010/16.html&query=BAE+and+Tanzania&method=boolean> (accessed May 29, 2011); CMS Cameron McKenna, "BAE 'accounting offence' settlement grudgingly allowed by Court," December 24, 2010 <www.law-now.com/law-now/baesettledec10.htm?cmckreg=true> (accessed May 29, 2011); Evans and Leigh, "Judge 'astonished' by corruption denials."

12 UK Trade and Investment, "Bribery Act," press release, April 4, 2011 <www.ukti.gov.uk/uktihome/aboutukti/item/129334.html> (accessed May 29, 2011).

13 Richard Tyler, "Bona fide corporate freebees must survive Bribery Act," *Telegraph,* November 8, 2010 <www.telegraph.co.uk>.

14 Michael Howie, "£20 Christmas tip is an illegal bribe, says council," *Telegraph,* February 20, 2011 <http://www.telegraph.co.uk/news/newstopics/howaboutthat/8335868/20-Christmas-tip-is-an-illegal-bribe-says-council.html> (accessed June 9, 2011).

15 Transparency International UK, "The 2010 UK Bribery Act: adequate procedures," p. 11.

16 Interview by author with Robert Sullivan, University College London, Spring 2011.

17 Ministry of Justice, *The Bribery Act 2010: Guidance,* p. 11.

18 Interview by author with senior legal practitioner, London, Spring 2011.

19 Ministry of Justice, *The Bribery Act 2010: Guidance,* p. 13.

20 McDermott Will & Emery, "The Bribery Act 2010: raising the bar above the US Foreign Practices Act, 2010," p. 4 <www.mwe.com/info/news/wp0910b.pdf> (accessed Feburary 2, 2011)

21 Bond Pearce, "Corporate hospitality could fall foul of new Bribery Act," July 7, 2010 <www.bondpearce.com>.

22 McDermott Will & Emery, "The Bribery Act 2010: raising the bar above the US Foreign Practices Act, 2010," p. 4.

23 "Joint prosecution guidance," p. 10.

24 Ministry of Justice, *The Bribery Act 2010: Guidance,* p. 14.

25 Lord Tunnicliffe: letter to Lord Henley clarifying Section 6 of the UK Bribery Act, January 14, 2010 <www.justice.gov.uk/.../letter-lord-henley-corporate-hospitality.pdf> (accessed June 9, 2011).

26 Interview by author with Vivian Robinson, London, Spring 2011.

27 Nick Kochan, "Delay of Bribery Bill won't buy time for firms," Risk.Net, March 1, 2011 <www.risk.net/operational-risk-and-regulation/feature/2027713/delay-uk-bribery-wont-firms> (accessed June 9, 2011).

28 Interview with Vivian Robinson.

29 G. Bayar, "The role of intermediaries in corruption," *Public Choice*, Vol. 122, Nos 3/4, 2005, p. 296.

30 R. Hague and M. Harrop, *Comparative Government and Politics*, Basingstoke: Palgrave, 2004, p. 61.

31 Interview with Vivian Robinson.

32 OECD, *Recommendation for Further Combating Bribery of Foreign Public Officials in International Business Transactions*, 2009, p. 4.

33 Russell Hotten "BAE is not afraid of the big bad Woolf Report," *Telegraph*, May 11, 2008 <www.telegraph.co.uk/finance/newsbysector/industry/2789757/BAE-is-not-afraid-of-the-big-bad-Woolf-Report.html> (accessed May 29, 2011).

34 McDermott Will & Emery, "The Bribery Act 2010: raising the bar above the U.S. Foreign Corrupt Practices Act," p. 14.

35 Interview with Vivian Robinson.

36 L. David-Barrett, *Avoiding Corruption Risks in the City: The Bribery Act 2010*, report prepared for the City of London Corporation by Transparency International, 2010, pp. 4–5.

37 Email correspondence between author and Gregory Husisian, Spring 2011.

38 Email correspondence with Gregory Husisian.

39 Interview by author with Barry Vitou, London, Spring 2011.

40 Interview with Vivian Robinson.

41 Interview by author with Robert Sullivan, University College London, Spring 2011.

42 Interview with Vivian Robinson.

43 Richard Tyler, "SFO to prosecute 'serious' overseas bribes," *Telegraph*, September 23, 2010 <www.telegraph.co.uk/finance/newsbysector/banksand finance/8019024/SFO-to-prosecute- serious-overseas-bribes.html> (accessed May 29, 2011).

44 "Joint prosecution guidance," p. 9.

45 Interview with Vivian Robinson.

46 Interview with Vivian Robinson.

47 Email correspondence with Gregory Husisian.

48 Interview with Vivian Robinson.

8 SPOTTING, STOPPING, AND COMBATING CORPORATE CORRUPTION

1 UK Ministry of Justice, "Consultation on guidance about commercial organisations preventing bribery (section 9 of the Bribery Act 2010)," Consultation Paper CP11/10, September 14, 2010 <www.justice.gov.uk/consultations/docs/bribery-act-guidance-consultation1.pdf> (accessed May 29, 2011).

2 Ministry of Justice, *The Bribery Act 2010: Guidance*, p. 25.

3 Ministry of Justice, *The Bribery Act 2010: Guidance*, p. 21.

4   Ministry of Justice, *The Bribery Act 2010: Guidance*, p. 20.
5   OECD, *Good Pratice Guidance on Internal Ethics, Controls, and Compliance,* Paris: OECD, February 18, 2010 <www.oecd.org/dataoecd/5/51/44884389.pdf> (accessed May 29, 2011).
6   Ministry of Justice, *The Bribery Act 2010: Quickstart Guide,* p. 5.
7   Ministry of Justice, *The Bribery Act 2010: Quickstart Guide.*
8   Ministry of Justice, *The Bribery Act 2010: Quickstart Guide,* p. 5.
9   Ministry of Justice, "Consultation on guidance."
10 Ministry of Justice, "Consultation on guidance."
11 Legal Week, "Anti-corruption practical guide for business," <www.legalweeklaw. com/download/anti-corruption-practical-guide-business-5152>.
12 Ministry of Justice, "Consultation on guidance."
13 Ministry of Justice, "Consultation on guidance."
14 Ministry of Justice, "Consultation on guidance."
15 Legal Week, "Guidance on corporate anti-bribery procedures," September 28, 2010 <www.legalweeklaw.com/download/guidance-corporate-anti-bribery-procedures-5481>.
16 OECD, *Good Pratice Guidance.*
17 Ministry of Justice, *The Bribery Act 2010: Guidance*, p. 22.
18 Association of Chartered Certified Accounants (ACCA), *Antibribery and Corruption Reporting Disclosures*, Sydney, NSW: ACCA Australia and New Zealand, August 2008 <ww.accaglobal.com/pubs/australia/general/research/ latest/ACC1528_BriberyReportMR.pdf?> (accessed May 29, 2011).
19 Alexandra Wrage, "How to maintain strong compliance in a weak economy", Corporate Compliance Insights <https://secure.traceinter national.org/news/articles-publications/documents/AW_Howto Main tainStrongComplianceinaWeakEconomy_CorporateComplianceInsights_0316 2010.pdf> (accessed June 9, 2011).
20 Wrage, "How to maintain strong compliance."
21 Wrage, "How to maintain strong compliance."
22 Wrage, "How to maintain strong compliance."
23 World Bank, "Standard anti-bribery code" <http://siteresources.worldbank. org/CGCSRLP/Resources/antibriberycode.doc> (accessed May 29, 2011).
24 Wrage, "How to maintain strong compliance."
25 Wrage, "How to maintain strong compliance."
26 Wrage, "How to maintain strong compliance."
27 Trace International, "The high cost of small bribes" <https://secure. traceinternational.org/documents/TheHighCostofSmallBribes.pdf> (accessed May 30, 2011).
28 Trace International, "The high cost of small bribes."
29 ECFA, "Policy on suspected misconduct, dishonesty, fraud, and whistle-blower protection" <www.ecfa.org/Content/Policy-on-Suspected-Misconduct-Dishonesty-Fraud-and-Whistle-Blower-Protection> (accessed May 30, 2011).
30 Global Infrastructure Anti-Corruption Centre (GIACC), "Anti-corruption program for companies" <www.giaccentre.org/project_companies.php> (accessed May 30, 2011).
31 GIACC, "Anti-corruption program for companies."
32 Public Concern at Work (PCAW), "Making whistleblowing work" <www.pcaw. co.uk/organisations/smes.htm> (accessed May 30, 2011).

33 Ministry of Justice, "Consultation on guidance."
34 Legal Week, "Anti-corruption practical guide for business."
35 Ministry of Justice, "Consultation on guidance."
36 Kent J. Schmidt, "Beyond the basics: implementing an anti-bribery programme that works," Dorsey & Whitney LLP, June 1, 2008 <www.dorsey.com/resources/ Detail.aspx?pub=3202> (accessed May 30, 2011).
37 GIACC, "Anti-corruption program for companies."
38 Legal Week, "Corporate anti-bribery procedures."
39 Mary-Jo Kranacher, "Creating an ethical culture," AllBusiness, October 1, 2006 <www.allbusiness.com/human-resources/employee-development-employee-ethics/4094432-1.html> (accessed May 30, 2011).
40 Charles D. Kerns, "Creating and sustaining an ethical workplace culture," *Graziadio Business Review*, Vol. 6, Issue 3, 2003 <http://gbr.pepperdine. edu/2010/08/Creating-and-Sustaining-an-Ethical-Workplace-Culture/> (accessed May 30, 2011).
41 GIACC, "Anti-corruption program for companies."
42 GIACC, "Anti-corruption tools: due diligence" <http://www.giaccentre.org/ due_diligence.php> (accessed May 30, 2011).
43 Charles D. Kerns, "Creating and sustaining an ethical workplace culture."
44 Legal Week, "Corporate anti-bribery procedures."
45 Ministry of Justice, *The Bribery Act 2010: Guidance,* p. 23.
46 Ministry of Justice, *The Bribery Act 2010: Guidance.*
47 Alexandra Wrage, "When reasonable is risky: the gifts and hospitality vortex", Trace International <https://secure.traceinternational.org/compliance/arti cles-publications/documents/AW_WhenReasonableIsRisky_Ethisphere_ Q1_2011.pdf> (accessed June 9, 2011).
48 GIACC, "Anti-corruption program for companies."
49 US Department of State, "2008 human rights report: Zambia," February 25, 2009 <www.state.gov/g/drl/rls/hrrpt/2008/af/119031.htm> (accessed May 30, 2011).
50 World Bank, "Standard anti-bribery code."
51 World Bank, "Standard anti-bribery code."
52 GIACC, "Anti-corruption program for companies."
53 GIACC, "Anti-corruption program for companies."
54 World Bank, "Standard anti-bribery code."
55 GIACC, "Anti-corruption program for companies."
56 UK Competition Commission, "Guidance on conflicts of interest," <www. competition-commission.org.uk/our_peop/conflicts_of_interest.htm> (accessed May 30, 2011).
57 Competition Commission, "Guidance on conflicts of interest."
58 World Bank, "Standard anti-bribery code."
59 Accunting Coach, "What is separation of duties?" <http://blog.accountingcoach. com/separation-of-duties-internal-control/> (accessed May 30, 2011).
60 Nick Szabo, "Patterns of integrity: separation of duties," 2004 <http://szabo. best.vwh.net/separationofduties.html> (accessed May 30, 2011).
61 John Gregg, Michael Nam, Stephen Northcutt, and Mason Pokladnik, "Separation of duties in information technology," Security Laboratory, February 18, 2008 <www.sans.edu/resources/securitylab/it_separation_duties. php> (accessed May 30, 2011).

62 Due Diligence.Net, "Due diligence" <http://www.duediligence.net/> (accessed May 30, 2011).

63 Ministry of Justice, *The Bribery Act 2010*, p. 28.

64 Ministry of Justice, *The Bribery Act 2010: Quickstart Guide*, p. 6.

65 GIACC, "Anti-corruption tools: due diligence."

66 OECD, *Good Pratice Guidance.*

67 Ministry of Justice, *The Bribery Act 2010: Guidance*, p. 16.

68 GIACC, "Anti-corruption tools: due diligence."

69 Legal Week, "Corporate anti-bribery procedures."

70 See for example <www.giaccentre.org/documents/GIACC_PACS_T4_Disclosure_Form_Nov08_.pdf>.

71 "Due diligence: checklist of question" <www.experienced-people.co.uk/1059-business-due-diligence/> (accessed May 30, 2011).

72 OECD, *Good Pratice Guidance.*

73 OECD, *Good Pratice Guidance.*

74 Legal Week, "Corporate anti-bribery procedures."

75 Legal Week, "Corporate anti-bribery procedures."

76 See Transparency International, "Integrity pacts" <www.transparency.org/global_priorities/public_contracting/integrity_pacts> (accessed May 30, 2011).

77 Association of Certified Fraud Examiners (ACFE), "Fraud-related internal controls: complying with Sarbanes–Oxley and SAS no 99," doc. no. 01-5409 <www.acfe.com/documents/Fraud-Internal-Controls-Excerpt.pdf> (accessed May 30, 2011).

78 ACFE, "Fraud-related internal controls."

79 William P. Olsen, *The Anti-Corruption Handbook*, Wiley, 2010.

80 Institute of Internal Auditors (IIA), American Association of Certified Public Accountants (AACPA), and ACFE, *Managing the Business Risk of Fraud: A Practical Guide* <www.acfe.com/documents/managing-business-risk.pdf> (accessed May 30, 2011).

81 NetLawMan, "Internet email and communications policy: monitoring employees" <www.netlawman.co.uk/info/email-policy.php> (accessed May 30, 2011); OutLaw.Com, "Monitoring your employees' emails legally" <www.out-law.com/page-460> (accessed May 30, 2011).

82 ACFE, "Fraud-related internal controls."

83 Olsen, *The Anti-Corruption Handbook.*

84 IIA, AACPA, and ACFE, *Managing the Business Risk of Fraud.*

85 IIA, AACPA, and ACFE, *Managing the Business Risk of Fraud.*

86 ACFE, "Fraud-related internal controls."

87 IIA, AACPA, and ACFE, *Managing the Business Risk of Fraud.*

88 Ministry of Justice, *The Bribery Act 2010: Guidance*, p. 29.

89 "Fraud whistleblower policy," October 21, 2008 <www.hhcpa.com/blogs/non-profit-accounting-services-blog/2008/10/21/fraud-whistleblower-policy/> (accessed June 9, 2011).

90 "Fraud whistleblower policy," October 21, 2008.

91 PCAW, "Making whistleblowing work."

92 PCAW, "Making whistleblowing work."

93 Practical Law Company, "Whistleblowing: a quick guide" <http://construction.practicallaw.com/6-500-1812> (accessed May 30, 2011).

94 PCAW, "Making whistleblowing work."
95 Evangelical Council for Financial Accountability (ECFA), "Policy on suspected misconduct, dishonesty, fraud, and whistle-blower protection" <www.ecfa.org/Documents/PolicyonSuspectedMisconductDishonestyFraudandWhistle-BlowerProtection.doc> (accessed May 30, 2011).
96 PCAW, "Making whistleblowing work."
97 Ministry of Justice, *The Bribery Act 2010: Guidance*, p. 30.
98 PCAW, "Making whistleblowing work."
99 ECFA, "Policy on suspected misconduct, dishonesty, fraud, and whistle-blower protection."
100 IIA, AACPA, and ACFE, *Managing the Business Risk of Fraud;* John Flaherty, "Role of auditors in the anti-corruption battle," International Anti-Corruption Conference (IACC), 1997 <www.8iacc.org/papers/jflaherty.html> (accessed May 30, 2011).
101 IIA, "What is internal auditing?" <www.iia.org.uk/download.cfm?docid= B576 DF82-7B56-4B85-96EDAF2B428D596D> (accessed May 30, 2011).
102 John Flaherty, "Role of auditors in the anti-corruption battle."
103 AICPA, "Management override of internal controls: the Achilles heel of fraud prevention" <www.aicpa.org/ForThePublic/AuditCommitteeEffectiveness/DownloadableDocuments/achilles_heel.pdf> (accessed May 30, 2011).
104 Nick Szabo, "Patterns of integrity: separation of duties."
105 AICPA, "Management override of internal control."
106 IIA, AACPA, and ACFE, *Managing the Business Risk of Fraud.*
107 Nick Szabo, "Patterns of integrity: separation of duties."
108 Legal Week, "Corporate anti-bribery procedures."
109 Ferret.Com, "Internal auditing: how often" <www.ferret.com.au/c/QA-Z-Systems-Coaching/Internal-auditing-How-often-n880392> (accessed May 30, 2011).
110 Reference for Business, "Audits, external" <www.referenceforbusiness.com/small/A-Bo/Audits-External.html> (accessed May 30, 2011).
111 Reference for Business, "Audits, external."
112 Reference for Business, "Audits, external."
113 Wise Geek, "What is an external audit?" <www.wisegeek.com/what-is-an-external-audit.htm> (accessed May 30, 2011).
114 Ministry of Justice, "Consultation on guidance."
115 Transparency International, *Business Principles for Countering Bribery*, 2nd English edition, 2009, Berlin: Transparency International <www.transparency.org/publications/publications/other/business_principles_for_countering_bribery> (accessed May 30, 2011).
116 Ministry of Justice, *The Bribery Act 2010: Guidance*, p. 33.
117 Olsen, *The Anti-Corruption Handbook.*
118 There are a number of lists of such countries, for example see <www.state.gov/p/inl/rls/nrcrpt/2007/vol2/html/80883.htm>; Grant Thornton, *Avoiding Corruption in Foreign Operations* <www.grantthornton.com/staticfiles/GTCom/files/services/Forensic%20accounting%20and%20investigative%20services/Gaming%20Management%20-%20Avoiding%20Corruption%20in%20Foreign%20Operations.pdf> (accessed April 2, 2011).
119 GIACC, "Anti-corruption program for companies."
120 Olsen, *The Anti-Corruption Handbook.*

121 Legal Week, "Dealing with fraud: the basics" <www.legalweeklaw.com/download/dealing-fraud-basics-5496>; GIACC, "Anti-corruption program for companies"; IIA, AACPA, and ACFE, *Managing the Business Risk of Fraud.*

122 Slaughter and May, "Corporate criminal liability update, the sentencing of Mabey and Johnson and possible prosecution of BAE Systems plc, October 2009 <www.slaughterandmay.com/media/1427267/corporate_criminal_liability_update_sentencing_of_mabey_and_johnson.pdf> (accessed June 9, 2011).

123 Davies Arnold Cooper, "A practical guide to the Bribery Act 2010," July 2010 <www.dac.co.uk/documents/resources/newsletters/The_corporate_dilemma_self_reporting_bribery_and_corruption> (accessed May 30, 2011).

124 Serious Fraud Office, "Should I self-report to the SFO?" <www.sfo.gov.uk/victims/corporate-victims/should-i-self-report-directly-to-the-sfo-.aspx> (accessed June 9, 2011).

125 Barry Vitou and Richard Kovalevsky, "Our predictions for 2011 – a round up" The Bribery Act, December 12, 2010 <http://thebriberyact.com/2010/12/12/december-newsletter-our-predictions-for-2011-a-round-up/> (accessed June 9, 2011).

126 UK SFO, "Approach of the Serious Fraud Office to dealing with overseas corruption," July 21, 2009 <www.sfo.gov.uk/media/128701/approach%20of%20the%20serious%20fraud%20office%20v6.pdf> (accessed May 30, 2011).

127 Legal Week," Dealing with fraud: the basics"; GIACC, "Anti-corruption program for companies."

128 Transparency International, "The 2010 UK Bribery Act: adequate procedures" <www.transparency.org.uk/attachments/138_adequate-procedures.pdf> (accessed June 9, 2011).

129 UK SFO, "Approach of the Serious Fraud Office to dealing with overseas corruption."

130 UK SFO, "Approach of the Serious Fraud Office to dealing with overseas corruption."

131 UK SFO, "Approach of the Serious Fraud Office to dealing with overseas corruption."

132 UK SFO, "Approach of the Serious Fraud Office to dealing with overseas corruption."

133 Ministry of Justice, *The Bribery Act 2010: Guidance,* pp. 23–43.

9 WHO WOULD BE A DIRECTOR?

1 Serious Fraud Office (SFO), "Mabey & Johnson Ltd sentencing," press release, September 25, 2009 <www.sfo.gov.uk/press-room/latest-press-releases/press-releases-2009/mabey--johnson-ltd-sentencing-.aspx> (accessed June 20, 2011).

2 SFO, "Mabey & Johnson Ltd prosecuted by the SFO," press release, July 10, 2009 <www.sfo.gov.uk/press-room/latest-press-releases/press-releases-2009/mabey--johnson-ltd-prosecuted-by-the-sfo.aspx> (accessed June 20, 2011).

3 SFO, "Mabey & Johnson Ltd sentencing."

4 SFO, "Mabey & Johnson Ltd: Former executives jailed for helping finance Saddam Hussein's government," press release, February 23, 2011 <www.sfo.gov.uk/press-room/latest-press-releases/press-releases-2011/mabey--johnson-ltd-

former-executives-jailed-for-helping-finance-saddam-hussein's-government. aspx> (accessed June 20, 2011).

5   SFO, "Mabey & Johnson Ltd: Former executives jailed."
6   SFO, "Insurance broker jailed for bribing Costa Rican officials," press release, October 26, 2010 <www.sfo.gov.uk/press-room/latest-press-releases/press-releases-2010/insurance-broker-jailed-for-bribing-costa-rican-officials.aspx> (accessed June 20, 2011).
7   Taken from the transcripts of the hearing,
8   SFO, "Insurance broker jailed."
9   SFO, "British executive jailed for part in Greek healthcare corruption," press release, April 14, 2010 h<www.sfo.gov.uk/press-room/latest-press-releases/press-releases-2010/british-executive-jailed-for-part-in-greek-healthcare-corruption.aspx> (accessed June 20, 2011).
10 Author interviews re Section 14 of the Bribery Act.
11 National Archives, Proceeds of Crime Act 2002, prospective provision 328 <www.legislation.gov.uk/ukpga/2002/29/section/328> (accessed June 20, 2011).
12 National Archives, Proceeds of Crime Act 2002, prospective provision 328
13 The confiscation provisions were described by Butterfield J. in R v Delaney; R v Hanrahan as follows:

> The provisions are and were intended to be Draconian. They apply only to convicted criminals. They are designed to ensure that criminals do not profit from crimes which they have committed, but which cannot be specifically identified yet alone proved against them. There is no injustice in the procedure.
> from papers for 1kbw, Criminal Justice Conference, Lewes, March 6, 2008 <www.1kbw.co.uk/__data/assets/pdf_file/0011/55793/Criminal_Justice_4_06032008.pdf> (accessed June 20, 2011).

14 Speech at S J Berwin, Corporate Investigations Group seminar, February 12, 2010 <www.sfo.gov.uk/about-us/our-views/director's-speeches/speeches-2010/the-corporate-investigations-group-seminar.aspx> (accessed June 20, 2011).

10   FORCES FIGHTING BRIBERY

1   Quoted in City of London Police, "About Overseas Anti Corruption Unit (OACU)," 2011 <www.cityoflondon.police.uk/CityPolice/Departments/ECD/anticorruptionunit/aboutus.htm> (accessed June 1, 2011).
2   Fulbright and Jaworski, "Two recent cases show UK is active in enforcement of anti-bribery laws," The In-House Lawyer, October 1, 2008 <www.inhouselawyer.co.uk/index.php/banking-and-finance/7438-two-recent-cases-show-uknis-active-in-enforcement-of-foreign-bribery-laws> (accessed June 1, 2011).
3   Nick Kochan, "UK set for clamp down on bribery and corruption", Operational Risk, October 28, 2009 <www.risk.net/operational-risk-and-regulation/feature/1560477/uk-set-clamp-bribery-corruption> (accessed June 9, 2011).
4   Jonathan Fisher, "How the Bribery Act brings the law of hidden consequences into play," Telegraph, January 21, 2011 <www.telegraph.co.uk/finance/your business/bribery-act/8271792/How-the-Bribery-Act-brings-the-law-of-hidden-consequences-into-play.html> (accessed June 1, 2011).

5   Interview by author with Barry Vitou, London, Spring 2011.
6   Richard Alderman, Speech to Transparency International Conference, Belgium, March 3, 2011, quoted on TheBriberyAct.Com, March 6, 2011 <http://thebriberyact.com/2011/03/06/richard-alderman-poca-face-corruption-money-laundering-key-theme-for-sfo-in-2011/> (accessed June 1, 2011).
7   SFO, "MW Kellogg Ltd to pay £7 million in SFO High Court action," press release, February 16, 2011 <www.sfo.gov.uk/press-room/latest-press-releases/press-releases-2011/mw-kellogg-ltd-to-pay-%C2%A37-million-in-sfo-high-court-action.aspx> (accessed June 1, 2011).
8   Barry Vitou and Richard Kovalevsky, "Don't get POCA'd," FCPA Blog, November 9, 2010 <www.fcpablog.com/blog/2010/11/9/dont-get-pocad.html> (accessed June 1, 2011).
9   Interview by author with senior British police officer, Spring 2011.
10 Interview with DI Whatmore, Metropolitan Police Service, Spring 2011.
11 Interview with senior British police officer.
12 Home Office, "Home Office to take lead on economic crime," Home Office Community Justice Portal, January 17, 2011 <www.cjp.org.uk/news/government-and-its-institutions/home-office/home-office-to-take-lead-on-economic-crime-17-01-2011/> (accessed June 1, 2011).
13 Stephen Parkinson, "Government scores 'own goal' in fight against white collar crime," E Financial News, January 24, 2011 <www.efinancialnews.com/story/2011-01-24/link-link-link> (accessed June 1, 2011).
14 Legal Week, "Government considers merging SFO into National Crime Agency" <www.legalweek.com/legal-week/news/1937893/government-considers-merging-sfo-national-crime-agency> (accessed Feburary 2, 2011).
15 Interview with DI Whatmore, Spring 2011.
16 City of London Police, "Overseas corruption assessment for The UK Bribery Strategy Group", draft report, January 15, 2010, pp. 88–9.
17 Interview conducted by author with senior British police officer, Spring 2011.
18 Jonathan Russell, "SFO urges companies to report corrupt rivals," Telegraph, January 16, 2011 <www.telegraph.co.uk/finance/yourbusiness/bribery-act/8262951/SFO-urges-companies-to-report-corrupt-rivals.html> (accessed June 1, 2011).
19 Interview by authors with Richard Alderman, Serious Fraud Office, Spring 2011.
20 Interview with DI Whatmore.
21 Fritz Heimann and Gillian Dell, "Progress report: enforcement of the OECD Anti-Bribery Convention," Transparency International, July 28, 2010.
22 Heimann and Dell, "Progress report."
23 Interview with DI Whatmore.
24 Interview with DI Whatmore.
25 Interview with DI Whatmore.
26 Richard Tyler, "Lord Goldsmith urges plea-bargaining in bribery cases," Telegraph, March 20, 2011 <www.telegraph.co.uk/finance/newsbysector/industry/8239575/Lord-Goldsmith-urges-plea-bargaining-in-bribery-cases.html> (accessed June 1, 2011).
27 Richard Tyler, "Bribery Act: SFO chief Richard Alderman sees UK courts as a stumbling block," Telegraph, January 20, 2011 <www.telegraph.co.uk/finance/yourbusiness/bribery-act/8269766/Bribery-Act-SFO-chief-Richard-Alderman-sees-UK-courts-as-a-stumbling-block.html> (accessed June 1, 2011).

28 Interview with Richard Alderman.
29 Heimann and Dell, "Progress report," p. 9.
30 Interview with Richard Alderman.
31 Interview with Richard Alderman.
32 Quoted in Trethowans Solicitors, "The Bribery Act 2010," December 13, 2010 <www.trethowans.com/news_resources/news/the-bribery-act-2010_3381/> (accessed June 1, 2011).
33 Quoted in Nick Clark, "Judge attacks SFO deal with Innospec," *Independent*, March 27, 2010, <www.independent.co.uk/news/business/news/judge-attacks-sfo-deal-with-innospec-1928636.html> (accessed June 1, 2011).
34 Interview with Richard Alderman.
35 Interview with Richard Alderman.
36 Interview with Richard Alderman.
37 Richard Tyler, "Lord Goldsmith urges plea-bargaining in bribery cases," *Telegraph,* January 5, 2011 <www.telegraph.co.uk/finance/newsbysector/industry/8239575/Lord-Goldsmith-urges-plea-bargaining-in-bribery-cases.html> (accessed June 1, 2011).

11 GLOBAL EFFORTS

1   Interview with DI Whatmore, Metropolitan Police Service, Spring 2011.
2   Trace International, *Global Enforcement Report 2010*, Annapolis, Md.: Trace International, 2010 <www.secure.traceinternational.org/compliance/documents/GlobalEnforcementReport9.20.10.pdf> (accessed June 1, 2011).
3   Authors' correspondence with Sam Eastwood, July 2011.
4   Trace International, *Global Enforcement Report 2010*.
5   Trace International, *Global Enforcement Report 2010*, pp. 2–3.
6   Egmont Group of Financial Intelligence Units, "Mission statement," 2011 <www.egmontgroup.org/about> (accessed June 1, 2011).
7   Council of Europe, "What is GRECO?" <www.coe.int/t/dghl/monitoring/greco/general/3.%20what%20is%20greco_EN.asp> (accessed June 9, 2011).
8   Quoted in Michael Robinson, "Global compliance challenges in 2010: Helga Kvamme on the EU's anti-corruption efforts," Bulletproof Blog, January 14, 2010 <www.bulletproofblog.com/2010/01/14/bulletproof-interview-special-%E2%80%93-global-compliance-challenges-in-2010-helge-kvamme-on-the-eu%E2%80%99s-anti-corruption-efforts-fcpa/> (accessed June 9, 2011).
9   Eurobarometer, *Attitudes of Europeans Towards Corruption*, 325 72.2, European Commission, November 2009 <http://ec.europa.eu/public_opinion/archives/ebs/ebs_325_en.pdf> (accessed June 9, 2011).
10 Monica Macovei, in EPP Group. "EU anti-corruption policy for a sustainable future," public hearing, press release, September 16, 2010 <www.eppgroup.eu/press/showpr.asp?PRControlDocTypeID=1&PRControlID=9645&PRContentID=16494&PRContentLG=en> (accessed June 1, 2011).
11 Macovei, press release.
12 European Council, "The Stockholm Programme: An open and secure Europe serving and protecting citizens," *Official Journal of the European Union,* No C115, 04/05/2010, p. 23 <eurlex.europa.eu/LexUriServ/LexUriServ.do?uri=OJ:C:2010:115:0001:0038:EN:PDF> (accessed June 1, 2011).

13   Robert B Zoellick, "Remarks for International Corruption Hunters Alliance,"
      Washington DC: World Bank, December 7, 2010 <www.worldbank.org.af/
      WBSITE/EXTERNAL/COUNTRIES/SOUTHASIAEXT/AFGHANISTANEXTN/0,,
      print:Y~isCURL:Y~contentMDK:22784346~menuPK:50003484~pagePK:2865
      066~piPK:2865079~theSitePK:305985,00.html> (accessed June 1, 2011).
14   World Bank, "First International Corruption Hunters Alliance meets at World
      Bank to accelerate global enforcement action," press release no. 2011/216/INT
      <http://web.worldbank.org/WBSITE/EXTERNAL/COUNTRIES/LACEXT/0,,co
      ntentMDK:22783894~menuPK:258559~pagePK:2865106~piPK:2865128~theS
      itePK:258554,00.html> (accessed June 1, 2011).
15   Authors' correspondence with Sam Eastwood, July 2011.
16   Fritz Heimann and Gillian Dell, "Progress report: enforcement of the OECD
      Anti-Bribery Convention," Transparency International, July 28, 2010, p. 9.
17   Joe Palazzalo, "Indonesia marks a first in AML enforcement," *Wall Street Journal*,
      Feburary 3, 2011 <http://blogs.wsj.com/corruption-currents/2011/02/03/
      indonesia-marks-a-first-in-aml-enforcement/> (accessed June 9, 2011)
18   Taiwan News, "Cambodia anti-drug chief faces corruption charge," January
      17, 2001 <www.taiwannews.com.tw/etn/news_content.php?id =1488504&
      lang=eng_news&cate_img=1037.jpg&cate_rss=General> (accessed June 9,
      2011).
19   MACC Background <www.sprm.gov.my/> (accessed June 9, 2011).
20   Datuk Seri Abu Kassim Mohamed, quoted in "MACC chief vows to probe
      every complaint," *The Star*, July 31, 2010 <www.thestar.com.my/news/story.
      asp?file=/2010/7/31/nation/20100731191317&sec=nation> (accessed June 1, 2011).
21   Willard Cheng, "Aquino still griping over SC ruling on truth commission,"
      ABS-CBN News, December 12, 2010 <www.abs-cbnnews.com/nation/12/30/10/
      aquino-still-griping-over-sc-ruling-truth-commission> (accessed June 9, 2011).
22   Rhodina Villanueva, "Obusmen claims credit for anti-corruption ranking"
      Philstar, October 31, 2011 <www.philstar.com/Article.aspx?articleId=625823&
      publicationSubCategoryId=63> (accessed June 9, 2011).
23   Ben Heineman, "The long war against corruption," *Foreign Affairs*, May/June
      2006<http://belfercenter.ksg.harvard.edu/publication/814/long_war_against_
      corruption.html>; Ross Lydall, "Evening Standard owner Levdevev to launch
      fund for free speech", November 15, 2010 <www.thisislondon.co.uk/standard/
      article-23897606-evening-standard-owner-alexander-lebedev-to-launch-fund-
      for-free-speech.do> (accessed June 9, 2011).
24   Paddy Rawlinson, "Any foreign investor knows Russia's been corrupt for centuries,"
      Guardian, December 14, 2010 <www.guardian.co.uk/commentisfree/2010/dec/14/
      russia-corruption-foreign-investors> (accessed June 1, 2011).
25   Alistair Dawber, "Bribery verdict shows peril of doing business in China,"
      Independent, March 30, 2010 <www.independent.co.uk/news/world/asia/
      bribery-verdicts-show-peril-of-doing-business-in-china-1930669.html>
      (accessed June 1, 2011).
26   Zhao Chenyan, "Bribery main reason for billionaires in prison," *ChinaDaily*,
      January 19, 2011 <http://usa.chinadaily.com.cn/china/2011-01/19/content_
      11888409.htm> (accessed June 1, 2011).
27   Eryn Correa, "China executes top corruption official for taking bribes,"
      University of Pittsburgh School of Law, December 31, 2010 <http://jurist.org/
      paperchase/2010/12/china-official-executed.php> (accessed June 9, 2011).

12 CURBING BRIBERY

1   City of London Police, "Overseas corruption assessment for The UK Bribery Strategy Group", draft report, January 15, 2010, p. 13.
2   Interview by author with senior British police officer, Spring 2011.
3   Serious Fraud Office, "Bribery Act 2010: Joint prosecution guidance of the director of the Serious Fraud Office and the director of prosecutions," London: Serious Fraud Office, <www.sfo.gov.uk/media/167348/bribery act joint prosecution guidance.pdf> (accessed May 28, 2011).
4   "Joint prosecution guidance," p. 7.
5   "Joint prosecution guidance," p. 9.
6   Interview with DI Whatmore, Metropolitan Police Service, Spring 2011.
7   Stephen Zimmerman, "Enforcing accountability: Italian company Lotti to pay US$350,000 in restitution to Indonesia after acknowledging fraudulent misconduct in a World Bank-financed project," World Bank press release 2011/279/INT <www.worldbank.org.md/WBSITE/EXTERNAL/COUNTRIES/ECAEXT/MOLDOVAEXTN/0,,contentMDK:22796379~menuPK:34463~pagePK:34370~piPK:34424~theSitePK:302251,00.html> (accessed June 1, 2011).
8   Interview with senior British police officer.
9   Interview with senior British police officer.
10 Fritz Heimann and Gillian Dell, "Progress report: enforcement of the OECD Anti-Bribery Convention," Transparency International, July 28, 2010, p. 9.
11 Nick Kochan, "UK set for clamp down on bribery and corruption," Operational Risk, October 28, 2009 <www.risk.net/operational-risk-and-regulation/feature/1560477/uk-set-clamp-bribery-corruption> (accessed June 9, 2011)
12 Kochan, "UK set for clamp down on bribery and corruption."
13 Barry Vitou and Richard Kovalevsky, "Debarment not mandatory for failure to prevent offence," The Bribery Act, March 31, 2011 <http://thebriberyact.com/2011/03/31/important-debarment-not-mandatory-for-conviction-of-failure-to-prevent-bribery-offence/> (accessed June 9, 2011)
14 FSA, "FSA fines Aon Limited £5.25m for failings in its anti-bribery and corruption systems and controls," press release, January 8, 2009 <www.fsa.gov.uk/pages/Library/Communication/PR/2009/004.shtml> (accessed June 1, 2011).
15 Interview with DI Whatmore.
16 FSA, Final Notice to Aon Ltd, January 6, 2009 <www.fsa.gov.uk/pubs/final/aon.pdf> (accessed June 1, 2011).
17 Kochan, "UK set for clamp down on bribery and corruption."
18 Richard Tyler, "Lord Goldsmith urges plea bargaining in bribery cases," Telegraph, March 20, 2011 <www.telegraph.co.uk/finance/newsbysector/industry/8239575/Lord-Goldsmith-urges-plea-bargaining-in-bribery-cases.html> (accessed June 1, 2011).
19 Simeon Igbinedion, "Corrupt multinationals and restitution," Guardian Nigeria, January 30, 2011 <www.ngrguardiannews.com/index.php?option=com_content&view=article&id=36899:igbinedion-corrupt-multinationals-andrestitution&catid=38:columnists&Itemid=615> (accessed February 2, 2011).
20 Interview by authors with Richard Alderman, Serious Fraud Office, Spring 2011.
21 Interview with Richard Alderman.
22 Stephen Zimmerman, "Enforcing accountability."

23 Siemens, "Siemens selects initial projects for US \$100 million Integrity Initiative," press release, December 9, 2010 <www.siemens.com/press/en/ pressrelease/?press=/en/pressrelease/2010/corporate_communication/ axx20101225.htm> (accessed June 1, 2011).
24 Siemens, "Siemens selects initial projects for US \$100 million Integrity Initiative," press release, December 9, 2010 <www.siemens.com/press/en/ pressrelease/?press=/en/pressrelease/2010/corporate_communication/ axx20101225.htm> (accessed June 1, 2011).
25 Interview with senior British police officer.
26 Interview with Richard Alderman.
27 Interview with Richard Alderman.
28 Interview with Richard Alderman.

CONCLUSION

1 Author's interview with local Cairo businessman.

APPENDIX 1

1 Transparency International, "Corruption crisis required coordinated response", Transparency International, July 18, 2011 <www.transparency.org/news_room/ latest_news/press_releases_nc/2011/2011_18_07_coordinated_response_ti_uk> (accessed July 20, 2011).
2 Victoria Howley, "Dealtalk: Newspaper's spin-off Murdoch's best hope for Sky deal", Reuters, July 19, 2011 <www.reuters.com/article/2011/07/19/us-news corp-sky-idUSTRE76I4OF20110719> (accessed July 20, 2011).
3 Laurence Knight, "*News of the World*: Counting the cost", BBC, July 7, 2011 <www.bbc.co.uk/news/business-14044052> (accessed July 20, 2011); Caroline Butcher, "Silverman Sherliker prepares for potential NotW class action", *The Lawyer*, July 8, 2011, <http://l2b.thelawyer.com/silverman-sherliker-prepares-for-potential-notw-class-action/1008557.article> (accessed July 20, 2011).
4 Nicole Kobie and Barry Collins, "Hackers wipe out all of News International's websites", *PC Pro*, July 19, 2011 <www.pcpro.co.uk/news/security/368734/ hackers-wipe-out-all-of-news-internationals-websites#ixzz1Se8rEDf5> (accessed July 20, 2011).
5 Graeme McLagan, "We've known about News of the World payments for years", *Guardian*, July 8, 2011 <www.guardian.co.uk/commentisfree/2011/ jul/08/news-of-the-world-payments-to-police> (accessed July 20, 2011).
6 Owen Bowcott, "News Corp board shocked at evidence of payments to police, says former DPP", *Guardian*, July 19, 2011 <www.guardian.co.uk/media/2011/ jul/19/news-corp-police-payments-macdonald> (accessed July 20, 2011).
7 Martin Bentham, "'Murdoch staff pay Met £100K in bribes': arrests imminent over illegal payments," *London Evening Standard*, July 7, 2011 <www. thisislondon.co.uk/standard/article-23967889-diabolical-practice-families-of-war-dead-were-hack-targets.do> (accessed July 20, 2011); Sandra Laville and Vikram Dodd, "News of the World paid bribes worth £100,000 to up to five Met officers", *Guardian,* July 7, 2011 < www.guardian.co.uk/media/2011/jul/07/ phone-hacking-bribes-five-police-officers> (accessed July 20, 2011).

8   Channel 4 News, "Yates: Police will be jailed over phone hack corruption" Channel 4 News, July 19, 2011 <www.channel4.com/news/stephenson-police-will-be-jailed-over-phone-hack-corruption> (accessed July 20, 2011).

9   Independent Police Complaints Commission, "IPCC Commissioner for London to oversee investigation into allegations that officers were paid by newspaper", July 7, 2011 <www.ipcc.gov.uk/news/Pages/pr_070711_hacking.a spx?auto=True&l1link=pages%2Fnews.aspx&l1title=News%20and%20press& l2link=news%2FPages%2Fdefault.aspx&l2title=Press%20Releases> (accessed July 20, 2011).

10 James Robinson and Charles Arthur, "News o f the World accused of paying police to track star's phones," *Guardian*, July 12, 2011 <http://www.guardian. co.uk/media/2011/jul/12/news-of-the-world-pinging> (accessed July 20, 2011).

11 Vikram Dodd, "How Sir Paul Stephenson's £12,000 spa break triggered downfall", *Guardian*, July 17, 2011 <www.guardian.co.uk/uk/2011/jul/17/ sir-paul-stephenson-spa-break-triggered-downfall> (accessed July 20, 2011).

12 Don Van Natta Jr, " Stain from tabloids rubs off on cozy Scotland Yard", *New York Times*, MSNBC, July 16, 2011 <www.msnbc.msn.com/id/43781013/ns/ world_news-the_new_york_times/t/stain-tabloids-rubs-cozy-scotland-yard/> (accessed July 20, 2011).

13 Transparency International, "Corruption crisis required coordinated response", Transparency International, July 18, 2011 <www.transparency.org/news_room/ latest_news/press_releases_nc/2011/2011_18_07_coordinated_response_ti_uk> (accessed July 20, 2011).

14 Robert Peston, US DoJ sounds out Serious Fraud Office on News International, BBC, July 18, 2011 <www.bbc.co.uk/news/business-14182445> (accessed July 20, 2011).

15 Gregory Husisian, correspondence with authors, July 22, 2011.

INDEX